Religion in the Age of Obama

Also available from Bloomsbury

Barack Obama: American Historian, Steven Sarson
The Bloomsbury Reader on Islam in the West, edited by Edward E. Curtis IV
We Are the Change We Seek, E.J. Dionne Jr. and Joy-Ann Reid

Belief and Religion in Barbarian Europe

Marilyn Dunn
University of Glasgow, UK

BLOOMSBURY ACADEMIC
LONDON • NEW YORK • OXFORD • NEW DELHI • SYDNEY

BLOOMSBURY ACADEMIC
Bloomsbury Publishing Plc
50 Bedford Square, London, WC1B 3DP, UK
1385 Broadway, New York, NY 10018, USA

BLOOMSBURY, BLOOMSBURY ACADEMIC and the Diana logo
are trademarks of Bloomsbury Publishing Plc

First published in Great Britain 2018
Paperback edition first published 2020

A catalogue record for this book is available from the British Library.

Library of Congress Cataloging-in-Publication Data
Names: Floyd-Thomas, Juan Marcial, editor.
Title: Religion in the age of Obama / edited by
Juan M. Floyd-Thomas and Anthony B. Pinn.
Description: 1 [edition]. | New York : Bloomsbury Academic, 2018. | Includes
bibliographical references and index.
Identifiers:LCCN2018009623(print)|LCCN2018025550(ebook)|ISBN9781350041066
(ePUB) | ISBN 9781350041059 (ePDF) | ISBN 9781350041035
(hardback) | ISBN 9781350041042 (nippod)
Subjects: LCSH: United States–Religion–History–21st century. | Religion
and politics–United States–History–21st century. | Obama, Barack–Religion.
Classifi cation: LCC BL2525 (ebook) | LCC BL2525 .R468155 2018
(print) | DDC 200.973/09051–dc23
LC record available at https://lccn.loc.gov/2018009623

ISBN: HB: 978-1-3500-4103-5
        PB: 978-1-3500-4104-2
     ePDF: 978-1-3500-4105-9
    eBook: 978-1-3500-4106-6

Typeset by Deanta Global Publishing Services, Chennai, India

To find out more about our authors and books visit
www.bloomsbury.com and sign up for our newsletters.

Dedicated to

Mrs. Lillian Floyd (1940–2017)
Reverend Anne H. Pinn (1931–2005)
and
Mrs. Desrine Mary Thomas (1945–2017)

Contents

Contributors

Keri Day received her PhD in religion from Vanderbilt University in Nashville, Tennessee. She earned an MA in religion and ethics from Yale University Divinity School in New Haven, Connecticut, and a bachelor of science degree from Tennessee State University in Nashville. Her teaching and research interests are in womanist/feminist theologies, social critical theory, cultural studies, economics, and Afro-Pentecostalism. Her published work includes the book *Unfinished Business: Black Women, the Black Church and the Struggle to Thrive in America* (2012).

Miguel A. De La Torre presently serves as Professor of Social Ethics and Latinx Studies at the Iliff School of Theology in Denver. A Fulbright scholar, he has taught in Indonesia, Mexico, South Africa, and Germany. Within his guild, he served as the 2012 president of the *Society of Christian Ethics*. Within the academy, he is a past-director to the *American Academy of Religion*; served as the past chair of the Committee for Racial and Ethnic Minorities in the Profession; served as the past chair of the Ethics Program Section; authored the "AAR Career Guide"; served on the Program Committee; and presently serves on the editorial board of *JAAR*. Additionally, he is the cofounder and present executive director of the *Society of Race, Ethnicity, and Religion* and the founding editor of the *Journal of Race, Ethnicity, and Religion*. Recently, he wrote the screenplay to a documentary on immigration, *Trails of Hope and Terror the Movie*, which has screened in over eighteen film festivals, winning over seven film awards.

Juan M. Floyd-Thomas is currently Associate Professor of African American Religious History in the Divinity School and Graduate Department of Religion at Vanderbilt University in Nashville, Tennessee. In his teaching and research interests as a religious historian, Professor Floyd-Thomas emphasizes religious pluralism within modern American society; race, ethnicity, and religion in US history; interdisciplinary approaches to the academic study of religious thought, especially philosophical, cultural, political, economic, and social scientific theories and methods for analyzing the intersections of popular culture and religion; the media interpretations and cultural images of African American religion; the varieties of African American religious experience; and African American churches and sociopolitical reform. In addition to having written numerous journal articles and book chapters, Floyd-Thomas is author of *The Origins of Black Humanism: Reverend Ethelred Brown and the Unitarian Church* (2008) and *Liberating Black Church History: Making It Plain* (2014) as well as coauthor of *Black Church Studies: An Introduction*

(2007) and *The Altars Where We Worship: The Religious Significance of Popular Culture in the United States* (2016).

Megan Goodwin received her PhD in religion and American culture from the University of North Carolina at Chapel Hill. Her work focuses on gender and sexuality, race, and contemporary American minority religions. A former Mellon postdoctoral fellow for creative and innovative pedagogy in the humanities, Goodwin is at work on her first monograph. The project explores late-twentieth and early-twenty-first-century American perceptions of religious difference as sexual and racial danger, using case studies of Mormon Fundamentalists, Muslims, and satanists. Another project she will undertake involves the operation of Islamophobia as an apparatus of white supremacy deployed against Muslim American women and women of color.

Alison Collis Greene is a historian of American religions and the twentieth-century United States, and serves as Associate Professor of American religious history at Mississippi State University. Her book *No Depression in Heaven: The Great, Depression, the New Deal, and the Transformation of Religion in the Delta* (2016) argues that the Great Depression and New Deal remade American religion just as it remade the nation's politics and social order. Set in Memphis and the Arkansas and Mississippi Delta, *No Depression in Heaven* weaves together the stories of ordinary believers, religious leaders, and grassroots activists to describe the collapse in voluntary and religious aid, the widespread demand for federal intervention, and a gradual disenchantment with the state among conservative Protestants in the 1930s. Greene's current research, for a manuscript tentatively entitled *God's Green Earth: Religion, Race, and the Land since the Gilded Age*, focuses on the racial and religious underpinnings of debates about the relationship between people and the land in the modern United States. Its characters are the farmers, rural reformers, civil rights activists, grassroots theologians, and civic leaders who fought to shape the nation's approaches to agriculture, conservation, and the environment.

Sylvester A. Johnson is the director of Virginia Tech's Center for the Humanities, and Professor of History in the department of religion and culture, as well as Assistant Vice Provost for the humanities. He focuses his research on the intersection of religion, race, and colonialism. He also has a particular interest in exploring humanity in the age of intelligent machines. Johnson is coeditor of the *Journal of Africana Religions*. His *African American Religions, 1500–2000: Colonialism, Democracy, and Freedom* was published by Cambridge University Press, and his *Myth of Ham in Nineteenth-Century American Christianity* garnered the American Academy of Religion's Best First Book Award. He is now coediting a volume on religion and the Federal Bureau of Investigation. He holds a doctorate in contemporary religious thought from the Union Theological Seminary.

Kathryn Lofton is a historian of religion, at Yale University, who has written extensively about capitalism, celebrity, sexuality, and the concept of the secular. In her work, she has examined the ways the history of religion is constituted by the history of popular culture and the emergence of corporations in modernity. Her first book, *Oprah: The Gospel of an Icon* (2011), used the example of Oprah Winfrey's multimedia productions to evaluate the material strategies of contemporary spirituality. Her second book, *Consuming Religion* (2017), offers a profile of religion and its relationship to consumption through a series of case studies including the Kardashian family and the Goldman Sachs Group. Her next book-length study will consider the religions of American singer-songwriter Bob Dylan. Lofton has served as an editor-at-large for the Immanent Frame; she has cocurated (with John Lardas Modern) a collaborative web project titled *Frequencies* and *Class 200: New Studies in Religion*, a book series with the University of Chicago Press.

Max Perry Mueller is a historian of American religion at the University of Nebraska-Lincoln. His research and teaching focuses on the intersection of religion, race, and politics in the nineteenth century. The central animating question of his scholarship is how the act of writing—especially the writing of historical narratives—has affected the creation and contestation of *race* as a category of political and religious division in American history. Mueller's first book, *Race and the Making of the Mormon People* (under contract, The University of North Carolina Press), analyzes the racialized scriptures, histories, and doctrines of the Church of Jesus Christ of Latter-day Saints as case studies to consider how nineteenth-century Americans turned to religion to solve the early American republic's "race problem." Other areas of research and teaching include the history of the American West, religion and modernity, religion and politics, and religion and journalism. Mueller's research and teaching also connect with his public scholarship. Mueller has written on religion, race, and politics for outlets including *Slate, The New Republic*, and *The Atlantic*.

Rebecca Todd Peters is a feminist and Christian social ethicist, whose scholarship focuses on questions of social ethics as they relate to economics, the environmental crisis, globalization, poverty, and women's access to reproductive health care. Peters addresses issues of conflict and social injustice in the world with the recognition that religion plays a significant role in shaping people's worldviews and moral ideas. Her most recent work is developing a Christian ethic of reproductive justice as the framework for thinking about women's whole reproductive lives, including everything from access to contraception to fertility treatments to unplanned pregnancies. She is examining many different sources, including history, social science, philosophy, and Christian tradition. This new project also focuses on helping people think in more sophisticated ways about how pregnancy challenges our existing moral categories of personhood and life. In addition, Peters writes about current events, theology, justice, and social change on her blog *"To Do Justice,"* which is featured on Patheos, an online site that hosts conversations on faith.

Anthony B. Pinn is currently the Agnes Cullen Arnold Professor of Humanities and Professor of Religion at Rice University. Pinn is the founding director of the Center for Engaged Research and Collaborative Learning, also at Rice University. In addition, he is the director of research for the Institute for Humanist Studies—a Washington,

DC–based think tank. Pinn's research interests include humanism and hip-hop culture. He is the author/editor of over thirty-five books, including *When Colorblindness Isn't the Answer: Humanism and the Challenge of Race* (2017); *Humanism: Essays in Race, Religion, and Cultural Production* (2015); *Writing God's Obituary: How a Good Methodist Became a Better Atheist* (2014); *Everyday Humanism*, Equinox (2014) (coeditor); *African American Humanist Principles: Living and Thinking Like the Children of Nimrod* (2004); and the novel, *The New Disciples* (2015).

Melanie Webb (Humanities and Liberal Arts Assessment Project) is a theologian and ethicist whose work focuses on political, theological, and philosophical constructs of flourishing societies. Her doctoral dissertation examines late antique reception of Roman and Christian virtue traditions through discourses of exemplarity, tracing in particular the expectations regarding personal and communal responses to sexual violence in the writings of Augustine of Hippo. She has over a decade of teaching experience in prisons, seminaries, universities, and online classrooms. At Princeton Theological Seminary, she piloted a certificate program at a local prison for both incarcerated and community students. In addition to her research with HULA, she is a research collaborator on the project Religious Education in Prisons (Louisville Institute/Villanova University), which is the first scholarly examination of religious education in prisons during the contemporary period.

Sharon Welch is a senior fellow of the Institute for Humanist Studies and a member of the Unitarian Universalist Peace Ministry Network. She served as provost and professor of religion and society at Meadville Lombard for ten years. Welch is the author of five books: *Real Peace, Real Security: The challenges of global citizenship*; *After Empire: The Art and Ethos of Enduring Peace*; *A Feminist Ethic of Risk*; *Sweet Dreams in America: Making Ethics and Spirituality Work*; and *Communities of Resistance and Solidarity*. Dr. Welch is also a regular contributor to *Tikkun* magazine, and is the author of many articles. Welch is the recipient of numerous awards, many of which recognize her excellence in teaching. Among these are the Internationalizing the Curriculum Course Development Award (2002) and the College of Education, High Flyer Teaching Award (several years). She also received the Annual Gustavus Myers Award: Honorable Mention for her 1999 book *Sweet Dreams in America*. She was awarded the honorary degree of doctor of sacred theology by Starr King School of the Ministry in May 2007.

Acknowledgments

The editors would like to begin this book by thanking those who helped carry it from idea to published book. We begin by acknowledging and thanking our families: Stacey Floyd-Thomas, Lillian Floyd-Thomas, Janet Floyd, Linda Bryant, Terry Bryant, Joyce Pinn, Ashely Bryant, Morgan Santana, and Ava Santana. And, we bring to memory the mothers to whom this volume is dedicated—Lillian Floyd, Anne Pinn, and Desrine Thomas—who departed the world far too soon. We wish that they could have seen this volume brought to fruition and we miss them more than words can ever possibly articulate. In addition, a host of friends provided good humor and robust support during this process, and we thank them all. We also want to express the deepest levels of appreciation to our editor, Lalle Pursglove, and the staff of Bloomsbury Academic for encouragement and patience as we missed deadline after deadline. Finally, we want to thank the contributors to the volume for their hard work.

Introduction

Juan M. Floyd-Thomas and Anthony B. Pinn

Whether one loved or hated him, it is undeniable that President Barack H. Obama Jr. has made a profound impact on both the United States and the larger world stage—as if he was the fulfillment of an ancient preternatural prophecy. With his historic election in November 2008 and subsequently his first inauguration in January 2009, millions of supporters, as popular news outlets attest, treated his emergence on the global stage as if they were bearing witness to the miraculous birth of a mocha-hued messiah. It was something of the perfect storm—the convergence of various anxieties over race relations, economic troubles, and political tensions. In such a cultural climate of measured despair, the "Yes We Can" optimism of President-elect Obama provided a glimmer of possibility, a way to maintain some hopefulness regarding the viability of the United States as a worthwhile experiment in democracy. His was an energetic and passionately articulated faithfulness to the potentiality of a unified and progressive nation. In articulating this vision, he captured the imagination and harnessed the energy of a diverse population.

He won a significant percentage of "independent" voters, suburban voters, the majority of young voters, a significant percentage of low-to-moderate income persons, and so on. And, of course, he gained the votes of a racially diverse range of voters.[1] In terms of individual responses to this historic election, and in addition to public gatherings of crying and joyful dancing and shouting, voters saw this as an opportunity for fundamental change. For some, it wasn't simply another presidential election cycle; their vote was for a deep shift in the very consciousness and self-understanding of the nation.[2] "Yes We Can" was more than a slogan; it became viral—with the help of artists like "will.i.am." It verbalized what some believed to be a new cultural perspective on the possibility of collective life. Put another way, "that simple theme of 'We Can' perfectly sums up the hope of an insurgent campaign. . . . It's a message that resonates especially strong with Obama followers. Politics should be all about doing the impossible."[3] A similar embrace of possibility was expressed on the international level by allies who see in the 2008 election at least the partial fulfillment of potential. In other words, "though many have denounced US power and unilateralism, they also seemed intent on putting the country back on a pedestal, and they fixed on Obama as their hope. Polls consistently showed that, if the rest of the world could vote, the Illinois Democrat would win by not a landslide, but an avalanche."[4]

Conversely, throngs of naysayers utterly despised him as the epitome of the Antichrist himself coming forth as the harbinger of white America's doomsday. In fact, one Catholic priest in the southern United States was reported to have informed his congregants not to "seek Holy Communion if they voted for Mr. Obama, because supporting him 'constitutes material cooperation with intrinsic evil' as the President-elect backs abortion rights."[5] Negative reaction to President-elect Obama's policy-related intensions came from the public and from elected officials. However, there was also hostility toward the 2008 election, for instance, that had little if anything to do with policy; rather, it spoke to the ongoing race hating marking the United States. From anxiety associated with a fear this election might just signal the collapse of the United States (the assumption being the United States is secure only if the whites are in charge) to verbalized wishes for a quick death for the president, the social construction of race attached to the most "powerful" politician in the United States sparked a fast and visceral reaction. More "polite" (to the extent this is possible) modalities of racial disregard were often replaced with one fueled by a sense of urgency. While some of what took place was little more than school children mimicking the worst of what they heard others say, or racist graffiti, these instances are tied to a larger display of racist response to the election of Obama—one that served to buttress and advance the aims of recognized hate groups. As the *Christian Science Monitor* reported,

> Supremacist propaganda is already on the upswing. In Oklahoma, fringe groups have distributed anti-Obama progapanda through newspapers and taped it to home mailboxes. Ugly incidents such as cross-burnings, assassination betting pools, and Obama effigies are also being reported from Maine to Alabama. The Ku Klux Klan has been tied to recent new events, as well. Two Tennessee men implicated for plotting to kill 88 black men, including Obama, were tied to the KKK chapter whose leader was convicted in a civil trial in Brandenburg, KY, last week, for inciting violence.[6]

Both public love and hate for Barack Obama resulted in curiosity concerning this man. Who is he? What's his story? His background? Such questions spoke to a desire for a narrative—something to explain his quick rise to the heights of power. And, to feed this curiosity, scholars, writers, and others produced materials at a rapid pace.

Writing the story

With his landmark election as the forty-fourth president of the United States, Barack H. Obama Jr. ignited a veritable flood of biographies, social and cultural analyses, and contemporary histories about modern democracy, civil rights, and postwar American race relations. The best of these books have attempted to examine America's tortured history of race relations through the prism of Obama's unique biography and unparalleled political ambitions.[7] Thinking of some of the cataclysmic events of the past few decades alone—the highly publicized and politicized murder trial of O. J. Simpson; the mass shootings at Columbine High School; the devastation of the Pentagon and World Trade Center by Islamic terrorists; the United States' retributive assault on Afghanistan in pursuit of the Taliban and al-Qaida; the invasion of Iraq that topples Saddam Hussein's regime; the burgeoning eruption of social media like

Facebook, Twitter, and Instagram; the ruinous man-made chaos following the natural disaster wrought by Hurricane Katrina; and the Great Recession of 2008–09—Barack Obama's rise to the presidency shares comparable power and prominence. These events share much in common. Each one in their own respective fashion affects the relationship of the United States and the larger world.

For many of us, these events have a deeply resonant place in our waking memories. Moreover, the sheer impact of these events is still unfolding in relevant yet wildly unpredictable ways. In this regard, Barack Obama has been a man of his times in the starkest terms imaginable. With its lengthy lyrical meditations on race and identity, Obama's memoir, *Dreams from My Father* (1995), has helped create a portrait of the young future president as a perpetual cultural outsider who was forced to deal with issues of belonging in a world marked by racial stratification. For instance, historian James T. Kloppenberg places Obama in the wider tradition of American political thought—the intellectual history of American democracy and philosophical pragmatism, as well as the social-cultural turmoil marking the twenty-year period of the 1980s through the 1990s. He situates Obama this way in order to understand the president's vision of American politics and culture.[8] Even as the world is beginning to tote up his legacies for the great "pissing contest" of op-ed history, we doubt anyone will be able to capture his saturation of our collective imagination.

Lest we forget, for any child born and raised during the first decade of the twenty-first century, that youngster had never known a world in which the president of the United States was not black. Although many might dismiss that perception simply as an aberration or possibly even a lacuna, such a new paradigm prompts one to inquire what that generational shift means, in the long run and, more importantly, what his lasting significance is? For the eight years of Obama's presidency, the photographs have been voluminous and varied; yet all of them strove to use the camera's eye in order to capture some new, mysteriously iconic manifestation of this unprecedented figure in world history. As Ta-Nehisi Coates writes, "Barack Obama's victories in 2008 and 2012 were dismissed by some of his critics as merely symbolic for African Americans. But there is nothing 'mere' about symbols. The power embedded in the word nigger is also symbolic. Burning crosses do not literally raise the black poverty rate, and the Confederate flag does not directly expand the wealth gap."[9]

Obama and religion

President Obama sharpened his intellectual abilities and interests at some of the most elite institutions around (i.e., Punahou Academy, Occidental College, Columbia University, and Harvard University Law School). Still, this is only his formal training. That is to say, it can just as easily be argued that his time spent worshiping at the Trinity United Church of Christ (UCC) for two decades was equally as influential in shaping his political and moral compass. During the 1980s and 1990s, Obama's intellectual evolution rested on intense study as well as practical experience at first as a community organizer in Southside Chicago and later as a University of Chicago law professor and Illinois state senator. The sum of his experiences made him a keen student of

American history in addition to being deeply appreciative of the contours of American democracy as a fluid ongoing conversation rather than a fixed predetermined destination. Kloppenberg observes that Obama's "predilection to conciliate whenever possible is grounded in his understanding of the history of American thought culture and politics" (83); yet critics would argue that Obama's sophisticated understanding of history and politics has been overwhelmed by the harsh realities of governance in an era of rabidly partisan national politics.[10]

Ever since the historic results of the 2008 US presidential election took root in the collective psyche of people worldwide, there has been a fairly consistent narrative about Obama's political ascendancy. In 2009, the essence of what could be deemed conventional wisdom about the meaning of Obama's election is as follows:

> American progressives have won a major victory in helping to defeat John McCain and placing Barack Obama in the White House. The far Right has been broadly rebuffed, the neoconservative war hawks displaced, and the diehard advocates of neoliberal economics are in thorough disarray. Of great importance, one long-standing crown jewel of white supremacy, the whites-only sign on the Oval Office, has been tossed into the dustbin of history.

Voicing beliefs readily espoused by folks across the broad swath of the nation's sociopolitical landscape, these writers also emphasize that "not only was a Black man elected president, but one whose name shouts its Third World otherness . . . . Obama's personal history is grounded in the multicultural and global reality of today's world."[11] By the time President-elect Barack Hussein Obama Jr. took center stage at Chicago's Grant Park to deliver his soaring yet sober victory speech, there were quite literally millions of US citizens of every walk of life weeping for joy and dancing in the streets over the unprecedented political sea change. As he said that day,

> if there is anyone out there who still doubts that America is a place where all things are possible; who still wonders if the dream of our founders is alive in our time; who still questions the power of our democracy, tonight is your answer.[12]

Whereas we would neither dismiss nor disparage the momentousness of Obama's election in popular memory both domestically and globally, it is presently necessary to tackle the critical task of comprehending the subsequent paradigm shift that occurred in the aftermath of his rise to presidential power as well as the redefinition of the body politic itself. Although the general opinion on contemporary US political culture tends toward stark polarization and rancorous discord, we contend that all of us are witnessing an era of heightened fragmentation and balkanization faced by both the right and the left. Yet, in the latter years of Obama's presidency, there was the parallel emergence of Black Lives Matter and the alt-Right that demonstrated racial divisions on a virtually Manichean level. Sadly, a historical era that once was presumed to be "post-racial" could be more accurately described as "most racial." What we noted in just a few examples at the start of this introduction represents a larger flood of animosity and disregard.

Before Obama's meteoric rise in American politics, the nation was subsumed under President George W. Bush's reign of ineptitude, terror, and belligerence, leaving many to honestly believe that there was nowhere else to go but get better. Into this chaotic fracas, McCain and Obama took on quasi-religious symbolism and accompanying mythology that bespoke the dire condition of the nation's reality at that moment. On the one hand, McCain's silver-haired suffering servant model stood rigid yet weary defense of the Republican Party's agenda defined by the misguided occupation of Iraq, the brokenness of the collapsing economic system, and the mounting toxicity within the nation's "culture wars." On the other, Obama arrived on the political scene as a sepia-toned smiling savior bringing an enlightened and impassioned gospel of hope and change which helped galvanize the disparate factions of the liberal-progressive partisans of the Democratic Party while also presenting a calm and cool demeanor sufficient enough to placate lingering doubts and biases among a reasonable number of moderate and independent voters. His political rhetoric, like that of his early years as a community organizer, were marked, at times, by a subtle appeal to the ethics of the social gospel—the idea that one's faith is best expressed not through doctrinal pronouncement but rather through action in the world. Even within his more secular professional activities, his intent is shaped through his Christian allegiance. The all-too-traditional closing of "God bless you, and may God Bless the United States of America" he uses when speaking is buttressed by a more heartfelt commitment to a liberal version of the Christian faith.

Regarding his religious life, Obama was clear: he rejects what he considers conversation that is divisive, language that does not encourage the best of our democratic principles and does not embrace our highest moral and ethical values. However, he embraces Trinity UCC's commitment to the social gospel, and he does so in a robust manner. It isn't clear that Obama is an advocate of black liberation theology (as Dr. Wright is), as opposed to a more general embrace of liberal religion's emphasis on active faith. His theological perspective seems to echo the sensitivity and the deep yearning for meaning and community of Howard Thurman, the religious realism of Reinhold Niebuhr, the religious engagement of sociopolitical life of Benjamin Mays, and the "beloved community" longed for by Martin Luther King Jr. And, unlike many African American ministers and professional writers of black theology, Obama attempts to speak to an appreciation for religious pluralism in the United States, the merit of difference, and a shared moral and ethical standard that cuts across religious traditions. And, he wants this expansive set of religiously inspired moral and ethical codes to inform public life.[13]

Considerations about how the current redefinition of the public sphere is vitally important to understanding how American society was being drastically remade in the age of Obama. Toward this end, cultural theorist Antonio Gramsci's formulation of hegemony in which elites maintain their societal dominance by means of both coercion and persuasion serves to foment a cohesive bloc that will serve as an identifiable social base within the body politic that galvanizes any alliances and coalitions. Unlike fashion, Gramscian analysis keeps us mindful that in order "to stay in power, all hegemonic blocs must maintain legitimacy with their social base."[14] While the hegemonic bloc coalescing around Obama is demographically wide and ideologically varied, the potential for an enduring generational shift in political economic and cultural orientation still remains rather tenuous and volatile—a fact about which the Obama administration appeared all too cognizant—as powerfully demonstrated by his White House's sympathetic overtures toward the Occupy Wall Street movement (circa 2012).[15] As we noted at the start of this introduction, the aggregation of environmentalists, organized labor, the LGBTQ community, civil rights activists, feminists, antiwar supporters, and an emergent constituency of millennial voters bitterly enraged by the abuses of the Bush-Cheney regime finally found a lynchpin in Obama. Thus, in a convergence of Jürgen Habermas's concept of public sphere as a place of "social life" devoted to negotiation and informed debate, as well as Nancy Fraser's more socially aware use of "counterpublics" as a means by which to capture and recognize the challenge to the inclusion of marginalized groups in the processes and debates shaping public life, it is the origination of any coalition in the late modern context that finds the diversity of the nation's demography potentially remaking the destiny of US democracy.[16]

Conversely, the hegemonic bloc that has constituted the right since the Nixon era took shape within the Republican Party around four main pillars: the Cold War/neoconservative military-industrial complex; the socially regressive evangelical Christians; wealthy Wall Street corporate interests; and race-baiting Deep South conservatives. More recently, however, the right wing had been whipped into a full-blown frenzy by the Tea Party as well as the alt-Right. The combined impact of these two reactionary factions of the conservative ecosystem was to deepen the ideological composition of the right so that it became more stridently anti-tax, anti-government, antiabortion, anti-LGBTQ rights, anti-immigrant, antiblack, and anti-Muslim bigotry. Even after the end of the Obama administration, this new constellation of far-right politics has stretched that longstanding political formation to its realistic breaking point. The situation has been so severe that even stalwart conservatives such as David Frum, George Will, and Jeff Flake—in keeping with the sensibility of the late William F. Buckley—admitted that their ideological camp faced stagnation due to having lost its way.[17] Nevertheless, it must be remembered that while the 2008 John McCain-Sarah Palin campaign was arguably one of the weakest, one of the most ideologically inconsistent tickets put forth by the GOP in the last half century, they still garnered about fifty-seven million votes.

Faithfulness

As a story of Obama's religious journey, *Dreams from My Father* serves as a testament of faith. It is a uniquely American tale of a seeker, an intellectually curious young individual from a very specific albeit shaky social location trying to cobble together a religious as well as racial identity out of myriad influences into a scheme that merges history with hybridity. Nevertheless, there is no reason why African Americans cannot or should not see the sometimes contradictory logic of Americanism as well as the complex web of religious concerns that Obama quite literally embodies, a legacy that is ultimately theirs as well. To be biracial, to have belonged to a nonreligious home and a Christian church, to have attended a largely Muslim school in Indonesia, to have lived and traveled extensively throughout the Global South during his formative years and even as a young adult, and ultimately embracing the black liberation theology espoused by Trinity UCC in urban Chicago, to be more than one thing and sometimes not fully anything—this is an increasingly common experience for Americans, including many racial/ethnic minorities. In terms of both his biological and biographical background, Obama expresses a thoroughly conflicted but resilient identity even before he utters a word. And yet it is precisely this level of complexity, with all of its intrinsic tensions, complicated contradictions, and ambiguous anxieties, that might ironically serve as the common ground shared by an increasing majority of Americans.

Obama has spoken often and eloquently about the importance of religion in public life. But, like many political leaders wary of offending potential backers in a society rooted in First Amendment rights, he has been less revealing about what he believes— about God, about prayer, about the connection between personal salvation and moral responsibility. In some respects, his reluctance is understandable in light of America's ongoing "culture wars." Obama's religiosity has been portrayed as unconventional and politically problematic based on a traditional political paradigm but might actually speak more honestly to the notions of lived faith at the dawn of the twenty-first century. By his own account, Obama was born, on the one hand, to a white American mother who was a Christian-turned-secular humanist and, on the other, to a native African father who was a Muslim-turned-atheist. Furthermore, because of an early childhood during which Obama grew up traveling and living all across the world with plenty of spiritual influences but without any particular religion, when describing his mother's approach to religion during his upbringing, he explains, "For all her professed secularism, my mother was in many ways the most spiritually awakened person that I've ever known. She had an unswerving instinct for kindness, charity, and love, and spent much of her life working on that instinct. . . . Without the help of religious texts or outside authorities, she worked mightily to instill in me the values that many Americans learn in Sunday school: honesty, empathy, discipline, delayed gratification, and hard work."[18]

Despite her own detachment from traditional religion, his mother made certain that he and his sister had what religious scholar Stephen Prothero would call "religious literacy"[19] in terms of a strong working knowledge of the world's major religions by ensuring they had access to copies of the Bible, the Quran, the Bhagavad Gita, and other holy books on their bookshelves. In short, one could easily say that Obama's connection to religion from childhood to young adulthood in any practical sense was quite complicated and, as his rhetoric would suggest, with lasting effect.

Therefore, when he made the journey to become an avowed Christian in the early 1990s having been baptized at Trinity UCC in Chicago by Rev. Dr. Jeremiah A. Wright Jr., Obama actually portrays a more contemporary vision of black religious faith formation. By his own admission, it was through his relationship with Wright and the congregation at Trinity UCC where he discovered the "power of the African American religious tradition" and bore witness to the possibilities of the black church as a space that could "spur social change." Furthermore, on the heels of this spiritual awakening, he explained: "I was able to see faith as more than just a comfort to the weary or a hedge against death; rather, it was an active, palpable agent in the world" that ultimately provided for believers "a source of hope."[20] Obama eloquently documented his religious journey and subsequent spiritual metamorphosis in his memoirs *Dreams from My Father* (1995) as well as *The Audacity of Hope: Thoughts on Reclaiming the American Dream* (2006), his polemic text outlining his political blueprints for the country written shortly after his Senate victory. It is clear from his writings as well as his public speeches that he has spent a considerable amount of time wrestling with religious ideas and issues.

Yet, in a bitter twist of fate, it would be Obama's commitment to the black church tradition that became a potentially devastating flashpoint of the 2008 presidential campaign. In March 2008, a media firestorm erupted when video excerpts of Wright Jr.'s sermons were taken out of context and picked up by worldwide media outlets. Republican rivals and conservative pundits frequently used Wright's words in order to question the patriotism of Obama, at that time a front-running Democratic presidential candidate. Since Obama and his family were members of Trinity UCC, the conservative media scrutiny over Obama and Wright's relationship made Trinity UCC a focal point during the political turmoil that unfolded from Wright's first appearances in the mainstream media to Obama's public resignation from Trinity UCC.

Despite a pastoral career that lasted nearly four decades, Wright will forever be linked to the historical 2008 presidential campaign of then senator Barack Obama. Although unwillingly thrust into the spotlight, the media attention could neither overshadow Wright's prophetic teachings nor define his life and ministry. Reflecting on this Wright-Obama controversy and its broader implications for how race, religion, and politics are debated in the public square, Anthony Pinn asks: "If one imagines that [Wright's] sermons probably average thirty minutes in length, what do we learn from a thirty-second or even three-minute clip? What of the better than sixty outreach ministries found at Trinity United Church of Christ? Do they speak to hopelessness, defeatism, and 'un-American' attitudes?"[21]

In a grandiose yet inevitable rush to judgment given the accelerated pace of the modern news cycle, the media generally overlooked the fact that Dr. Wright had been a legendary faith leader and human rights activist in Chicago's South Side community. Celebrated by Democratic and Republican politicians alike, Wright had worked tirelessly to unite social justice and divine justice for poor and marginalized peoples both in the United States and worldwide. A lifelong proponent of higher education as a means of personal and communal empowerment, Wright has four earned degrees: a bachelor of arts and master of arts in English from Howard University, a master of arts in the history of religions from the University of Chicago Divinity School, and a doctor of ministry from the United Theological Seminary under the tutelage of Rev. Dr. Samuel DeWitt Proctor. In addition, he is also the author of numerous scholarly articles for academic journals as well as being the author of numerous texts that are widely used in seminaries and theological institutions across the globe: *What Makes You So Strong?*, *Good News: Sermons of Hope for Today's Families*, *Africans Who Shaped Our Faith* and *When Black Men Stand Up for God*, *Blow the Trumpet in Zion!: Global Vision and Action for the 21st Century Black Church*, and most recently *A Sankofa Moment: The History of Trinity United Church of Christ*.

Moreover, as senior pastor emeritus of Trinity UCC in Chicago, IL, where he served faithfully for thirty-six years, Wright combined his studies of African traditional religions, African/African American musicology, and the historic black church tradition with his academic studies of Judeo-Christian thought to develop some fifty pioneering ministries, including the HIV/AIDS outreach programs, two senior housing complexes, a federally funded child care program for low-income families, and Trinity UCC's Kwame Nkrumah Academy. Wright has inspired not only his congregation but an entire nation to imagine a more progressive and prophetic example of church leadership by moving ministry, as he often proclaims, "from theory to praxis." Since 2003, Wright also has been a cofounder and board member of the Samuel DeWitt Proctor Conference, a national network that serves thousands of pastors, lay leaders, and community activists in addition to preparing the next generation of those working for social justice. In this fashion, Wright continues to serve as a mentor and role model for an entire generation of clergy, activists, and scholars seeking to that which addresses the needs of the community as well as enriching the faith-filled lives and guaranteeing the human dignity of all people. Even as the media firestorm surrounding his controversial sound bite became ratings fodder for conservative politicos and right-wing media pundits, his long and esteemed career in ministry has been grossly obscured from popular memory as a whole. Nonetheless, the relevance of his ministry reaches far beyond his pastorate at Trinity UCC. Wright's ministry has transcended to a global stage with a liberating message of freedom, justice, and equality.[22] Rather than coming to the matter of faith bound by preexisting issues of traditionalism or preordained notions of black racial identity to dictate his decision to affiliate himself with any given church, President Obama's relationship to the black church tradition under the spiritual guidance of Wright is the result of clear choice instead of being the result of coercion, chance, or circumstance.[23]

In our consideration of crafting a volume on the various ways religion takes shape in the age of Obama, we are well aware and fully understand the innate challenges of distilling a potentially sprawling chronological period and thematic issue(s) such as trying to grapple with the historical epoch we are succinctly calling the "age of Obama." To that last point, the scale and scope of the "age" is broad, allowing each contributor to tackle it as they see fit. In this sense, some of the essays begin with the initial interest in Obama as a potential candidate, while others are more firmly lodged in the period of his campaign and terms in office. For instance, in the aftermath of the 2016 presidential election, Stephen Marche wrote:

> The Obama years, unlike the '60s, have a definite end date. January 20, 2017. No doubt the man will not simply vanish—hopefully he will write an elaborate, gossipy memoir—but it was never Obama himself who defined the Obama years. It was the fact that such a man was in power. It was witnessing him daily move with and inside and around the machineries of the world. His legacies are sizable no doubt, on the scale of LBJ or FDR: the salvation of the global economy, the reintroduction of the idea of government initiative as a positive force in American life, the first US commander-in-chief to refuse to serve as the world's policeman. But the significance of those legacies will be established 50 or a hundred years from now. His legacy will be determined by human fate, not policy.[24]

In so many ways, Obama very often has been portrayed and perceived as the people's president. On his very first full day, he froze White House salaries for the duration of the Great Recession in solidarity with the multitude of American citizens who were struggling through financially dire times. On the first day of any new venture, when most folks would stand somewhat dazed and confused as they sought to gain their bearings, the new administration under Obama used the early days of his presidency as the time to make change. And throughout the eight years of his presidency, he continued to do so. As one of his most laudable achievements, he worked with the Democrat-controlled Congress to establish the Affordable Care Act (a.k.a. Obamacare), which provided health insurance for more than twenty million previously uninsured Americans. A hallmark of his time as the nation's commander-in-chief was not just his leadership in the capture and assassination of Osama bin Laden, the mastermind of the 9/11 terrorist attacks, but also the fact that he ended the Pentagon's "don't ask, don't tell" policy, thus allowing LGBTQ military personnel to serve proudly and openly. Under his watch, marriage equality in the United States became legalized, thanks to a Supreme Court decision. Obama also implemented the Lilly Ledbetter Fair Pay Act, which restored basic protections against pay discrimination for women and other workers in the hopes of improving overall conditions for the nation's workforce; and in his efforts to address mounting concerns about the criminal justice system, he granted over 1,000 pardons for thousands of nonviolent drug offenders en route to much-hoped-for reforms in America's mass incarceration system.

The story of Obama's religious journey is a distinctively contemporaneous narrative of our time. Always drawn to life's deepest philosophical quandaries from an early age, Obama embarked on a spiritual quest in which he tried to reconcile his rational side with his yearning for transcendence. Even though he "found Christ" in his own personal life, that did not mean he stopped asking questions. His biography has been framed around him being a seeker striving to chart his own path forward as an intellectually curious individual from a valid albeit volatile personal background. As he explained in his 1995 memoir *Dreams from My Father*, Obama spent much of his life trying to cobble together a religious worldview as well as racial identity out of myriad influences into a scheme that merges contemporary history with cultural hybridity. "I'm on my own faith journey and I'm searching," Obama has stated publicly, adding that, "I leave open the possibility that I'm entirely wrong."

Through the various phases of his personal evolution, Obama has spoken often and eloquently about the importance of religion in public life. But, like many politicians wary of offending prospective voters as well as potential donors, he often has been less than forthcoming about what he believes—about God, about prayer, about the connection between salvation and personal responsibility, visions of moral authority and social justice, and thoughts on just war and peacemaking. However, since Obama's political ascendancy within the US electoral politics more than a decade ago, widespread rumors about his religious identification have also persisted among throngs of conservatives in the United States. For instance, in a 2008 *Newsweek* poll, 12 percent of registered voters incorrectly believed Obama was Muslim while more than a quarter of them wrongly believed he was raised in a Muslim household and was educated in a madrassa. Among die-hard conservatives, these misconceptions have persistently dogged Obama throughout his years in office. What is more, as E. J. Dionne Jr. and Joy-Ann Reid observe, "given the profound divisions that grew during the Obama years, it is paradoxical and even tragic that Obama dedicated so much of his rhetorical firepower to the task of conciliating religious white conservatives to his vision, only to look on those divisions deepened. Even gifted preachers can fail in their task of conversion."[25]

Despite living in a society rooted in First Amendment rights, Obama's religiosity has been portrayed as unconventional and politically problematic based on a traditional political paradigm but might actually speak more honestly to the notions of lived faith in the early twenty-first century. Even as he identified himself as a "skinny kid with a funny name" in his landmark 2004 Democratic National Convention keynote address, there has been something significant about Obama being a biracial political leader with an Arabic name attempting to navigate the United States through some of its most drastic demographic and sociopolitical transitions in more than a century. Whether one looks to the Global War on Terror or the Great Recession or the rise of the Tea Party or #Black Lives Matter or even #Oscars So White protests, Obama not only has been a polarizing figure in global culture and politics but, more importantly, has been a prism through which we can examine the social, political, cultural, and yes religious trajectories of our current day and time.

What this volume offers

All that we have presented up to this point begs a set of questions: what can be said about religion within the age of Obama? What does religion tell us about the nature and content of his presidency, and what's more, what does examination of religion during that period tell us about the nature and place of religion within US public life more generally? This volume aims to address these questions from a variety of vantage points.

This said, *Religion in the Age of Obama* focuses on the significant transformations within religion and society during the late twentieth and early twenty-first centuries, making these sophisticated ideas and complex issues accessible to the general public. The presidency of Barack Obama is unique in a variety of ways, beyond the obvious introduction of race into politics in a manner that changes the grammar and vocabulary of power. In addition to the aggressive turn of the right to create a political blockade against the president's agenda, there is the less frequent attention to the dimension of religion. From his personal faith, to projected faith as political counterpoint, to the manner in which the Obama presidency is alternately haunted by the rise of various politicized forms of religious fundamentalism and yet also shadowed by the growth of the "nones" and the decrease in particular modalities of Christianity, religion matters in the age of Obama.

While there are numerous books written on the presidency of Obama, few of them address dimensions of religion. Even works by religion scholars such as Gary Dorrien, Eddie S. Glaude, and Michael Eric Dyson offer insights that are multidimensional and international in scope. This volume emerges at a critical time when the study of religion continues to explicitly participate in national and transnational conversations on topics such as race, gender, sexuality, secular humanism, church-state relations, immigration, and other related matters.

Although there have been a wide array of volumes discussing various aspects of the Obama presidency, any works addressing the impact and issues of religion in relationship to the contemporary era in the field of religious studies and theology remain consistently underrepresented. Without question, there is much more to be said concerning not only Obama's own religious perspective but also the meaning and impact of religion in our time. *Religion in the Age of Obama* seeks to fill this gap by offering a multidisciplinary and international conversation concerning the nature and meaning of religion in public during this unique period of "American" politics. It offers analysis of Obama's religiosity and its relationship to his vision of public life, but it also provides discussion of the manner in which the general ethos of religiosity and non-religiosity has shifted over the past decade.[26] Our intent with this volume is the presentation of a plausible cartography of the "look" and function of religion within the context of public life, and to present this cartography with as much graphic depiction and detail as one book can muster.

Structure

Some of the chapters explore religion explicitly, while others offer religion as only the shadow of assumed moral and ethical sensibilities that are—or should be for some— operative within public life. We don't see these differences as a shortcoming in that they mirror the manner in which religion is discussed and operative within the United States. That is to say, the impact of religion in US public life—for good or ill—isn't limited to issues of explicit participation in religious communities; it is also felt in the manner in which the rhetoric used within public space is often tied to the language and ideological platforms of what we have come to call American religion(s).

This volume is divided into three parts. The first, "Faith in Public," contains chapters exploring—from various vantage points—the public intersection of government and personal faith claims. This portion of the book begins with a discussion of Romney and Obama. Max Perry Mueller explores the dilemma of public faith through attention to the religious commitments of Romney and Obama during their bid for presidential nominations. In doing this, Mueller highlights the tensions between personal religious beliefs and more general perceptions of proper faith. For Romney the challenge entailed the actual nature of Mormon beliefs over against popular perceptions. And for Obama the dilemma involved the nuance of his Christian faith over against what was perceived as the radical beliefs of Rev. Dr. Jeremiah Wright. To rectify this situation, both Romney and Obama made public their belief claims so as to render themselves acceptable and nonthreatening. Mueller examines this public presentation of faith through two speeches—"Faith in America" by Romney and "A More Perfect Union" by Obama—and highlights the manner in which both speeches aim to position the candidate in terms of presence within a particular and marginalized culture context, yet part of the broader framework of American life.

This chapter is followed by Kathryn Lofton's exploration of the relationship between Oprah Winfrey and Barack Obama. As the chapter points out, Oprah's "effect" involves a manner of commodification by means of which identity transformation takes place through "confessions, conversions, and popular showcases of pluralism." This process is not simply commercialization, according to Lofton; rather it is also a process of spiritualization, to the extent it shapes markers of identity that "sale" and also mark lasting ideals. The campaign of Obama leading to his inauguration as the first African American president of the United States benefited from this "Oprahfication" but, in a manner unusual for Oprah, it also involved her more direct involvement in politics—campaign appearances and fundraisers. According to Lofton, there is something about the commodification of Obama that positioned him for so many voters as a savior with the capacity to nudge the United States to be its better self. The chapter casts this attitudinal shift, this specter of hope, in terms of a "modern revival."

The next chapter in this section is by Sylvester A. Johnson. In it he explores what he labels one of the most significant reactions to the election of President Obama— the argument he was a Muslim and hence a threat to the integrity and security of the nation. Despite his public pronouncements of Christian faith and his headline-grabbing feud with Rev. Dr. Jeremiah Wright over theology, many argued he was a Muslim—how could he not be with that name and look, they reasoned. Despite so much evidence to the contrary, as Johnson outlines, this thinking persisted through Obama's second term in office. What accounts for this? In response to this question, the chapter suggests it is tied to a palatable sense of (white Christian) nationalism that casts Muslims as an external threat to democracy and to the ongoing threat of the racialized "Other." Whatever its origin, this assumption Obama is a Muslim, or at least a Muslim sympathizer, flies in the face of his foreign policy.

The final chapter in this part, by Melanie Webb, situates a concern with levels of incarceration during the Obama presidency, and uses Augustinian theology as a way of forging a new sense of relationship as interdependence between "our humanity and the humanity of those most denigrated by our carceral practices." In making this argument, the chapter also interrogates the impact of plea deals on the nature and application of mercy.

The second part of the book addresses the politics of moral vision. Moving away from strict attention to religious belief and communities, the chapters in this part address a more general concern with the moral-ethical underpinning of activities and policies during the Obama years. It begins with Alison Collis Greene's examination of the manner in which the Obama presidency marked not a decline in the influence of religious organizations in public life, but rather an increased presence of such organizations within government thought and policy. The chapter offers an important historical overview of aid provided by religious organizations, and the economic-historical developments that limited such aid and fostered greater governmental assistance; but this came with a price, so to speak. With time, Greene argues, religious organizations would come to dispense federal dollars as subsidiaries of this expanding "welfare state." During the Obama presidency, a graphic sign of this continued and growing collaboration is the federal funds available for helping the disadvantaged funneled through faith-based organizations whose theological commitments often run contrary to secular, governmental policies. As the chapter outlines, there is a clear tension between the moral vision of these organizations and the secular responsibilities of governmental agencies. The undercurrent of this connection too easily becomes a moral vision requirement on the part of citizens in order to receive aid.

Next, Rebecca Todd Peters examines economic conditions over the past decade—the Obama years—for what those conditions, as markers of a crisis of capitalism (e.g., increased wealth for a select few), tell us about the election of Donald Trump. Through this examination, Rebecca Todd Peters exposes what the she labels the "moral bankruptcy of capitalism" as a root cause for the discontent and disillusionment to which the Trump campaign responded. Numerous factors figure into the concealment of capitalism's moral failure, and the process of mystification that conceals this problem shaped public discourse in ways that favored Trump's scapegoating rhetoric within white, working-class circles that sought a rationale for their economic troubles (and evangelical who detested what they perceived as a turn away from family values) that, from their perspective, were linked to the Obama presidency.

Megan Goodwin's contribution explores what can often be a troubled relationship between proclaimed moral values and the requirements of public life. That is to say, the *Burwell v. Hobby Lobby* lawsuit addressing whether the corporation is required to provide contraceptive services for employees points on the conflict between personal moral values and political and economic structures that impact the larger public. Pointed out through this investigation is a tension between conservative Christian values and rights associated with a more secular view of democratic life. Through this discussion, Goodwin highlights the manner in which religious freedom and the exercise of that freedom over against bodily agency—particularly in relationship to women of color—arguments and debates marked the Obama years.

Next, Juan M. Floyd-Thomas offers a discussion of the "just war" tradition from its roots in Augustinian thought to contemporary articulations. The chapter grapples with how US foreign policy has been shaped not only by President Obama's own interpretation of just war theory but also by vocal dissent from the likes of Obama's former pastor, Rev. Dr. Jeremiah A. Wright Jr., and hip-hop artist Lupe Fiasco to the ongoing global war on terror. Toward this end, Floyd-Thomas explores the work and writings of the aforementioned figures as three distinctive foci of concern and the respective modalities each one represents in terms of racial and religious perspectives on global matters of war and peace.

The final portion of the book—"On Race/ing Belief"—explores the manner in which embodied human difference and issues of justice played out during the Obama presidency. This section begins with a chapter by Keri Day, in which she discusses the impact of "Christian religious fundamentalisms" on an exclusionary white nationalism-leaning mode of white populism—resulting in a reconfiguration of race and issues of justice. The argument involves speculation on the manner in which these fundamentalisms have rendered whiteness hyper-visible and thereby framed a narrative of white people as under the threat of being marginalized if not wiped out. In this way, the gains of racial minorities—with the presidency of Obama (and the subsequent election of Donald Trump) as a prime marker—are believed to come at the expense of whites as the new oppressed figures in American life. Day continues by asserting that the best of the African American progressive religious tradition has the potential to aid with the development of a counter to this anti-pluralism white populism.

That chapter is followed by Anthony B. Pinn's discussion of the manner in which the Black Lives Matter movement, which emerged during the age of Obama, challenges prevailing assumptions regarding the centrality of religious leadership in justice work. The chapter also presents the manner in which Black Lives Matter disrupts the traditional narrative of American progress. Pinn argues that in place of religious (i.e., Christian) leadership and inevitability of progress, Black Lives Matter offers a more humanist ethic framed in terms of a race-conscious moralism.

Next, Miguel A. De La Torre frames Trump's attitude toward immigration in light of a rather problematic and reactionary stance demonstrated by Obama. Borrowing the label of the "deporter-in-chief" and tying it to the atrocities taking place along the "border," the chapter argues that the eight years of the Obama presidency were marked by a failure to produce progressive and affirming policies regarding immigrants. Within the chapter is a critique of Obama's failure to apply the "virtue of hospitality" that one might assume is connected to his stated moral and ethical sensibilities derived from his faith. Still, even the application of a sense of hospitality is, according to De La Torre, an incorrect response in that it is premised on an erroneous sense of ownership of the land called the United States, and a failure to acknowledge political abuse and resource theft that allowed for the growth of this nation.

The section ends with Sharon Welch's consideration of a two-part question regarding politics and race: "what enabled the first victory of Barack Obama, and what propelled the backlash?" Welch seeks to address these questions by means of a "conversation" with select figures working on these issues, thereby giving the chapter a dialogical feel. Using this approach, the chapter interrogates the parameters of religious-prophetic imagination as well as the religious and ethical challenges of maintaining justice work in the current political-cultural climate of the United States.

With the various chapters taken together, the book covers with some detail the period of Obama's campaigns and terms of office, and does so from a variety of vantage points and using a range of methodological and theoretical tools. In this way, it offers important insights. Yet, there are shortcomings to this project, and we admit to them without hesitation. For example, future work on this topic would benefit from more attention to the global context or greater exploration of various religious communities than we were able to provide here. While several chapters of this volume venture to offer reflection on a more global impact of the Obama years, the volume is limited to a presentation of the domestic impact of the age of Obama as an initial starting point for what we hope will be a longer engagement on the part of numerous scholars. Lasting roughly a decade in length, this period influenced and informed so many structures of thought, social experience, and public activity in the United States that, we believe, attempting to focus on domestic circumstances is a justifiable starting point.

The potential of Obama's presidency (as the first African American president) was widely recognized as a somewhat unique opportunity to rethink the United States. As political commentator Andrew Sullivan wrote in *The Atlantic* (December 2007):

Obama's candidacy in this sense is a potentially transformational one. Unlike any of the other candidates, he could take America—finally—past the debilitating, self-perpetuating family quarrel of the Baby Boom generation that has long engulfed all of us. So much has happened in America in the past seven years, let alone the past

40, that we can be forgiven for focusing on the present and the immediate future. But it is only when you take several large steps back into the long past that the full logic of an Obama presidency stares directly—and uncomfortably—at you.[27]

Mindful of these words, as well as so many other similar statements, the goal of this volume is to "stare" back, so to speak, and reflect on the relationship of religion to some of the most critically significant issues situated within the Obama years.

The success or failures associated with his presidency—whether or not it was a transformative administration—will be hotly debated in academic and popular circles for years to come. However, while not unusual in itself—presidential administrations frequently have to withstand such retrospective scrutiny—there is still something about these years in particular. It seems clear in hindsight what so many people either anticipated or feared in relationship to this grand democratic experiment called the United States merits consideration. Hence, we feel that more focused attention on the domestic sphere is a good framing mechanism for this book. Even now, we believe the book offers a vital invitation to discuss the wider, more global implications of the Obama presidency. And, in this way, it encourages deeper and more sustained attention to the pros and cons of religion in public not just for now but for years to come.

Part One

Faith in Public

Religion (and Race) Problems on the Way to the White House: Mitt Romney and Barack Obama's "Faith" Speeches

Max Perry Mueller

Religion problems on the way to the White House

During the 2008 presidential campaign both Barack Obama and Mitt Romney confronted "religion problems" that they and their backers worried would derail their pathbreaking roads to the White House. For the former governor of Massachusetts Mitt Romney, his membership in the Church of Jesus Christ of Latter-day Saints (LDS) created a rift among white evangelical Protestants whose support he needed to become the first Mormon presidential nominee of a major US political party.

Like the Southern Baptist Conference's Dr. Richard Land, some prominent evangelical leaders urged the faithful to look beyond what they viewed as Mormonism's heretical beliefs about Jesus Christ, biblical canon, and prophecy, and instead pay attention to Romney's shared conservative values. Yet others joined televangelist Bill Keller in arguing that true Christians cannot vote for a follower of "false Gospels and false religions like Mormonism." In October 2007, Keller sounded the alarm when Romney emerged as the front-runner in first-in-the nation Iowa caucuses. The stakes could not be higher, Keller said. Elevating Romney to the "highest visibility, highest power" would lead more to convert to the "Mormon cult," the followers of which "are all going . . . to hell."[1] The Reverend Richard Cizik, an influential figure in the thirty-million member National Association of Evangelicals, was less alarmist than Keller. But he also worried that too many Christians were ready to "jump on the Romney bandwagon" before Romney explained how his religion—which Cizik also said was not Christian—shaped the presidential hopeful's "personal integrity" and policy positions.[2]

Past persecution against the Mormons—including against Romney's own ancestors and family members—and present-day anti-Mormon animus among many white conservative evangelicals certainly weighed on Romney's mind.[3] For most of his career in public life, Romney chose to say all but nothing about his devout Mormon faith or his extensive service within the LDS Church, which included a stint as the Boston area's highest-ranking Mormon official. Nevertheless, by December 2007, Romney realized that his own silence on the Mormon question had created a vacuum that others were happy to fill with their only slightly veiled anti-Mormon invective.[4] This approach was especially true for Mike Huckabee, the former Baptist minister and the former governor of Arkansas, who by December had caught up with Romney in the Iowa polls.

For then US senator Barack Obama, the "religion problem" that seemed like it might prevent him from becoming the first African American to win a major party presidential nomination arose from his relationship with the Reverend Dr. Jeremiah Wright. The longtime senior pastor of Trinity United Church of Christ in Chicago, Illinois, Wright led a young Obama to Christ in the late 1980s when Obama was working as a community organizer. To many in the greater Chicago area as well as to many black Christian leaders around the country, Wright was a celebrated voice, known for calling attention to injustices in America and abroad. But Wright became a national figure in March 2008 during Obama's improbable ascent to front-runner status in the Democratic primary race. Highly edited, decontextualized clips of two of Wright's sermons, in which the preacher declared US domestic and foreign policy racist and imperialistic, were broadcast ad nauseam on cable news outlets. As the man seeking the American presidency, pundits on the left and right were aghast that Obama had ever turned to the "anti-American" Wright for spiritual guidance.[5] In early March 2008, when the Wright controversy became the dominant election story, Barack Obama came to a similar conclusion as Romney did about his own religion problem. Staying silent about Jeremiah Wright only ceded precious ground to his political foes who, in turn, were ready, willing, and able to mischaracterize Obama's faith to their advantage.

This chapter examines Mitt Romney's "Faith in America" speech, delivered in December 2007, and Barack Obama's "A More Perfect Union" speech, delivered in March 2008. The purpose of doing so is to determine what lessons can be drawn from these two speeches about how American politicians from religiously and racially marginalized communities have argued—with varying degrees of success—for the acceptance of themselves as candidates and their kind as citizens in the American republic. This chapter makes no empirical claims about the impact of these two controversies on the 2007–08 presidential campaign. Nor does it make any empirical claims to determine if these two speeches solved Romney or Obama's "religion problems."[6] Instead, what follows are qualitative assessments in two parts. First, this chapter contextualizes these speeches in the fraught religious and racial histories from which they emerge. Namely, this chapter traces how, as "problem" peoples, Mormon Americans and black Americans have existed within but not fully *of* the (white) American republic.[7] And second, this chapter examines how (the Mormon) Mitt Romney and (the black Christian) Barack Obama attempted to talk their way into the most exclusive club that, up until that point in American history, would not have them as members: the American presidency.

I argue that the main historical lesson to draw from this unique moment in American presidential politics is the persuasive power of speaking *from* a specific (even suspect) American religious and/or racial culture, while also speaking *to* the broader American culture. In "Faith in America," Romney not only continued to avoid speaking as a Mormon. He also tried to rebrand Mormonism so that it would be palatable to the white evangelical Christians who have long held his faith at arm's length. Instead, in "A More Perfect Union" because Obama spoke from within the black church tradition and connected this tradition to the broader sweep of American history, Obama's speech was more successful than Romney's in the short term, and more enduring in the long run.

When religion problems are race problems, too: Barack Obama

Obama's religion problem was also a "race problem." In fact, during the 2008 presidential election, the race and religion problems were so interconnected that debates about Obama's religious background, which the public clamored for, served as a proxy for talking about Obama's race, which was more or less verboten.[8] It was not just that for three decades Obama was a member of a church whose controversial pastor served as his chief mentor in the Christian gospel. It was also that this church was an unapologetically "black church"—the only truly independent black institution in American history. As Clarence E. Walker and Gregory D. Smithers have put it, "for more than two hundred years, the black church has provided African American people with the faith, strength, and social services needed to survive in a country that has enslaved them, discriminated against them, lynched them, and legally segregated them from white Americans."[9] Adopting the Puritan jeremiad tradition, leaders of these institutions—from Denmark Vesey's role in the 1820s slave rebellion in South Carolina and Martin Luther King Jr.'s role in the civil rights battles of the 1950s and 1960s, to Jeremiah Wright's denunciation of America's imperialistic foreign policy in the 2000s—have spoken "truth to power." But, exactly because of its economic and cultural wealth, its influence on black American life and politics, and its independence from white America, the "black church" and the ministers who led them have also been a target of suspicion, scorn, and sometimes violence from "white Americans [who] have harbored suspicions about its true objectives." As such, Walker and Smithers write, truth-speaking ministers have often "struck fear into the hearts of white America."[10]

This fear got a full airing in 2008 as the nation contemplated the possibility of its first black president. During the twelve weeks between March 10 and June 1, by a 12-to-1 ratio, the Obama-Wright relationship was mentioned in the American press—the vast majority of which were negative—compared to the relationship between Obama's general election opponent John McCain and the two controversial pastors with which he was most associated, the antigay and anti-Islam crusaders John Hagee and Rod Parsley.[11] Let's examine one of the more pointed of the 6,103 Obama-Wright press items produced during this period. Two days after the Wright controversy first broke, writing for the *National Review*, on March 15, 2008, Mark Steyn suggested that the promise of Obama—the half-black half-white "symbol of [American] redemption and renewal"—is a hallow one. Obama's message was designed to make "upscale white liberals feel good about themselves." But white America—white liberals, no exception—should beware. Steyn suggested that Obama's relationship with the Reverend Wright meant that his candidacy was just as dangerous in its racial myopia as black presidential hopefuls of the past, including the "Reverend Al Sharpton or the Reverend Jesse Jackson or the rest of the racial-grievance mongers." The difference was that Obama could win. This meant that a (black) man whose (black) spiritual mentor preached that the "United States brought the death and destruction of 9/11 on itself" could soon occupy the White House.[12]

Steyn and Obama's other political enemies were happy to assume that Obama's religion was the same as Wright's. But it wasn't—not completely. If Jeremiah Wright practiced and preached three interrelated political theologies that dominated the post–civil rights black church—the jeremiad tradition, black liberation theology, and black nationalism—Barack Obama accepted (and later preached himself) only the first two. However, Obama replaced black nationalism with the politics of respectability.[13]

To be sure, Wright's post-9/11 sermons were provocative. But they were intended to be. They belonged to the American tradition of the jeremiad—established by Wright's Congregationalist spiritual ancestor John Winthrop—in which American preachers have long warned of divine retribution when the nation has failed to live up to the covenantal promises it made with God. For example, echoes of antislavery jeremiads of the past appear in Wright's sermon, "Confusing God and Government," in which Wright chastised a nation founded on liberty but denies it to its black citizens. The "government gives them [black Americans] drugs, builds bigger prisons, passes a three-strike law and then wants us to sing 'God Bless America,'" Wight declared. "No, no, no, not God Bless America. God damn America, that's in the Bible for killing innocent people, God damn America for treating our [black] citizens as less than human."[14]

In his other most infamous sermon, Wright combined the old jeremiad theology with the relatively new theology of black liberation. In "The Day of Jerusalem's Fall," which he preached in Trinity just days after 9/11, Wright argued that the terrorist attacks signaled "America's chickens are coming home to roost." God's wrath against the once-favored United States was the result of the nation's own violent imperialist past—the forceful removal against Native Americans; the enslavement of African Americans—and the government's recent support of racist regimes in South Africa and Israel. Wright, who in the 1970s reshaped Trinity's theological outlook based on James H. Cone's foundational black liberation texts, taught that God took special offense at such violence. God expressed special favor for poor and oppressed peoples who, in recent world history, have most often been synonymous with black and brown peoples.[15]

Yet the line between black people's status as God's "favored" people due to the oppression they face as well as black people's status as God's "chosen" people due to some birthright, is a fine one. And Wright often operated on the other side of that line. Against the economic and political conditions that discounted black American lives, Wright promoted an Afrocentric theology that essentialized blackness as the first, not the last, of God's peoples. In his sermons, Wright often labeled black Americans "Africans." And he described African Americans' dehumanizing time in America as a historical aberration. In the grand sweep of history, Wright preached that Africa—not Europe—had produced the world's great innovators of civilization, democracy, and Christianity itself.[16] Wright thus shared with James Cone, with the (pre-Hajj) Malcolm X, and with the 1970s Black Power movement, the belief that the "Negro" in America must throw off the oppressive weight of what W. E. B. Du Bois famously called "the veil," which produces in him an overriding sense of "double-consciousness."[17] In doing so, the Negro would emerge as the singular being God created and destined him to be: the African.[18]

Then in his twenties, Barack Obama first sought out Jeremiah Wright in 1988. Obama hoped to convert the influential Chicagoland pastor to Obama's brand of grassroots, social justice organizing. But it was Wright's ability to recast the quotidian struggles of contemporary black Americans into epic sagas that converted Obama to Wright's brand of liberation theology. As Obama explained in his first memoir *Dreams from My Father*, "my spirit" first came alive when Wright preached his sermon, "The Audacity of Hope." As black preachers have done since the days of slavery, Wright connected contemporary black Americans' struggles against race-based political abuses and economic exclusion with the biblical "stories of David and Goliath, Moses and Pharaoh, the Christian's in the lion's den, field of dry bones," Obama writes. "Those stories—of survival, and freedom, and hope—became our story, my story; the blood that had been spilled was our blood, the tears our tears."[19]

Obama took from the "Audacity of Hope"—which would serve as the title and the organizing principle for his political memoir—not a post-racial message. Instead he took from it a transracial (in addition to trans-class, transnational, transgendered, and later transsexual) message that Obama believed all oppressed people could make their own. "Our trials and triumphs became at once unique and universal," explains Obama in *Dreams from My Father*, "black and more than black." But Obama writes that he also intuited the limits of the "black church" itself. He recognized that to make this "black and more than black" story truly universal—in order to move "beyond our narrow [racialized] dream—meant answering a political call to carry 'the spirit' he encountered on Sundays in Trinity out into the world and apply it 'through action.'"[20] In 2008, thirty years after he first encountered Wright's brand of black Christianity, as a presidential candidate Obama would be called to explain how this race-specific religion, which seemed to outsiders to exclude nonblacks in its vision of community and salvation, could shape him into the racially transcendent politician he presented himself to be.

When religion problems are race problems, too: Mitt Romney

Although it was certainly less evident than Obama's, Mitt Romney also had a race problem during the 2008 campaign. As W. Paul Reeve has argued, non-Mormon Americans long viewed the Mormon people as both a religious *and* a racial other. The Mormons' nineteenth-century enemies considered Mormon polygamy as so unnatural that offspring produced in polygamous homes were viewed as racially degenerate.[21] Mormons, like the Jews, Irish, and other not-quite-white cultural and ethnic minorities, responded to their racialization by asserting their (relative) whiteness in contrast to the blackness of African Americans. In their exegeses of the Bible and of Mormon-specific scriptures, in Utah territorial laws legalizing a form of "African" slavery, and in blackface minstrelsy performances, Mormons denigrated African Americans. They deemed black people unworthy of full citizenship and unworthy of enjoying the full blessings of the Mormon gospel. It was as recently as 1978 that the LDS Church lifted its bans on people of African descent from entering the Mormon priesthood and temples. But Mormons overcorrected in their pursuit of acceptance by white Christian America. In the nineteenth century, Mormons weren't white enough; by the time Romney was running for president in the early twenty-first century, they were so white as to be viewed with suspicion.[22]

In 2007, the Mormons' own imitation of (or perhaps more aptly, *signification*) on the image and ethos of "white Christian America"—their dress, their demonstrations of patriotism, their devotion to faith and family, their erstwhile racism, and their roles in the culture wars—struck many white evangelicals as landing somewhere in the uncanny valley.[23] This was particularly true of Mitt Romney, whose patrician pedigree, perfect family, and perfect hair made him look *too* presidential. In May 2006, after Romney gave a commencement address at Coe College in Iowa, one GOP blogger captured a sentiment shared by many GOP voters. Romney's "robotic" appearance made sense when they learned that he was a Mormon. "Look at that dude," the blogger wrote. "Lantern-jawed, excellent physical shape, jet-black hair with graying temples, crisp suit, and too long in the tanning booth. He's a caricature of your slick and soulless politician."[24]

Like the religion that he embodied, Romney had succeeded in becoming the exemplar American. He was wealthy, healthy, and handsome beyond his years. He was prolific at producing children and grandchildren who were also wealthy, healthy, and handsome. He was also the son—it's worth mentioning—of another successful businessman and popular governor, George W. Romney, who, exactly forty years before, had his own (unrealized) presidential ambitions. Mitt Romney's mother also ran unsuccessfully for the US Senate in 1970. The younger Romney was motivated, at least in part, to run in order to establish his family as one of the dynasties of American politics.[25] But in 2007, as one New Hampshire GOP primary voter described him, Romney was just "a little too perfect."[26] His perfection made voters and observers so uncomfortable that they wanted to undress him—almost literally. It became a sport, of sorts, to try to spot wrinkles in Romney's tailored suits that might be "Mormon underwear," the garments that Mormons wear under their clothes as part of their devotion to modesty. *The Atlantic*'s Andrew Sullivan posted images of models sporting the sacred garments, though he wished he had some "visuals" of Romney himself.[27] Maureen Dowd suggested that, to the well-established question that reporters like to pose to presidential candidates, "boxers or briefs[?]," because of Romney, there now existed a third possibility, "the [Mormon] Garment."[28] The "underwear" question served as a synecdoche for a larger constellation of questions about Mormon secrecy and insularity, which some believed masked insincerity. Electing Romney might mean installing a member of a cunning "cult" in the Oval Office, the ultimate coup of the cabal from Salt Lake City who would remake America in its image.

Since the moment he announced his White House bid in January 2007, as Romney's candidacy grew in strength, so did the volume and velocity of questions—coming from everyday voters, pundits, as well as rival politicians—about his religion. Mormons looked like, talked like, and walked like them—perhaps even better than them. But in early December 2007, as Romney was campaigning in Iowa, a Pew poll found that

36 percent of white evangelical Protestants—the core of the GOP base—said they were less likely to vote for a Mormon presidential candidate. No other segment of the electorate signaled such a strong opposition to Mormonism.[29] Not coincidently by that time, Mike Huckabee had propelled himself into a tie with Romney in Iowa. And he did so in no small measure by playing up his evangelical-insider status and contrasting it with the specter of Romney's Mormonism.[30]

"Faith in America"

Until December 2007, Romney had been reticent, if not recalcitrant, about discussing his personal faith. He was deeply cognizant that it could be a liability among many white evangelical Republican voters. Yet Romney's campaign insiders, as well as GOP pundits, urged Romney to face the "Mormon problem" head on or risk having his campaign submerged by it.[31] In an attempt to right his foundering campaign and to lay out his vision for the role that religion should play in American public life more broadly, on December 6, Romney delivered a speech entitled, "Faith in America," at the George H. W. Bush Presidential Library in College Station, Texas.[32]

From the outset of his speech, Romney made clear that there was a clear precedent in coming before the American people to answer questions about how his faith would inform his presidency. "Almost 50 years ago another candidate from Massachusetts explained that he was an American running for president, not a Catholic running for president." And this president, then Senator John F. Kennedy, also did so in Texas. On September 12, 1960, before the Greater Houston Ministerial Association, Kennedy responded to charges from anti-Catholic nativist groups that as president Kennedy would carry out a counter-Reformation, forcing American Protestants to live under "papal oppression" and pervert American "religious freedom."[33] "Like him" Romney continued, without ever actually naming Kennedy, "I am an American running for president." And like Kennedy, Romney proposed to the American people that he'd separate the presidency—long considered the seat of America's "civil religion"—from his faith.[34]

Because of the historic conflation between (white) American Protestantism and the (white) American state, past Protestant presidential candidates—including recent ones like Jimmy Carter and George W. Bush—had the privilege of presenting themselves as the (white) "evangelical" candidate.[35] Romney recognized that even though it led him to hold the same views on abortion and homosexuality as white evangelical Americans, his Mormonism afforded him no such privilege. "I do not define my candidacy by my religion," Romney said. And like Kennedy before him, Romney asked to be judged on his political merits, not on his religious affiliation. Romney thus sought to assure GOP primary voters that they need not worry he'd seek to make America Mormon. There would be no late-night phone calls from the Oval Office to the prophets in Temple Square. "Let me assure you that no authorities of my church, or any other church for that matter, will ever exert influence on my presidential decisions." "The obligations of the office and the Constitution," Romney said, would trump "doctrine of any church" in a Romney Administration.[36]

And yet in his speech, Romney also attempted to present himself as a kind of pluralist, who regards other faiths with admiring envy. "In every faith there are features I wish were my own: I love the profound ceremony of the Catholic Mass, the approachability of God in the prayers of the Evangelicals, the tenderness of spirit among Pentecostals, the confident independence of the Lutherans, the ancient traditions of the Jews, unchanged through the ages, and the commitment to frequent prayer of the Muslims."[37] Romney celebrated these diverse forms of religion in America. He also implied that "while differences in theology exist between churches in America," when expressed in "the public square" these theologies reinforce "a common creed of moral convictions." As such, Romney argued that the best Americans have always been religious Americans. "Whether it was the cause of abolition, or civil rights, or the right to life itself, no movement of conscience can succeed in America that cannot speak to the convictions of religious people."[38]

By championing religion's historical role—but not *a specific religion*—to expand Americans' freedoms and protect the most vulnerable, Romney aligned himself to another twentieth-century president, Dwight D. Eisenhower. In 1952, as the Cold War with the Soviet Union intensified, Eisenhower famously quipped, "Our form of government has no sense unless it is founded in a deeply-felt religious faith, and I don't care what it is." Eisenhower believed that Americans' faith in the "Judeo-Christian concept . . . [that] all men are created equal" could serve as a buttress against the godless communism of the Soviet Union.[39] To be sure, it did not present the same existential threat to American democracy as communist statism. But Romney also warned of the creep of "the religion of secularism" in which some Americans conflate the insidious effort "to remove from the public domain any acknowledgment of God" with the celebrated (Jeffersonian) "notion of the separation of the church and state." And yet not all religions are created equal. In fact, according to Romney, when taken to extremes one religion, namely, "radical violent Islam," is "infinitely worse" than secularism because it "seeks to destroy" America. The "radical Islamists" hate "religious freedom" because they believe that all of humanity should be converted to Islam, even by "conquest" or "violent jihad." Just as the state should not destroy religion, Islamic "theocratic tyranny" cannot be allowed to become the state, explained Romney, as it is in certain parts of the world.[40]

Thus in "Faith in America," Romney implied that the more religious America is, the freer it is; Islam is a noted exception. But if Islam is the least of the Abrahamic Faiths, or at least the one with the greatest potential for extremism, Romney also implied that the Christian faith is the greatest in America because it was the first. The nation's Founders created a constitutional system that "proscribed the establishment of a state religion" because of their faith in God, not despite it. "It was in Philadelphia that our founding fathers defined a revolutionary vision of liberty, grounded on self-evident truths about the equality of all, and the inalienable rights with which each is endowed by his Creator." This nation was founded "Under God," Romney said. If he were elected, Romney implied that he'd protect the nation's acknowledgments to God—"on our currency, in our pledge, in the teaching or our history"—and protect the right to proclaim God "during the holiday season, [in] nativity scenes and menorahs . . . in public places."[41] In his speech announcing his candidacy for the White House in February 2007, Romney rejected calls by the likes of Barack Obama to immediately end the war in Iraq.[42] But in December that same year, he promised to end the war on Christmas, a position that he certainly hoped would resonate with the white evangelical Christian voters to whom his speech was chiefly addressed.

In "Faith in America," Romney said a lot about "religious freedom" and "religious liberty," phrases he used three times and five times respectively. He said a lot about how religious freedom in America created a freer, more equal America. And he said a lot about what he called the two greatest threats to American religion and American freedom: extreme secularism and extreme Islam. But in a speech purportedly about Romney's own faith he had very little to say. Romney uttered the word "Mormon" only once; he referred to "my faith," "my church," and "my religion" three times each. (He never mentioned the official name of his church: the LDS Church.) Romney did acknowledge that his faith was a significant issue for some voters. "They would prefer if I would simply distance myself from my religion." But Romney said that he would not do so, even if "a confession of my faith will sink my candidacy." Instead, in the face of that possibility, Romney said, "I believe in my Mormon faith and I endeavor to live by it. My faith is the faith of my fathers—I will be true to them and to my beliefs."[43]

What exactly did Romney tell America about these beliefs? Romney ventured to answer only one theological question about Mormonism: "What do I believe about Jesus Christ?" But in posing this question, what Romney really attempted to do is answer the biggest question that white evangelicals had about Mormonism: "Are Mormons Christians?" "I believe that Jesus Christ is the Son of God and the Savior of mankind," Romney stated. Romney acknowledged, "My church's beliefs about Christ may not all be the same as those of other faiths." But if Christians are defined by their faith in Christ, then according to Romney, Mormons, like Protestants and Catholics, Lutherans and Methodists, Pentecostals and Baptists, are Christians.[44]

Seeking to win over white evangelical voters, in "Faith in America," Romney attempted to map out common ground upon which they both could meet. Shared faith in Christ was a logical and theologically sincere place to start. Yet in presenting Mormonism as (just another) Christian faith in America, Romney (all but) failed to account for the history of his faith in America. In his only sideways nod to the Mormons' history as a pariah people, Romney noted that while America's first colonies were founded by religious people seeking "religious liberty," these same religious freedom seekers "denied it to others. Because of their diverse beliefs, Ann Hutchinson was exiled from Massachusetts Bay, a banished Roger Williams founded Rhode Island, and two centuries later, Brigham Young set out for the West."[45]

By citing Young, Mormonism's second prophet who took over the majority of the faithful after Joseph Smith's assassination by an anti-Mormon mob in 1844, Romney did include Mormonism in his history lesson of religious intolerance in America. But in his anodyne formulation—the Mormons "set out for the west"— Romney also stripped from this history the truth that the Mormons were more akin to religious refugees fleeing west for their lives than pioneers. He also stripped from this history its theological importance for the Mormons. The Mormons reframed this exile as an exodus, in which they, with Young serving as their Moses, became the latter-day Israelites escaping from the American Egypt to find refuge in their

Zion in the Intermountain West.[46] Romney also failed to account for the historical irony of a Mormon presidential candidate denigrating Islam (in an extreme form) as incompatible with the American way of life. At the start of the twentieth century, even after the LDS Church officially abandoned polygamy, Mormonism was itself called "the Islam of America." Sultan-like polygamists were depicted as making "dupes and slaves" of the women forced into "moral perversity," fathering a degenerate, less-than-white race, and governing their desert kingdom as a tyrannical theocracy.[47]

In "Faith in America," Romney attempted to champion the history of "faith in America." That is, he sought to celebrate the history of religion's role in making the American experiment a success. But in deploying this not-so-subtle wordplay, Romney also (all but) failed to place the history of his own faith *in America*. This was perhaps a missed opportunity. He could have tracked how Mormonism first came to be because of America's religious liberty; how Mormons themselves became religious exiles because of religious intolerance; and how Mormons overcame this intolerance to become exemplary faithful, patriotic, (and white) productive Americans—to the point that an exemplary faithful (and exemplary white) Mormon might even become a major party presidential candidate.

Romney attempted to make his speech a demonstration of his own "faith in America." He wanted to show that he had faith in the American electorate. "Americans do not respect believers of convenience," he said. Instead, Romney believed that they would respond favorably to a strong declaration of faith. And it was those who believed otherwise who actually did not have faith in America; "they underestimate the American people." "Religious tolerance," Romney said, "would be a shallow principle indeed if it were reserved only for faiths with which we agree." And yet Romney demonstrated that his own faith in America was limited. Perhaps believing that to speak directly to Mormonism's "unique doctrines and history" would drive away evangelical voters, he presented Mormonism as (just another) form of Christianity. Romney hoped to show that he was similar enough to white evangelicals, whose backing he desperately needed, to be palatable, even if he'd never be preferable.

"A More Perfect Union"

Three months after Romney delivered "Faith in America," Barack Obama's candidacy was also in turmoil because of his own religious (and racial) background. On March 13, CBS News first ran excerpts of Jeremiah Wright's controversial speeches. Wright quickly became the dominant story of the campaign. Reporters, pundits, and voters asked, did Obama share Wright's race-specific—many called them racist—views about America's past and present? If so, how could Obama be the president for all Americans?

Unlike Romney, who many believed took too long to address Americans' concerns about his Mormonism, Obama responded quickly to the growing questions about his affiliation with Jeremiah Wright. On March 14, Obama published a short essay in the *Huffington Post* in which he called Wright's statements "about our country, our politics, and my political opponents" "inflammatory and appalling."[48] That same day, Obama's campaign announced that it had dropped Wright from its African American Religious

Leadership Committee.[49] Perhaps practicing the political adage that Obama's future White House Chief of Staff Rahm Emanuel popularized, "never let a serious crisis go to waste," Obama and his speechwriters sprang into action. Over the next few days and nights, they composed a speech that they hoped would not only explain Obama's relationship with Wright and with the "black church" that Wright represented. They hoped to place this relationship—and Obama's candidacy itself—into the larger sweep of America's racial and religious history, and into the (never finished) work of achieving the promises of the nation's founding generation.[50]

On March 18, at Philadelphia's Constitution Center, Obama delivered "A More Perfect Union." If Mitt Romney's choice of location was intended to echo Kennedy's address from 1960, Obama's (borrowed) provenance was even older and more august. "We the people, in order to form a more perfect union," Obama began his speech by quoting the preamble of the Constitution, which he noted, was written 221 years ago, "in a hall across the street." Like Romney, Obama pointed out the irony that America's Founders were descendants of religious refugees "who traveled across an ocean to escape tyranny and persecution," only to enact tyranny and persecution on others. But Obama focused on America's persecution of the racial other, not the religious one. From the outset, the Constitution and the union that it was written to forge were "stained by this nation's original sin of slavery," Obama said. In this incipient union, one (white) people's freedom, Obama implied, was contingent, on the enslavement of a (black) other.[51]

Obama spoke of the constant need in American history for prophets and protestors to draw attention to the imperfection of this union. "Words on parchment would not be enough to deliver slaves from bondage," Obama said. "What would be needed were Americans in successive generations who were willing to do their part—through protests and struggles, on the streets and in the courts, through a civil war and civil disobedience, and always at great risk—to narrow that gap between the promise of our ideals and the reality of their time." In his speech, Obama acknowledged—and once again repudiated—Wright's "controversial" and "inflammatory" rhetoric. But Obama also explained that as a "fierce critic of American domestic and foreign policy," Wright also fit squarely into this lineage of Jeremiah-like, truth-telling justice fighters. And Wright spoke these truths, Obama implied, not out of hatred for America but, as a former marine, respected scholar, and preacher, out of dedication to it. Throughout his career, Wright modeled the best of the black church tradition. "By housing the homeless, ministering to the needy, providing day care services and scholarships and prison ministries, and reaching out to those suffering from HIV/AIDS," Obama explained that Wright served communities that the rest of American society—including the American government—had neglected.[52]

Obama highlighted the basic theology that informed Wright's community work. In fact, in his speech, Obama quoted directly from his first memoir, *Dreams from My Father*, in which he describes Wright's "Audacity of Hope" sermon. It was common "hope," Obama learned from Wright's black liberation theology, as much as common "tears" and "blood," that connected "the stories of ordinary black people" in modern-day Chicago with the stories of the ancient Israelites and the first Christians. To be sure, Obama did not shy away from criticizing Wright for turning these stories, which

Obama understood as "unique and universal, black and more than black," into the sole providence of black Americans. Obama acknowledged that "anger" poisoned some of Wrights views. Wrights "remarks . . . weren't simply a religious leader's efforts to speak out against perceived injustice," Obama said. "Instead, they expressed a profoundly distorted view of this country—a view that sees white racism as endemic."[53] But Obama's message was that Wright's occasional descent into black nationalism was the exception. In emphasizing Wright's "Audacity of Hope" sermon, Obama hoped to show that on most Sundays, Wright preached Christ-like unity; the controversial sermons of damnation and wrath against white America were the outliers.[54]

In their speeches, Romney described secularism and (extremist) Islam as the greatest threats to the expansion of liberty in America; Obama described racial strife as the greatest impediment to a more perfect union. Romney pledged that he would be the pro-religious growth president—or at least religious growth of a certain (Judeo-Christian) kind. He promised that he would expand religious freedoms (for some) because he believed that more (good) religion meant more liberty for all. Yet Romney shied away from offering his own religion's history as a symbol of what those expanded religious freedoms can yield. Obama, however, offered his family history—"the son of a black man from Kenya and a white woman from Kansas"—as a model bridge that had successfully spanned the chasm between black and white America. "I was raised with the help of a white grandfather who survived a Depression to serve in Patton's Army during World War II . . . I am married to a black American who carries within her the blood of slaves and slaveowners—an inheritance we pass on to our two precious daughters." His history was American history, Obama explained: "in no other country on Earth is my story even possible."[55]

In his speech, Obama leveraged his black *and* white histories and identities to represent the best of twentieth-century America. An insider to both, the biracial Obama engaged in bidirectional respectability politics, hoping to (re)introduce one America to the other. As a grandson of the Greatest Generation, for white America, he walked through the opened doors of a "black church" on the Southside of Chicago. There, as a young man, he was brought to Christ and witnessed on many Sundays that "the doctor and the welfare mom, the model student and the former gang-banger" worshiped together side by side. "Trinity's services are full of raucous laughter and sometimes bawdy humor. They are full of dancing and clapping and screaming and shouting that may seem jarring to the untrained ear." Obama explained—in a rhetorical style that was a study in contrast to Wright's bombast—the untrained (white) ear might be jarred by "black anger" about the legacy of racial injustice, which continues to produce failing schools, unemployment, and mass incarceration.

Furthermore, as a latter-day member of black America's Talented Tenth, Obama opened the doors of a white home in Kansas to find a woman who "worked a bomber assembly line at Fort Leavenworth" during World War II and later "helped raise me, a woman who sacrificed again and again for me, a woman who loves me as much as she loves anything in this world."[56] But in this same home, Obama's grandmother also "once confessed her fear of black men who passed her by on the street, and who on more than one occasion has uttered racial or ethnic stereotypes that made me cringe." Obama explained that this "white resentment" toward racial others derives from the fact that hardworking people like his grandmother "don't feel that they have been particularly privileged by their race." But now they see their jobs disappearing due to globalization and automation, while "they hear an African-American is getting an advantage in landing a good job or a spot in a good college because of an injustice that they themselves never committed."[57] Obama's Kansas grandmother's racial resentments were particular to her. But in Obama's speech, these views also served as a proxy for those of other downwardly mobile white Americans who, as Thomas Frank observed in *What' the Matter with Kansas*, exchange at the ballot box their economic interests for promised victories in the culture wars.[58]

In his speech, Romney refused to disown the "faith of his fathers"; he could not separate his own (racial and religious) identity from his and his family's membership in the LDS Church. Likewise, while calling attention to the limitations of the black and white community that they represented, Obama said, "I can no more disown him [Wright] than I can disown my white grandmother." In this regard, Obama proposed that the nation follow his lead and empathize with both black anger and white resentment as a step toward overcoming the present "racial stalemate." For white America, "the path to a more perfect union means acknowledging that what ails the African-American community does not exist in the minds of black people." For black America, "that path means embracing the burdens of our past without becoming victims of our past . . . [and it means] binding our particular grievances . . . to the larger aspirations of all Americans: the white woman struggling to break the glass ceiling, the white man who has been laid off, the immigrant trying to feed his family."[59]

From these mutual expressions of empathy, Obama envisioned that a new era in American politics would emerge. It would embrace the idea "that your dreams do not have to come at the expense of my dreams; that investing in the health, welfare and education of black and brown and white children will ultimately help all of America prosper." Obama proposed that this new era be forged out of two old theologies. First, as the "world great religions demand," and as "[Judeo-Christian] scripture tell us," "Let us be our brother's keeper. Let us be our sister's keeper," Obama said. Second, Obama proposed a renewed faith in America's own greatest religion: the gospel of "self-help." By "taking full responsibility of our own lives" and by taking responsibility for the upbringing of their children, American fathers must teach their children "that while they may face challenges and discrimination in their own lives, they must never succumb to despair or cynicism; they must always believe that they can write their own destiny."[60]

Obama's emphasis on the importance of fathers being present—in large measure to catechize their children in the American gospel of self-help—is notable because of Obama's own father's absence. Clearly, in the care of mothers and grandparents (all but) fatherless children can grow up to be productive workers, engaged citizens, and caring parents. In March 2008, as he delivered an address to the nation from Philadelphia's Constitution Center, then senator Barack Obama was the living embodiment of this fact. And yet, Obama's address was, in large measure, about his father. Specifically, it was about his spiritual father, Jeremiah Wright, and that father's faith. Contrast this with Romney. More than from his own father, Romney took on the "dreams from his mother," as a 2012 *Time* profile described his role as a surrogate and confidante to his mother Lenore Romney during her 1970 bid for the US Senate from Michigan. Mitt Romney also learned from his mother to be wary—perhaps overly wary—about how much to give of himself to the public.[61] This is evident in his "Faith in America" speech; Romney leaned away from the religion problem. In his own speech, Obama leaned in; he mentioned "Reverend Wright" by name fourteen times. In doing so, Obama contextualized for the mostly white electorate whose support he needed to win the Democratic nomination the unique role that the black church had played in America's past and present.

E. Franklin Frazier famously called the "Negro Church" "a Nation within a Nation" because black churches provided black Americans the material, political, and spiritual sustenance and cultural norms to which they were long denied access in the larger (white) American nation. In "A More Perfect Union," Barack Obama refused to disown the father who had welcomed him into this nation and who introduced him to the beauty and power of the black Christian experience. But in the very audacity required for him to run to become the first black president of the (white) American nation, Obama demonstrated that he refused to have his dreams or his "destiny," and that of the coalition "of white and black, Latino and Asian, rich and poor, young and old" that he represented, be limited by his spiritual father's notion of that nation.[62]

Conclusion: When one religion problem becomes another

In "Faith in America," Mitt Romney tried to present himself not as a Mormon, whose faith and familial history exemplify at once the ideals and limitations of the history of religious freedom in America. Instead, he tried to present himself as an ahistorical Christian. Beyond his faith in Christ and in American liberty, the "unique doctrines and history" of Romney's particular religion need not concern the voting electorate. In any event, beyond how these beliefs required him to defend "the right to life," the sanctity of traditional marriage, and the sacrality of the Christmas season, Romney promised not to bring these particular beliefs into the White House with him.[63]

"Faith in America" dominated the news in the GOP primary race for several days after Romney delivered it in Texas. Initially, the response seemed positive. Romney garnered praise from pundits on the left and right. Focus on the Family's James Dobson called "Faith in America" "a magnificent reminder of the role religious faith must play in government and public policy."[64] But on the ground in Iowa where it counted most, Romney did not succeed in persuading white evangelical voters to put their support behind him. In fact, some evangelicals were appalled that Romney would claim to be Christian at all. Romney lost the Iowa caucus to Huckabee 27 percent to 34 percent and never regained his front-runner status. In early February he withdrew from the race after Senator John McCain emerged as the presumptive nominee. Postmortems of Romney's campaign focused on the religion problem as the deciding factor. According to some reports, even Romney himself believed, "had he been a Baptist, for example, he may not of have lost the Iowa caucuses—a devastating setback to his early surge strategy."[65]

Romney's Mormon problem did not go away when he ran again four years later. A hit Broadway show, the LDS Church's own "I'm a Mormon" international media campaign, and Romney's win in the GOP nominating contest brought unprecedented attention to Mormonism. During this "Mormon Moment" old slurs against Mormonism—that it was a "cult," that it was a cover for a massive untaxed business empire, to name just two—resurfaced. But new Mormon problems also emerged. Notably, as Romney, the devout Mormon, tried to unseat Barack Obama, America's first black president, questions about his church's (never-fully repudiated) antiblack theologies and its history of excluding people of African descent from full church membership came into sharper relief. Some Mormon critics believed that if Romney was successful at winning the White House, because he and his church exemplified the "whitest" of white America, it would signal a return of pre–civil rights era white supremacy in American politics and culture.[66]

Romney's anti-Mormon critics had the right idea, but the wrong man at the wrong time. In 2016, it was Donald Trump's primary and Electoral College victory in the general election that signaled a "whitelash" to President Obama's progressive, pluralistic, multicultural America. Of all people, Mitt Romney emerged as one of the most vocal NeverTrumpers. He did so in large measure because of his devout Mormon faith. In fact, in March 2016 just before the Utah primaries in a speech at the University of Utah, Romney gave his strongest repudiation of Trump. The speech was thoroughly—though not explicitly—Mormon. Speaking to his fellow Mormons, who prize honesty, modesty, personal character, and service to others, Romney labeled Trump "a con man, a fake" who "mocked a disabled reporter, who attributed a reporter's questions to her menstrual cycle." Not only does he prey on the weaknesses of others to hock his often-worthless wares and services. Romney also said that Trump preys on Americans' economic and security fears to make "scapegoats of Muslims and Mexicans immigrants."[67] In alluding to Trump's proposed Mexican border wall and Muslim travel ban, Romney addressed both the Mormons' past and present persecution as a religious community. Mormons, of course, know something of being scapegoats; their history is replete with periods of state-sponsored persecution and even anti-Mormon violence.[68] But Romney also hoped to convince Mormons to reject Trump because of the church's international growth; Mexico is today the home to more Mormons outside of the United States than any other country.[69]

In the primary, Utah roundly rejected Trump. But, even with the anti-Trump conservative Mormon Evan McMullin on the ballot as a third-party candidate in the general election, most Republican Mormons ultimately came home to the party. As a result, Trump easily won Utah's six electoral votes. However, to the chagrin of many Mormons, the famed Mormon Tabernacle Choir sang at Trump's inauguration.[70] Even more alarming, Romney himself was briefly being considered as a contender to be Trump's secretary of state. While many saw Romney's willingness to work with a man whom he despises as cowardly capitulation, it could also be interpreted as an act of patriotism, as a largely vain attempt at providing professional leadership at the State Department that just might help the United States avoid international disaster. The Trump years might provide Mitt Romney, arguably the most famous Mormon in the world, and the LDS Church itself ample time to articulate "faith in America," especially faith in America's legal and cultural legacy of supporting religious liberty for all.

Thus, Mitt Romney's presidential legacy as a Mormon has yet to be written, if not as President Romney then perhaps as Senator Romney, a vocal critic of President Trump. Similarly, the legacy of President Obama and his religion problem(s)—the parts for which he is accountable and the parts he is not—began with his March 2008 "A More Perfect Union" speech. Pollsters and pundits in the weeks after the speech and historians since have argued that not only did Obama steady his campaign. With the nation's eyes on him, Obama so successfully seized the opportunity to frame his racially (and religiously) transcendent politics that it just might have won him the White House.[71]

Still Obama's critics focused not on what Obama did in the speech, but what he didn't—disown Wright outright. While for much of the nation "A More Perfect Union" helped answer questions about Obama's (rumored) black church radicalism, the right pounced on Obama's refusal to break completely with Wright to suggest that Obama ascribed to even more dangerous radicalisms, rumors which would follow Obama throughout his presidency. In his May 2008 *National Review* cover story on Jeremiah Wright, Stanley Kurtz forwarded a "scholarly" version of the right-wring conspiracy theory that had been circulating on the Internet for years. Conflating fears about Obama's racial and religious identities, conservatives spun a narrative about Obama's attraction to anti-American figures like Wright that allegedly spoke to some natural or nurtured foreignness in Obama's personal and familial history. According to their logic, it wasn't just that Obama was himself un-American and un-Christian, but rather that he was certainly never an American much less a Christian.[72]

The rise of the thoroughly debunked "birtherism" into the national political discourse dovetailed with the Jeremiah Wright controversy. So did claims that Obama was a secret Muslim.[73] As an official presidential candidate, Donald Trump launched his own path to the White House by scapegoating Mexicans and later Muslims. But it is important to recall that Trump's divisive presidential bid unofficially began a few years earlier when he emerged as the nation's "birther-in-chief." Due at least in part to Trump's efforts, among Obama critics the percentage of Americans who believed that Obama was a Muslim grew during his presidency. A CNN/ORC poll from September 2015 found that 29 percent of American adults (and 43 percent of Republicans) believed that Obama was a Muslim, while only 39 percent of American adults correctly identified Obama as a Christian.[74]

Yet, at the end of his presidency, Obama was more Christian than ever. For example, his 2015 eulogy of Clementa C. Pinckney, the state senator and the senior pastor of Mother Emmanuel A.M.E. Church in Charleston, South Carolina, who was assassinated along with eight other worshippers by a white supremacist during a weekday Bible study at the church. Famously, during the eulogy, Obama preached on "grace" which, he explained, in the "Christian tradition . . . is not earned . . . [but] is the free and benevolent favor of God, such a reflection prompted him to spontaneously sing the chorus of Amazing Grace."[75] And yet, it is among the most painful paradoxes of the Obama era that a president of deep faith, unparalleled exegetical acumen, and Christ-like empathy was so despised by so many of his fellow (white) Christian Americans.

It is a painful paradox that perhaps more than any other president in modern presidential history, a man who spoke powerfully about how his faith has shaped his own personal history—and spoke of the histories of both the white and black Americas that raised him and that he sought to serve as president—could not unify the union he dreamed of helping to perfect. In the spirit of Obama's (and Wright's) audacity of hope, the age of Obama need not end with the advent of Trump era. Perhaps Americans can return and renew this hope by reading Obama's words, and find in them not just the messages of a former president but also those of a prophet who brought forth an as-yet unheeded jeremiad rooted in black liberation and respectability politics.[76]

Political Spirituality, or the Oprahfication of Obama[1]

Kathryn Lofton

First, you need a name. Not just any name. An unusual name: a biblical misspelling, maybe, or an invocation of some distant land. No matter what, the name needs an O. The O will come in handy when you need to summon a common sphere, encourage chanting, or design an expansive logo. Never deny its replication. Never avoid its allusion. Never miss an opportunity for its branding.[2] An O is a space anyone can fill with anything.

Second, you need a life. Not just any life. A life that is ready to be a story, prepared for metaphor, assembled in advance by memoir, by professional mode, or by fictional expectation. If Aaron Sorkin or Alice Walker is not available for the scribing, you must be prepared to tell your story yourself again and again, mentioning its familiar bits like tired icebreakers to loosen the uncomfortable, the unfamiliar, and the closet racists. Advertise your chronological or genealogical messiness: the hardscrabble youth, the absent parent, the nonnuclear family, the experiments with drugs, the cultural patois that produced your singular self. Tell the story like it is utterly improbable that it happened, even as you knew, you knew from the beginning that you were destined. The more you say it, the more it will become the new normal. Your small, sweeping, rural, urban, abusive, tender, confusing, and familiar tale of ascent is what they have been waiting to hear. The American Dream is no conjure. It is you.[3]

Third, you will need a crew. Not many people: just enough to create a familiar inner circle of stand-up, saucy influences. A truth-telling African American female intimate is a must. So is a tall, experienced white man. Whereas the white guy can be crass, even obnoxious, the woman must know the value of strategic silence. She also should relax her hair. Obviously, she must look fantastic, always. Her control over her aesthetic will suggest in part that she is tamed.

Keeping great people close is important because you will often feel alone. Being alone is strange, since it is your burden to be that which nobody can dislike, to which everyone wants to be near. Prepare yourself: this is an exhausting sort of friendliness. Rick Warren and Gene Robinson must feel comfortable next to you. Starlets and statesmen must respect you. Bill Cosby must like you. White women need to feel safe with you. Homosexuals must love you, even as you sometimes co-opt their affections and ignore their causes. Resist the temptation to call old friends who may infect you with toxic associations. Celebrate mothers and family but steer clear of feminists and fathers. Mourn the loss of mid-century America even if it was the America that segregated you. Assign a family life you never had; endorse the nuclear sweetness your childhood biography lacks. Eschew race reification, but cultivate black institutions early. Their loyalty will supersede your betrayals. Connect personally with Africa. Connect with Peoria. Connect with the Bronx. Vacation on the Pacific Rim, but be from Chicago. *Be* Chicago. Attend Jeremiah Wright's church. Use the music of U2 and Stevie Wonder, and any high-spirited progressive-friendly country you can find. Get a dog.[4]

Fourth, you will need a style. This manner will help you endure some hard knocks. Inevitably, some people will call you the Antichrist. Others will call you a sellout. Some will call you a cult leader. Take these assaults with nonchalance. Make criticism about you seem silly, cynical, even bigoted. Through it all, master the encompassing hold, the sense that you are accessible to everyone. Yet retain an incommensurable mystery. Keep people guessing: does she mean it? What does he *really* believe? Some will regard this as an admirable equanimity, while others will see it as a shallow capaciousness. No matter. You will counter those claims with discipline, with consistency, with extraordinary prescience.[5] You will confound expectations over and over again. Your mistakes will be translated as incidentally brilliant. You will possess a preternatural ability to give people what they want, to know what they need, to sell what they will buy. Prepare yourself for the resultant sale of yourself. You have to get over any anxieties about your own assimilation, incorporation, and amalgamation. Be the commodity. Put your O everywhere. Your iconography is how they brace against the disappointments of your humanity.

Fifth, you will need to be ambivalent. You have always been neither here nor there, neither us nor them, and neither of or outside. You have always been able to see from many perspectives, to appeal to many sorts of people, to believe many different things. You do so even as you are fiercely moral, upstanding, and almost pious. You are, as everyone knows, a Christian. Even more: a Protestant. But you dabble in everything, never shying away from the Quran or kabbalah, Jewish professors, or Eastern spiritual advisers.[6] You pick up what you need from where in order to understand who you are and why others are as they are. You are open for a spiritual journey, even as you are clear about what finally you believe. You are the ambiguity of your epoch, the middle that makes the mass, the crossroads of a country that excited your youth, raped your ancestral continent, and claps now for your beautiful children. You are a global distribution suffused with spiritual truth. You are motivated with missionary zeal to convert everyone, unrelentingly, to change. You make them believe their best lives are yet to come. You make it impossible to look away, to hate, to dissent, or to change the channel. You make us feel *good*, finally. You are our redemption.[7] And you are our satisfaction at the possibility of a secular that made it all so.

* * *

As I wrote those words in the days before the inauguration of Barack Hussein Obama in January 2009, the world seemed to be in a state of perpetual postcoital sighing. After a two-year bated breath, a nation of new believers could, finally, exhale: we did it, they hummed, it has happened. Hope lives. Diversity thrives. America *is.*

Historians make lousy politicians and religionists make even dodgier prophets, but from the minute Barack Obama took a Springfield, Illinois, stage in February 2007 and said, "I am as you are," it seemed more plausible than not that he could run the board. Those resistant to his possible victory were in part protective of his symbolic meaning. Yet the phrase "no one will ever elect a black man president in America" was said often by observers who would, absolutely, vote for a black president. "I'll admit that when Obama first entered this race, my jaded friends and I rolled our eyes," reported one writer in *The Washington Post*, explaining that they reflexively "doubted the humanity of the people he needed to convince in order to win."[8]

The nation waited nervously, watching the romantic comedy play out. Typical intervening problems ensued, including appearances of several stock archetypes. There was the shadowy figure from the past, offering information to threaten the relationship; the dorky but super-prepared gal competitor, reminding the audience that in love, good people get hurt; the disturbingly uninformed but superhot girl, reminding the audience that looks can be deceiving; and the grumpy old wiseacre man, the one with the story of torturous times and more socioeconomic sway. In the end, he is the one who contorted the most and did, with his old heroism and aching body, hit home a taste or two of guilt. But those are the breaks. Love isn't love if it hasn't met reasonable alternatives, and turned them down; if it hasn't heard some tough things, and moved beyond; if it hasn't seen the darker side of human sadness, and felt redeemed. Any good requited love story requires the looming sense of its own implausibility in order for the release, for that final embrace to feel so won. They did it, you smile in the dark theater, they beat them all. Yes, we can. Yes, we can. Yes, we can.

Rimming the route to Oz was a very specific Glinda, the divine Miss O. She was there, if occasionally hidden from view. Sometimes she preached before a podium, proud. Other times, she joined the masses, with tears streaming down her face as she stared up at the stage where he stood. Her varied positions reflected her own multivalent occupations, as she simultaneously played cheerleading promoter, platinum donor, and average voter. She repeatedly refused credit for his success, saying that it wasn't anything she had done. His Spirit had permeated the masses, she said, and this spirit reminded people not only of who he was, but also of what they could be.

The relationship between Oprah Winfrey and Barack Obama is not only the relationship between plug and product, between the endorser and the endorsed. It is more: it is a correlation between two products that format themselves in strikingly similar ways. *Oprahfication* describes a type of commodification in which the personal is commercialized and spiritualized through confessions, conversions, and popular showcases of pluralism. When journalists or pundits refer to this phenomenon, they mean to be derogatory. They mean to say that once upon a time we didn't talk about our emotions or personal problems but now we do because she made it legitimate programming. Any subject, once Oprahfied, does not talk about structures and systems. Instead, they tell stories and solicit yours. They ask to hear specifically about your past and present troubles so as to set the stage for the moral in the story. Oprahfication isn't just the increased phenomenon of telling our private lives in public places; it is also the smoothing-out procedure that follows those disclosures. Once the story is said, we got good at saying what it means. Generic slogans about change wrap up the particular story of suffering. Describing Obama as "Oprahfied" emphasizes that the nation was readied, in part, for receipt of him by her. We were ready to get personal about our presidents.

This was her first real foray into electioneering. Despite her domineering symbolic heft on behalf of and in service to her nation, the presidency had never been seriously considered by her. When an interviewer asked Oprah in 1997 if she'd consider a run for the presidency, her reply was that "television is more powerful than politics."[9] Embattled Illinois governor Rod Blagojevich, desperate for any distraction from his prosecutor's glare, considered offering Barack Obama's vacated Senate seat to Oprah. "She was obviously someone with a much broader bully pulpit than other senators," he told *Good Morning America*.[10]

In reply to these compliments, she flicked away political life like a minor orbiting moon of a distant planet. What she did as talk show host was more potent than elected office, she said. She had more freedom, and more regular access to regular folks, than any DC insider. Yet this disinclination toward electoral politics should not suggest that she was apolitical. As demonstrated by the work of Janice Peck, Winfrey's project possesses political consequences and political descriptions even as it evades political issues. Since the switch to "Change Your Life TV," Winfrey has avoided debates on abortion or gay marriage, choosing instead to spotlight the difficulties facing young mothers and the happy lives of "out" fashion designers. A 2001 episode of *The Oprah Winfrey Show* on war encapsulates her emphasis. "As we all face here the possibility of war and question whether it is a choice we should make here at our crossroads in humanity, it is important, I think, to realize and to remember what the real face of war is," she announces before a montage of children in war-torn countries, "What it looks like, what it feels like, and what it does to humanity."[11] The personal story is the only war story she wants to share. Get into the person whom war affects, she argued, and you find the political morality nations should follow.

Never a politico like her talk show predecessor (and personal hero) Phil Donahue, Oprah finds her strongest sway by the hearth and in the home. Donahue was to liberalism what Oprah is to neoliberalism, with his assembling of debates and her assembling of affects. Directing readers, consumers, and voters to focus upon the domestic and the sentimental is an emphasis with a long political genealogy. The Oprah difference is to remind any viewer—Democrat or Republican—that priority one is care not of politics, not of other people, but of *you*. Care of nation will radiate from that self-nursing.

Her "Change Your Life Television" ferried politics from legislative bickering to pastel portraits. In the 2000 and 2004 elections, she interviewed each of the major party candidates separately and evenly, focusing more on family and hobbies and personality than positions on the economy or the environment. Her reasons for avoiding campaign interviews till then were eye level: "I've interviewed thousands of people over the years, but until today I've stayed away from politicians, really for one main reason: I—I—I never felt like I could have a real, real honest conversation with—there's this—kind of this wall that exists between the people and the authentic part of the candidate."[12] People suspected from her pet issues that she was a Democrat; people guessed from her income bracket she was a Republican. But no one knew for sure what her electoral preferences were. Then, in 2004, she saw Barack Obama give his address at the Democratic Convention, and she said to herself, "I think this is the One."[13] In 2008, she broke her voting silence and committed to limited campaign appearances and major fund-raising efforts on his behalf. Her repeated rationale for her entrance into this election was how perfectly Obama meshed with her ideal of the singular self. "I don't consider myself political, and I seldom interview politicians," she would repeat, "So when I decided to talk with [Obama], people around me were like, 'What's happened to you?' I said, 'I think this is beyond and above politics.' It feels like something new."[14] Obama was a candidate she believed transcended the pettiness of a two-party system to meet her in her undivided O.

Voting viewers predicted hers would be an influential endorsement. "I think Oprah is John the Baptist, leading the way for Obama to win," observed one Iowa caucus voter.[15] On the other hand, some media reports suggested that this endorsement cost Winfrey some Nielsen points, that she had expended her most valuable gift, her opinionated neutrality. Whatever costs there were, none diluted her own sense of product clarity. The endorsement of him, against all Nielsen tugs, proved again that the product was not the manipulation of market researchers, but was hers and hers alone. Obama was, like the items on the monthly *O, The Oprah Magazine* "O List," just another thing that Oprah thought was *just great*. That greatness has no podiums or positions. Like a purse, an ice cream flavor, or an Oprah Book Club selection, Oprah's presidential nominee was an extension of her partiality as her brand. It also turned out that, like most everything else, her taste was her nation's preference.[16] He won.

Now Oprah and Obama are names locked into documentary fusion. Forever, they will be the double-Os in the textbook, famous for what they are, and what they have done with the telling of who they are. "What Obama did, he's run as an American who is black, not as the black American," Colin Powell observed, "There's a difference . . . He ran honestly on the basis of who he is and what he is and his background, which is a fascinating background, but he didn't run just to appeal to black people or to say a black person could do it. He's running as an American."[17] This is an elision of the truth, since Obama ran as a conscious color palette, as a man whose conjure of his colors defined his manhood and cosmopolitan citizenship, shaping and naming and infusing his every motion. To Oprah, he would say, "I had to reconcile that I could be proud of my African-American heritage and not be limited by it," and she would reply, "that's now my favorite Barack Obama quote!"[18] In the naming of no limits, in the making of self black but not broken, not bitter, not sad, and not trapped, Obama became, as political scientist Ross K. Baker would remark, "the post-polarization candidate" just as "Oprah is a post-polarization celebrity." They find themselves, united together, in a compromised civility their corporate merger supplies.

In a lecture at the New York Public Library, novelist Zadie Smith spoke about the voice she grew up with in the London district of Willesden, and the voice she "added" when she went to Cambridge. For a while, and sometimes still, she slipped back and forth between her dialects. But now "this voice I picked up along the way is no longer an exotic garment I put on like a college gown whenever I choose—now it is my only voice, whether I want it or not. I regret it; I should have kept both voices alive in my mouth." Smith admires the way Barack Obama has had "more than one voice," and the way he used this plurality to posit himself as a Dream City, a collective space for people from nowhere to find themselves, finally, somewhere cool, somewhere that celebrates who they are now rather than wherever weird from whence they came. "Throughout his campaign," Smith continued,

> Obama was careful always to say we. He was noticeably wary of "I." By speaking so, he wasn't simply avoiding a singularity he didn't feel, he was also drawing us in with him. He had the audacity to suggest that, even if you can't see it stamped on their faces, most people come from Dream City, too. Most of us have complicated back stories, messy histories, multiple narratives.[19]

The key pronoun is the repeated "we." This collective supplies a seeming contrast between Oprah and Obama, since Winfrey rarely speaks of a "we," instead reiterating the authority of her "I." This is because Oprah believes that her "I" represents us. Oprah is, in this way, more exterior than Obama in her incorporations. She knows that what she is building is a consensus invented through her taste, a postulated us designed expressly for *us* by *her*. Obama, on the other hand, seeks to name common values that are not personal—even as his life story exhibits them, even as he argues for his particular story to win the election. He names the "we" but steers away from his I. "We're not as divided as our politics would indicate," he will say:

> You meet with the average person—I don't care if they're Republican, Democrat, conservative, liberal—they don't think in labels, they're not particularly ideological, everybody is sort of a mix of what you might consider some liberal ideas, what you might consider some conservative ideas. But there is a set of common values that everybody buys into: Everybody thinks you should have to work hard for what you get, everybody believes that things like equal opportunity should be real, not just a slogan.[20]

What are those common values? Smith's praise of Obama's Dream City invites real questions about the connection between campaigning and governing, between advertisement and application. Estimations of Obama's policies will be the work of future historians. What is pressing for this work is the problem of the common, for an *I* or a *we* posited to be you and me. It seems that the representative value of Oprah Winfrey and Barack Obama is in part their ability to name a collective that seems permeable and plural while also restricting it, bounding it by values and rules that won them their place in the pantheon of American ascent and assimilation.

Barack Obama is not the first president to be conscious of his iconography. But he is the first president since Teddy Roosevelt to have become iconic before he was even elected. And managing iconicity was not easy to do while leading the federal government. Despite Obama's repeated promise that his administration would be the most open and transparent in American history, reporters and government transparency advocates said they were disappointed by its performance in improving access to the information they need. "This is the most closed, control freak administration I've ever covered," said David E. Sanger, veteran chief Washington correspondent of *The New York Times*, in 2013.[21] To be sure, the Obama administration distributed vast amount of representations of the White House, including curated pictures of the Obama family and strategic promotions of policy maneuvers, sometimes with Hollywood celebrity endorsements. However, with some exceptions—such as putting the White House visitors' logs on the whitehouse.gov website and selected declassified documents on the new US Intelligence Community website—most observers felt it disclosed too little of the information most needed by the press and public to hold the administration accountable for its policies and actions.

Obama's White House officials objected to such characterizations, citing statistics showing that Obama gave more interviews to news, entertainment, and digital media in his first four-plus years in office than Presidents George W. Bush and Bill Clinton did in their respective first terms, combined. "The idea that people are shutting up and not leaking to reporters is belied by the facts," Obama's press secretary, Jay Carney, said. The White House says they are saying more, and showing more, than any other White House; the world says they are keeping too quiet on the details that really matter. But the White House doesn't acknowledge the distinction between the maintenance of Obama's brand and the disclosure of administrative information.

And the former is something at which Obama, over time, became even better than Oprah. Even if you don't like Obama as president, you do know about his basketball games, his ferociously disciplined schedule, and his relentlessly sanguine attitude. You know about his physical features, and his wife's every outfit innovation. He learned how to lasso his weirdness into a coherent form that would be perfect, someday, on a coin.

The lessons become clearer. How now to Oprahify yourself? Make your past, your peculiarity, your irreconcilability into a garnish for your J. Crew cardigan. Take the hard stories from before, and capture them in an amulet that you string about your neck, and color-code with the outfit assembled for your long day. Toss the sari over your shoulder to reveal the navy knit sheath beneath. Fling a father's abandonment onto a book placed on a shelf organized by the color of the spines. Nab the childhood abuse and smack it into a sound-bite submission. This isn't Victorian curio containment, nor is it ribald plurality. This is collage collected carefully by scrapbook handbooks that tell you which wardrobe item to keep (the always-classic Oxford shirt) and what to relinquish (mama's unloving gaze), which memory to encapsulate and which to let go. This is how you, too, can become an icon.

This is not a new dream. Obama is, as many have said before, a familiar sort of savior, offering a recognizable call for national, personal, and spiritual change. We have tried before to release ourselves from precedent, and we have tried through many men to redeem ourselves.[22] We have also tried in our rituals, our theologies, our purchases, and our makeovers to rid the world of ethnic rumbling and sleek our motley collectives into productive social calm. What makes Obama different is that he is so very good at it, at the talk and the modeling, the dreamscape and the productivity, that he convinces us, better than anyone before, that we should feel good about the costs of his incorporations. Feel good because we do, in the final hour, want to feel what he proposed. We want to be inspired. We want to feel good. We want to know change over and against the messes that we know can never contain, and will never stop making. At the appointed hour, the television is on, and we wait, humming and hoping for the same spirit, again. Only time will tell just what we lost when we threw ourselves, so eagerly, into him, into her, into the stories and wars and speeches and serials that form the flames of this, our modern revival.

A Muslim in the White House? Race, Islam, and the Presidency of Barack Obama

Sylvester A. Johnson

When the people of the United States elected Barack Obama to the presidency in 2008, the nation and the international world were rocked by a mixture of surprise, awe, relief, and resentment. Nations abroad viewed the election of the nation's first black president as a sure indication the United States had embraced the racial diversity of its constituency. Many countries critical of US imperialist ambitions wondered aloud whether the election of a nonwhite president might attenuate what had been an aggressive paradigm of foreign policy. White Christian nationalists within the United States pointed to the election as irrefutable evidence vindicating their longstanding claims that inferior races were taking over their nation. African Americans voiced pride of membership in a nation that had long spurned them as outsiders, as the Obama victory seemed a culmination of a long history for inclusion. White antiracist activists were equally enthused, as many of them had worked during the campaign to challenge skeptical whites to vote based on platform issues instead of eschewing a black candidate.[1]

Of the various responses to Obama's election to the presidency, one of the most significant and enduring was the claim that US citizens had elected a Muslim to the White House. This assertion was bizarre and peculiar for many reasons, not least because Barack Obama was a practicing Christian who had never been a Muslim. In fact, he had openly and repeatedly identified his Christian affiliation throughout the campaign. Perhaps the most memorable instance of this occurred during his public denunciation of Jeremiah Wright, the African American Christian minister under whose pastoral leadership Obama had worshiped when he affiliated with the Trinity United Church of Christ.[2]

Despite its complete lack of basis in fact, however, the claim that Obama was a Muslim became a lasting phenomenon with considerable reach. During Obama's 2008 campaign, the claim he was a Muslim circulated so widely that it became a palpable dynamic during the election. Two years after the election, moreover, the Pew Research Center conducted a survey that found 18 percent of Americans still believed Obama was a Muslim. This situation prevailed despite repeated newscasts that critiqued this false claim and that explicitly publicized Obama's Christian affiliation. As shocking as this might seem, the number of Americans who believed Obama was a Muslim actually increased during his second term as president. A CNN/Opinion Research Corporation poll found in September 2015 that 29 percent of all respondents expressed their belief that Obama's religion was Islam. The percentage among regular Republican voters was even higher—43 percent. In a separate poll of Republican primary voters conducted by Public Policy Polling, 54 percent of respondents identified Obama as a Muslim, with an additional 34 percent expressing uncertainty. This was by no means a purely Republican phenomenon, however, as 15 percent of Democrats polled in 2015 believed that Obama was a Muslim; many of these same Democrats, presumably, voted for Obama.[3] All of this means that throughout the entirety of Obama's two-term tenure as president of the United States, a vast segment of voters continued to believe they were under the administration of the nation's first Muslim president.

How does one make sense of what appears on the surface as a blatantly counterfactual claim that was repeatedly shown to be false? How might one account for the tenacity and expansiveness of US Americans' belief that a Muslim was serving as the nation's president? Of even greater complexity is the linkage between this perception—indeed, a deep conviction—and politics. What does it reveal about the relationship between religion and US nationalism? About the import of being a US American?

In this chapter, I examine the claim that Obama was a Muslim in order to interpret the role of race and religion during the Obama presidency. I will show that this assertion was contextualized by a Western practice of rendering Muslims as a cohesive population whose political loyalties are incommensurate with the security of the Western nation. In tandem with this, I argue that the unabated currency and symbolic power of Obama's putative Islamic presidency emerged through a particular history of racializing Islam that in turn has thrived because US Christians have imagined a spectral symbiosis of Islam and racial blackness.

"Assalaamu alaykum": The Cairo speech

Few presidential speeches have met with the scale of enthusiasm and disdain as did President Obama's public address in Egypt during the summer of 2009. In many ways, in fact, the early period of Obama's presidency was indelibly marked by this historic speech in Egypt's capital city of Cairo. For the international community, the address was a sure sign that the US American empire was changing its ways to become less unilateral, less aggressive, and more cooperative and respectful of other nations' sovereignty. For his domestic critics, this speech was a coming-out speech of a closeted Muslim, as it functioned as evidence that Obama was secretly a member of the international Muslim community.

Expressing his gratitude for the hospitality with which he had been met in Egypt, Obama immediately announced that he had arrived carrying both "the goodwill of the American people" and "a greeting of peace from Muslim communities in my country: Assalaamu alaykum." Those final words—assalaamu alaykum—taken literally constituted merely a common greeting of peace and wholeness to the recipient, a common posture of auspiciousness that underlies most greetings in languages and cultures (such as the English "hello") throughout the world.[4] But words always transcend simply literal meanings. This Arabic phrase has long been employed as a Muslim greeting by non-Arabic speakers, just as the Hebrew "shalom" (peace) has come to function as a Jewish greeting. In the skeptical reading of his critics, Obama was "signifying" or performing his Muslim identity in a manner completely recognizable to other Muslims. The idea that he was doing so as president of the United States, purportedly a Judeo-Christian nation—outraged white Christian nationalists back at home. As striking as this was, however, it was only the beginning to a series of rhetorical moves that further cemented the appearance that Obama was performing his true Muslim identity.

This matter of a Muslim greeting seemed small in comparison to what followed: Obama repeatedly quoted from the Quran to rationalize and underscore important points of his speech. In all fairness, one should recognize that Obama's engagement with religious scripture was carefully scripted and, by design, hewed to a series of dignified and evenhanded quotes and allusions referencing the major biblical religions—Christianity, Islam, and Judaism. As his critics noted, however, key aspects of Obama's speech to Egypt's citizens were pathbreaking and stridently unconventional. He repeatedly referred to the book of Islamic scripture as the "holy Koran." This is the standard way English translations of the Quran are titled, just as "holy Bible" is employed to title English translations of Christian scripture. But until Obama's delivery, US presidents had never employed such terminology publicly, to refer to the Muslim book of scripture. This achieved multiple effects, among which was signaling to his predominantly Muslim audience that an American Christian president could recognize and respect the authority and status traditionally associated with the Islamic book of scripture. Indeed, it would be naive to think Obama's team of speechwriters was unwitting in this regard.

Beyond this, Obama plainly recognized and praised the long history of religious tolerance in Islamicate polities, a tradition that has contrasted sharply with the murderous intolerance of Christian states toward Muslims and Jews. In this way, Obama departed sharply from the typical Western derision of Islam as endemically violent and intolerant, a vilifying style of representation that usually employed Wahabism as the paradigmatic expression of Islam.

Aside from these relatively benign remarks, there were other, more compelling reasons for the shock and backlash that Obama generated with his remarks, and they merit serious examination. Among the most important was his critique of Western colonialism as a meddlesome history that had undermined the best interests of Egypt and other predominantly Muslim polities. At the time of his visit, Hosni Mubarak held the Egyptian presidency. The Mubarak administration, which had held power since 1981, exemplified how the United States exercised colonial power through structuring satellites states whose leaders were US-supported dictators following the directives of the United States. It was in this context that Obama unleashed his first talking point of the speech—Western colonialism. After briefly acknowledging that the "relationship between Islam and the West" included "centuries of coexistence and cooperation," he also pointed to the role of the Crusades—"religious wars"—and other brutal conflicts that ingrained deep hostilities and antagonism. More importantly, Obama pointed to tensions that "more recently" resulted from "colonialism that denied rights and opportunities to many Muslims." In addition, he referenced the role of anti-Muslim policies during the Cold War, by which "Muslim-majority countries were too often treated as proxies without regard to their own aspirations."[5]

And there it was. Less than three minutes into a major policy speech in the Middle East during his first six months in office, Obama had lent his own voice to a foundational critique of Western colonialism that was surely a shock to his Egyptian audience, not to mention the US Americans listening from back home. Even a pedestrian student of history and foreign policy could immediately recognize that such concepts as "colonialism," "proxy," and "aspirations" (of the national sort) were the root elements of anticolonial struggles to replace the status of satellites states with actual sovereignty, of which Egypt's own history of resistance against the British and US imperialism was an exemplum—it was still a US satellite state.

It was just minutes after this opening that Obama then quoted the "holy Koran" to underscore the importance of honest, truthful speech. This quote from Muslim scripture, along with his Arabic greeting, drew some of the most enthusiastic cheers and applause from his audience. He quickly followed this by plainly and unequivocally stating, "I'm a Christian." But what followed became fodder to further fuel the ire of domestic Christian nationalists who regarded Obama as a Muslim imposter. He relayed that his father was from "a Kenyan family that includes generations of Muslims." Obama then shared that his childhood was marked by years spent in Indonesia, a nation with the world's largest population of Muslims. He recalled that the start and end of each day during his Indonesian childhood was marked by the "azaan"—the Muslim call to prayer. Beyond inscribing Islam into his autobiographical reflections, Obama summarized in broad strokes some of the pivotal ways that global civilizations—including the West—were indebted to Islam for such foundational contributions as mathematics (algebra), architecture, and education (the university).[6]

War on terror, war on Islam?

Claiming that the United States was at war against terror was itself a problematical trope for Obama during his 2008 presidential campaign. He was aware of the criticism that terrorism was more akin to an amorphous phenomenon than to a discrete enemy of a sovereign state against which war could be waged. So, he avoided the phrase and emphasized in contrast that the United States was fighting against al-Qaeda operatives and their networks of violence. Over the course of his presidency, however, this gradually shifted to include the language of war "against terrorism." As national security practices of the United States increasingly became rationalized against the "Muslim enemy," moreover, the Obama administration began leaking information to the press about its aggressive measures against Muslims abroad suspected of planning attacks against the United States or other Western targets.

Of paramount importance was the Obama administration's very public admission that it was targeting Muslims abroad by using drones to kill those suspected of having links to terrorism. From Pakistan to Somalia to Yemen, this approach to killing

Muslims outside the United States became a defining aspect of his presidency. This strategy combined extrajudicial killings of people with confirmed involvement in military operations with the so-called signature strikes, which profiled Muslim males whose ages roughly corresponded to that suitable for military duty; loosely interpreted, this latter approach encompassed males ranging from adolescents to seniors.[7] Human rights organizations such as Amnesty International and Human Rights Watch repeatedly condemned these attacks, as they worked by identifying targets whose activities approximate the "signature" of known terrorists. It came as little surprise that such a tactic resulted in the deaths of innocent civilians, as the killing pattern worked by targeting people who had never been formally classified as terrorists. Rather, their actions merely appeared similar to those of known sponsors or agents of organized violence.[8]

The morbid results lent credence to longstanding claims that the United States based its foreign policy on enmity against Muslims. In Yemen alone, the United States employed 131 drone attacks (along with 16 airstrikes) between 2002 and 2016 to kill 1,242 Muslims. During the same period in Pakistan, the United States used more than 400 drone strikes to kill 3,623 Muslims. Human rights organizations repeatedly detailed the deaths of hundreds of Muslim civilians with no ties to military activity (whether or not designated as terrorism by US officials) because of these attacks. Media observers such as the Bureau of Investigative Journalism (BIJ), moreover, have confirmed the use of so-called double-tap attacks, by which US drone operators kill targets, wait for rescuers to arrive, then kill those as well. The BIJ also confirmed that the United States employed a slight variation—a recurring pattern of drone attacks on mourners who hold funerals for those killed in the initial attacks. Even the US government itself, however, has occasionally conceded that drone attacks have killed people with no suspected ties to militant activity. This was precisely the scenario in December of 2013, when a US drone strike in Yemen killed twelve innocent civilians, as a result of which the United States paid $1 million in restitution.[9]

The Obama administration inherited what began as an innovation of military engagement under the administration of George W. Bush and transformed it into a centerpiece of its policy for engaging predominantly Muslim nations of the world. This inheritance, furthermore, went far beyond drone warfare. Bush had made continual use of the Joint Special Operations Command (JSOC), the secretive military force that included such famous military groups as the Green Berets and the Navy SEAL teams. Once he assumed the presidency, Obama quickly expanded the use of JSOC, with up to fifteen operations occurring during a single night.[10]

The fundamental issue with the Obama administration's use of drones to kill Muslims was not technology per se but politics. Drones are unequivocally more precise than traditional airstrikes (i.e., using human-operated fighter jets). Moreover, drone killings often occur after lengthy periods of surveillance using unarmed drones with highly sophisticated cameras that can resolve the individuals faces of possible targets from miles away (surveillance drones deployed in 2014 could operate for days on end from an altitude of over 80,000 feet). This creates an unprecedented ability to confirm the identity of the people being targeted. All of this means that the number of uninvolved civilians killed by US military strikes has actually decreased with the growing use of drones and the decreasing use of traditional fighter jets over the past decade.[11]

One need only take seriously, however, the plight of those Muslims abroad who have survived the killing of their family members through drone strikes (including those killed at funerals) to understand the limits of championing the unprecedented precision of drone technology. The issue is not technological precision but, rather, the fundamental ethics of the United States murdering Muslims by categorizing them as terrorists and thereby denying their right to any rights as human beings. This drone technology has enabled the United States to place virtually any spot on the globe under attack. This has occurred in simultaneity with the US national security paradigm of conceiving terrorism as a Muslim category: as employed by the US military complex, terrorists are Muslims whose very ideas and actions the United States perceives as opposing the strategic interests of US dominance. This means that Muslims throughout the world are now routinely subjected to the threat of death, regardless of their innocence with respect to any criminal or violent acts. That is a political condition, not merely a technological one. For this reason, when US think tanks such as the Stimson Center equivocate by arguing that drones save lives, they are making a moot point that easily functions to mislead the public by suggesting that such killing is compassionate and just.[12]

Racializing Islam

US national security paradigms for engaging the world's Muslims have not only reshaped policies abroad but have also reconstituted domestic engagement with American Muslims. Consequently, the nation's Islamic population has been continually targeted as a threat to internal security, a condition enabled by treating Muslims as a cohesive population who share an essential nature that structures their putative incommensurability with Western civilization. In this way, historical developments in national security practices have rendered American Muslims as a racial population who collectively threaten both the American way of life and the literal lives of non-Muslim Americans.

Although US law enforcement entities have regarded Muslims as a security threat since the early twentieth century, much of the policy infrastructure at work during the Obama presidency resulted from the political backlash that followed the events of 9/11. For instance, the Patriot Act, which was legislated during George W. Bush's tenure, legalized game-changing practices such as the new surveillance guidelines and warrantless detention of noncitizens suspected of terrorism. The administration of George W. Bush even oversaw the creation of a Muslim registry, in 2002. Known as the National Security Entry-Exit Registration System, it required more than 80,000 people in the United States from predominantly Muslim countries to register with the Department of Homeland Security. Many of these Muslims were indefinitely detained or deported. To his credit, Obama ended this registry system upon entering the White House.[13]

This pattern of interpreting Islam through the categories of terrorism and national security is reminiscent of the treatment blacks have experienced as a result of racial counterintelligence practices in law enforcement. In the case of African Americans, federal and municipal law enforcement entities created strategic alliances during the 1960s and 1970s to neutralize black political movements. The Federal Bureau of Investigation (FBI) identified black political activism as the chief threat to internal security during the late 1960s—J. Edgar Hoover placed it ahead of even the communist "threat" to internal security. The bureau also militarized municipal police departments and set up intelligence divisions within them. This new iteration of US law enforcement devastated black communities by adopting mass incarceration as a weapon of racial repression. By the 1980s, the criminalizing practices that targeted black political activists had become the standard treatment against blacks in general, regardless of their politics.[14]

The connection between the racial profiling of blacks and the security profiling of Muslims has been examined in several contexts. Perhaps most notable is the critique that the black scholar and activist Cornel West proffered in the wake of President Obama's response in July of 2013 to the racially motivated murder of the black teenager Trayvon Martin. After George Zimmerman, Martin's killer, was acquitted and set free, Obama addressed the public by identifying personally with Martin, stating that upon first learning the child had been murdered while walking home, Obama's initial thoughts were that "this could have been my son." He went on to say, "Trayvon Martin could have been me 35 years ago."[15] As his tenure in office had been marked by very few direct statements concerning race, Obama's decision to communicate such explicit empathy and solidarity toward Martin's family met with rapt attention in the national media. West, who had always challenged the ethics of Obama's position on foreign policy particularly, was quick to assert that Obama himself was a "global Zimmerman" who had tried to "rationalize the killing of innocent children, 221 so far, in the name of self-defense." West was speaking of Obama's oversight of US drone killings in Pakistan, Yemen, and Somalia.[16] West also highlighted the federal government's 2012 designation of Assata Shakur as a "most wanted terrorist," a status warrant that had never occurred until Obama's presidency. This was the same designation the Department of Justice had applied to Osama bin Laden, and it meant that Shakur might become a target of an extrajudicial killing through conventional or covert means.

West's characterization of Obama highlighted the tensions and ironies of the Obama presidency against the backdrop of fallacious assertions that his was a Muslim presidency and in the wake of Obama's vocal commitment to opening a new chapter in US relations with predominantly Muslim polities. More importantly, in a national media context that typically operated under a gentlemen's agreement to censor any explicit references to Zionism and US empire, West nudged the nation toward engaging these factors in foreign policy. As a result, the Obama administration's policy of drone warfare against Muslims gained more explicit recognition within the broader context of race and empire.[17]

Obama and the black Muslims

For most of the nation's history, blacks constituted the overwhelming majority of Muslims. This began to change after the Hart-Cellar Act of 1965 ended the immigration quota system. As a result, immigrants (mostly nonblack) began to constitute an increasing proportion of the US Muslim population. Because the US Census Bureau does not collect information on religious identification, no official government count of Muslims exists. However, nongovernmental organizations have made several efforts to estimate the religious constituency of the United States. The Pew Research Center, more notably, estimates that Muslims account for 1 percent of the population (about 3.2 million Muslims) and are projected to become the nation's second largest religious demographic by 2040 (after Christianity).[18]

During the election of 2008, white media companies devoted the usual pattern of scrutiny toward Barack Obama's relationship with organized forms of black religion. The white media's response to his racial blackness, in fact, significantly heightened the scrutiny of Obama's ties to black religious institutions. This has routinely meant gauging the relationship of presidential candidates to respectable forms of black religion—the "black church," loosely equated with mainline black denominations such black Baptists and Methodists, whose formal theology is identical to that of mainstream white denominations. By contrast, other forms of black religion have been deemed anathema—the Nation of Islam (NOI), most notably. Throughout 2008, concerns over Obama's ties to black religion were dominated by his relationship to black liberation theology (as embodied in Jeremiah Wright) on the one hand and to Louis Farrakhan and the NOI, on the other.[19]

Although most racially black Muslims in the United States affiliate with the Sunni sect of Islam, it is the NOI that has long been the most visible in the US imagination. In the minds of many if not most US Americans, the country's Islamic blacks are largely indistinguishable from members of the NOI. More importantly, it appears that black Americans generally are regarded as suspected members (honorific, in a perverse way) of the NOI. This dynamic has rendered a "Farrakhan litmus test" that black Americans must pass on the way to achieving political legitimacy in the eyes of white Americans.

As bizarre as such a phenomenon might seem, it can be explained. The dynamic is rooted in decades of national security practices that have relegated the NOI to the status of a "hate-group." The designation originated in the FBI's historic efforts to vilify and delegitimize black "militants." As the FBI employed these terms, "hate-group" and "black militants" designated black people who opposed white supremacy and participated in any of the multiple activist movements to end apartheid and to advance racial equality in the United States. This designation applied regardless of whether such groups embraced armed resistance to white violence. This is why the FBI classified Martin Luther King Jr.'s Southern Christian Leadership Conference as a "hate-group" along with the NOI. After several decades, however, this propagandistic rendering of the NOI achieved the status of official doctrine for corporate media, academic textbooks, and many academic experts. (By contrast, no media company or religion scholars have designated the FBI as a hate-group, despite the fact that the bureau has targeted, criminalized, abducted, tortured, and even murdered blacks, Hispanics, and Native Americans to perpetuate racism and inequality.)[20]

For his part, the renowned minister Louis Farrakhan, who has led the NOI since the 1970s, was unwavering in his positive assessment of Barack Obama through the 2008 election. Approximately one month before Obama took his oath of office, Farrakhan was interviewed by Al-Jazeera and responded to numerous questions about the implications of Obama's ascent to the presidency. When asked about the greatest challenges Obama would face, Farrakhan rather presciently noted his first challenge would be "to remain alive" and expressed his hope that "the secret service will be on their watch."[21]

Farrakhan's enthusiastic assessment of Obama's administration, however, quickly changed as US foreign policy toward predominantly Muslim nations during Obama's presidency became salient. Few developments rivaled Obama's support of NATO's decisive efforts in 2011 to overthrow Libya's government led by Muammar Gaddafi. As a self-identified pan-Africanist, Gaddafi had established a lasting reputation as a devoted supporter of Third World liberation movements, especially those of black Africans fighting for independence from white colonialism. He contributed funds and military personnel to anticolonial movements throughout the African continent, helping to shift the balance of power over several decades. The United States had long supported efforts to destabilize Libya. So, when civil war erupted in that nation, it created an opportunity to culminate a favored political objective.[22] As part of this effort, Obama tapped Harvard University professor Samantha Power to head a task force investigating the human rights situation in Libya. Power quickly delivered a damning if arguably disingenuous assessment that charged Gaddafi with genocide against the Libyans seeking to overthrow their government through war.[23]

In the weeks and months following the overthrow of Libya's government, local anti-government forces began rounding up black residents and killing them, an action that solicited no human rights investigations or condemnation from Power and her task force. In fact, the abductions and murders of blacks in post-Gaddafi Libyan were not even judged newsworthy by most mainstream media companies in the United States. For his part, Obama had repeated Power's claims that Gaddafi was committing genocide. No such language was forthcoming when US-backed militias in Libya began killing blacks. In light of such, the Obama administration's militarism in Libya—along with that of NATO—functioned harmoniously with the established anti-blackness of Western colonialism while opposing an Islamic government whose political philosophy was shaped by roughly one century of pan-Islamic and pan-African movements that opposed white racism and Western colonialism.[24]

US-led efforts to topple Libya's government eventually led to the killing of Gaddafi's family. In the spring of 2011, NATO forces executed a missile strike against Gaddafi's home. The missile attack succeeded in killing members of Gaddafi's family who were present; the Libyan president himself survived. The murder of Gaddafi's family members heightened the urgency of calls for charging the United States and other Western nations with terrorism. Even before the killing of Gaddafi's family members, for instance, Farrakhan pointed to the fact that the United States contributed both weapons and funding to the Israeli Defense Force, whose continual killing of

Palestinian civilians was repeatedly condemned by human rights organizations and by the United Nations.

As the NOI's chief minister, Farrakhan critiqued the very fundamentals of Obama's actions against the Libyan government.[25] The NOI leader also pointed to a further irony. At the very time President Obama was calling for the resignation or removal of the Libyan president, white nationalists throughout the United States were demanding that Obama resign or be forcefully removed from office. As early as 2009, during Obama's first year in office, thousands of white protestors rallied on the National Mall to extirpate what they called a socialist take over by a president whose imagined crimes ranged from being a socialist to being a Muslim. The most immediate factor identified in the public rhetoric was Obama's call for US Congress to legislate the reform of healthcare to expand insurance coverage for the nation's citizens and to rein in the runaway increases in the cost of healthcare. This initiative became the Affordable Care Act of 2010.[26]

As the tactics of anti-Obama demonstrators revealed, however, the underlying concern was not healthcare but Obama himself. The most extreme critics branded him a veritable imposter who had managed to penetrate into the sacred office of the presidency. Although Obama won both the popular vote and the Electoral College in an open, democratic election, it was clear enough in the first six months of his presidency that he would have to contend with an unrelenting assault on his legitimacy, a dynamic that played out continually in the most public and flamboyant ways. During the Republican-led government shutdown of 2013, for instance, the white nationalist "patriot" Larry Klayman of Freedom Watch expressed his outrage that the United States was being "ruled by a president who bows down to Allah." Denying that Obama was "a president of 'we the people,'" Klayman joined Texas Republican senator Ted Cruz and Alaskan governor Sarah Palin to lead others in a mass demonstration where he issued an ultimatum: "I call upon all of you to wage a second American nonviolent revolution, to use civil disobedience, and to demand that this president leave town, to get up, to put the Quran down, to get up off his knees, and to figuratively come out with his hands up."[27] As with earlier mass demonstrations, the 2013 march on Washington wed a rejection of government spending to a much more visceral and contentious assertion that Obama was an alien presence, not of the American but of an inherently alien Muslim people. Klayman shrewdly interwove the racial specter of "the Muslim enemy" with the handily arousing jeremiad of a white nation under siege.

The military dimensions of this white nationalist demographic emerged in clearer dimensions the following spring, in 2014, when hundreds of other white nationalists "patriots" organized a march in Washington to demand that Obama and his administrative Cabinet resign immediately and surrender their leadership of the federal government.[28]

The historical relationship between Farrakhan and Gaddafi only heightened the urgency of these developments. In 1996, following a personal meeting between Gaddafi and Farrakhan, the Libyan president had pledged $1 billion to the NOI. The US government immediately blocked the gift, adhering to its continuing claims that Libya was a supporter of terrorism.[29] The Libyan president did eventually contribute a relatively small donation of $5 million to the NOI, thereby cementing a mutually supportive relationship between the American Muslim group and the Libyan nation. The symbolic import of this, furthermore, was to underscore that the NOI was a nodal point in a global Islamic community. In this way, the NOI was repeating a long tradition of African American Muslims expressing their participation in a global Muslim diaspora from their location within the United States.

Global responses to Obama

By the time he left office in January 2017, Obama had earned the distinction of presiding over an unending series of formally declared wars. He was certainly not the first, as the United States was continually at war with Indigenous American nations during the 1800s and executed covert and illegal wars throughout the latter half of the twentieth century—these were not formally declared but were wars nonetheless. More unusual was his distinction as a winner of the Nobel Peace Prize in October 2009—only three other US presidents have shared this honor.[30] Obama's status as a Nobel laureate only heightened the tensions marking the long arc of his tenure in the White House. He had campaigned on the promise of ending CIA torture, reining in an aggressive US military foreign policy, and de-escalating an ill-fated occupation of Iraq, whose invasion he argued distracted US resources from more legitimate targets. From his stated commitment to closing Guantanamo Bay to scaling down the US nuclear arsenal to advance the ultimate goal of a world free from nuclear weapons, Obama's keen vision for a more just global order was attractive to an international audience because it valorized respect for sovereignty and human rights over US unilateralism. In fact, in its public announcement of the prize, the Nobel Prize Committee explicitly named Obama's vision for "a world without nuclear weapons." The committee also remarked that he had "captured the world's attention and given its people hope for a better future."[31]

It is not difficult to appreciate the committee's optimism. Obama's election came on the heels of George W. Bush's administrative legacy marked by the Patriot Act, the US invasion of Iraq, the documentation of torture and abuses at Abu Ghraib, the escalation of CIA torture at a global constellation of black sites, and a flagrant disregard for repeated alarms over US human rights abuses voiced by global stakeholders. So, there is no mystery to the fact that the world greeted Obama with a deep sigh of relief and a renewed commitment to global governance marked not by US hegemony but by mutual respect upheld by standards of human rights.

In retrospect, however, it is now evident that the Obama presidency actually built on the Bush administration's bellicose legacy and even surpassed the Bush watermark of military aggression in a few respects. For instance, the Bush administration embraced drone technology for surveillance following the invasion of Afghanistan in 2001 and then of Iraq in 2003. The CIA delivered its first weaponized drone strike using a Hellfire missile in the Afghan province of Paktia on February 4, 2002. They were targeting someone they believed was Osama bin Laden, but they merely ended up killing civilians scavenging for scrap metal.[32] Such a tragic, unjustified murder was yet a small precursor of things to come. What emerged as an experimental and marginal use of drones under Bush's presidency accelerated exponentially under Obama's presidency. This robotic, remote warfare began as a trickle of weaponized drones and became a full-fledged program of targeted killing administered by the CIA and US Special Forces (the JSOC). This sharp increase was due not so much to any sinister motives from Obama as to the familiar exponential pace of technological development and mainstream political distractions in the Pentagon; as the capacity for robotic warfare accelerated, so too did the ease with which the nation's military leaders could justify aggressions with minimal danger to loss of US military personnel.

Equally important were the practical advantages of drone technology, as it enabled the United States to violate the sovereignty of nations such as Pakistan, Yemen, Somalia, and Afghanistan with minimal danger to US military personnel.[33] Despite these complexities, the material consequences were profoundly diametric to the change that Obama's campaign portended. By 2015, following his resignation as secretary of the Nobel Prize Committee, Geir Lundestad reflected that the committee had hoped to encourage Obama to confidently pursue his ambitions and regretted that such had not transpired.[34] Lundestad's comments resonated with the general sentiment that there loomed a substantial gap between Obama's campaign vision of a kinder, gentler US hegemony and what actually transpired—the normalized targeted killing of Muslims abroad.

Guantanamo Bay

If the abuses at Abu Ghraib became the most visible symbol of America's anti-Muslim violations of human rights, Guantanamo Bay emerged in an arguably similar fashion for the Obama administration. The United States first appropriated the naval base in the early 1900s when it held Cuba as a colony. Even after Cuba's 1959 revolution secured its status as a sovereign state, the United States refused to end its possession of the Cuba-owned naval base. Thus, it remained a striking irony that while the United States continually rationalized efforts to overthrow Cuba's national government because of human rights violation, the naval station embodied, according to human rights organizations worldwide, the most strident forms of detainee abuses on record. Following the events of 9/11, the naval base became the central location for detaining Muslims throughout the world who were identified as suspected actors with ties to terrorism. Since 2001, 780 Muslims have been detained at Guantanamo Bay. More than 500 would be released during Bush's administration. As a result, when Obama took office, he inherited custody of 242 Muslims.[35]

During his campaign, Obama seemed to appreciate the gravity of both the substance and the optics that Guantanamo created. It was essentially functioning as a Muslim detention center, and the men taken there were abductees. The treatment of the Muslim men, furthermore, was characterized by torture (so-called harsh interrogation) and marked by protest, typically in the form of hunger strikes. Obama campaigned on the promise of closing the detention center. Once in office, however, he found this politically difficult. The detainees at Guantanamo, according to US intelligence officials, were high-level terrorists so dangerous that they were classified as "enemy-combatants." This designation functioned to deny them any right to have rights. To date, many of the Muslims who were abducted and taken to the base—the official terminology of the CIA is "extraordinary rendition"—have never been charged with any crimes. Among these are detainees who were abducted as long ago as 2003.[36]

Much to Obama's chagrin, his Republican opponents and other right-wing critics turned Guantanamo into a political football. They easily exploited the anti-Muslim racism that had emerged so powerfully after the federal government had propagandized Muslims as terrorists. A growing number of US citizens no longer cared or even realized that white Christians commit most acts of domestic terrorism. In their minds, terrorists were Muslims and Muslims were terrorists who posed a surreal threat to the very lives of all Americans. In such an ideological climate, Obama's political opponents charged that he was playing fast and loose by planning to remove Muslim terrorists from Guantanamo Bay and to relocate them in proximity to vulnerable American citizens. Such a reckless move, they argued, would endanger the lives of everyday Americans and end with the most hostile terrorists escaping and running amok within the heart of a vulnerable nation.

Such a ruse elided the fact that convicted terrorists had already been detained throughout the United States in super-maximum security prisons, a practice going back decades. It came as little surprise, however, that such a disingenuous ploy proved highly effective, as it generated a backlash against Obama's efforts to close the Guantanamo detention center. Few US politicians were willing to speak out on behalf of the human rights of Muslims abductees housed there, even in instances where prisoners had never been charged with any crimes and might never be charged. Consequently, Obama ended his two-term presidency in January of 2017 having failed to fulfill a major campaign promise from 2008, one that bore directly on the lives of Muslim abductees.

To his credit, however, Obama did secure the transfer, repatriation, or resettlement of 197 Muslim detainees by the time he left office, as his administration worked with dozens of countries who accepted the men, most of whom had never been charged with any crimes. Despite this, the fact that Muslims continued to be detained there underscored a growing sense that the United States was indeed continuing the torture and other human right violations from the early 2000s. In this way, it was evident that Obama was continuing to enable a national security paradigm that targeted Muslims with the most strident forms of human rights violations.

Conclusion: The longue durée of the "Muslim Enemy"

In order to understand why numerous US Americans have continued to identify Obama as a Muslim throughout his entire presidency, it is essential to recognize how religion has shaped nationalism in the United States and, more broadly, in the West. More specifically, we must ask, How does the specter of a Muslim in government— or Muslim governance—contrast with Christian governance over the longue durée of Western politics and since the recent turn of the century? Were one to assume that US nationalism is a strictly secular phenomenon—in the sense of having been emptied of theological or otherwise religious formations—it might seem misguided to concern ourselves with an account of religion to explain politics. At this point, however, there is solid consensus among experts that secularism has never produced the extinction of religion in the West. In one elegant formulation, it is Christianity itself that has generated multiple "formations of the secular" that Western states have championed to cure the putative disease of religion (in this instance, Islam) among non-Western peoples.[37]

Throughout the history of Christianity, since the emergence of Islam, Christian states have judged Muslims to be traitors waiting to overthrow their state—the enemies within. This same practice prevailed toward Jews. But unlike Jews, Muslims possessed vast empires that rivaled or exceeded in scale those of Christians. In fact, it was often the case that an empire such as that run by the Ottomans dwarfed small Christian polities such as Lisbon and England.

The United States was founded as a settler state, a polity crafted and maintained by and for white settlers and their white descendants. The very history of US democracy and rights, for this reason, has been a history of nonwhites (politically dominated races) seeking to change the fundamental character of the settler state from one of racial enmity to multiracialism. As this primordial racism has been demonstrated at length elsewhere, there is little originality in observing that the United States and other settler states created structures of democracy for settlers and their racial progeny. The political system of racial freedom was integral to exterminating Indigenous nations, destroying indigenous sovereignty, enslaving abducted peoples (particularly Africans and Indigenous Americans), and instituting apartheid as a central paradigm for managing resources such as schools, healthcare, employment, and policing.

By the 1600s, the specter of the Muslim in US colonialism soon pivoted from analogical claims (identifying Indigenous Americans as Muslims in New Spain, for instance) to militancy in the form of freedom wars waged by enslaved African Muslims in the Americas.[38] By the early 1900s, as the United States began to colonize polities with significantly Muslim populations (fighting "Moros" in the Philippines is a classic example), the larger system of European colonialism was reaping a whirlwind of anticolonial resistance. From pan-Islamist movements in Egypt to Muslim sovereignty struggles in South Asia, West Africa, and Iran. So palpable was the anticolonial surge in colonized Muslim polities that white racists such as Lothrop Stoddard and John Mott named Islam as a special scourge.

At the same time, the fall of the Ottoman Empire in 1920 implied a victory that had been fought for many centuries—the strain of Christendom against Islamicate polities. The Western rhetoric of this conflict hearkened back to the Crusades of the twelfth century, a practice that has been kept alive by anti-Muslim authors such as Bernard Lewis and Samuel Huntington. It is certainly true that Christians had targeted Muslims (as well as Jews) as inherent, "natural" enemies of Christian states since the age of the Crusades. The larger history of Islam and Christianity, however, cannot be reduced to this single dynamic. One need only consider the history of Christian-Muslim relations in Istanbul (first created as Constantinople to be an imperial Christian city par excellence) or the history of Muslims and Christians in Egypt. More importantly, the Western antagonism toward Islam during the twentieth century was due to the political conditions of that time. Namely, the violent efforts of Western empires—France and Britain, particularly—to colonize and dominate Muslim polities inspired anticolonial movements that, quite predictably, drew on local religious and political paradigms to produce what has been called "Islamism."

There is another important element of this association that is especially formative for the United States. For most of US history, blacks have constituted the majority of the nation's Muslim population. Not until 1965 did the Hart-Cellar Act remove quotas that prohibited large numbers of immigrants from predominantly Muslim countries. In fact, the strident critiques of white racism popularized by the American Muslim minister Malik Shabazz (more commonly known as Malcolm X) serves as a parallel to the formidable resistance to colonialism that became associated with pan-Islamic movements globally.

As Obama ascended into the ranks of a finalist for the US presidency and subsequently clinched the election, he became easily legible as a political imposter to Christian nationalists. At its core, asserting that President Obama is a Muslim marked him as a foreigner and as an outsider—an alien ruler of the body politic. As a Muslim (albeit an imagined one), he is the quintessential enemy of the racial civilization called the West. In this light, the demands by white activists to remove Obama from office iterated the Crusaders' demand that Christian lands (i.e., Europe) be ruled by Christian (read "European") princes.

Toward a "Culture of Mercy": Augustine, Pope Francis, and the Transformation of Moral Imagination

Melanie Webb

The people who need to be "rehabilitated" . . . are those whose minds and bodies have been warped by false value systems that convince them that some people must die so they can live, many must starve so they can eat, all must slave so they can enjoy rest.[1]

Women at Alderson Federal Prison, West Virginia, 1971

In 2015, both Pope Francis and President Barack Obama visited correctional facilities in America. In doing so, they amplified national attention on the enormous US prison population and the ever larger number of Americans with incarcerated or formerly incarcerated loved ones. America's criminal justice system constitutes a moral crisis. It is by now well established in our national consciousness that America has the highest rate of incarceration of any nation: America has 5 percent of the world's population and 25 percent of the world's prison population.[2] Less well known is the reality that America now has more prisons and jails than degree-granting institutions of higher education.[3] Incarceration is an overwhelmingly common part of the American experience, and therefore an important area of concern both for American society as a whole and for congregations across America.

Conversations around reducing the American prison population often focus on sentencing reform for nonviolent offenders, who are incarcerated for "property or petty drug offenses, that would not warrant a sentence in many other countries."[4] As important as these initiatives are, they rely upon an implicit distinction between good criminals ("nonviolent offenders") and bad criminals ("violent offenders") that is common to discussions regarding criminal justice reform.[5] By seeking to justify the harm done through our criminal justice system to some on account of their status as "violent offenders," however, we blind ourselves to the societal self-wounding that is exposed by and enacted through the entire system of mass incarceration.[6]

This chapter explores Augustinian theological resources by which we might envision a set of social relationships that recognize the connection between our humanity and the humanity of those most denigrated by our carceral practices. Pope Francis and Augustine both note the relationships of interdependence on which a society's flourishing depends. Pope Francis suggests that the social values exhibited through the American criminal justice system—that it normalizes and creates the expectation that our society's children will suffer—indicates that our society is "'condemned' to remain a hostage to itself, prey to the very things which cause that pain."[7] Pope Francis is building on an Augustinian insight: a society cannot be happy if its members are not happy. Augustine writes, "The happiness of a city and of a human do not, after all, arise from different sources; for a city is nothing other than a concordant multitude of humans."[8] Nonviolent and violent offenders are among our society's members. To think that we can be happy even as we lock up and lock out vast segments of our children, our neighbors is to delude ourselves. Our fear of, and disgust toward, one another dehumanizes not only those of whom we are afraid, but also ourselves, and further damages our capacity for flourishing.

On March 13, 2015, Pope Francis declared a Year of Jubilee for all those imprisoned across the world. At the year's conclusion, on November 20, 2016, he issued an apostolic letter. In response to the dehumanizing realities of incarceration, Pope Francis argues instead for a "culture of mercy based on the rediscovery of encounter with others, a culture in which no one looks at another with indifference or turns away from the suffering of our brothers and sisters."[9] The opening of the letter grounds all following references to mercy in the encounter between Jesus and "the woman taken in adultery":

> *Misericordia et misera* is a phrase used by Saint Augustine in recounting the story of Jesus' meeting with the woman taken in adultery (cf. Jn 8:1-11). It would be difficult to imagine a more beautiful or apt way of expressing the mystery of God's love when it touches the sinner: "the two of them alone remained: *mercy with misery.*" What great mercy and divine justice shine forth in this narrative! Its teaching serves not only to throw light on the conclusion of the Extraordinary Jubilee of Mercy, but also to point out the path that we are called to follow in the future.[10]

Pope Francis attributes his opening words to the Roman African bishop, Augustine of Hippo (354–430): *misericordia et misera*, translated as "mercy with misery." The phrase comes from a sermon given as part of a series on the Gospel of John, in which Augustine discusses the encounter between Jesus and the woman supposedly caught in adultery. Pope Francis interprets this story as a "beautiful" and an "apt" expression of God's love "when it touches the sinner"—that is, in the context of his letter, those who are sentenced to imprisonment.

This chapter will proceed in two parts. First, we will delve into the portion of Augustine's Commentary on the Gospel of John that Pope Francis cites in order to consider the dynamics of mercy. Second, we will consider how the prevalence of plea deals impacts our understanding of the dynamics of mercy. In conclusion, we will turn to a 1971 call from women at Alderson Federal Prison to consider how an Augustinian "culture of mercy" might motivate initiatives toward de-carceration.

Misericordia et Misera: Augustine's
Commentary on the Gospel of John, 33

Core to the "culture of mercy" for which Pope Francis advocates is the belief that transformation is possible: "mercy is this concrete action of love that, by forgiving, transforms and changes our lives."[11] Pope Francis frames his apostolic letter by citing Augustine's description of the moment when Jesus and the woman are left alone: "mercy with misery." Before Augustine arrives at this phrase, however, he discusses the sociopolitical challenges to Jesus's capacity to be present to the woman accused of adultery. The sermon encompasses three pericopes: Jn 7:40-44; 7:45-52; and 7:53–8:11, and reads the pericope of the woman caught in adultery (Jn 7:53–8:11) as a commentary on the two prior passages. My reading will focus on the character of Nicodemus in the second pericope; Nicodemus asks a question of his fellow religious leaders that sets the stage for our reading of the passage about the woman accused of adultery. We will then turn our attention to Augustine's detailed interpretation of the story of the woman accused of adultery.

Nicodemus, judgment, and the heart's prejudices

The themes of judgment and recognition are at the forefront of Augustine's sermon. He begins his sermon by noting the activity of the Holy Spirit in the nascent recognition of Jesus's role within the community. In the first pericope (7:40-44), the crowd is said to wonder if he is a prophet or Messiah. The temple police, with orders from the religious leaders, have been sent to arrest Jesus and were among the crowd; they did not succeed but "returned innocent of the crime, and filled with wonder."[12] Their innocence is, on Augustine's telling, a result of Jesus's unwillingness to be arrested: "they were not able [to arrest him] because he was unwilling."[13]

While Jesus's identity is the focus of the first pericope, the second pericope raises the question of Nicodemus's identity. Let us walk through the passage and Augustine's reading of it. The text of the second pericope (7:45-52) presents the conversation between the temple police and the religious leaders, when the former return without having arrested Jesus. Having heard his teaching, the temple police report that "never has anyone spoken like this!" (7:46). The religious leaders deride the people for attending to Jesus's teaching, saying that they do not know the law. One of the religious leaders, Nicodemus, however, interjects: "Our law does not judge people without first giving them a hearing to find out what they are doing, does it?" (7:51). The other religious leaders do not answer this question, but instead suggest that Nicodemus might himself be from Galilee, insisting that their scriptures nowhere attest to a prophet arising from that region.

Of this behind-the-scenes interaction between Nicodemus and his fellow religious leaders, Augustine preaches:

> *Nicodemus*, however, was *one of the Pharisees, who had come to the Lord by night* [Jn. 3:2]; he was not an unbeliever, but he was afraid. . . . Nicodemus was well

aware, or at least he believed, that if only they would be willing to listen to him patiently, they themselves might become like the men they'd sent to arrest him, who had chosen to believe. *They replied to him* just as they had to them, out of the prejudice of their hearts: "*Surely you are not a Galilean as well?*"[14]

Augustine notes how Nicodemus emerges, at this point in the gospel, as a grounded voice among the anxious religious leaders. There are three main points to draw from this passage. First, Augustine points out that Nicodemus is a member of the religious leaders' class; he is one of them, and they speak freely with him of their plans to entrap Jesus. He has also previously been drawn to the teachings of Jesus, coming to him under the cover of night and receiving the invitation to be born anew. Nicodemus's clandestine visit made clear, as Augustine says that "he was not an unbeliever, but he was afraid." While previously he was not ready to be associated with Jesus, now he challenges the fear that animates the other religious leaders' impulse to arrest Jesus by appealing to his community's regard for the law.

Second, Augustine attributes to Nicodemus confidence in the transformability of his peers: he thinks that, if only they would listen, they too might believe. Augustine sees Nicodemus's question as a shrewd attempt to create the conditions in which they might listen to Jesus: "Surely our law does not judge (*iudicat*) a human unless he has first been heard before it and it knows what he's doing?" Such a suggestion gets Nicodemus classed with Jesus as a Galilean—and their reply comes "out of the prejudice of their hearts" (*ex praeiudicio cordis sui*). Augustine implicitly contrasts the law and the religious leaders' hearts; they do not seek how the law judges (*iudicat*) Jesus because they are acting out of the prejudice (*praeiudicio*) of their hearts. Their prejudice prevents them from acting in accord with their own commitment to God's law and from seeing Jesus's life and ministry as an expression of that law.

Third, Augustine does not see the suggestion that Nicodemus is a Galilean as a supposition regarding his actual birthplace, but says that "they were implying that he'd been led astray by the Galilean."[15] Nicodemus, having previously attempted to hide his association with Jesus, is now accused of being one of his followers because he interprets the law as requiring truthfulness and justice, and so evading prejudice. The religious leaders, evading his question about the law, find Nicodemus guilty by association, without giving him a hearing either.

The gospel text (as it is extant for both Augustine and ourselves) then transitions to another court scene. Augustine reads the exchanges between Jesus and the religious leaders through the lens of a test or temptation, like those presented in the synoptic gospels: Jesus is at the temple, and he is being asked to prove his legitimacy according to standards that are not his own.

Jesus, the accused, and the accusers

Having looked at salient elements in the first two pericopes, we will walk through Augustine's interpretation of this pericope in three stages: the test, the response, his call to his congregants, and the result of Jesus's private exchange with the accused woman.

First, though, let us begin with the text. Since the majority of Augustine's sermon focuses on Jn 7:53–8:11, I present these verses in full here:

> **7:53** Then each of them went home, **8:1** while Jesus went to the Mount of Olives. **2** Early in the morning he came again to the temple. All the people came to him and he sat down and began to teach them. **3** The scribes and the Pharisees brought a woman who had been caught in adultery; and making her stand before all of them, **4** they said to him, "Teacher, this woman was caught in the very act of committing adultery. **5** Now in the law Moses commanded us to stone such women. Now what do you say?" **6** They said this to test him, so that they might have some charge to bring against him. Jesus bent down and wrote with his finger on the ground. **7** When they kept on questioning him, he straightened up and said to them, "Let anyone among you who is without sin be the first to throw a stone at her." **8** And once again he bent down and wrote on the ground. **9** When they heard it, they went away, one by one, beginning with the elders; and Jesus was left alone with the woman standing before him. **10** Jesus straightened up and said to her, "Woman, where are they? Has no one condemned you?" **11** She said, "No one, sir." And Jesus said, "Neither do I condemn you. Go your way, and from now on do not sin again." (NRSV)

The test

On the day following his attempted arrest, Jesus descends once again from the Mount of Olives to the temple.[16] The people come from their homes, and the religious leaders come via someone else's home. The setting is, at first, a classroom—"he sat them down and began to teach." The teaching, though, is interrupted, as Jesus is challenged to a test of judgment. The scene shifts to a court setting, with the religious leaders as prosecutors, Jesus as judge, and the woman as silenced defendant. Behind the courtroom bar sits the crowd, those who have come to hear Jesus teach, as they had the day before. Though the religious leaders had not answered Nicodemus's question about the law ("Surely our law does not judge a human unless he has first been heard before it and it knows what he's doing?"), they now draw on the law to demand that Jesus condone the death penalty for a woman they have accused of adultery.

Augustine wonders what the line "so that they might be able to bring a charge against him" might mean: "To bring a charge on what grounds? Surely they hadn't caught him in some criminal act! Or were they implying that the woman had some connection with him?"[17] Augustine does not arrive at an answer, but comments that "they had noticed that he was exceedingly mild, exceedingly gentle."[18] From this insight, Augustine invokes Ps. 45(44):4 to suggest other attributes of Jesus that are on display in the passage: "march forward in prosperity, and reign, for the sake of truth, and gentleness, and justice."[19] Augustine riffs on this line, presenting these qualities as Jesus's own: "he brought the truth, then, as a teacher, gentleness as a liberator, justice as a judge."[20]

Augustine ventriloquizes the religious leaders scheming among themselves about how to trap Jesus by pitting these characteristics against each other: "he's thought to be truthful; he seems to be gentle; we must look for a way of slandering his justice. Let's present him with a woman caught in adultery; let's tell him what the Law instructs in cases like hers. Then, if he orders her to be stoned, he'll be lacking in mercy; but if he decrees that she should be released he'll lose hold of his justice."[21] They anticipate that he will err on the side of gentleness, and call for her release. If he does, they will accuse him of being "an enemy of the law," which they consider "a capital offense" that would let them stone him along with the woman.[22] But Jesus does not let these men turn his classroom into a courtroom. Instead, he continues with his plan to teach.

The response

Jesus shrewdly evades their trap by saying that whoever is without sin is to cast the first stone. Augustine remarks, "Look how full of justice it was, how full of gentleness and truth! . . . What wisdom in that answer!"[23] Jesus's justice, gentleness, and truth, for Augustine, yields wisdom. The first consequence that he notes is in consonance with Nicodemus's confidence that his peers were transformable, if only they would listen to him: "how did it open the door for them into themselves? . . . They saw an adulteress, they didn't notice themselves."[24] Previously, they replied to Nicodemus "out of the prejudice of their hearts,"[25] and now Augustine remarks that "they were engaging in false accusations out of doors, so to speak, but they failed to examine their own indoors."[26] Jesus's gentleness is not, as they anticipated, directed only at the woman whom they accused. Rather, Jesus's gentleness opens their hearts to themselves.

Having spoken, Jesus then writes in the sand. Though the text indicates that he uses a stick, Augustine reads it as Jesus's finger and draws a parallel with the law written by the finger of God. The law was written on stone because, as Augustine says, "they were hard," but Jesus writes "on the earth, because he was looking for fruit."[27] On Augustine's telling, the law written in stone calls for stoning; yet Jesus, his finger to the earth, calls forth fruit. Augustine also alludes here to the parable of the sower, in which seed is spread on four different kinds of ground, including stony and soft earth.

Yet, those who are using the woman as a prop for their own religious authority are not, for Augustine, stony ground. Previously having only seen the woman as guilty, "the men then turned their attention to themselves, and confessed their guilt simply by departing."[28] Augustine seems to think that the religious leaders, in this moment, see themselves clearly. They leave not because they have been defeated, nor because Jesus is once again unwilling to be arrested. Rather, they leave one by one because his teaching has softened their hearts from stone to earth. This is a remarkable reach beyond the text, but Augustine goes even further. The people who had gathered for Jesus's teaching are entirely soft earth, ready to bear fruit under the force of a plow: "the others [in the crowd] were hit by his justice as if it were a wooden club; they looked within themselves, and they discovered their own guilt."[29]

The image of the "wooden club" (*trabalis*) might also be read another way. Though we do not know how Augustine's Latin Bible rendered Mt. 7:3,[30] the Vulgate reads: "Quid autem vides festucam in oculo fratris tui et **trabem** in oculo tuo non vides?"[31] That is, "How can you see the fleck in the eye of your brother and not see the club (*trabem*) in your own eye?" Edmund Hill, in a footnote to his translation of Augustine's sermon on John 8, suggests "a spear as thick as a beam" for *trabalis*.[32] Jesus addresses their penchant for justice by confronting them with their own spears. Jolted and now with clearer eyes, "they looked within themselves."[33] Jesus freed them from their judgment of the other so that they might know themselves. Meeting themselves, "they discovered their own guilt."[34] The "weapon of justice" is confrontation with their own guilt. To the credit of accusers and crowd alike, seeing guilt in themselves unravels their concern with the guilt of the woman.

Call to congregants

Before we turn to the exchange between Jesus and the accused woman, let us consider Augustine's challenge to his own congregants. Augustine situates this direct address between his discussion of the religious leaders and his discussion of the crowds, placing his congregants within the scene. He considers them among those Jesus is teaching in these lines, and turns the call to look within toward his congregants: "each one of you should reflect upon yourself, should enter within yourself, should mount the tribunal of your own mind, should arraign yourself before your own conscience, and should force yourself to confess."[35] Augustine's recommendation is, in effect, that each congregant should follow the path taken by the religious leaders in response to Jesus's rebuff and by Augustine himself in his *Confessions*. Augustine presses his congregants to consider their own hearts, and appeals to 1 Cor. 2:11, "for no man knows what belongs to him, except the spirit of the man which is within him."[36] Augustine has turned to this passage before.

In *City of God* 1.26, Augustine writes, "It is through the ear, then, that we become aware of the conscience; we do not presume to judge those things which are hidden from us."[37] While knowledge and vision are often aligned, here Augustine represents the conscience as something out of view, which must be heard rather than seen.[38] Augustine does not specify precisely whose "conscience" or "ear" is at issue here. This ambiguity is an important component of his lesson. It is not only that we come to know others through listening; but we also come to know ourselves better through being heard.

The things hidden from us, then, are not only matters pertaining to our neighbors but also to ourselves. In *City of God* 1.26, Augustine quotes 1 Cor. 2:11 to dissuade readers from believing that they know what was happening in the hearts of others apart from hearing testimony from those others. In Commentary on the Gospel of John 33:5, he turns to the same passage to discourage listeners from imitating the religious leaders and passing judgment on the accused woman or others in the story (such as the religious leaders!), and instead encourages them to examine their own hearts. The upshot, for Augustine's listeners and for those in the pericope alike: "either release the woman, or else accept the penalty of the Law along with her."[39] That is, if you would have her stoned, then be stoned with her. Indeed, we have all harmed others; do we have the courage to recognize the severity of that harm? In this way, Augustine suggests that a recognition of shared humanity yields empathy and solidarity.

Augustine challenges his congregants to see themselves clearly and, like the religious leaders and the crowd, to leave the accused alone with Jesus.

The result

Now comes the line on which Pope Francis relies for his letter: "the two of them were left, pity and the pitiable (*misera et misericordia*),"[40] or, as Pope Francis renders it, "mercy with misery." While the religious leaders are said to seek Jesus's unjust arrest "out of the prejudice of their own hearts (*sui cordis*)," Augustine identifies Jesus as *misericordia*, as placing his heart with those in misery. Pope Francis inverts Augustine's Latin; where Augustine writes *misera et misericordia*, Pope Francis quotes *misericordia et misera*. In doing so, Pope Francis emphasizes the preeminence of mercy in the encounter. Augustine anticipates that the woman is terrified, suggesting that she knows who Jesus is, that he is without sin, that he could—according to the terms he set before the others—be justified in casting the first stone. While his command caused the men to examine themselves, it likely caused her—Augustine adds—"to expect to be punished by him, *in whom no sin* could be found."[41]

Augustine presents his listeners with the same voice that spoke justice, but that now speaks gentleness: "Has no one condemned you?" She bears true testimony regarding her neighbors and herself: "No one, Lord." Jesus then replies: "Neither will I condemn you." Augustine feigns perplexity: "Why is this, Lord? Are you on the side of sinners, then?"[42] Rather, Jesus's response to the woman caught in adultery acknowledges the harm that she is accused of doing, but rejects punishment as the solution: "Go your way, and from now on do not sin again" (8:11). As Pope Francis challenges Catholics and his readers worldwide to recognize, justice is enacted through healing presence—*misericordia et misera*, "mercy with misery."[43]

* * *

The story of the woman caught in adultery is beloved for many reasons. In it, Jesus challenges the religious leaders with both justice and gentleness; they consider the woman's sins worse than their own, and Jesus sends them away to search their hearts, to recognize the harm that they have done, and to scrape out the prejudices that stunt the circulation of love. Jesus gives the woman a second chance, saying, "Neither do I condemn you. Go and sin no more." For this reason, Pope Francis celebrates it as a grounding narrative for a faithful Christian response to those who have harmed others or otherwise broken the law. The criminal defense lawyer Bryan Stevenson also turns to the passage as he articulates how he has come to understand his role as a "stonecatcher":

> I also reminded people that when the woman accused of adultery was brought to Jesus, he told the accusers who wanted to stone her to death, "Let he who is without sin cast the first stone." The woman's accusers retreated, and Jesus forgave her and urged her to sin no more. But today, our self-righteousness, our fear, and our anger have caused even the Christians to hurl stones at the people who fall down, even when we know we should forgive or show compassion. I told the congregation that we can't simply watch that happen. I told them we have to be stonecatchers.[44]

We should seek, that is, to be present to those accused and convicted of crimes, to deflect the cruelty aimed at them, and provide hope for a different future. Stevenson is concerned that the culture of punishment—motivated by our self-righteousness, fear, and anger—will continue as long as we want to spare ourselves the risk of intervening as stonecatchers. To catch stones, one has to stand with those being stoned; one has to risk "encounter with others," turning toward "the suffering of our brothers and sisters"[45] and seeking, with any means at one's disposal, to alleviate that suffering and to prevent its continuation.

Plea deals and the woman accused of adultery

Mercy means not only recognizing those in prison as our neighbors but also recognizing the damage done through false accusations. In America, roughly 95 percent of felony cases that are not dismissed are settled without a trial. Instead, prosecutors offer defendants a "plea deal," that is, a wager: take the certainty of a light(er) sentence by pleading guilty to all charges, or risk a more severe sentence by insisting that your case go to trial.[46] Because of the prevalence of plea deals within our taxed criminal courts, we are unable to assess whether convictions account for the harms experienced by victims.[47] Brady Heiner has argued that "the systematic practice of plea bargaining . . . functions massively and predominantly as a form of procedural entrapment."[48] When discussing those who are incarcerated, then, we might ask with Nicodemus: "surely *our* law does not judge a person before it has given him a hearing and knows what he is doing?"

Nicodemus's question about the religious leaders' eagerness to arrest Jesus as well as Jesus's response to the woman accused of adultery might also be read as encouragement to develop a healthy suspicion of those who are eager to see others punished. Justice is, as Augustine insists, both gentle and truthful. Justice not only extends mercy to those who have harmed others, but also recognizes the severe injustice of false accusation. The call, then, is not only to mercy but also to epistemic humility regarding accusations. This woman is brought to Jesus by men who claim to have caught her "in the very act of committing adultery." It's remarkable how often we believe them! Jesus knew not to take them at their word.

Perhaps Jesus recalled, while he wrote in the sand, a similar story, included in the Septuagint, the story of Susanna and the elders. While bathing in her garden, Susanna was approached by two elders of the city and given this ultimatum: have sex with us, or we testify that we found you in your garden having sex with a young man—and then we try you for adultery. She refused the deal, and was brought before the community's court which tried and convicted her of adultery, condemning her to death. The prophet Daniel, however, discerns the prejudice at work in her condemnation; he halts proceedings, cross examines the elders, convicts them of "bearing false witness against [their] neighbor," and they are stoned to death.

As he makes markings in the sand, perhaps Jesus is also mulling over Daniel's cross examination of Susanna's accusers and its result—the execution of the elders. With this backdrop, Jesus's delayed reply takes on different significance: "let the one who is without sin cast the first stone." Perhaps the religious leaders also know Susanna's story, and so catch Jesus's drift as they depart in silence.

The possibilities of false accusation also exploit the vulnerabilities of those considered suspicious or dangerous on account of societal prejudices, such as sexism, racism, classism, xenophobia, homophobia, or transphobia. Higher rates of crime and of imprisonment are indicators of social inequality,[49] while states and countries that invest in social welfare have significantly lower incarceration rates.[50] In many cases, those who are imprisoned and the survivors of crime come from the same communities that suffer from poverty, lack of educational opportunity, and other social inequalities.[51] Harsh conditions within our prisons, then, deleteriously impact not only those who might make reparations for harms done but also the lives of those seeking to recover from the harm that they have experienced.[52]

Jesus's interaction with the woman "caught" in adultery directs us toward epistemic humility as a mode of interacting with one another in justice, gentleness, and truth. Reading the story of the woman "caught" in adultery through the lens of Susanna's story centers the recognition that we do not know whether she was guilty of that which she was accused of doing. Jesus's exhortation "go and sin no more" does not specify what kind of sin any more than it specifies the sins of the religious leaders or the crowd; the story is silent on that point. Instead, the narrative directs us to examine our own hearts in order to root out prejudice and cultivate mercy. We can say, however, that, like the religious leaders and the crowds, the accused woman leaves Jesus's presence with the challenge to live free of condemnation and free of the drive to condemn others. In a society that turns to litigation and incarceration as modes of justice, we are directed through these passages to seek not punishment but transformation in our pursuit of the beloved community.

Concluding thoughts

In 1971, in the aftermath of the uprising at the Attica men's prison in New York, women at Alderson Federal Women's Prison (West Virginia) wrote: "The people who need to be 'rehabilitated' . . . are those whose minds and bodies have been warped by false value systems that convince them that some people must die so they can live, many must starve so they can eat, all must slave so they can enjoy rest."[53] The logics of punishment that motivate distinctions between, for instance, "violent" and "nonviolent offenders" continue to deceive us into believing that our well-being depends on doing violence to (one) another rather than redressing legacies of inequality, racism, and poverty. With a clear view of what our society loses through incarceration, the women of Alderson argue that "we need to rid ourselves of prisons. They are a danger to society . . . because they try to erase from our consciousness people who could possibly bring about exciting changes in our social order."[54]

Ruth Gilmore notes that the prevailing logic of American practices of incarceration is not "rehabilitation" but "incapacitation."[55] According to Gilmore, "incapacitation doesn't pretend to change anything about people except where they are. It is in a simpleminded way, then, a geographical solution that purports to solve social problems."[56] It aims to remove people from view, and to disconnect them from forms of community that promote the well-being of all. Or, as Allegra McLeod puts it, we are "banishing and relegating to civil death any person convicted of serious crime."[57] In so doing, we are "condemning" our society to "remain a hostage to itself."[58]

The women of Alderson draw our attention to society's exclusions and direct our attention to societal prejudices regarding what is necessary to secure our safety and well-being, which require reevaluation. Our current prison system bolsters our tendency to fail in recognizing one another's value. We cannot *see* the harm we do to others, but instead must listen to and trust the testimony of those who have survived the brutalities and banalities of incarceration in America.

The woman whom Jesus tells to "go and sin no more" is precisely the person best positioned to lead us beyond the structural sins that placed her in such a vulnerable position in the first place. To live out the example of Jesus as "mercy with misery," as Pope Francis renders Augustine's phrase, is to recognize the liberatory gift of being present with those who are despised and feared within our society. We too are hostages of the normalization of their pain, "prey to the very things which cause that pain."[59] It is also to recognize that, having relied on the functioning of the American criminal justice system for our sense of safety and stability, we are despised and feared by those who have survived its horrors. We mistake our misery for happiness, not knowing what we lose by locking up and locking out our neighbors and our own children.

For Pope Francis, the effect of Jesus's mercy is to "[help] the woman look to the future with hope and to make a new start in life."[60] It is not just those who are caged in our prisons who are in need of mercy; rather, we who have been complicit in or who have actively sought their caging need mercy. Lasting and substantive criminal justice reform demands a transformation of moral imagination that bridges demographic cleavages endemic within contemporary American society, and that recognizes those who have harmed others as enduringly human in our regard for and responsibility to them. "Mercy . . . must continue to be *celebrated* and *lived out* in our communities."[61] Not just those who have been labeled "prisoner" and "criminal," then, but those of us who have been seduced into embracing these terms as salient for navigating our own social relationships need merciful encounters that expose "the deepest desires hidden [in the heart of each person]."[62] As we come ever more clearly to recognize the structural sin of our distorted criminal justice system, mercy might likewise make it possible for us to envision a future that is desirable for all of our society's members and to make efforts toward realizing that future.

Part Two

The Politics of Moral Vision

The Welfare of Faith

Alison Collis Greene

"The question we ask today is not whether our government is too big or too small, but whether it works—whether it helps families find jobs at a decent wage, care they can afford, a retirement that is dignified." Barack Obama's first inaugural address in 2009 seemed a repudiation of his predecessor, George W. Bush, who shrank domestic programs in favor of sharp tax cuts for wealthy Americans even as defense spending ballooned. "The nation cannot prosper long when it favors only the prosperous," Obama went on. "The success of our economy has always depended not just on the size of our gross domestic product, but on the reach of our prosperity, on the ability to extend opportunity to every willing heart—not out of charity, but because it is the surest route to our common good."[1]

Democrats celebrated Obama's "echoes of Jefferson, Lincoln, and Roosevelt," and many hoped most fervently that he would emulate the latter.[2] Liberals and church-state separation advocates expected the new president to fulfill his campaign promise to reform the controversial Bush-era Office of Faith-Based and Community Initiatives and return to Roosevelt's emphasis on federal aid administered through public agencies. Many expressed disappointment when Obama simply renamed the organization the Office of Faith-Based and Neighborhood Partnerships (OFBNP), appointed Pentecostal minister Joshua DuBois to head it, and vaguely promised that it would make its programs more transparent and recruit a broader spectrum of religious agencies into cooperation with federal ones. Yet that office, since 2013 headed by church-state separation attorney Melissa Rogers, has also worked to advise the administration in negotiations with religious bodies over same-sex marriage and women's health coverage under the Affordable Care Act (ACA). Those battles, as well as the ongoing if largely unnoticed work of the OFBNP, have demonstrated the degree to which explicitly religious and proselytizing bodies have entwined their work ever more closely with that of the federal government in the decades since the New Deal.[3]

Seventy-six years before Obama entered the White House, Franklin Roosevelt took office during an even bleaker economic depression than that of 2008, and in the face of worldwide financial and political instability. He stood on the steps of the Capitol building and pronounced Americans' commitment to one another and the nation a "sacred obligation," and then concluded with a prayer that God bless and protect the nation and his administration's effort to preserve it.[4] Roosevelt populated his Cabinet with more Catholics and Jews than any president before him, he cultivated a close relationship with the liberal Federal Council of Churches, and he spoke often of the New Deal's welfare and reform programs as an outgrowth of a century of Catholic, Jewish, and Protestant social activism.[5]

Yet Roosevelt separated the work of the expanded federal state from that of private and religious agencies whose efforts he—and many Americans—deemed "scattered, uneconomical, and unequal."[6] Harry Hopkins, head of Roosevelt's largest relief program, the Federal Emergency Relief Administration (FERA), announced in the summer of 1933 that his agency would work only through other public agencies, not through private and religious ones. In practice, FERA's work often took place with the cooperation of local churches, and organizations like Catholic Charities quickly learned how to reclassify their work as public. The New Deal's commitment to local administration of federal programs also guaranteed at least the indirect participation of religious leaders and churches that had long helped to distribute social services in tandem with public agencies. Nonetheless, Hopkins's largely successful effort to draw a line between church and state relief provided a blueprint for the administration's subsequent programs, from the Works Progress Administration to the Social Security Administration.[7]

Both Roosevelt and Obama rode into office on a wave of desperation and hope, on the promise that they would harness the power of the federal government to restore the nation to prosperity. When Obama shepherded the ACA through Congress, liberals celebrated his success in achieving one of Roosevelt's unmet goals.[8]

The comparisons ended there. When Roosevelt took office, Americans clamored for the federal government to intervene in the suffering they faced—and many churches led the way. From left to right, North, South, and West, religious leaders celebrated the handoff of social welfare from church to state and heralded the New Deal as the realization of their own reform efforts and aspirations. Christian organizations gradually reclaimed a role in distributing aid, however, supported by federal funds. First, the federal government funneled post–World War II international relief funds through predominantly mainline and Catholic organizations. Many conservatives protested the shift as an encroachment on religious liberty that would make religious agencies accountable to the state. Yet the trend continued into the 1950s. Church-state collaboration in social action increased again with Lyndon B. Johnson's Great Society programs of the 1960s, which favored cooperation with voluntary agencies over direct federal action. By this time, sectarian hospitals and social service agencies of all types found federal support irresistible, even as conservatives attacked the growing welfare state. Bill Clinton provided still more direct sectarian access to public welfare funds in 1996, when he signed off on the Charitable Choice provision to the 1996 welfare reform law. By Obama's inauguration, Christian organizations simultaneously controlled and denounced federal support for those in need.[9]

Franklin Roosevelt oversaw the creation of the federal welfare state; Barack Obama worked to hold together what remains of it. Yet Obama's major domestic efforts, including the OFBNP and even the ACA, represent an extension of a privatized, associationalist state that resembles Herbert Hoover's vision of federally supported voluntarism as much as it does Franklin Roosevelt's vision of a coherent federal welfare state. This privatization preceded Obama's tenure, and his attempts to push it back—in the form of single-payer health care, for instance—have met with quick and vehement opposition. Furthermore, the longstanding and increasing separation of federal funds from federal agencies and oversight and their administration through voluntary and religious bodies obscures the essential role of taxpayer dollars in maintaining private and religious social services. By the 1990s, Catholic Charities, Lutheran Social Ministries, and a majority of the nation's Christian child service agencies relied on public funds for more than half their income. Bush's faith-based initiatives extended an already established trend by allowing churches themselves, and not just religious charities, to receive taxpayer dollars.[10] Yet those same churches and agencies denounce the welfare state for usurping their moral authority even as they depend on federal funds to extend it.[11]

Public arguments about the relative effectiveness of federal and voluntary aid agencies build on two contradictory historical narratives, both of which take Roosevelt's New Deal as a turning point. Advocates of a privatized state, or of a shrunken state that turns over the functions of social welfare to voluntary agencies, stress the pre–New Deal power of charitable institutions to care for the needy. Most successfully put forward by historian Marvin Olasky, whose work helped to reshape the 1990s debate over welfare reform, this narrative describes a golden age of mutual concern and support among Americans that lasted from early America to the 1930s. Then, according to Olasky, the New Deal began to undermine Americans' innate compassion by creating an impersonal and permanent welfare state that rendered the poor helpless and dependent. In 2012, Franklin Graham, son of Billy Graham and head of Samaritan's Purse—an evangelical agency that has drawn heavily on federal funds for its international aid work—put the popular expression of this position most succinctly. In an interview with ABC's Christiane Amanpour, Graham explained, "A hundred years ago, the safety net, the social safety net in the country was provided by the church. . . . But the government took that. And took it away from the church." What the churches lost, according to this narrative, was not just a public role in charity but also the moral authority to cultivate good citizens by tying aid to prescribed behaviors.[12]

Scholars and activists who defend the welfare state even as they seek to redress its inequities tell a different story, one in which churches play very little part. Scholars of poverty and welfare, like Michael Katz and Theda Skocpol, demonstrate that, as Katz put it, "American public welfare has a very old history. Public funds have always relieved more people than private ones." From disaster relief to veterans' pensions to funds for mothers and orphans to municipal poor relief, state aid for people in need expanded dramatically in the nineteenth and early twentieth centuries, and religious agencies lost ground to charity organization societies that blended public and private aid. Yet both these nonsectarian agencies and public ones built on the private agencies' work and their racialized and gendered notion that some poor people deserved help and some did not. The New Deal wove these inequities into a social safety net that disproportionately benefited white men even as it forced women and minorities to submit to insulting means tests, when it covered them at all. For many scholars and activists, the appropriate redress for the New Deal's injustices is not to dismantle or privatize welfare but to restructure it on a more equitable model.[13]

The divide between these two narratives is clear. Advocates of voluntarism point to churches' and private organizations' illustrious history of caring for those in need; advocates of a federal safety net point to the longstanding role of state and public agencies in individual welfare, even before the federal government intervened in the 1930s. Both camps focus primarily on the urban north and west, however, where both private and public agencies proved most powerful. In short, both focus on the best version of their preferred model.

But what of the places where people relied almost entirely on a very limited scope of voluntary, largely church-based aid right up to 1933? What kind of help did they offer, to whom, and under what conditions? Did they deem it to be enough? How did they fund their work? How did they navigate the greatest economic crisis since the Civil War? And how did their work change in response to the New Deal?

Memphis, Tennessee, and the surrounding Delta regions of Mississippi and Arkansas provide one set of answers to these questions. Memphis and the Delta make for an interesting case study because the region lacked the state and municipal relief that historians of welfare have stressed as a predecessor to the New Deal, and because it boasted the private, primarily religious sources of aid that conservatives celebrate— and which proved inadequate in the best circumstances and disastrous in the worst. The Great Depression crippled the efforts of even the most robust public and private agencies across the nation. For instance, Lizabeth Cohen has examined the extensive public, ethnic, and religious safety nets that supported Chicago workers in the 1920s and shown how rapidly they collapsed with the onset of the Great Depression. Chicago workers demanded that the federal government step in and organize to ensure that they could help shape its efforts. Even in places like New York City, where both municipal and private relief expenditures soared during the Depression, the increased help could not match the need brought on by a national unemployment rate of 25 percent and widespread hunger and homelessness. Southern cities generally provided less public aid than their northern and Midwestern counterparts, and the rural South provided less still. Rather than rallying around their suffering community members when the Depression began, already-weak southern aid structures folded, leaving people in need with nowhere to turn. Neither the New Deal's public antecedents nor its private alternatives could address the region's widespread suffering and starvation. Here, the necessity of federal intervention in the Great Depression is clear.[14]

Both Memphis and the Delta relied almost entirely on voluntary aid until the 1930s. While relief in the Delta proved patchwork and sparse, Memphis boasted a well-organized Community Fund, a nonsectarian central source of charity and social services whose member organizations were overwhelmingly religious. In 1930, Memphis was a city of 250,000, the nation's thirty-sixth largest. Memphis was majority white and over a third African American; much of the Delta was majority black. Thus, the region also provides some insight into the distinct forms of aid available to black and white southerners in a Jim Crow order. Significant populations of Catholics and Jews and strong Catholic and Jewish charities in the city further illuminate the distinct operations of Catholic, Jewish, and Protestant aid societies.[15]

The South's first serious foray into public aid came during the Civil War and in its aftermath, in the form of state pensions for Confederate veterans. States also funded prisons and asylums, and many cities operated poorhouses for the indigent and elderly. The pensions—the South's only real form of relief—went only to white men; poorhouses were sometimes available for African Americans but often were not. In 1898, after two devastating yellow fever epidemics, Memphis established a city hospital that included wards for both black and white patients, and for a brief period in the 1920s the city distributed privately donated milk to needy infants of both races. Between 1911 and 1930, most states established small Mothers' Aid funds. These funds, designed to provide pensions so that widowed or abandoned mothers could care for their children at home rather than institutionalizing them, supported only whites in Memphis and the Delta, reached only a few hundred families altogether, and provided a few dollars a month at best. Before the New Deal, that was the extent of public aid in the region.[16]

Private charities, most of them religious, accounted for 76 percent of per capita expenditures on relief in Memphis in 1930, and for nearly 100 percent in the Delta. Those organizations made no pretense of serving all equally. Between the Civil War and the Great Depression, Protestant women's societies and home missions organizations built schools, hospitals, orphanages, and settlement houses to reach the city's needy whites, but they served only those they deemed deserving and appropriately deferent. Concerned that their members not be deemed a burden on the larger Protestant community, Catholic and Jewish charities served members of their own communities first, but in Memphis the Catholic House of the Good Shepherd cooperated with the city's juvenile court system to house both Catholic and non-Catholic girls who were deemed troubled. The Jewish Neighborhood House fed poor children of all backgrounds. Black churches and fraternal orders provided the only source of support for most African Americans in need, and they established schools, medical facilities, and insurance programs in both city and countryside.[17]

Yet the need these various organizations sought to alleviate far outpaced the resources they could gather even before the Depression. For families that did not need the institutional help religious societies favored but faced chronic poverty and hunger, little help was available at all. Southern charities generally ascribed chronic poverty to individual shortcomings and deemed it the responsibility of extended families and churches to care for their own members. Only the Salvation Army offered a comprehensive soup kitchen, and it served only white men and boys in Memphis. People in the countryside relied entirely on informal aid, or—more frequently—went hungry, as state-level nutrition studies clearly demonstrate. But the constant requests for support from underfunded voluntary societies, and their stories of families helped (rather than those they missed), could easily leave the impression that anyone who truly needed help had only to ask.[18]

In 1923, several of the city's charitable organizations consolidated their fund-raising efforts under the umbrella of the Memphis Community Fund, which vowed to reduce the pleas for help and increase the efficiency of aid. The Community Fund's member agencies almost exclusively served whites, and even for them it proved inadequate. The fund met its minimal fund-raising goals in its founding year, and then failed to reach them again for a decade. Its organizers, who believed that poverty generally resulted from individual failures, lamented that they could not raise the funds even to help those few souls they deemed both needy and worthy of help.[19]

And then disaster struck. The 1929 stock market crash left Memphians and Delta residents unfazed, their fortunes tied instead to the cotton and the agricultural market. But a record-setting drought in the spring and summer of 1930 parched the cotton in the fields as the prices for what little remained plummeted to a third of the previous year's rates. Food crops shriveled alongside the cotton, and farmers faced a long winter with neither food to store nor income for basic staples. Then, a wave of bank failures swept the region, and even those who had managed to put by a little money saw their savings disappear. With federal support, the Red Cross provided minimal emergency aid starting in December, often distributed through churches whose members so universally suffered that they could not aid one another without outside help. But the help was not enough, and reports soon emerged of people walking miles for food, their feet wrapped in sacks, and of "frantic women begging for medical aid for babies dying of malnutrition or the many forms of disease that attack the underfed and underclothed." Some of those people arrived only to find that their townships or county Red Cross chapters had run out of ration cards and refused to provide aid without them.[20]

The private aid organizations that had proudly proclaimed their success at caring for all who really needed help now faced three crises at once. First, the number of people seeking help skyrocketed very quickly. Second, the defense that many of the poor deserved their lot fell apart in the face of widespread environmental and economic crisis. And last, donations to charities and churches plummeted and any savings they had often vanished in the same bank failures that crushed farmers and the middle class.

Churches and charities tried to help. In December of 1929, the Salvation Army—a member of the Community Fund—had served 1,700 meals; by December of 1930, that number had ballooned to 6,500 meals and by April of 1931 to 10,250 meals. Also a men's shelter, the Salvation Army drained its pool to make room for extra pallets on the pool floor.[21] But many agencies cut back. In 1931, the Community Fund pared its fund-raising goals to a minimum, and it still brought in only $462,344 of its $609,553 goal—a 24 percent shortfall.[22] Many women's clubs, fraternal orders, and other quasi-religious private organizations suspended their work or disbanded.[23]

Churches fared still worse, often struggling just to keep their doors open. Between 1929 and 1932, national income dropped by more than 50 percent. Wage earners' income sank by 60 percent; salaried workers' by 40 percent. Because of the drought and the lost cotton crop, that loss came earlier to Memphis and the Delta. Until 1933, church giving held steady as a proportion of national income, but a 50 percent loss nonetheless proved crippling at the very moment that demands on church resources escalated. More ominously, the churches cut benevolent spending first.[24] As the president of the cash-strapped Southern Baptist Convention put it in 1931, "we are putting off the Lord's cause while we try to settle with our other creditors."[25] When the money ran out, the churches turned their spending inward, not outward.

As they faced the suffering before them and their own inability to alleviate it, even conservative religious leaders joined social workers and hungry Americans to call for federal intervention. In January 1932, Herbert Hoover's administration established the Reconstruction Finance Corporation (RFC), which Congress authorized to provide emergency loans to banks and corporations, and in July Congress expanded its powers to provide loans to states and municipalities for public works projects that would employ out-of-work citizens. States often disbursed those funds through private agencies like the Memphis Community Fund, cementing their support. Yet the measure did little to stem the deepening Depression. Democrat Franklin Roosevelt trounced Hoover in the 1932 election, largely on the promise that he would use the power of the federal government to address the Depression. Even as many Protestants protested Roosevelt's vow to oversee an end to Prohibition, southern clergy enthusiastically supported the new president's first efforts to address the Depression.[26]

The barrage of legislation that Roosevelt signed in 1933, in what would become known as the First Hundred Days, included the creation of an agency that drew a clear line between federal and private relief: the FERA. The FERA replaced Hoover's RFC loans with grants to the states for relief projects. Headed by Iowan Harry Hopkins, FERA was the first program to put federal funds not only toward employment relief but also toward direct aid for the suffering, in whatever form city and state aid administrators saw fit. It was also the program that most directly engaged with work once conducted by private aid organizations.[27]

In June 1933, Hopkins stipulated that as of July 1 only public agencies could administer federal FERA funds. With so much at stake both financially and politically, Hopkins wanted to avoid the problems and complaints that proliferated about the inadequate, incompetent, and dishonest administration of Hoover's RFC by cronies of the politicians in charge. Yet he also had to honor Roosevelt's commitment to maintain local control of aid. Public aid on the RFC's scale was such a novelty that many states— particularly in the South—lacked the infrastructure and experience to administer it, and many had simply subsidized private work rather than establishing new public programs. As Josephine Brown, a social worker and FERA field agent, explained, Hopkins's decision meant "the financing and administration of public benefits for persons in need was definitely established as being the responsibility of government and not of private citizens, however organized or however charitably disposed."[28] Leaders of private and religious agencies often simply transitioned to public positions, while other private agencies—like Catholic Charities in Chicago—gained public certification. Hopkins's decree nonetheless established a clear public-private boundary both for FERA and for subsequent New Deal programs.[29]

Government aid quickly outpaced that of all private agencies, because it could leverage a vastly larger pool of resources. Across the nation, but especially in places like Memphis and the Delta that had offered little aid to the poor, New Deal spending made previous private contributions look like pocket change. At the peak of private giving, in 1931, Memphians raised $0.88 in aid per person, $0.75, or 85 percent of it, private. By 1934, the New Deal in full swing, Memphians received $7.21 per capita in aid for direct relief and work relief. Private contributions that year amounted to only $0.13 per capita—1.6 percent of the total. By comparison, the average aid per person in the nation's 116 major urban areas increased from $2.36 per person, 29 percent ($0.45) of it private, in 1931 to $16.51 per person in 1934, with only 1.8 percent ($0.15) provided by private sources. Nationally, but even more so in Memphis, this was a striking reversal. In just five years, as federal dollars provided the work and food Memphians so desperately needed, private aid dropped from nearly three-quarters of relief spending in the city to less than 2 percent. The shift from private to public responsibility for the needy could hardly have been more dramatic.[30]

The swing from private to public aid was easier to track in the city, but it was even more pronounced in the countryside, where fewer resources of either kind were available. In the Delta, neither public nor private charity was organized enough to provide accurate reports before 1933. By the end of July 1933, FERA had made grants to every state and the District of Columbia. Between January 1933 and December 1935, eleven states—including Arkansas, Mississippi, Tennessee, and most of the South—received more than 90 percent of their total work relief funds from the federal government.[31]

Because it was the only New Deal agency to provide direct aid to the needy, FERA proved particularly important to religious leaders. People had finally begun to receive the help that they so desperately needed, and that the churches and civic organizations had proven unable to provide. Now those people began to turn to the state rather than to local religious groups for both material aid and personal guidance. Some clergy celebrated the transition and asked for more. A white Arkansas Sunday School Superintendent wrote to the nonexistent "Welfare Society" in Washington, DC, to ask for help with a pair of tough local children. "If you have a place for such lads, to have them reformed," wrote the superintendent, "the community would be much pleased." He was almost certainly disappointed to receive a quick response from Eleanor Roosevelt's secretary reporting that the federal government could do nothing to address the matter, which instead "would come under the jurisdiction of local authorities."[32]

This emphasis on local distribution of federal aid secured the support of white southerners who distrusted the federal government's commitment to the region's Jim Crow capitalist economy, but ministers concerned with social and racial justice denounced FERA's unequal implementation. Local relief administrators often represented the economic elite, and they structured the new system to humiliate those who sought help and to deny them when possible. Southern capitalism depended on a dual wage system that kept African American workers poor, and local administration guaranteed the perpetuation of that system. One Mississippi minister wrote to Roosevelt to "call attention to the Southern negro who has not had a square deal of the many projects since the depression."[33]

Yet black religious leaders also applauded signs that the Roosevelt administration cared more for African Americans' safety and well-being in the South than had previous administrations. In 1934, Harold Ickes, Roosevelt's Secretary of the Interior and head of the Public Works Administration, created an "Interdepartmental Group Concerned with Special Problems of Negroes" to push for inclusion of African Americans in the major New Deal programs. Though the group had little power, its existence seemed a hopeful step. The overall standard of living for black workers who kept their jobs also increased a little as their employers found a way to cheat the government and stopped working so hard to cheat their workers.[34]

Although its separation of public and private relief work proved more durable, FERA was itself a temporary measure, intended only to meet the immediate physical needs of people devastated by the Depression. The program expired in 1935, replaced in part by two programs at the heart of Franklin Roosevelt's Second New Deal: the

Works Progress Administration and the Social Security Act. Perhaps because these two programs created permanent structures that overlapped with work that churches had once done, in September 1935 Roosevelt's administration sent a letter to the nation's clergy asking for feedback on them. He received more than 12,000 replies within two months, a full 84 percent of which proved generally favorable in tone, particularly toward the Social Security Act, which made provisions for the elderly, the orphaned, and the disabled.[35]

"Above all else, as I see it, is your Social Security Program," wrote the editor of the South's major white Methodist journal. "For the first time in our history we have a National Administration that is seeking to realize practically all the objectives of the 'Social Creeds' of the Churches—Catholic, Protestant, Jewish."[36] For religious leaders like this one, the welfare state represented a religious achievement rather than an encroachment on the churches' work. Indeed, it freed the churches to focus on supplementary care or to return to a focus on evangelism.

But a few clergy expressed concerns that would grow more widespread by the late 1930s, particularly among conservative and evangelically oriented white Protestants. Although Social Security excluded domestic and agricultural workers, and thus most southern African Americans, some whites nonetheless complained of the "high cost to the white population" of Social Security because "one-half of the citizenry pays a very small part of the taxes."[37] Others feared their loss of power over white community members as well. One Mississippi Presbyterian and self-proclaimed "southern democrat" worried that the state had severed the church's hold on community members who now had someplace else to find help. "Where they once had community contacts for cooperation and sympathy they now look to the Government for all," he declared.[38] It is possible that federal aid made it easier for some poor families to disconnect from middle-class churches where they felt out of place. Now, they had options other than local paternalism, and clergy already inclined to question the New Deal expressed both alarm and outrage.

Although dissent against the New Deal grew in Memphis and the Delta, and across the South, during the late 1930s, Roosevelt's programs remained popular in the region and its churches for decades. Black and white workers proved loyal to the president they credited with pulling them out of the Depression, as did much of the region's middle class. Some southern whites defected from the Democratic Party because they believed that the New Deal threatened white supremacy in the region, but the South's Republican turn lay in the future. The memory of the inadequacy of private relief and its utter collapse in a moment of crisis still fresh, southerners in the 1930s and 1940s embraced the nascent welfare state.[39]

Soon, however, American religious institutions also began to take roles not only complementary to the welfare state but integral to it—and funded by it. After World War II and increasingly as the Cold War dragged on, both secular and religious nonprofits worked as subsidiaries of the federal government to provide overseas relief, education, and aid. As the domestic welfare state expanded under both Republican and Democratic presidents from the 1940s to the 1960s, federal officials increasingly relied on private subsidiaries, including religious organizations, to administer new programs. Lyndon Johnson's War on Poverty sped this transition, its most important provisions for health and child welfare often administered through subsidies to religious hospitals and church-based child care providers.[40]

As conservative critics of the welfare state rose to power in the 1980s and 1990s, they pushed further privatization of services. By the 1980s, the National Association of Evangelicals and other conservative organizations that had once spurned government support now embraced tax credits for private child care, fought for public vouchers to parochial schools, and relied heavily on federal support for international missionary and relief work.[41] But it was Democrat Bill Clinton who signed the Personal Responsibility and Work Opportunity Reconciliation Act into law in 1996, and with it Charitable Choice, a provision that ensured that religious providers received equal consideration in competition for federal funds and removed stipulations that those providers qualify for tax-exempt status.[42]

His successor, George W. Bush, more famously established the White House Office of Faith-Based and Community Initiatives, which allowed churches themselves, and not just religious charities, to receive federal funds. Obama promised more transparency about the disbursement of federal funds to proselytizing bodies in his continuation of the faith-based initiatives effort. Yet even as he has shifted emphasis from such programs, the funding for them remains robust. As the welfare state shrank, then, it also made an increasing proportion of its remaining funds available to explicitly religious providers.[43]

Indeed, many religious organizations rely so heavily on federal dollars today that they would likely fold without them. More than eighty years since the New Deal first established a federal safety net, it is difficult to imagine the United States without such basic protections for its citizens. Many conservatives and libertarians call for just that, however, recalling an American past that never existed, in which unfettered capitalism ensured a robust economy and in which the deserving poor received what they needed from generous private and religious charities. Those very charities have become so deeply entwined in the federal government in the post–World War II decades that in dismantling the welfare state they also risk dismantling themselves. In short, religious and private agencies grow fat on federal dollars that allow them to extend their moral and political authority with little oversight. In a deceptive sleight-of-hand and a bald-faced denial of history, anti-government Christian conservatives like Franklin Graham demand an end to the very federal programs that they—and many far more vulnerable Americans—rely on to survive.

The Mystification of Capitalism and the Misdirection of White Anger

Rebecca Todd Peters

The 2016 US presidential election highlighted sociocultural tensions confronting advanced democracies across the Western world. From Hillary Clinton's "basket of deplorables" to Donald Trump's braggadocio attitude toward sexually assaulting women, the election rhetoric was shot through with intense emotions and perspectives about how we think and act on our attitudes about race, class, and gender in the United States. It is not inconsequential that the culturally charged rhetoric of this campaign followed eight years of the country's first black president. In liberal and Democratic circles, Hillary's loss was largely blamed on working-class whites and white evangelicals (two groups with significant overlap); while in some conservative and alt-right circles, Trump's win was regarded as a repudiation of liberal politics and a vindication of whiteness, white values, and white political power.[1] The anger and frustration of working-class whites received a lot of attention in the weeks and months following the election as a largely surprised white, urban public sought to analyze and understand Trump's election. While there is general agreement that the core of white working-class anger is rooted in economic dislocation, there has been too little critical examination of the economic circumstances, policies, and priorities that generated that dislocation.

In this chapter, I will argue that the economic marginalization of the white working class is indicative of a larger crisis that threatens human and planetary well-being. While conveniently masked by the Great Recession and the collective struggle for economic recovery that has marked the last ten years, the more serious crisis that we face is the crisis of capitalism, particularly in its neoliberal form. Neoliberalism, the dominant form of capitalism shaping the global economy for the past thirty-five years, focuses on the three goals of privatization, deregulation, and increased trade and promises to increase growth and prosperity through decreasing government involvement in the economy.[2] Neoliberalism replaced the social equity or welfare liberal economic approach, which holds both that the state has a significant role to play in the economy through guaranteeing a social safety that ensures no one falls into poverty and that the state sometimes needs to provide an economic stimulus to a sluggish economy. From a purely macro-economic perspective focused on rising GDPs, neoliberalism has delivered on its promises—increasing production efficiency, maximizing profits, and generating vast amounts of wealth around the globe.

The crisis is not that neoliberalism has failed, but rather that it has succeeded spectacularly. The wealth that neoliberal economic globalization has generated over the past thirty-five years is flowing exactly where it was intended to flow—to the owners of capital, the existing economic elite. In fact, the top 1 percent in the United States is approaching a marginal stake of 24 percent of the fiscal income in the United States, a level not seen since 1928, just before the market crash that ushered in the Great Depression. We got close in 2007 when levels hit 22.8 percent, right before the market crashed, ushering in the Great Recession. Alongside the phenomenal economic growth accompanying the global shift to a neoliberal economy, there has been a corresponding stagnation in the wages of the workers. In the United States, the wages of workers who fall into the bottom half of earners have dropped their share of income from roughly 20 percent of the total between 1962 and 1980 to 12.5 percent in 2014, while the top 1 percent doubled their share of income to over 20 percent.[3] The increasing inequality in the United States is not simply that the rich are making more money but that the working class is making substantially less, and the combined factors are contributing to an economic divide between rich and poor not seen in the United States since before the Gilded Age.

While the reasons for the growing economic inequality are extraordinarily complex, our ability to engage in productive debates about these problems and about the very role and function of political-economies and the health and future of our markets in the United States has fixated on arguing about which version of capitalism we ought to follow—social equity or neoliberal. As a country, we are largely unwilling or unable to acknowledge that the true crisis that we face is the moral bankruptcy of capitalism. Our collective inability to adequately recognize the moral failings of capitalism are a result of the mystification of capitalism, which functions to hide its flaws and valorize its potential as the economic salvation of humanity. This crisis of capitalism is fundamentally an epistemological crisis in which the human community has forgotten that the primary purpose of a political-economy is to support and promote human flourishing.

Mystification is a distortion of reality (or history) that functions to impede people's capacity to think critically and rationally about a subject. Marx famously denounced bourgeois accounts tracing the origins of capitalism to the hard work of Europeans as mystifying the more sinister origins of capitalism in the exploitation and extraction of resources associated with colonialism.[4] Mystification causes people to misunderstand or misidentify the causes and determinations of problems, thus making it difficult to address the root causes of social problems. The mystification of capitalism in the United States functions to prevent people from accurately identifying the sources and causes of our economic distress and prevents US Americans from addressing the very real political, social, and economic problems that face us in the twenty-first century. To say that US Americans have a mystified relationship with capitalism is to acknowledge that capitalism is not merely an economic system but that it has a potent psychological role in our social identity as well.

Twenty years ago, religious studies scholar David Loy argued that capitalism should be understood as our common religion because it has come to fulfill a religious function for us, namely, both explaining the world and our place in it and shaping and forming the dominant values that guide interpersonal and social behavior. In short, Loy argued that "the market" had become our god.[5] The influence and power of capitalism to shape social values and communal expectations has only increased over the past twenty years as people increasingly embrace the cult of individualism that undergirds the foundational myths of this country. From the American Dream, which seeks to define hard work as the road to success to its accompanying bootstrap theology, the foundational myths of this country are grounded in an individualism that holds people personally responsible for their successes and failures. Ironically, the bootstrap theology that promotes and supports the rugged individualism undergirding US American identity is actively hostile to the actual history of community and cooperation that shaped a variety of communities that worked together to build this country. It is also deeply at odds with the communal character of Biblical teachings about human flourishing and abundant life.

Blind faith in the promise of capitalism to bring democracy to the world, to provide access to the American Dream, and to eliminate global poverty is only possible in the midst of a fog of mystification that distracts our attention from the looming crises that threaten the health and well-being of all of the world's people and the planet that we share. In this chapter, I will outline how three important factors have coalesced to conceal the moral dangers inherent in capitalism and mystify our understanding of capitalism. These factors include the following: (1) the economic benefits of early forms of capitalism in the Fordist era; (2) the anti-communist and pro-capitalist hysteria of the Cold War; and (3) the mythology of the American Dream and its emphasis on rugged individualism. I then turn to discussing how mystification deflects public attention from the crisis of capitalism and how it contributed to Trump's appeal among white, working-class voters. The chapter concludes with a discussion of how the epistemological crisis of capitalism is preventing the development of robust twenty-first century models of political-economies that promote human flourishing and planetary well-being.

The mystification of capitalism

The story of capitalism begins in the eighteenth century with the rise of the Industrial Revolution. Technological innovations like the invention of the cotton gin and the development of the steam engine laid the ground work for the shift from craft guilds and the small-scale local production of goods to the mass production of consumer goods through the factory system and eventually the assembly line. These technological advances in the production of goods functioned to transform the largely rural and agricultural economies of the eighteenth century and helped to facilitate the rise of urban populations. Initially, factories were built in cities due to their need for workers. Eventually the increased mechanization of work reduced the number of jobs in the agriculture and craft sectors and younger people began moving to the cities in pursuit of factory jobs.

Factories in the nineteenth century were notoriously dangerous and exploitative of wage laborers. These conditions mobilized workers, Christian activists, and unions to lobby for governmental regulations to protect workers from the abuses of capitalism.[6] Karl Marx's trenchant description of capitalism as rooted in the exploitation of labor for the enrichment of the capitalist owning class was born out of the abuses and excesses of the Industrial Revolution and the unregulated form of capitalism that reigned in the nineteenth century. Marxian critiques of capitalism were also influential in the rise of the Social Gospel Movement and Christian socialism which sought to mediate the most harmful effects of industrial capitalism and to create a more just economic order.[7] It wasn't until 1938 that the Fair Labor Standards Act was passed in the United States, ushering in a new kinder and gentler form of capitalism that offered protection for workers from the exploitation of owners in the form of important safety regulations and labor laws that standardized the forty-hour work week, established a national minimum wage, ensured provisions for overtime pay, and prohibited child labor. Tragically, however, these benefits were not extended to large numbers of black workers as both farmworkers and domestic workers were excluded from the Act, both jobs heavily filled by black workers at the time.

In many places, factory work had already begun to change voluntarily in the late nineteenth and early twentieth centuries as some capitalist owners of factories and production facilities sought to shape work environments that provided for the health and well-being of their workers rather than simply viewing them for the use value of their labor. Robert Owen was an early pioneer of an alternative vision of industrial production that sought to shape the structures of economic production in ways that shared the economic benefits with the workers. His philosophy was labeled as utopian and laid the groundwork for the development of socialism and the other economic arrangements that focused on sharing the economic benefits of production, including worker-owned cooperatives. Henry Ford was another early economic radical who recognized that his workers were also potential consumers and that they needed to be paid wages that allowed them to fully participate in society, including having the capacity to own and drive the cars they were helping to produce. His philosophy of mass production accompanied by high wages for workers was known as Fordism and became the dominant model of capitalism in the United States. This model of capitalism drove the postwar boom that built the middle class and allowed for a level of disposable income that created the economic model of accumulation and mass consumption that continues to shape daily life in the United States.

With the rise of the tensions between the USSR and the United States in the postwar period, anti-Soviet attitudes were stoked by triumphalist and nationalist messages that promoted the United States and our interest in capitalism at the expense of the USSR and the alternative economic model that they represented. Marxism, socialism, and communism were vilified and demonized and US American citizens who believed in alternative forms of arranging economic policies and markets were hauled before Congress and their lives, careers, and reputations were ruined. The denigration of the USSR continued throughout the Cold War and the fall of the Berlin Wall was celebrated in the United States as the symbolic triumph of capitalism over socialism and communism. In assessing the changes happening around the world in 1989,

Francis Fukuyama commented that "the twentieth century saw the developed world descend into a paroxysm of ideological violence, as liberalism contended first with the remnants of absolutism, then bolshevism and fascism, and finally an updated Marxism that threatened to lead to the ultimate apocalypse of nuclear war." He interpreted the collapse of communism in 1989 not as an end of ideology, but as the "unabashed victory of economic and political liberalism."[8]

The "liberalism" that Fukuyama championed and sold to adoring publics in the West was the ideology of neoliberalism that had been ushered in by the Reagan-Thatcher revolution in the 1980s. A new world order that promoted a Western model of laissez-faire capitalism as the reigning model for organizing economic behavior around the globe. While the theoretical foundations of this model of free-market capitalism had been laid by economist Friedrich Hayek in the 1930s and 1940s and further developed by Milton Friedman in the 1950s and 1960s, their work did not gain much credibility until the 1980s. Friedman himself noted, "people are not influential in arguing for different courses in the economy. . . . The role of people is to keep ideas alive until a crisis occurs. It wasn't my talking that caused people to embrace these ideas, just as the rooster doesn't make the sun rise. Collectivism was an impossible way to run an economy."[9] The Reagan-Thatcher revolution of the 1980s turned the theoretical arguments of Hayek and Friedman into the public policies that shaped a new era of neoliberalism.

The third factor that contributes to the mystification of capitalism in the United States is our persistent collective dependence on the mythology of the "American Dream." This "Dream" promotes the belief that America is a land of opportunity and that upward mobility is possible if you work hard enough.[10] This dream is not only rooted in a rugged individualism associated with our colonial history as a pioneer nation, it was reinforced with the idealization of capitalism as having "won" the Cold War. A perspective exemplified in Margaret Thatcher's popular "TINA" claim that "There Is No Alternative" to free-market capitalism.

It might be a bit of an understatement to say that Americans are deeply invested in capitalism. Capitalism has been presented as the core of economic success in the United States. Capitalism has been equated with opportunity, hard work, and social mobility. In fact, US Americans have been sold the idea that capitalism *is* the American Dream. Consequently, when US workers experience economic dislocation that result from neoliberal economic policies they are unable to identify the correct source of that dislocation. While strategies like the automation of jobs, relocating production facilities to lower wage countries, and eliminating the "middle-man" appear to increase economic efficiency by cutting production costs and increasing profits, they have also resulted in a cumulative massive loss of jobs over the past thirty years. Perhaps even more importantly, the jobs that have been lost to this increased "economic efficiency" were often high-wage, stable blue-collar, and middle-management jobs—a class of jobs that have all but disappeared. Since the GDP and the stock market have continued to climb in the United States, our economy is widely regarded as stable, productive, and growth-oriented. This rosy economic picture, however, belies the transformation of our labor market which has replaced a large part of our solid, middle-wage, middle-income jobs that include salaries and benefits with part-time, contingent, low-wage work.

Mystification deflects attention from the crisis of capitalism

The crisis and transformation in the US auto industry illustrates how the mystification of capitalism works in our country. In 1970, General Motors (GM) was the largest private employer in the United States. They paid $17.50 an hour plus health, pension, and paid vacation benefits. Based on the consumer price index, the purchasing power of that $17.50 an hour wage would be the equivalent of almost $113,000 in 2016. These were the jobs that created a vibrant and healthy middle class in the postwar United States. Compare that to today's largest employer, Walmart, with its 1.5 million US workers.[11] According to Walmart, full-time workers make an average of $13.38 an hour and their part-time workers make an average of $10.58 an hour.[12] This means that a full-time worker at Walmart who works 40 hours a week, 52 weeks a year, would make roughly $27,800 annually—four times less than their GM counterpart almost fifty years ago. If that full-time Walmart worker is also the head-of-household of a family of four, their salary puts them $459 below the 2017 federal poverty line, a measurement that is widely regarded by poverty experts as woefully inadequate. Identifying the twenty-first-century economic reality as one where many of the nations' full-time working class are living at or near poverty is the context within which we must consider the moral and social value of capitalism.

The displacement of GM by Walmart as the nation's largest employer epitomizes the shift in the labor market in this country from stable, middle-income jobs to poorly paid contingent work. Shifts in the labor market are also a reflection of the shifting global economy. Plant closures and massive job cuts in the mid-2000s signaled significant economic distress in the auto industry. In early 2006, for example, Ford and GM cut approximately 60,000 jobs and announced closures of over two dozen plants over the next six years. Unfortunately, these job cuts and plant closures were not enough to keep the companies afloat, and the auto industry in the United States struggled to remake itself in the midst of the Great Recession with significant aid from the US government. One version of GM's recovery plan called for a 98 percent increase in auto manufacturing intended for US markets to take place in Mexico, China, South Korea, and Japan.[13] While it was clear during the Great Recession that the US auto industry was floundering, the discussions about how to save GM and Chrysler were focused primarily on assisting these entities as business corporations, not on recognizing and encouraging the social and economic contributions that these industries make to our society as a whole by serving as integral elements of a larger social fabric. Namely, the purpose and function of a business is more than simply to make a profit. Businesses offer goods and services that contribute to improving the quality of life of community members; they provide jobs and contribute to the economic and social well-being of a community by paying taxes and supporting community endeavors. Buying into the premise that the primary function of business is generating profits is a result of the mystification of capitalism that impairs our ability to recognize the social and moral duties of businesses that exist alongside the ability to turn a profit.

Examining the US auto industry offers a lens into what happens when profit is the primary factor driving economic decision-making. As domestic auto sales declined in the latter half of the twentieth century due to increased competition from Germany,

Japan, and then Korea, GM did not respond by stepping up their game and making better cars. Through the 1970s and 1980s, US car manufacturers attempted to stave off economic disaster through protectionist policies that limited the number of imports. When these policies ran out of steam in the 1990s, GM shifted their economic model from investing in improving the quality and production of their product to an economic growth model rooted in finance.[14] GM executives repositioned their profits from making money on cars sold to making money on the financing of car sales. In 2004, 80 percent of their profit came from General Motor Acceptance Corporation (GMAC), their financial arm. While this shift garnered short-term financial gains, by failing to invest in improving their actual products, these "car makers" not only lost any competitive edge they might have had in the market, they also lost the credibility of their name brand as the quality of their products fell in public estimation. By the summer of 2009, GM was facing bankruptcy and sought a bailout from the federal government in partnership with Chrysler and Ford. In the end, $80.7 billion of Troubled Asset Relief Program (TARP) funds were allocated to the Big Three automakers. While the majority of that money was recouped over the next five years, $10 billion of US taxpayer dollars ultimately financed an industry that had failed to do its job. GM is a prime example of how the mystification of capitalism has created an economic system that no longer functions to contribute to the well-being of society. In a strict neoliberal, laissez-faire model of capitalism, GM and Chrysler's economic crisis should have served as the ultimate demise of poorly run companies that had failed to stay competitive in a changing market. However, the fact that one million jobs were on the line meant the car companies were deemed "too big to fail" due to the damaging ripple effect their bankruptcy would have on an economy already in recession.

That the mystification of capitalism blurs our senses is evident in the way in which political and economic debates are primarily focused on defining what is the "best" form of capitalism. In the midst of a culture that worships capitalism and markets; too many US Americans believe that there is no alternative to free-market capitalism. We saw this in the debate of the auto-industry bailout as politicians weighed the pros and cons of government involvement with an industry deemed "too big to fail." While economists and politicians may divide themselves into the two camps that can be described as neoliberals and social equity liberals, these two "sides" are functionally engaged in a Pyrrhic battle over what role government should play in the regulation of capitalism, not in any substantive debate about the moral or economic adequacy of capitalism as an economic system. As each side develops arguments to support their position toward government involvement in the economy, their approaches to economic stability and political-economy both remain deeply tied to the economic dominance of capitalism as the superior mechanism for ordering economic activity in our country and globally. As long as both sides continue to believe in the promises of capitalism, that the profit motive and self-interest are truly the only way to order our economies, then the primary political task will simply be to debate the extent of government involvement in the economy. Meanwhile, the mystification of capitalism has contributed to more serious social and political problems.

How Trump exploited the mystified
sensibilities of white America

Donald Trump's campaign took advantage of the mystification of capitalism by offering economically anxious white voters scapegoats to blame for their troubles as a substitute for substantive analysis of the real economic crisis of capitalism. His authoritarian approach to governing offered the illusion of control with concrete "solutions" to fabricated problems. While Trump didn't invent the problems of immigration, terrorism, and trade, he manipulated these issues to shape narratives of danger and uncertainty that exploited the economic dis-ease of working-class, white US Americans. Trump transformed his narratives into a xenophobic and hateful version of American exceptionalism that traded on an American Dream mythology rooted in white privilege, white prosperity, and ultimately white supremacy. His racist and xenophobic rhetoric played into the rising racial resentment among some white US Americans about the normalization of black leadership that accompanied a black president.[15] While Obama appealed to a liberal base interested in social change related to race, inclusion, and other values associated with a social democratic vision of identity, politics, and governance, Trump's election represented a 180 degree reversal of that sentiment, capitalizing on a broad spectrum of white voters who experienced feelings of disenfranchisement, loss of power, and insecurity during the Great Recession (and, truth be told for many years prior to that as well) that happened to coincide with the Obama presidency.[16]

Hearkening back to an idyllic bygone era of American "greatness" that was presented as synonymous with economic prosperity, safety, and homogeneity, Trump's populist appeal to "Make America Great Again" was aimed at anxious white voters. His nostalgic promise was also racially coded in complex ways. For working-class whites who felt that they had been left behind by the massive transformation of the economy over the last thirty years—the message appealed to their desire to regain their footing as solidly middle-class citizens. Sixty-six percent of whites without a college degree voted for Trump.[17] For evangelical whites who felt that the country has lost its moral center with increasing civil rights for LGBT citizens and what they see as the loss of "traditional family values"—the message signaled a return to a set of conservative Christian values.[18] Eighty percent of white evangelicals voted for Trump.[19] On the other hand, for many people of color, the "Again" aspect of Trump's agenda functioned as a jingoistic call to return to a vaguely unidentified US American past associated with racial violence and the civil exclusion of minorities in the form of segregation, internment camps, and the acceptability of blatant and explicit racism and racial prejudice. A perspective reinforced by Trump's campaign promises to "build a wall," and start a "Muslim registry," promises that traded on highlighting the otherness of immigrants who Trump cast as compromising the safety and security of US America's. Under the protection of mystification, Trump was able to manufacture scapegoats for the public and divert attention from the real crisis that we face as a nation and the crisis that we face as a global community—the economic crisis of capitalism.

From an economic perspective, Hillary Clinton was only marginally better in that she too is an apologist for capitalism, she just approaches it from the social equity side. In the Democratic world, inequality is something to be managed through government policies. To be sure, redistribution is essential for any society that seeks to ensure the safety and well-being of its citizens when that society lacks a functioning economy that is able to provide jobs that pay workers a living wage, sufficient affordable housing and high-quality day care to meet demand, and exceptional education that effectively prepares children and young people to participate in society. In the absence of any serious critique of the capacity of capitalism to function as an effective economic tool for shaping healthy societies, policies of redistribution play an important moral role in addressing poverty and economic marginalization.

The problem, however, is not that we are shifting from an industrial economy to an information economy and thus dislocating workers who need to be retrained for a new set of jobs. After all, innovation and change are hallmarks of human society and labor markets reflect this reality. In every age, there are issues of economic dislocation as well as questions of who has access to "good" jobs—jobs that offer the opportunity for independence and security for oneself and one's family. The problem is that the economic logic of capitalism is *structured* to benefit the few at the expense of the many—whether that is an industrial economy or an information economy. The economic system of capitalism, particularly neoliberal or laissez-faire capitalism, is designed to transfer wealth to the owners of capital. When the Industrial Revolution began, working-class people had to fight for the protections against exploitation that built the middle class in most industrial countries. Unions organized workers so they could engage in collective bargaining and governments implemented labor and environmental regulations that protected workers and the environment from the exploitative actions of industrialists seeking to maximize their profits. Shaping industrialization into an economic model that offered jobs that paid a living wage is the result of people working together to create a just economic system. These jobs allowed for the development of a self-sufficient middle class throughout the twentieth century. This shifted when companies in the industrialized world realized that profits could be increased by moving production to low-wage countries with little to no environmental or labor regulations.

The crisis that we face today is no longer simply a crisis of capitalism. Given the mystified relationship that US Americans hold with capitalism, we now face an epistemological crisis, a crisis in which we have misunderstood the fundamental purpose of an economy. Markets and businesses should be understood as the mechanisms to shape a healthy society rather than simply tools to create wealth. The creation of wealth in a capitalist system is a creation of private wealth that leads to individual prosperity for a few. The creation of wealth is not synonymous with the creation of a healthy society. The purpose of a market is to facilitate the trade of goods and services in order for people to live together in a community. The purpose of an economy is to help shape and guide those markets in ways that build flourishing societies. Economies and markets do not function magically outside of human control and organization. Economies always and only ever exist inside political communities. Economies are always shaped by political considerations, this is why they are better understood as political-economies.

The moral crisis of capitalism

It is time for us to ask some deeper moral questions about capitalism in both its neoliberal and social equity forms. What are we to make of the fact that while Walmart is the nation's largest private employer and the largest overall employer in twenty-five states, only 48 percent of Walmart employees have health insurance?[20] Or the fact that 56 percent of state and federal spending on public assistance contributes to subsidizing low-wage employers like Walmart and McDonalds when their employees don't have enough food or can't afford health insurance?[21] Or what about the fact that a recent study found that only 25 percent of jobs in this country fall into the category of "good jobs" when that is defined as paying at least $32,000 a year and offering health care and pension benefits?[22]

The massive outsourcing of jobs that has accompanied the growth of neoliberal economic policies over the past thirty years has brought with it increasing economic divides within first-world countries. Census data shows that income inequality in the United States has risen consistently over the past forty years with increasing numbers of affluent and poor and a shrinking middle class.[23] Poverty rates in the United States have steadily increased in the twenty-first century, from 11.3 percent in 2000 to 13.5 percent by 2015, representing 11.5 million additional people living in poverty.[24] A total of 41 percent of those people living in poverty were working full time or part time.[25] However, it is difficult, if not impossible, for people who work low-wage service jobs (which are often the only kinds of jobs available to low-skilled workers) to pull themselves above the poverty line. Increasingly, middle- and upper-middle-class families struggling with job loss are finding it difficult to feed their families. When capitalism is presented as the solution to our problems, workers like these are blamed for their poverty while corporate leaders and CEOs are exempt from criticism. Ultimately, we are unable to engage in rigorous critique of the fundamental principles of capitalism that are contributing to the rise of economic inequality.

Even before the economic downtown, the proponents of neoliberal economic globalization argued that the current restructuring and retooling of the US economy was simply the market at work. The unionized jobs of the auto or textile industry that offered living wages and decent benefits were marked as "dinosaurs," relics of an old world order. Businesses simply don't have to pay what they used to in wages, not in a globalized economy—not when they can outsource parts manufacturing or even open assembly plants in developing countries where the wages are much, much lower. Why pay a United Auto Worker in the United States $28 an hour when they can pay pennies on the dollar to a Mexican, Korean, or Chinese worker?[26] The logic of the system is clear—when you lower production costs, you raise profitability. The mystification of capitalism has placed a veil over our eyes that prevents us from questioning the fundamental tenet of a capitalist ideology—that maximizing profits is the essential element of a stable and functioning economy and that profits are the preeminent corporate goal.

In the 1980s, the logic of neoliberalism took hold of global international financial institutions through the increasing implementation of austerity policies and structural adjustment loans that sought to control the growing debt crisis in the developing world. The severe social impact of neoliberal economic globalization on the health and well-being of the world's poorest people was immediately apparent in many two-thirds world countries that were still struggling to overcome the cultural, political, and economic devastation of colonialism. The colonial histories of exploitation in countries like Ghana, the Philippines, and Jamaica contributed to the ability of workers and activists in many debt-ridden countries to challenge the structural adjustment policies that threatened their health and livelihood.[27] Poor and working-class people in the Global South who did not idolize capitalism or see it as their salvation immediately and clearly identified the neoliberal policies of the International Monetary Fund and the World Bank as the cause of the economic strife that unsettled the lives of the working poor in countries across the Global South, and they organized to challenge and resist the neo-colonization of their countries, their economies, and their bodies.

Despite similar social and economic shifts in the US economy in the 1990s and 2000s, cultural attitudes about the superiority of the economic model of capitalism throughout the Cold War shaped a culture in the United States that resulted in people who are unwilling and often unable to engage in the kind of serious economic critique that marked resistance to neoliberal globalization in the two-thirds world. Absent a compelling economic analysis of the problems in the labor market in the United States, many white working-class workers during the Obama presidency misidentified the cause of their economic distress. Unable or unwilling to blame capitalism and the policies of neoliberalism for their economic and social dislocation, the white working class sought other ways to understand their economic and social hardships.

The economic woes of the white, working class are real but they were not caused by minorities, women, or immigrants. White working-class economic dislocation is a result of capitalism and its core operational principle of profit maximization. Furthermore, the pitting of the white working-class against minorities is hardly a new tactic in the history of the United States.[28] Working-class and poor people, regardless of their race, ethnicity or immigration status are rarely the primary policy concern of the majority of politicians.[29] It is only when we demystify capitalism that workers, politicians, and the business community will be able to recognize that the health and well-being of our communities and our country requires a robust economic model that properly identifies the moral role that businesses and corporations play in our world. Only then will we be in a position to develop a twenty-first-century economy that reflects social justice by balancing attention to individual initiative and hard work with economic and social provisions that promote the common good.

Costs of Corporate Conscience: How Women, Queers, and People of Color Are Paying for Hobby Lobby's Sincerely Held Beliefs

Megan Goodwin

Congress shall make no law respecting the establishment of religion, or prohibiting the free exercise thereof.

First Amendment to the Constitution of the United States

The exemption sought by Hobby Lobby and Conestoga would override significant interests of the corporations' employees and covered dependents. It would deny legions of women who do not hold their employers' beliefs access to contraceptive coverage that the ACA would otherwise secure . . .

In sum, with respect to free exercise claims no less than free speech claims, "your right to swing your arms ends just where the other man's nose begins."

Justice Ruth Bader Ginsburg, dissenting on *Burwell v. Hobby Lobby*

In June 2014, the US Supreme Court favored closely held corporations' scientifically inaccurate but sincerely held beliefs over the federal government's compelling interest in securing American women access to cost-free contraception—as well as over their women employees and dependents' right to all contraceptive methods approved by the Food and Drug Administration (FDA), guaranteed by the Patient Protection and Affordable Care Act (ACA, colloquially known as Obamacare). In her dissent to *Burwell v. Hobby Lobby*, Justice Ginsburg alleged that the Court conflated the sincerity of these corporations' beliefs with the substantiality of the burden placed on closely held conservative Christian corporations by requiring those corporations to facilitate access to legal contraceptives for their employees. That is, the Court valued the protection of corporations' free exercise of religion over the bodily autonomy of its women laborers and employees' women dependents.[1] Limiting women employees and dependents' access to contraception not only compromises the agency of adult women, but also places a disproportionate burden on employees and dependents of color.[2]

One of *Burwell*'s most significant precedents is its successful deployment of the Religious Freedom Restoration Act (RFRA) in defense of for-profit conservative Christian conscience. In addition to undermining the ACA's contraceptive mandate, *Burwell* ignited a firestorm of state-level religious freedom proposals attempting to "protect" for-profit Christian businesses that sincerely believe they should not have to serve queer people. *Burwell*'s legacy, then, is not merely the Court's preference for corporate religious exercise over women's bodily agency—which, as I will show, adversely affects women of color to a disproportionate degree—but also executive and legislative attempts to leverage for-profit corporate conscience against the rights and full personhood of LGBTQ Americans.

Constitutional protections for American religious liberty are few in number and often elusive in intent. The Constitution of the United States enshrines only three protections for religion. The first, Article VI Paragraph 3, ensures that no religious test may be required to qualify for any American "office or public trust." The second and third reside in the First Amendment, which begins "Congress shall make no law respecting an establishment of religion, or prohibiting the free exercise thereof." The first clause forbids the establishment of religion, preventing the federal government from endorsing or financially supporting one religious tradition to the exclusion of others. The second clause, disallowing the prohibition of free exercise, is the subject of this chapter. *Burwell v. Hobby Lobby* is remarkable in its extension of "free exercise" to for-profit corporations.

In "a decision of startling breadth," *Burwell* extended the constitutional protections of religious freedom to the "familiar legal fiction" of corporations-as-people—and specified that the people those corporations represent are their shareholders, officers, and employees, in that order.[3] In doing so, the Court effectively valued for-profit religious conscience—and financial interests—over the bodily agency of corporations' women workers and employees' women dependents. In regarding conscience over contraception, this decision ensures disproportionate weight on women of color.[4] And *Burwell*'s legislative aftermath has seen state-level RFRAs weaponize for-profit Christian conscience against LGBTQ Americans. Thus, in this chapter, I propose that *Burwell* defines religion not simply in terms of mainstream Christianity, but as white heterosexual male religio-capitalist commitments—at the expense of the bodily autonomy, livelihoods, and lives of American women, queers, and people of color.

How much free exercise cost?
Religious conscience and the Sherbert Test[5]

Among these three vulnerable and intersecting populations, women's disenfranchisement is perhaps most historically linked to the Court's understanding of religious free exercise. Indeed, the definition of the free exercise of religion has been written on the bodies of American women. Denials of women's bodily agency bookend the Supreme Court's history of free exercise: the earliest definition of the clause denied women lawful entrance into plural marriages; the most recent prioritizes the sincerely held beliefs of closely held corporations over the federal government's compelling interest in providing comprehensive reproductive health care to American women.[6]

Burwell also represents a significant departure from the Court's historic regulation and frequent defense of the free exercise of minority religious practices. Of the roughly seventy cases heard by the Court in its ongoing assessment of the boundaries of free exercise, the majority were brought for or against practices and practitioners of American minority religions, which is to say religious traditions (like Judaism and Islam) and Christian denominations (like Seventh-day Adventists and Latter-day Saints [LDS]) that fall outside the purview of mainstream, predominantly white Christianity. Nineteen of these cases pertain to the Watch Tower Bible and Tract Society, better known as Jehovah's Witnesses, alone. Until the late twentieth century, Supreme Court free exercise case law as consistently, almost exclusively, focused on the adjudication of minority religious practices.[7]

Burwell's most significant judicial free exercise antecedents—*Reynolds v. United States* (1879) and *Employment Division of Oregon v. Smith* (1990)—both involve minority religious parties. The latter directly contributed to the passage of the federal RFRA (1993)—the grounds upon which the Court found the ACA's contraceptive mandate unconstitutional for closely held for-profit corporations with sincerely held (though, again, scientifically inaccurate) beliefs about contraceptive methods. Through *Burwell*, the Roberts Court reinvigorated *Smith's* trajectory away from the use of free exercise arguments to protect minority religious practices and toward the constitutional provisions for "religious freedom" as protecting conservative Christian beliefs.

The Court first defined free exercise in *Reynolds v. United States* (1879), ruling that the religious duty of the LDS to enter into plural marriages did not outweigh federal laws prohibiting bigamy.[8] The plaintiff, George Reynolds, testified that

> it was the duty of male members of said church, circumstances permitting, to practise polygamy; . . . that this duty was enjoined by different books which the members of said church believed to be of divine origin, and, among others, the Holy Bible, and also that the members of the church believed that the practice of polygamy was directly enjoined upon the male members thereof by the Almighty God, in a revelation to Joseph Smith, the founder and prophet of said church; that the failing or refusing to practise polygamy by such male members of said church, when circumstances would admit, would be punished, and that the penalty for such failure and refusal would be damnation in the life to come.[9]

His Mormon faith, in short, encouraged him to enter into polygynous marriage.

In response, the Court acknowledged that the First Amendment guaranteed free exercise, but insisted that the Constitution only guarantees free exercise of "mere opinion." Congress, the Court maintained, "was left free to reach actions which were in violation of social duties or subversive of good order," even those actions justified by faith. In a unanimous opinion, Justice Waite wrote that "laws are made for the government of actions, and while they cannot interfere with mere religious belief and opinions, they may with practices."[10] Allowing religious beliefs to excuse otherwise-illegal practices "would make the professed doctrines of religious belief superior to the law of the land, and, in effect, to *permit every citizen to become a law unto himself.*"[11] The first definition of free exercise, then, is freedom to believe. Religious practice cannot flout secular law, and individual conscience may not be allowed to countermand governmental authority.

According to the opinion, the survival of the American state required the sublimation of religious allegiance to federalism.[12] "Government could exist only in name" if individual citizens were allowed to flout federal and state laws based on their private religious beliefs.

While the justices agreed with Thomas Jefferson's insistence upon "a wall of separation between church and State," the practice of polygamy was so "odious" as to be impermissible.[13] The Court justified its interference with the LDS's religious practices on behalf of the "pure-minded women" who were "to be the sufferers" of this presumably barbaric practice.[14] It is ironic, then, that *Reynolds* and three subsequent Supreme Court cases denied women the right to enter into plural marriages and disenfranchised the adult women of the Utah Territory.[15] This is to say that the judicial provenance of free exercise definitions originates with forbidding adult women from entering into unconventional family structures and denying them the vote.[16] The Court's understanding of free exercise is inextricably rooted in both the limitation of women's bodily agency and the sublimation of individual religious conscience to governmental authority.

Despite this beginning, the Supreme Court tended toward making space for practical religious difference through most of the twentieth century.[17] The clearest defense for permitting religious conscience to supersede government regulations occurred in *Sherbert v. Verner* (1963), in which the Court ruled unconstitutional the denial of unemployment benefits to a Seventh-day Adventist woman, Adeil Sherbert, who was fired for refusing to work on Saturdays, the Adventist sabbath.[18] This case instituted the Sherbert Test, which requires the government to prove it has a compelling interest in infringing upon free exercise and that that infringement constitutes a substantial burden on the religious party in question. If there is a compelling interest in the requirement that constitutes a substantial burden on that religious party, the government must pursue the least restrictive means of fulfilling that interest. The Sherbert Test informed all Court definitions of free exercise until *Employment Division of Oregon v. Smith* (1990).

Prior to Smith, the post-*Sherbert* Court had grown increasingly liberal in its allowance for religious obligations to displace governmental authority in the name of free exercise. *Smith* sharply reversed that direction. The Rehnquist Court ruled that "general laws of neutral application"—in this case, anti-narcotics regulations—motivated by a compelling government interest may be constitutional even if they present a substantial burden upon religious exercise, effectively doing away with the Sherbert Test.[19]

Noting that a number of states permitted the sacramental use of peyote, Justice Antonin Scalia asserted that "to say that a nondiscriminatory religious practice exemption is permitted, or even that it is desirable, is not to say that it is constitutionally required, and that the appropriate occasions for its creation can be discerned by the courts."[20] That other states had accommodated the Native American Church by making exceptions for members' use of peyote in ritual did not make otherwise-neutral narcotics regulations unconstitutional, nor should the Court necessarily determine whether such accommodations were appropriate. *Smith* prioritized compelling government interest in laws that do not specifically target religious actors or institutions over the substantiality of the burden those laws might impose upon said religious parties.

Writing for the majority, Scalia noted that the *Smith* opinion might well disadvantage members of minority religions:

> It may fairly be said that leaving accommodation to the political process will place at a relative disadvantage those religious practices that are not widely engaged in; but that unavoidable consequence of democratic government must be preferred to a system *in which each conscience is a law unto itself* or in which judges weigh the social importance of all laws against the centrality of all religious beliefs.[21]

Smith, like *Reynolds*, weighed the considerations of unlawful practices motivated by religious conscience against compelling government interests and decided in favor of the latter. Scalia went so far as to note that the decision specifically disadvantages "those religious practices that are not widely engaged in"—which is to say practices more common in minority religions like the Native American Church—but failed to acknowledge that members of such movements are also often racial minorities and thus doubly disenfranchised by the decision.

The *Smith* opinion met with widespread disapproval and public censure, particularly among religious communities. A politically and religiously diverse coalition of more than sixty religious groups successfully lobbied Congress to pass the RFRA (1993) to countermand *Smith*.[22] RFRA observes that a generally applicable and otherwise neutral law can substantially burden religious actors "as surely as laws intended to interfere with religious exercise" and that in *Smith*, "the Supreme Court virtually eliminated the requirement that the government justify burdens on religious exercise imposed by laws neutral toward religion."[23] To this end, RFRA mandates that "government shall not substantially burden a person's exercise of religion even if the burden results from a rule of general applicability" unless there is a compelling government interest in seeing the law enforced. If such a compelling interest exists, the government must find the least restrictive means of enforcing said law. In essence, then, RFRA restored the Sherbert Test.

With the Religious Land Use and Incarcerated Persons Act (RLUIPA; 2000), RFRA has extended considerations of free exercise beyond the designations of the First Amendment and has been explicitly invoked to protect vulnerable religious minority populations. Since their passage, the RFRA and RLUIPA have primarily functioned to secure members of minority religions—including Wicca, Islam, Buddhism, Santeria, and Centro Espírita Beneficente União do Vegetal (a group that uses ayahuasca sacramentally)—rights to practice freely.

Though the Act was found unconstitutional at the state level in *City of Boerne v. Flores* (1997), RFRA still has bearing on federal matters—including President Obama's ACA (2010). *Burwell v. Hobby Lobby* successfully used RFRA—passed in large part to correct the disenfranchisement of minority religious practice—to argue for exceptions to ACA federal mandates on the basis of broad protections for conservative Christian conscience.

As Sullivan notes in "The World That Smith Made," *Smith* and its legislative and judicial aftermath represent a departure from free exercise adjudication as seeking limited exceptions to secular law toward suing for broad "jurisdictional demands for church autonomy or even church sovereignty."[24] This trend is clear in the adjudication of free exercise during the Obama administration.

Only fifteen of the seventy-one free exercise cases heard from 1878 to 2017 involved mainstream Christian appellants or defendants; a third of these cases were brought during the Obama presidency.[25] Four of the five free exercise cases brought before the Court since Obama's inauguration involve mainstream Christian parties, and with the exception of *Christian Legal Society v. Martinez*, all were decided in favor of those parties. And among these cases involving mainstream Christian parties, *Burwell* has done the most to steer the purview of free exercise from the protection of minority religions toward reinforcing Christian primacy within the American body politic.

Conscience versus contraception

The history of American women's struggle for reproductive autonomy has always been entwined with battles of Christian conscience, but Christian conscience with regard to contraception and abortion has shifted dramatically since Margaret Sanger said that "the greatest sin in the world" was to bring unwanted children into it.[26]

The history of Christian conscience with regard to contraception is complicated. The hierarchy of the Catholic Church has consistently opposed "artificial" birth control and abortion, and Protestant attitudes toward both have changed dramatically in the past 150 years.[27] In the mid-nineteenth century, 75–90 percent of women seeking abortion were married Protestants who did not want more children—which ignited nativist anxieties about Catholic children eventually overwhelming the US population.[28] In her *Good Catholics: The Battle over Abortion in the Catholic Church*, journalist Patti Miller identifies 1930 as the tipping point for Christians and birth control: in this year, the Anglican Church—the most influential Western Christian church of its time—officially permitted married couples to use contraception.[29] Other Protestant denominations followed suit, "signaling that contraceptives had gained moral and social legitimacy," Miller observes.[30] For much of the twentieth century, contraception was not an especially fraught issue for most non-Catholic Christians.[31]

How, then, does allowing employees and their dependents cost-free access to contraception become such a grave matter of conscience for closely held for-profit Protestant companies?

The answer lies, in part, on what I call the catholicization of public morality, or the adoption of Roman Catholic sexual morality as the justification for and articulation of national values.[32] The 1970s saw the consolidation of disparate Protestantisms into a powerful and politically cohesive interest group, the New Christian Right, who joined with Roman Catholic bishops to decry national moral decay—which both groups saw as most clearly evidenced in non-normative sexual and gender practices. Unmarried contraception use and abortion were high among the list of symptoms of America's "moral decline," which directly threatened national integrity.[33]

While much has been made of the influence of Protestant sexual ethics in shaping American public morality, less scholarly attention has been paid to the ways Roman Catholicism has helped shape normative American sexuality. As Tracy Fessenden notes in her 2008 "Sex and the Subject of Religion," the Church put forward its twentieth-century sexual ethics in universal terms—indeed, the regulation of sex and gender became the primary, if not only, means through which modern Catholicism attempted universality and absolutism.[34] Catholic sexual ethics were presented as universal because they were ostensibly grounded in natural law, and thus applied equally to the faithful and non-faithful alike. This universality politicized Catholic pronouncements on sexual practices, leading to Church arguments that contraception, abortion, and homosexuality were best understood as moral (rather than specifically religious or purely political) matters.[35]

Especially in the wake of the 1968 papal encyclical *Humanae Vitae*, best known for its condemnation of artificial birth control, the Church emerged as an arbiter not merely of Roman Catholic sexual ethics, but of American morality writ large. The Magisterium's firm public stance embracing conservative sexual ethics aided unprecedented alliance building with American evangelicals and arguably contributed to Catholics' increased political influence in the 1970s and 1980s.[36] At its political height, the so-called Moral Majority included evangelical Protestants, antiabortion/contraception Catholics, some orthodox Jews, and the Church of Jesus Christ of Latter-day Saints.[37]

The Moral Majority's acceptance of Catholic natural law as an articulation of national values becomes particularly pertinent to *Burwell* when we consider Pope John Paul II's consistent, even "militant," conflation of contraception with abortion.[38] John Paul II warned against a "contraceptive mentality" that valued independence and personal pleasure over allegiance to God, and attributed societal decline to women's selfishness, as manifest in their desire for reproductive autonomy.[39] Under Reagan, Roman Catholic sexual ethics increasingly informed domestic and foreign policy.[40] Leaders from both sides formalized the political alliance among conservative Protestants and Roman Catholics in March 1994 with the signing of the "Evangelicals and Catholics Together" declaration.[41] Likewise, George W. Bush made overtures to the Roman Catholic electorate as part of his "compassionate conservatism" platform.[42] This cemented the political union among Roman Catholics, conservative evangelicals, and the Republican Party.[43]

Far right antiabortion activists began adopting Catholic rhetoric conflating abortion and contraception.[44] By the mid-1990s, social conservatives—including the US Catholic Conference, the National Right to Life Committee, and the Christian Coalition—had begun targeting access to contraception through legislative opposition to Title X, which provides federal support to young and low-income women in need of contraception and family planning counseling.[45] Miller attributes intensified religiopolitical opposition to contraception to an increased viability of contraceptive equity measures attempting to ensure that health coverage plans covered birth control pills like any other prescription medication.[46] Though almost all women use contraceptives at some point in their lives, insurance companies had largely omitted contraceptive coverage—making women's out-of-pocket medical expenses 70 percent higher than men's.[47] Once insurers began covering Viagra in 1998, however, arguments against paying for "lifestyle choices" fell short and contraceptive coverage measures increasingly passed state legislatures.[48]

Conservative Christian opponents, Protestant and Catholic alike, rallied around arguments that intrauterine devices (IUDs) and newly approved emergency contraceptive pills were abortifacients because these could prevent a fertilized egg from implanting on the uterine wall.[49] This claim countermands the American Medical Association's definition of pregnancy as beginning at implantation. Nevertheless, early-twenty-first-century Catholic bishops and their allies increasingly opposed insurance coverage for emergency contraception (EC) and IUDs, claiming that requirements for contraceptive coverage would violate the religious freedom of both insurers and employers morally opposed to abortion.[50]

Miller attributes this conflation of contraception and abortion directly to the efforts of US bishops, but notes that the argument was quickly adopted by other conservative Christian interests—including Walmart's famous refusal to carry EC in its stores.[51] By 2004, the president of the Southern Baptist Theological Seminary, Albert Mohler, was urging evangelicals to reject the "contraceptive mentality" and quoting John Paul II's assertion that widespread use of birth control had decoupled sex from reproduction and led to "near total abandonment of Christian sexual morality."[52] That same year, "Catholics and Evangelicals Together" declared a "new pattern of convergence and cooperation" on a "culture of life" increasingly opposed to contraception.[53] This convergence carried political weight as well: the Republican Party abandoned its longstanding support for contraception and increasingly attacked family planning funding.[54]

In 2005, George W. Bush signed an appropriations bill that included the first federal conscience clause, exempting health care entities from providing services in contradiction of their religious obligations.[55] By 2008, the Bush administration had passed provisions allowing almost any health worker to opt out of providing services to which she was morally or religiously opposed.[56] Advocates for women's health vocally protested such measures, not only because they compromised patients' access to care, but because the language codifying these "conscience exceptions" explicitly conflated abortion and contraception.[57]

The Obama administration steered sharply away from conscience exemptions while noting that federal law still allowed providers to refuse to provide abortions.[58] In August 2011, the Department of Health and Human Services (HHS) determined that all employer-based health plans should be required to provide cost-free access to all contraceptive methods approved by the FDA as part of HHS's proposed rules for the ACA's preventative services.[59] Despite extraordinary legislative obstruction to affordable access to contraception, 98.2 percent of US women who have had sex had used at least one method of birth control by 1998.[60] After the ACA mandated coverage for cost-free contraception, women's out-of-pocket expenses for oral contraceptive pills dropped from 20.9 percent to 3 percent, accounting for two-thirds of the drop in spending for retail drugs from 2012 to 2014.[61] The contraceptive mandate is also a considerable cost saver for the 70 percent of reproductively capable women currently using some form of birth control.[62]

Which is why the inclusion of a contraceptive mandate in the ACA was, to borrow the unforgettable words of former vice president Joe Biden, "a big fucking deal."[63]

By providing cost-free access to contraception, the ACA has arguably done more to prevent abortions than any other legislation in US history.[64] A study by the Guttmacher Institute attributes the United States' historically low abortion rate to increased use of contraception among American women—particularly the use of IUDs to prevent pregnancy.[65] With EC, IUDs are precisely the contraceptive methods to which the defendants in *Burwell*—Hobby Lobby Stores, Inc., Mardel, and Conestoga Wood Specialities Corporation—object to so strenuously on the grounds of sincerely held Christian belief.

Conestoga, Mardel, and Hobby Lobby's sincerely held belief that EC and IUDs are abortifacients lacks credible medical or scientific substance, but religion is protected by the Constitution in ways that scientific and medical knowledge are not. Writing for the majority, Justice Samuel Alito offers that "the Hahns and the Greens and their companies [Hobby Lobby/Mardel and Conestoga respectively] sincerely believe that providing the insurance coverage demanded by the HHS regulations [i.e., contraceptive mandate] lies on the forbidden side of the line [between religious beliefs and work found morally objectionable] and it is not for us to say that their religious beliefs are mistaken or insubstantial."[66] For this reason, Alito maintains, "the mandate clearly imposes a substantial burden" on the beliefs of the owners of the three companies.[67] Given the provenance of conservative Christian conflation of contraception and abortion, it is not surprising that the owners of these companies would object to the use of birth control methods they consider to be abortifacients.

What is surprising is the Court's recognition of for-profit corporations as entitled to the protections of free exercise guaranteed by the RFRA. Alito notes that the Court has already recognized corporations as religious plaintiffs and defendants, as in *Braunfeld v. Brown* (1960) and *Gallagher v. Crown Kosher Supermarket* (1960); the justice does not stress that—unlike *Burwell*—both cases involved members of a minority religion (i.e., Orthodox Judaism) but does glancingly mention that the Court found against blue laws being religiously discriminatory.[68] *Braunfeld* and *Gallagher* both establish a precedent for the "familiar legal fiction" of recognizing corporations as persons. The Court further fails to recognize distinctions between for-profit and nonprofit corporations, and notes that HHS has already made accommodations for nonprofit corporations that object to the contraceptive mandate on religious grounds.[69] For these reasons, the ACA's contraceptive mandate cannot be the least restrictive means of enforcing the government's compelling interest in providing cost-free access to contraception—meaning *Burwell* fails the Sherbert Test, and is thus unlawful under the RFRA.

Refuting arguments that *Burwell*'s precedent for overly broad objections of religious conscience to federal law, Alito responds that the decision pertains *only* to the contraceptive mandate and not other medical procedures contraindicated by religious belief—such as blood infusions for Jehovah's Witnesses, or psychiatric treatment for Scientologists—specifically because the latter have been traditionally covered by private insurance plans.[70] That is to say that *Burwell* can safely decide against women's entitlement to cost-free contraceptive access because private insurance companies have historically impeded women's access to contraception.

Alito further emphasizes that the Court is deeply concerned for corporations' "full participation in the life of the nation"; for this reason, the Court is eager to accommodate the sincerely held beliefs of closely held corporations like Hobby Lobby.[71] "Protecting the free-exercise rights of corporations like Hobby Lobby, Conestoga, and Mardel protects the religious liberty of *the humans who own and control those companies.*"[72] The opinion conjectures that the impact of the *Burwell* decision on the thousands of women who work for Hobby Lobby, Mardel, and Conestoga will be "precisely zero," because the government can—and should—absorb the cost of the corporations' conscientious abstentions.[73]

There are two significant assumptions in the Court's opinion: first, that the "people" these corporations represent are not the workers of the corporations in question, many of whom do not share the Greens and Hahns's belief system; and that the American taxpayers—including the women disenfranchised by this decision—should subsidize said corporations' religious objections despite a compelling government interest to the contrary. Here we see the Court's articulation of religion as the religio-capitalist commitments of conservative Christians, and the weighting of those religio-capitalist commitments heavily over the bodily autonomy of women employees and dependents.

Justice Ruth Bader Ginsburg's scathing dissent focuses at length on the extent to which the majority opinion overextends RFRA, conflates the defendants' sincerity of belief with the substantiality of the burden placed upon their beliefs by the ACA's contraceptive mandate, and fails to propose a less restrictive means of carrying out the government's compelling interest in securing American women cost-free access to all FDA-approved methods of birth control.

With the majority, Ginsburg reiterates the government's compelling interest in women's health care. Her dissent begins by quoting *Planned Parenthood of Southeastern PA v. Casey* (1992): "the ability of women to participate equally in the economic and social life of the Nation has been facilitated by their ability to control their reproductive lives." Ginsburg notes that women of childbearing age paid 68 percent more for health care before the ACA, and that costs prevented many women from accessing reproductive health care at all—some 17 million women were left uninsured. The contraceptive mandate furthers a compelling government interest in "public health and women's well-being. Those interests are concrete, specific, and demonstrated by a wealth of empirical evidence."[74] The dissent further emphasizes that the methods to which Hobby Lobby et al. object, specifically IUDs, are both more expensive and more effective than other methods of contraception.[75] *Burwell* directly affects thousands of Hobby Lobby, Mardel, and Conestoga's women employees and dependents, many of whom do not share the beliefs of the Greens or the Hahns.

It is for this reason, she insists, that Congress vetoed a conscience amendment to the ACA, and why she argues that *Burwell* represents a massive overextension of RFRA.[76] Congress intended a "far less radical purpose" in passing the RFRA, and could never have meant its definition of free exercise to be "so extreme."[77] RFRA was, Ginsburg insists, meant to reinstate the Sherbert Test, not to "unsettle other areas of law."[78]

She writes, "no tradition, and no prior decision under RFRA, allows a religion-based exemption when the accommodation would be harmful to others—here, the very persons the contraceptive coverage requirement was designed to protect."[79] Ginsburg is explicit: the Court's definition of free exercise in *Burwell* comes at the expense of American women's bodily autonomy and full civil participation.

Free exercise, Ginsburg asserts, must "yield to the common good" of fellow citizens.[80] Citing *United States v. Lee* (1982), in which the Amish defendant claimed Social Security violated his community's commitment to caring for their elderly, Justice Ginsburg quotes: "When followers of a particular sect enter into commercial activity as a matter of choice . . . the limits they accept on their own conduct as a matter of conscience and faith are not to be superimposed on statutory schemes which are binding on others in that activity."[81] Ginsburg further observes that many state-level religious freedom cases have been based on racist and homophobic beliefs, and wonders if this extension of RFRA now exempts those biases.[82]

Burwell's grossest overreach, according to Ginsburg, is the "passing strange" extension of free exercise protections to for-profit corporations.[83] Religion is for "natural persons, not artificial legal entities," she emphasizes, and citing Justice Stephens in *Citizens United* (2010), observes that "corporations have no consciences, no beliefs, no feelings, no thoughts, no desires."[84] For-profit corporations are sustained by their workers, who by law cannot be hired on basis of religion, nor should the Court assume that those workers share the religious commitments of the corporations' owners or shareholders.[85] Ginsburg warns that "the Court's expansive notion of corporate personhood . . . invites for-profit entities to seek religion-based exemptions from regulations they deem offensive to their faith."[86] Justice Ginsburg's warning bore out, as I will discuss in the next section.

Ginsburg ultimately insists that *Burwell* does not require the Court to assess the sincerity of for-profit corporations' beliefs, but rather to assess whether the requested accommodation of those beliefs deprives others of their lawful rights.[87] While confirming the sincerity of said beliefs, Ginsburg asserts that the connection between those beliefs and the acquisition of birth control by an employee or her dependent is "too attenuated" a connection "to rank as substantial."[88] The corporations are not required to purchase or provide contraception, and should an employee or her dependant share the Hahns and Greens's beliefs, she need not purchase contraception.[89] "Any decision to use contraceptives made by a woman covered under Hobby Lobby's or Conestoga's plan will not be propelled by the Government, it will be the woman's autonomous choice, informed by the physician she consults."[90] Justice Ginsburg finds women's entitlement to bodily agency more substantial than the burden placed on Hobby Lobby et al. and its incorporate beliefs.[91]

Ginsburg adamantly denies that a less restrictive means exists than ACA's contraceptive mandate as written. "A 'least restrictive means' cannot require employees to relinquish benefits accorded them by federal law in order to ensure that their commercial employers can adhere unreservedly to their religious tenets," she maintains.[92] By privileging for-profit corporate Christian conscience over women's bodily autonomy, Ginsburg observes that the Court has consigned the American taxpayers to "pick[ing] up the tab."[93] The tab is considerable: by 2014, publicly funded family planning programs will have saved the federal government over $13 billion a year.[94]

Burwell redefined free exercise by extending the protections of the RFRA to for-profit corporations. In doing so, the Court lent momentum toward adjudication of free exercise privileging Christian primacy in the American body politics, and signaled its willingness to pass along the cost of that privilege to the taxpayers disenfranchised by the decision.

The cost of Christian conscience: Who pays and how

Winnifred Sullivan, Sarah Imhoff, and other religious studies scholars have demonstrated that the American legal system in general and the Supreme Court specifically understands "religion" in emphatically Christian terms.[95] This is certainly the case in *Burwell*, both in Alito's opinion and in Ginsburg's dissent. This should be enough to concern scholars of American political religions, as *Burwell* has made significant inroads toward eroding RFRA as protection for minority religions in favor of shoring up conservative Christian rights of conscience. This decision marks an important shift toward increased constitutional protections for conservative Christians, who increasingly perceived themselves as embattled during Obama's two presidential terms—a sense of religious embattlement not unrelated to increased white racial anxiety, as reflected in the outcome of the 2016 election.[96]

Justice Ginsburg's insistence that women's full participation in the American body politic requires reproductive agency is spot on. Not only does reproductive bodily agency increase women's personal earning potential, effective family planning programs that include access to contraception benefit the nation's economy and decrease poverty.[97] Unexpected pregnancies are costly and can be detrimental to the health of both mother and child.[98]

However, Ginsburg's dissent fails to consider the extent to which *Burwell* particularly affects women of color. Recent surveys suggest that 69 percent of pregnancies among black women and 54 percent of pregnancies among Hispanic women are unintended, compared to 40 percent among white women; women of color possessing lower socioeconomic status were more likely to experience unintended pregnancy in each of these racial groups.[99] Less access to contraception ensures more unintended pregnancies, which can result in increased abortion rates or, in cases when abortion is financially unfeasible, unintended pregnancies carried to term. (The latter disproportionately affects black women.)[100] Women of color, particularly young women of color, have demonstrated difficulties in accessing high-quality contraceptive services and in using their preferred methods of contraceptive consistently and effectively over time.[101] Poor women of color experience unintended pregnancy at disproportionately high rates, placing them at higher health risks over the course of their lives.[102] Ginsburg is right to note the substantial burden placed on American women by *Burwell*, but she falls short of considering the imbalance of that burden with respect to women of color—15 million of whom are of reproductive age and covered by private insurance.[103]

Burwell's successful use of RFRA to defend conservative Christian morality also inspired an eruption of religious freedom legislation at the state level: whereas nineteen states had RFRAs before the 2015 legislative session, an additional seventeen states put RFRAs on their 2015 legislative agendas.[104] Arkansas signed its "Conscience Protection Act" into law in April 2015. Though Governor Asa Hutchinson refused to sign it as written, the bill as passed by the state's congress originally included language that extended the definition of "person" to include corporations, allowing for-profit businesses to claim entitlements to religious freedom.[105] Then governor Mike Pence signed Indiana's infamous RFRA into law in March 2015, allowing individuals and corporations to assert the right to free exercise of religion.[106] Both bills as written included explicit protections for for-profit businesses owned by conservative Christians opposed to serving LGBTQ persons, though Indiana's legislation faced such national backlash that Pence was forced to amend the act to explicitly prohibit discrimination against queer people.[107] *Burwell* sparked widespread legislative movement toward lending the protection of the state to conservative Christian sexual ethics.

Burwell's reification of religio-corporate personhood entitled to free exercise protections has done much to embolden conservative Christian appellants to the Court. The case and its aftermath demonstrate a broad and politically potent anxiety among conservative white Christians, expressed through attempts to "protect" for-profit Christian businesses by regulating public sexuality: both through restricting women's access to FDA–approved contraceptive methods and by disincentivizing public expressions of queer identity, specifically but not exclusively expressions related to same-sex marriage.[108]

This is to say that by privileging for-profit corporate Christian conscience over women's bodily autonomy, *Burwell* has passed the cost for the nation's health back onto the taxpayers. In *Good Catholics*, Patti Miller proposes that conservative Christian opposition to women's reproductive agency is rooted in the conviction that women who have sex—particularly unmarried women who have sex—and "control their fertility [are] doing something fundamentally illicit and shouldn't expect anyone else to pay for it."[109] But if Congress is to fulfill its compelling interest in public health and women's well-being, the taxpayers will pay for corporate Christian conscience.

Beyond *Burwell*

The death of Antonin Scalia, the remanding of *Zubik v. Burwell* to lower courts, and the appointment of Neil Gorsuch have left the judicial future of reproductive rights uncertain.[110] The forty-fifth president's administration has signaled its allegiance to corporate Christian conscience and a "culture of life."[111] The president's mostly insubstantial Executive Order "Promoting Free Speech and Religious Liberty" explicitly promised further considerations of "conscience protections with respect to preventive-care mandate."[112] The current secretary of the HHS is a vocal opponent of the contraceptive mandate, going so far as to say that it "trampl[es] on religious freedom and religious liberty in this country."[113] Price has also insisted that no woman, "not one," has struggled to afford birth control, despite evidence to the contrary.[114] The woman overseeing Title X for HHS, Teresa Manning, insists that contraception doesn't work, and has publicly said that "family planning is what occurs between a husband and a wife and God."[115] At the same time, progressive Congressmen Joe Kennedy and Bobby Scott reintroduced the "Do No Harm" Act in July 2017, intended to amend RFRA to "clarify that no one can seek religious exemption from laws guaranteeing fundamental civil and legal rights."[116]

With the Senate's recent—and dramatic—failures to repeal and replace (or merely repeal) "Obamacare," the future of the contraceptive mandate and free exercise is murky. As it stands, we can only note that the Court's first definition of free exercise demanded surrender of individual Christian conscience to federal law, while its most recent definition requires the surrender of federal law to individual (corporate) Christian conscience.

Black Prophetic Discourse and Just War Theory in the Age of Obama

Juan M. Floyd-Thomas

On the June 20, 2011, episode of the top-rated *The O'Reilly Factor* Fox News television program, conservative pundit and author Bill O'Reilly hosted a segment featuring a 29-year-old hip-hop artist and devout Muslim named Lupe Fiasco. Fiasco had released a politically charged song entitled "Words I Never Said," in which, among a number of provocative statements, the rapper proclaimed that President Obama was a "terrorist." While antiwar activists and radical intellectuals previously had raised similar accusations toward US presidents, it was previously deemed improbable that a hip-hop artist would level such charges against the nation's first black president. Given the prevailing sensibility of many right-wing media pundits, this interview illustrates a somewhat paradoxical twist for Fox News. Fiasco's remark created an opening for O'Reilly to launch a tirade wherein he berated hip-hop music and its adherents for being irresponsible, irrational, and ill-informed while also standing in defense of President Obama. O'Reilly dutifully presented his talking points, chief among them being "Obama is not a terrorist" although somewhat disingenuously. Then O'Reilly turned to Fiasco with the greatest level of condescension and contempt imaginable, by first lecturing the rapper that the word "fallacious" means wrong, and then making the inane observation that few fans of hip-hop have doctorates in political science, thus negating their credibility for criticizing the American government in any manner. Still operating under the assumption that they were engaged in an actual debate, Fiasco countered O'Reilly's taunts by stating that his grievances were not just with the Obama administration, but with militaristic US foreign policy and the root causes of terrorism, finding critical fault with all American presidents. However, the interview eventually spiralled downward into frivolity.[1]

Aside from the curious obsession that O'Reilly and his conservative cohorts have had with maligning rappers, the steady inclusion of hip-hop music and culture into mainstream American society rendered O'Reilly's outrage rather banal and quaint. Yet the story would be incomplete without some additional sparring after the show aired. Later that same evening, Lupe Fiasco went online via blogs, websites, and social media platforms to complain that some of his sharpest arguments were edited out of the segment prior to broadcast. For example, he tweeted the claim that US military manuals "teach you how to be a terrorist" to the more than 670,000 followers of his Twitter account, quickly adding that his father had been a Green Beret and that he himself is "not against the military." Meanwhile, O'Reilly's television program simply moved on to another "hot button" topic the following night in order to satisfy its viewers' interests.

My initial fascination in this exchange is multilayered. First, having heard the song and being familiar with Fiasco as an artist and activist, I am intrigued about why he would ever agree to sit for an interview with O'Reilly. Next, despite my avid and avowed support of President Obama, the song's provocative ideas about the lack of critical discourse concerning the correlation of the nation's domestic woes to American foreign policy and military power compelled me to consider what sort of reception both the lyrics and the lyricist garnered more generally. Lastly, this brief albeit provocative exchange between Bill O'Reilly and Lupe Fiasco reflects the contemporary public sphere as an increasingly fractured arena of thought and discourse where we are supposed to resolve the important issues of our time. Put another way, how can "the prophetic" find its way into mainstream discourse within a highly toxic, rapidly splintering, and ideologically balkanized public sphere especially in talking about issues of war and peace.[2]

For more than two decades, I have been pondering the implications of the so-called global war on terror in general and America's broader strategic interests in the Middle East in conjunction with just war theory. In the following pages, I evolve my attention toward prophetic discourse about war and peace operates within the contemporary framework of the global public square. It was in writing an earlier article, "More than Conquerors," that helped move my thoughts on US foreign policy beyond sheer antagonism toward Bush-Cheney-era neo-conservatism and toward a bona fide critique of Obama's reworking of liberal interventionism.[3] Beginning with a brief examination of the "just war" tradition from its roots in Augustinian thought to contemporary articulations, that article juxtaposes the broad contours of President Obama's foreign policy in juxtaposition to two formidable figures in his intellectual formation that would make him an important exemplar of the just war moral tradition, namely, Reinhold Niebuhr. I grapple with how US foreign policy has been shaped by President Obama's own interpretation of just war theory as influenced by his reading of Reinhold Niebuhr. Next it will also revisit Obama's former pastor, Rev. Dr. Jeremiah A. Wright Jr.'s commitment to black Christian antiwar tradition was reminiscent of Rev. Dr. Martin Luther King's pacifism. Finally, I will consider hip-hop artist Lupe Fiasco's condemnation of America's prosecution of the ongoing global war on terror, which brings to mind the activism of Malcolm X. Although Obama, Wright, and Fiasco are from different generations and have taken preeminence in their respective fields of expertise—reformist politics, religious ministry, and conscious hip-hop music—these three native sons of Chicago exemplify a capacity to tell often difficult, distasteful truths about America's role in the world prompted by their deeply held beliefs. Toward this end, I explore the work and writings of the aforementioned figures as three distinctive foci of concern and the respective modalities each one represents in terms of racial and religious perspectives on global matters of war and peace.

"Fighting for the Juster Cause": The roots of the just war theory

When looking at how this "just war" tradition takes shape, the theologian Augustine of Hippo is most helpful in discerning the rudiments of Christian attitudes on war and peace. In a classic argument raised in his masterwork *The City of God*, Augustine asserts that "now when victory goes to those who were fighting for the juster cause [*sic*], can anyone doubt that the victory is a matter for rejoicing and the resulting peace is something to be desired?" Additionally, Augustine sought to provide an answer to the question about whether a Christian could rightfully answer the call to military duty and still have a clear conscience before God? Although no conclusive statement was rendered in terms of the average layperson, it is during the fourth and fifth centuries that church decrees and doctrines establish that priests and monks were to be exempted from military actions. As it is widely understood, embedded within the broader contours of Augustinian thought, just war theory addresses the morality of the use of force in three parts: when it is right to resort to armed conflict (the concern of *jus ad bellum*); what is acceptable in using such force (the concern of *jus in bello*); how to achieve justice through war termination and peace agreements as well as the trying of war criminals (the concern of *jus post bellum*)—this latter issue being raised by the unfortunate realities of our modern era.

When pared down to its most fundamental levels, the core principles of the just war doctrine in the contemporary era can be reduced most succinctly to the following factors: *proportionality, discrimination,* and *minimum force*. First, proportionality regards the force used must be relatively equal to the wrong endured, and appropriate to the possible good that may result from engaging in warfare. As a consequence, the more disproportional the number of collateral civilian deaths, the more suspect will be the sincerity of a belligerent nation's claim to the justness of a war it initiated. Next, discrimination is the process by which the military action should be directed toward enemy combatants who were declared wrongdoers, and not toward civilians caught in circumstances they did not create. The prohibited acts include bombing civilian residential areas that include no military targets and committing acts of terrorism or reprisals against ordinary civilians. Moreover, there are a number of just war thinkers who believe that this directive forbids the use of weapons of mass destruction of any kind for any reason whatsoever. Finally, minimum force is a principle of just war meant to limit unnecessary death and excessive destruction. It is important to note that this notion differs from proportionality insofar as the amount of force proportionate to the goal of the mission might exceed the amount of force necessary to accomplish that mission. In the pages that follow, I discuss the mutability of just war theory with regard to how Obama, Wright, and Fiasco each viewed the form and function of American foreign policy.

"Acknowledging the hard truth": Barack Obama's Niebuhrian geopolitics

On December 9, 2009, then US president Barack Obama and his entourage went to Oslo, Norway, to receive the Nobel Peace Prize. Although there was much scuttlebutt surrounding the supposedly premature nature of him being given the prestigious award, the nation's first African American president had to address an even more critical problem: how to reconcile the receipt of this august commendation as a global peacemaker while facing the reality of his administration's commitment to the two ongoing wars in Afghanistan and Iraq? During his acceptance speech, Obama briefly yet effectively summarized the broad outline of just war theory. According to Obama, "over time, as codes of law sought to control violence within groups, so did philosophers and clerics and statesmen seek to regulate the destructive power of war. The concept of a 'just war' emerged, suggesting that war is justified only when certain conditions were met: if it is waged as a last resort or in self-defense; if the force used is proportional; and if, whenever possible, civilians are spared from violence."[4]

In his Nobel acceptance speech, President Obama asserted: "perhaps the most profound issue surrounding my receipt of this prize is the fact that I am the Commander-in-Chief of the military of a nation in the midst of two wars. One of these wars is winding down. The other is a conflict that America did not seek; one in which we are joined by 42 other countries—including Norway—in an effort to defend ourselves and all nations from further attacks."[5] Furthermore he stated, "I do not bring with me today a definitive solution to the problems of war. What I do know is that meeting these challenges will require the same vision, hard work, and persistence of those men and women who acted so boldly decades ago. And it will require us to think in new ways about the notions of just war and the imperatives of a just peace." However, in an interesting attempt to merge these disparate concerns, Obama invoked the memory of devotees of nonviolent activism of Mahatma Gandhi and Martin Luther King Jr. while defending his need to prosecute war when necessary by dint of his sworn duty as president. According to the president, "We must begin by acknowledging the hard truth: we will not eradicate violent conflict in our lifetimes. There will be times when nations—acting individually or in concert—will find the use of force not only necessary but morally justified."[6] Given that critical tension within his statement, if a transformative figure such as Obama cannot figure a way forward beyond global conflict, how can any of us truly make sense of matters of war and peace in our contemporary world?

When thinking about US foreign policy over the course of the past half century, it is vitally important to acknowledge the true nature of Obama's outlook on the US role in contemporary international affairs broadly speaking. To be honest, there was a great deal of disingenuous outrage on both sides of the political landscape during Obama's presidency regarding his administration's approach to the use of American power globally. On the one hand, the US conservatives (as one could reasonably expect) generally denounced President Obama's foreign policy goals and actions but were wildly inconsistent in their attacks; it was not uncommon for right-wing politicians and pundits to accuse Obama repeatedly for being too timid and reckless in his views on numerous issues of foreign relations simultaneously. On the other hand, there was also a disgruntled contingent of liberals and progressives who harbored serious grievances about Obama's policy decisions that seemed to be not just the continuation but also even the expansion of principles and practices established during George W. Bush's presidency.

The willful disregard for Obama's innately reserved albeit hawkish bent in foreign policy matters is hugely suggestive of the heartfelt desire held by the liberal-progressive coalition comprising the Democratic Party's core constituency to pretend that the foreign wars it has dutifully prosecuted for nearly a decade—as well as the continued killing of innocent people for which it is responsible—have not inflicted any lethal damage on the world stage. Part of that discomfort is due to the cognitive dissonance about liberal interventionism within the soul of the American Left concerning their uneasy relationship to the American war machine. Striving to establish themselves in stark contradistinction to the warmongering Republican Party of the last half century, the Democrats have quite often branded themselves self-righteously as the enemies of rampant militarism, privilege, racism, intolerance, and endless violence. In spite of this legitimate posture at the heart of the Democratic Party's ideological core, these ideals fly directly in the face of the realpolitik demands of governance. This is made all the more visible when viewed through the party's dogged efforts under Obama to ignore, or even actively support, strategic interests and policies which kill large numbers of innocent people from Pakistan, Libya, Somalia to Yemen, Iraq, and Gaza, but which receive scant attention in the mainstream media due to the race, religion, nationality, ethnicity, poverty, and distance of these victims with the perverse aura of invisibility that these factors lend to imagination. Even more vital is the contradiction that arises when we have to grapple with what it means to have Obama, with all of his overtures toward transparent pragmatism and transformative principles in terms of US foreign policy, administering covert lethal operations coordinated via a secretive protocol in defense of an open and free society.

But a major part of this minimization is a misperception of the political importance of these wartime policies on the home front. From the beginning of his candidacy through the 2008 Democratic primaries, Barack Obama strategically positioned himself as a vehement critic and vocal opponent of endless warfare, inveighing against both of his political rivals, Hillary Clinton and John McCain, while doing so. In the hopes of avoiding any revisionist effort underway in the service of hagiography by falsely depicting those who pointed this out as being gullible believers in Obama's possible dovishness and antiwar credentials, the reality is that those of us who were swayed by the efficacy and even-keeled nature of Obama's antiwar stance often made a tacit bargain that there was no reason to believe Obama would actually always be dovish if he were elected but rather would use his war-making powers in a sagacious manner, like Plato's revered philosopher-king. Virtually echoing Obama's 2002 disdain for the Iraq conflict as a "dumb war," liberal pundit Peter Beinart wrote *The Good Fight*, a book advocating for the establishment of a smarter, more muscular and principled approach to US foreign policy by liberals and progressives.[7] Even though Obama had clearly articulated his own mind on these matters much earlier, a polemic like this indicates a clear indication by the center-left members of the Democratic Party establishment to "get tough" in their use of American military might. Indeed, even before Obama's prolonging the wars in Iraq and Afghanistan (which he openly denounced years earlier) as well as his calls for greater bombing runs and more systematic use of drone strikes to his unclear approach to the Syrian crisis, there were ample reasons to doubt that he alone could ever honestly usher in a Democratic era of dovishness in any real sense. But the point was that Obama's antiwar posturing during his political ascent revealed a key issue in terms of how politically potent as a campaign approach opposition to the ongoing military conflicts had become. In truth, Obama gained much traction in 2008 because of how unpopular the prospect of endless war and rampant militarism had become within the psyche of a war-weary nation.

Despite criticism from either ideological extreme, an honest evaluation of Obama's perspective on the scope and uses of American power requires closer scrutiny. Although many observers might chart Obama's political ascent to his 2004 Democratic National Convention keynote speech, I would contend that this emergence on the world stage actually took place two years earlier. In 2002, Obama, then a relatively unknown Illinois state senator, delivered a powerfully clear and strident speech opposing the Iraq War at a rally in Chicago. In a particularly thorny political climate in the wake of the post-9/11 terror attacks, such an outspoken stance denouncing the machinations by the Bush White House that led to the US military invasion and subsequent occupation of Iraq was a move deemed both bold and rare at the time. Yet, as I have argued elsewhere, many of Obama's earliest, most ardent supporters on the American left willfully mistook his unequivocal rejection of the Bush administration's war in Iraq for a pacifist inclination that he never actually held. Truth be told, aside from his wholesale rejection of the American military adventurism in Iraq, Obama largely possessed centrist-right foreign policy views that were very much in keeping with his immediate presidential predecessors, George H. W. Bush, Bill Clinton, and George W. Bush.[8]

Given this concern, there was a remarkable tightrope walk that had to be conducted by President Obama in terms of minimizing the effectiveness of his opponents' bloc while maintaining his core support. The persistence of the continued global war on terror has been an intriguing arena in which the Obama administration wrestled mightily with these concerns. From day one of his presidency, there was the looming burden of the ongoing wars in Afghanistan and Iraq, with those conflicts ultimately becoming the longest and second longest wars in our nation's history, respectively, on his watch. Although Obama was eventually able to de-escalate America's military adventure in Iraq during his time in office, both conflicts regrettably became twin millstones around Obama's neck. Furthermore, the irrepressible desire among Obama's greatest supporters came from those who welcomed a national security policy and diplomatic approach by his administration informed by mindful multilateralism and responsible nation building with a focus on political solutions rooted in soft power as opposed to the unilateralism and preemptive military interventionism that was the stock-in-trade of the Bush White House.

Over the course of eight years, the Obama administration's foreign policy had a whole host of strategic interests in the hopes of improving the United States' relationship with the larger world. Faced with the pronounced anti-Americanism around the globe that accompanied the negative impact of George W. Bush's government, the Obama White House promised a considerable sea change in strategic vision. Weary of costly military adventures and frustrating diplomatic engagement especially in the Middle East, President Obama's policy in the region proved increasingly cautious and even circumspect in nature. This new direction in the Arab world was most clearly illustrated by the president's famous 2009 Cairo speech and the administration's subsequent response to the Arab Spring belies much of the optimism that his comments generated. Among other commitments, Obama swore in his Cairo speech to renew the Arab-Israeli peace process in the hopes of establishing a two-state solution based on 1967 borders. Also, while openly rejecting the use of American military intervention as a means of promoting democracy, Obama restated that his consistent opposition to the Iraq War would not lessen his administration's commitment to democratic governance, free trade, regime transparency, nation building, the rule of law, and civil liberties.[9] Moreover, activists seeking the establishment of liberal democracy in the region saw considerable hope in Obama's words that advanced US strategic interests such as combating global terrorism, achieving a lasting Arab-Israeli peace settlement, increased diplomatic engagement with Iran and Syria, marked expansion of women's rights globally, and ending the repression of religious minorities.[10] Despite the fact that his Cairo speech had a critical impact in sparking the "Arab Spring," Obama's pro-democracy agenda actually contained no programmatic initiatives to democratize the Gulf Kingdoms of the Arab world.[11]

In retrospect, Obama's overall foreign policy agenda was marked by a multiplicity of factors that included the following: the desire to end the wars in Iraq and Afghanistan; the capture and killing of Osama bin Laden; the failure to close Guantanamo Bay prison camp; the aversion to military force; the extension of the USA Patriot Act; the expansion of the National Security Agency's surveillance program; the increased latitude of the Foreign Intelligence Surveillance Act court system; the administration's aggressive pursuit of whistleblowers such as Edward Snowden, Chelsea Manning, and Julian Assange; and the goal of pivoting US foreign policy attention to Asia. All of this contributed to his realist-idealist vision of what Fareed Zakaria has dubbed a "post-American world" focused not on the collapse of America but the "rise of the rest" within a reconstituted global order.[12] Yet Zbigniew Brzezinski, former president Jimmy Carter's National Security Advisor, observes that President Obama inherited a nation that lost an integral sense of its overall mission in the world. He explains how:

> The tragedy of September 11, 2001, fundamentally altered America's own view of its global purpose. Building off of the public's basic ignorance of world history and geography, for the demagogically inclined Bush administration to spend eight years remaking the United States into a crusader state. The "war on terror" became synonymous with foreign policy and the United States . . . neglected to build a strategy that addressed its long-term interests in an evolving geopolitical environment. Thus, America was left unprepared—thanks to the confluence of the above—to face the novel challenges of the twenty-first century.[13]

However, the Obama administration's inability to secure a long-term security agreement with Iraq resulted in the removal of US combat troops in 2011 that has contributed immeasurably to Iraqi instability. President Obama's reluctance to fully engage US military and diplomatic power in the Arab world exacerbated regional instability and alienated traditional allies. The rising sectarian conflict and resurgent jihadist violence throughout the Middle East and North Africa only reinforced the Obama administration's desires to disengage further from mounting turmoil in the region as witnessed in Syria and Libya.

Based on that state of affairs, the fate of Afghanistan and Iraq remained atop the list of the most enervating foreign policy challenges for Obama. In terms of the Afghan conflict, a sizable number of Americans still view our military efforts there as a "just war" against the vestiges of the Taliban and al-Qaeda, who attacked the United States, a viewpoint solidified by the covert military raid that led to the killing of Osama bin Laden. The execution of bin Laden in May 2011 marked an undeniable turning point in the global war on terror.

Given the events of the prior decade, Obama's Nobel Prize speech notably served as an opportunity to seriously reexamine the long and winding trajectory of the US war machine from 9/11 to the present. Amid the deluge of scandal, incompetence, and opacity emanating from the George W. Bush White House, the soothing calm and focused efficiency of the Obama era was a welcome relief. The reality was that Obama had not yet begun a full term as president but walked into the West Wing faced with, among a whole of host of problems, a largely mishandled war in the Middle East that desperately needed to be brought under control in relatively short order. Spend even a few moments studying the evolution of the Pentagon and Langley during the Obama era and you will find that very little has changed in their post-9/11 trajectory. Covert operations continued relatively unabated throughout the Arab world. Increasingly, the United States maintained its forces in Iraq and Afghanistan, became directly involved in toppling Muammar Gaddafi's regime in Libya, and became more deeply entrenched in Somalia and Syria. If anything, the CIA and US military are currently much less restrained and are in greater control of their decisions—a development that arguably creates policy rather than implements it—than they were under Obama. Hence, this transition has removed effective civilian oversight of the world's most lethal fighting force at a crucial moment in world affairs.

Years from now, when historians and researchers examine the Obama era with unfettered access to declassified documents and first-person accounts from key players (including the former president himself), it is certain that among the greatest beneficiaries of his presidency in terms of sheer structural power will be the unelected institutions of the US national security apparatus, namely, the military and CIA. But it would be a mistake to attribute this exclusively to Obama. To be clear, during the 2016 presidential campaign, the leading presidential candidates—Donald Trump, Hillary Clinton, and yes, even Bernie Sanders—all made clear that they supported and would continue the "targeted killing" program. Dating back to 2001, George W. Bush, Dick Cheney, and Donald Rumsfeld used 9/11 as a rationale to unleash the most unsavory forces in the national security apparatus. Driven by the nexus of neoconservative hawks both in the Bush White House and think tanks, they empowered the elite Joint Special

Operations Command to wage a global, covert war replete with operations kept secret even from US ambassadors and the State Department. The CIA set up global black sites for rendition and conducted heinous acts of torture with the White House's blessing.

While Barack Obama certainly did roll back some of the most glaringly blatant activities enthusiastically endorsed by Bush-Cheney administration, he was also a diligent and disciplined manager of the American empire. In key ways, Obama served as a launderer for operations of some of the most aggressive forces in the US arsenal. He used his credibility among liberals—as well as the derision hurled at him by conservatives who tirelessly vilified him as a secret radical Kenyan Muslim socialist— to legitimize assassination and covert offensive military actions as lawful, moral, and necessary. The patently false allegations from the right that Obama was somehow a pacifist dove only served to undermine the severity of military and paramilitary actions he authorized and expanded.

Despite their obvious lethality, weaponized drones were merely an instrument and never intended to be a policy unto itself. Although much attention has been paid to the technology and ethics of remote killing, the focus on drones actually has been in many ways a digression from a deeper, more meaningful debate.[14] Meanwhile the overall discussion that should occur has to be a broad examination of the state's power over life and death. Whether extrajudicial killings are carried out by drones, manned aircraft, covert special forces operators on the ground, or remote controlled explosive device, the end result is ultimately the same. For the sake of sheer honesty and accuracy, it is vital for all Americans to understand that, in its purest, most unmitigated form, the policy has always been state-sanctioned assassination.

In the waning months of the Obama presidency, the administration revealed some details on its secret drone-based US assassination program in a rather slow, unsatisfactory fashion. For instance, there were admissions that a small number of civilians had been killed but this fact was offset by earnest declarations that drone strikes were lawful and generally accurate. Nevertheless, even after Obama exited the White House, the public still remained largely in the dark about the secret process used to decide whose name gets placed on the proverbial kill list as well as the criteria used to determine if those people will receive the death penalty without even the pretense of a trial. There was no public accounting by the Obama administration for the countless special operations ground raids conducted across the globe. Those raids and the drone strikes continued somewhat unabated but during White House press conferences the majority of the Washington press corps was more focused on whether enemy combatants or US military personnel are killed rather than the fate of foreign civilians.

To its credit, the Obama White House zealously promoted efforts to create what it called a "durable legal and policy framework to guide our counterterrorism actions." Nevertheless it shrouded that framework in secrecy, thereby precluding a robust, full-fledged democratic debate over the growing practice of remotely killing unarmed, unknown, and unintended people as targets of the US government's foreign policy goals. Needless to say, there is zero to no chance whatsoever that any such debate will happen under Obama's successor, Donald Trump, so the best information available to the public on how the assassination program functions is derived from the end of Obama's time in office.[15]

When Obama publicly stated that a small number of civilians had been killed in drone strikes, he said he felt "profound regret," specifically about Western hostages accidentally killed in a strike on al-Qaeda. In the end, Obama told the public as many as 116 civilians may have been killed in drone strikes conducted during his time in office. Still the administration's statistics were highly misleading. Thanks to verified secret US military documents obtained by *The Intercept*, investigative journalist Jeremy Scahill reported that the Obama administration as a matter of policy classified unknown persons killed in airstrikes as "enemies killed in action," even if they were not the originally intended targets. During a five-month period in Afghanistan, for example, nearly 90 percent of those killed in one high-value campaign were not the intended targets. Between January 2012 and February 2013, US special operations airstrikes killed more than 200 people, only 35 of whom were actually the intended targets. All of these victims were labeled "enemies killed in action" as per Obama-era policies.[16]

After many years of warfare, the US military has developed extensive intelligence networks on the ground in Afghanistan and Iraq. Outside of those declared war zones—for instance, in Yemen and Somalia—the White House's remote killing program had to rely on far weaker, less dependable intelligence sources, which the military's own documents acknowledged is markedly more inferior and unreliable in nature. As a result, the accuracy of its targeting judgments in those regions was likely to be even worse with a heightened risk of collateral damage and unintended loss of life. According to one classified slide, as of June 2012, Obama had authorized the assassination of sixteen individuals in Yemen. Yet, during that same year, US airstrikes had killed more than 200 people in that country. Despite the level of administration's high standards on accountability and transparency, the Obama White House never explained either the identities of the majority of victims or any rationale for why they were killed. Conversely, to date, at least seven US citizens were killed under this policy, including a 16-year-old boy. Only one American, the radical preacher Anwar al-Awlaki, was said to have been the "intended target" of a drone strike.[17]

Even though assassination is obviously a charged term, the prohibition against its use as a political tool actually has been a critical concern at the highest echelons of US government for several decades. In 1976, following Church Committee recommendations regarding allegations of assassination plots carried out by US intelligence agencies, President Gerald Ford signed an Executive Order banning "political assassination." President Jimmy Carter subsequently issued a new order strengthening the prohibition by dropping the word "political" and extending it to include persons "employed by or acting on behalf of the United States." In 1981, President Ronald Reagan signed Executive Order 12333, which remains in effect today. The language seems clear enough: "no person employed by or acting on behalf of the US government shall engage in, or conspire to engage in, assassination." Congress, despite commissioning a report on the subject from the Congressional Research Service, has avoided legislating the issue or even defining the word "assassination." An extrajudicial killing of a person who poses no imminent and immediate threat to citizens of the United States, in a country with which the United States is not at war, carried out by agents of the US government is an assassination. Regardless of any jargon or euphemism one wishes to deploy—targeted killing, military action, or signature surgical strike—when a civilian noncombatant is killed by such an action, it is murder pure and simple.

Whether or not one might have had deep trust in the Obama administration's use of this sort of power (admittedly, I was cautiously critical in my support of Obama's foreign policy approach), the question at stake was always about the absolute rather than abstract impact of this policy development. The institutionalization of a program of drone-based murders of any and all individuals deemed as threats to national security—through secret processes without the benefit of either indictment, trial, or appeal—enshrined a policy of assassination in direct violation of Executive Order 12333 and, furthermore, due process of the law within our political culture, and thus bequeathed to his successor Donald Trump.

The unprecedented powers the CIA and the Pentagon have attained through Democratic and Republican administrations alike should be a permanent focus of media coverage. History has shown that the unelected national security apparatus does not surrender its newly acquired powers willingly. Many liberals ignored these issues during the Obama presidency. From the time of his initial opposition to the Iraq War in 2002, Obama was never quite the naive pacifist that either his most ardent supporters or more strident critics presented him as at the time.[18] What Obama sought and desperately needed was a nuanced theology that would suitably fit his often stoic, professorial temperament, which would be a huge evolutionary leap from the instinctively Manichean views of the Bush-Cheney years. As noted in the op-ed pages of *The New York Times*, President Obama found just such an instrumental guide to navigating the world via the works of Reinhold Niebuhr especially his 1952 book *The Irony of American History*. "If we should perish," Niebuhr argues, "the ruthlessness of the foe would be only the secondary cause of the disaster. The primary cause would be that the strength of a giant nation was directed by eyes too blind to see all the hazards of the struggle; and the blindness would be induced not by some accident of nature or history but by hatred and vainglory."[19] On the one hand, Obama readily embraced Niebuhr's notion that "the compelling idea that there's serious evil in the world, and hardship, and pain." On the other, he understood that "we are immersed in world-wide responsibilities; and our weakness has grown into strength."[20] Obama embraced from Niebuhr "the sense we have to make these efforts knowing they are hard, and not swinging from naive idealism to bitter realism." Moreover, while not fearful to use terms such as "imperialism" and "hegemony" in America's role in the world, Niebuhr indicates that

> our culture knows little of the use and the abuse of power; but we have to use power in global terms. Our idealists are divided between those who would renounce the responsibilities of power for the sake of preserving the purity of our soul and those who are ready to cover every ambiguity of good and evil in our actions by the frantic insistence that any measure taken in a good cause must be unequivocally virtuous. We take, morally hazardous actions to preserve our civilization.[21]

The real question for Niebuhr is whether or not one can articulate a morally cogent geopolitical worldview, even one inundated with irony and nuance. For those charged with the responsibility of governance, what matters is whether it is fitted to the situation, and whether it is executed effectively. While the distinctions between "realists" and "idealists" emphasize disposition instead of doctrines. Niebuhr understood that decision-making was an entirely different process than theologizing.[22] What mattered in politics was not how choices were framed but how they were made. Therefore, the litmus test for Obama was discerning a sane, smart foreign policy could be assessed only on the grounds of its successes and failures, rather than its coherence or intellectual lucidity. The difficulties faced by the Obama administration in foreign affairs have not been conceptual but rather strategic and tactical. What we are left with is not so much an "Obama doctrine" in a classical sense as an "Obama worldview." Why does this matter? Because, in spite of the continued secrecy and cynicism, it is only through self-awareness and acknowledging the hard truth that Obama attempted to move the nation toward a more mature and meaningful appreciation of its place in history.

"It's in the Bible": Jeremiah Wright's condemnation of the American empire

On April 13, 2003, Rev. Dr. Jeremiah A. Wright Jr. delivered a forty-minute-long sermon at Trinity United Church of Christ in Chicago's South Side neighborhood entitled "Confusing God and Government." However, for those of us watching and listening to the video footage years later, it is better known as the sermon that contains the now infamous "God Damn America" sound bite that almost decimated the Obama presidential campaign in March 2008. Despite the ways in which this sermon ignited such a firestorm of negative reaction, it would be safe to argue that even now, most Americans still have neither explored to the sermon in its entirety nor looked at its significance beyond its role in prompting the severing of the relationship between the Obamas and Dr. Wright. It is important to assess Wright's "Confusing God and Government" sermon as a searing indictment of US domestic and foreign policy, and as outlining the critical failure of the black church tradition to take a more outspoken stance on matters of war and peace. Therefore, aside from the initial shock of his choice of words in condemning the United States for its long history of brutality and inhumanity toward marginalized Others (especially people of color), the recent controversy surrounding Rev. Dr. Jeremiah Wright Jr.'s "Confusing God and Government" sermon illustrates all too clearly the consistent and continuing reluctance of many black religious leaders to challenge the US government and the larger society on its sins, both past and present.

Wright's scriptural text was derived from Lk. 19:37-44 (NRSV). In this sermon, Wright spoke about the imperial Roman domination of Israel during Jesus's lifetime as led by Pontius Pilate but it was plainly clear throughout his sermon that he was making a direct analogy to the war that President Bush had initiated in Iraq a month earlier. Throughout his prepared remarks, the pastor had peppered his sermon with very striking critical points. For instance, "war does not make for peace," he said. "Fighting for peace is like raping for virginity." Wright got to the core premise of his sermon, remarking that "a lot of people confuse God with their government." By this point, Wright openly criticized the Bush White House and its supporters for using godly language to justify the Iraq War. The crux of the controversial statement related to government mistreatment of African Americans, Wright preached: "The government gives [blacks] the drugs, builds bigger prisons, passes a three-strike law and then wants us to sing 'God Bless America.' No, no, no, God damn America, that's in the Bible for killing innocent people."[23] He even goes so far as to equate Americans using God as a means of condoning the US war in Iraq as being a latter-day version of the Crusades as being comparable to Islamic extremists declaring death to America as Allah's mandate for jihad. Wright elaborates by saying, "We can see clearly the confusion in the mind of a few Muslims, and please notice I did not say all Muslims, I said a few Muslims, who see Allah as condoning killing and killing any and all who don't believe what they don't believe. They call it jihad. We can see clearly the confusion in their minds, but we cannot see clearly what it is that we do. We call it crusade when we turn right around and say that our God condones the killing of innocent civilians as a necessary means to an end. We say that God understand collateral damage. We say that God knows how to forgive friendly fire."[24] Hitting the emotional and rhetorical peak of the sermon, Wright begins to recite a litany of governmental abuses and atrocities enacted around the globe but with a strict focus on the United States and its mistreatment of its citizens of color.

As he drew to his sermonic close, Wright illustrated his threefold critique of government insofar that governments lie; governments change over the course of time; and finally he states that governments fail. Wright expounds upon this last issue by stating, "Where government fail, God never fails. When God says it, it's done. God never fails. When God wills it, you better get out the way, cause God never fails. When God fixes it, oh believe me it's fixed. God never fails. Somebody right now, you think you can't make it, but I want you to know that you are more than a conqueror through Christ. You can do all things through Christ who strengthens you." Sensing the uneasiness that his provocative statement would raise among members of the congregation, Wright told the people, "Tell your neighbor [God's] (going to) help us one last time. Turn back and say forgive him for the God Damn, that's in the Bible though. Blessings and curses is in the Bible. It's in the Bible." Then Wright proceeded to talk about the salvation of Christians through the death of Jesus Christ. The sermon ended with a congregational song proclaiming, "God never fails."[25]

Broadly speaking, we must consider how utterly deafening the silence of the black religious leadership has been on global matters of war and peace in the decades since Dr. Martin Luther King Jr.'s death. On April 4, 1967, Dr. King delivered a now legendary sermon entitled "Beyond Vietnam" at the Riverside Church in New York City. In order to fully understand the need for all people of genuine faith and good conscience in this era to develop an antiwar position which is thoughtful, intentional, and consistent, we need to briefly contextualize the causes as well as consequences surrounding King's vigorous albeit short-lived attempts in the last years of his life to foment a black Christian antiwar stance in order to address the great American military quagmire of his lifetime, namely, the Vietnam War. This should be instructive to all of us not only as we are still dealing with the ongoing impact of our military engagement in Iraq and Afghanistan over the past fifteen years during the recent Bush and Obama presidencies but also the imminent threat that looms large as Donald Trump, the current part-time occupant of the White House, seems absolutely eager to rev up the American war machine to previously unprecedented levels. Toward that end, I want to quickly emphasize how Dr. King's "Beyond Vietnam" sermon both in its historic context and its hermeneutical content illustrated a helpful framework wherein the Church could provide a prophetic witness in its quest for peace while holding a more meaningful and truthful definition of patriotism to bear.

Unquestionably, King's message was a major media event particularly because, as the internationally renowned leader of the nonviolent civil rights movement in the United States, Dr. King chose this historic Riverside Church and its prestigious pulpit as the prime venue to address his stance on US foreign policy in general and his views on the Vietnam conflict in particular. Even though he had briefly spoken out against US involvement in Southeast Asia in 1965, it was the increasing pressure from aides and confidantes such as Rev. James Lawson and the late historian Vincent Harding—who has been credited as the speech's ghostwriter—that finally convinced King to end his silence about America's military conflict with Vietnam. More importantly, King's "Beyond Vietnam" sermon was a risk of faith in the most Kierkegaardian sense because he knew full and well that opposing the war would certainly create bad blood between him and President Lyndon Johnson precisely at the time when the civil rights movement needed more presidential support in order to guarantee social and economic gains at home.

While there is not enough time and space right now to go into full detail about the Dr. King's views on internationalism, anti-imperialism, anti racism, nonviolence, and ending poverty, please know that these elements are evident as early as his years of seminary training and graduate education. When Dr. King stood behind the sacred desk that is the pulpit of the Riverside Church in the full glare of the media spotlight, he had to address the great question that swirled above him like so many storm clouds, namely, "why break his silence" when supposedly "peace and civil rights don't mix?" In response to this speculative concern, Dr. King offers several reasons why ending the Vietnam War and inevitably all wars had become a centerpiece of his prophetic ministry.[26]

Taking into consideration the vast potential of President Johnson's Great Society initiatives to recreate the United States with a domestic agenda for all Americans that was supremely liberal and humane, King argues that domestic policy was going to be compromised by the nation's military expenditures in Southeast Asia. As Dr. King comments, he had high hopes for the Great Society program but "then came the buildup in Vietnam and I watched this program broken and eviscerated as if it were some idle political plaything of a society gone mad on war." King's opposition to the Vietnam War on the grounds that the war was taking money and other vital resources that could have been spent on the War on Poverty. From the civil rights leader's perspective, Congress was simultaneously spending more wealth and legislative clout on the use of military force overseas while having virtually nothing left to spend on anti-poverty programs. He summed up this aspect by saying, "A nation that continues year after year to spend more money on military defense than on programs of social uplift is approaching spiritual death."

Once he revealed his manifold vision for opposing the American war in Vietnam, Dr. King suffered possibly the worst backlash of his career. Even though King is now lionized as the American patron saint of peace and nonviolent social change, it is important to remember that, upon delivery of this sermon, he was demonized and skewered by the federal government, the national media, and the general public. In many regards, the most alarming backlash to King's comments came from members of the black middle class who had previously been the chief beneficiaries, if not the strongest supporters, of King's prophetic ministry up to then. As a matter of fact, King was denounced in many circles as "traitorous" for his remarks.

Simply put, with the exception of prophetic leaders such as Wright, the black church tradition has paid too little attention to Christian attitudes toward issues of war and peace in recent times. Since the start of the twenty-first century, there have been mixed signals regarding the complicated relationship of black people and US foreign policy. In the last two decades alone, there have been isolated cases when a handful of individual pastors or prominent activists offered fulsome critiques of American imperialism's impact at home and abroad. Meanwhile, such an overwhelming silence represents an utter failure of black religious leadership collectively to address the role of the United States in creating global conflicts much less providing possible correction to said crises.

Even as the scandal based on Wright's incendiary rhetoric surfaced at the height of the 2008 Democratic primary season, then senator Obama shocked both critics and supporters alike when he delivered his widely celebrated "A More Perfect Union" speech (a.k.a. the "Race" speech) on March 18, 2008.[27] Among the plethora of things that have been said about that oratorical masterpiece, I would suggest that the speech was an extremely artful dodge not necessarily in its expressed content (that's a matter for another conversation altogether) inasmuch as it totally avoided the actual central critique of Wright's controversial sermon. Oddly enough, even as Obama's renowned speech on race was intended to short-circuit a near-catastrophic controversy, his rhetorical exercise showed that he and his advisors chose race rather than US imperialism as the lesser of two evils.

Furthermore, the media firestorm unleashed by the preacher's sound bite became fixated upon the perennial and precarious ways in which race and religion in terms of black liberation theology have played themselves out in American life rather than dealing with the concerns broached by Wright's message, namely, a long history of American militaristic aggression and imperial hubris rapidly approaching its zenith with the global war on terror. Even if countless American citizens heard bits and pieces of the sermon, it seems that hardly any of them actually listened to it and its deeper meaning. Rather than running from Dr. Wright and his remarks, African American religious scholars, leaders, and faith communities ought to see this moment as an opening, an opportunity in order to revive a much-needed conversation about the role and responsibility of the black church tradition to confront the powers that be on all matters that affect the chances for human flourishing, especially this nation's ability to wage war and make peace in this world.

"My problem is I'm peaceful": Lupe Fiasco and prophetic Islamic hip-hop

Returning to the event that prompted much of this reflection, I have been working in various ways to incorporate the often submerged and overlooked hip-hop generation within the broader discussions of the recent past. As such, while briefly turning to the words of Lupe Fiasco who is among a small but significant number of hip-hop artists who has merged his musical creativity and political convictions in ways concerned with the breaking silence about the patent absurdity of fighting perpetual war in pursuit of perceived peace. During a 2011 CBS News interview, Lupe Fiasco explained: "The biggest terrorist is Obama in the United States of America. I'm trying to fight the terrorism that's causing the other forms of terrorism. You know the root cause of terrorists is the stuff the US government allows to happen. The foreign policies that we have in place in different countries that inspire people to become terrorists."[28]

Better known by his stage name Lupe Fiasco, he was born Wasalu Muhammad Jaco on February 16, 1982, in Chicago, Illinois into a West African immigrant household as one of nine children. His parents were Shirley, a gourmet chef, and Gregory, an operating plant engineer. His father was a particularly intriguing influence in Fiasco's childhood. In addition to his work as an engineer, his father also had been a member of the Black Panther Party, a prolific African drummer, martial arts instructor, and owner of army surplus stores. Moreover, Fiasco was raised Muslim on Chicago's West Side in Madison Terrace housing project. As an academically high achieving student born into a hardworking and politically engaged black immigrant Muslim family from an urban neighborhood heavily infested with drugs and gangs, there is no question that his worldview was shaped and informed by a constant interplay of local realities and global concerns in both his art and activism. Fiasco has produced politically charged music since the earliest days of his career but it is important to note that he has produced numerous songs that have been explicitly geared with an eye toward matters of global political sensibility such as "American Terrorist," "Little Weapon," "Muhammad Walks," "State-Run Radio," and others.

While Lupe Fiasco's vocal criticism of contemporary politics is quite pointed and poignant, it is hardly a pioneering effort either for him as a musical artist or hip-hop as a genre. During the 1980s, hip-hop music evolved from mere party music to protest music with songs like Grandmaster Flash and the Furious Five's "The Message" and Run DMC's "Hard Times." By the late 1980s and early 1990s, there were numerous hip-hop artists such as Boogie Down Productions, Public Enemy, X-Clan, Arrested Development, Poor Righteous Teachers, Brand Nubian, Wu-Tang Clan, Nas, Common, and others whose musical output was infused with racial pride, religious principles, and radical politics. In addition to Lupe Fiasco, there are numerous hip-hop artists such as Yasiin Bey (aka Mos Def), Rhymefest, Jay Electronica, Busta Rhymes, Q-Tip, and Ali Shaheed Muhammad who are adherents of various Islamic traditions. More than that, there have been several instances when members of the hip-hop generation have spoken to matters directly related to Middle Eastern geopolitical issues. What is more, Islam has been a vital element of hip-hop music and culture since its inception in the 1970s. "For over a century," Hisham Aidi posits, "African American thinkers—Muslim and non-Muslim—have attempted to harness the black struggle to global Islam, while leaders in the Islamic world have tried to yoke their political causes to African American liberation."[29] Whether recognized as Arabic, Afro-Asiatic, or black Muslim in nature, the incorporation of Islamic influences and concepts into hip-hop has been undeniable in building bridges between Middle Eastern geopolitics and black religious radicalism.[30]

Allow me to provide a few examples of like-minded hip-hop artists who have also produced insightful musical critiques of US foreign policy especially in the Middle East. For instance, the hip-hop duo Eric B and Rakim's "Casualties of War" (1992) relates to the experiences of a morally conflicted black soldier during the first Gulf War in which the United States led a multinational military coalition that invaded Iraq during the George H. W. Bush administration. Most notable for its immediacy and prescience about the extent of racism and imperialism at work in US foreign policy as relates to Rakim's Islamic faith as a Five Percenter, he also grapples with the twin concepts of moral injury and post-traumatic stress disorder, growing realities for countless US troops in contemporary conflicts. Often heralded as classic New York hip-hop album, Capone-N-Noreaga's *The War Report* (1997) constructed a mythological superimposition wherein the Queen's natives reimagined New York borough's Lefrak Housing Projects as an Iraqi war zone. Even their abbreviated moniker—CNN— not only recalled rapper Chuck D's famous statements about hip-hop as a source of street reportage but also invoked the news network's near omnipresence during the Persian Gulf War and its aftermath. "PLO Style," a song on Wu-Tang Clan member Method Man's debut album, derives its name from the controversial Palestinian Liberation Organization, a group designated as a terrorist organization by both the United States and United Nations until 1991; since then, the PLO has transitioned itself past its legacy of organized acts of attrition and retribution against Israel into a more political, diplomacy-oriented group. Still, in his comments about the song's origins, Method Man recounts that he and his friends used to frequent a pro-PLO store in their Staten Island neighborhood, and often caught glimpses of intimidating, gun-toting figures in photos taken in Palestine and put up proudly on display at the shop. "The same way Wu Tang respected how the kung fu dudes [were] doing their thing . . . we respected how the PLOs [*sic*] got down," Method says in the clip. "They're freedom fighters and we felt like we were fighting for our freedom everyday, too, where we lived at."[31] In a song eerily similar to Dr. Wright's infamous 2003 sermon, Nas's "What Goes Around" inveighs against the brutal inhumanity of American imperialism both at home and abroad as a contributing factor to the rise in Middle Eastern terrorism that led to the 9/11 attacks among other horrific events; in this fashion, the legendary Queensbridge rapper situated the global war on terror within a historical and global frame of reference that accentuates retributive blowback as much as clashing religious principles or ideological perspectives.[32] Shifting attention from the macro outlook to the microcosmic, Rhymefest's "Bullet" devotes a verse to the life of a young man who joins the US National Guard due to a lack of gainful employment and positive life options in his hometown who inadvertently finds himself deployed and subsequently killed in Iraq as part of a larger military adventure without either a clearly defined mission or truly achievable goals.[33] In a rather Spartan yet incendiary musical invective,

Killer Mike's "Reagan" concisely outlines a case for distrusting the US government's ulterior motives for military interventionism in the region from the Reagan to Obama eras. As these and other examples prove, Fiasco's "Words I Never Said" as a particularly blunt song protesting US foreign policy was neither isolated nor inconsistent within hip-hop music and culture.

In his song "Words I Never Said," Fiasco illustrates the realities of his millennial generation where he rhymes about the geopolitics in tandem with domestic woes. In the song's lyrics, Fiasco outlines a list of concerns such as maldistribution of wealth, the sensationalism and superficiality of the contemporary news media, racial prejudice and cultural insensitivity by ideological spokespeople, the declining state of the American Dream, an expressed desire to pursue nonviolent resolution to global conflicts, and a growing sense of disconnection of citizens from their elected government. Toward that end, Fiasco exhibits his distrust of the voting process within the American political process by saying,

> That's why I ain't vote for him—next one either/
> I'm a part of the problem, my problem is I'm peaceful
> And I believe in the people.

But Fiasco is also mindful to raise the argument about Islamic extremism as well by saying,

> Now you can say it ain't our fault if we never heard it
> But if we know better than we probably deserve it
> Jihad is not a holy war, where's that in the worship?
> Murdering is not Islam!
> And you are not observant
> And you are not a Muslim

It also cannot be emphasized enough that in the closing lines of his 1964 Oxford Union speech, Malcolm X made a somewhat similar declaration about his own ideological as well as theological shift away from black nationalism toward a radical humanism infused with revolutionary internationalism. "And I, for one will join with anyone," Malcolm X stated, "don't care what color you are, as long as you want to change this miserable condition that exists on this earth."[34] He went on to comment about the importance of Islam for those back home in the United States, saying that "America needs to understand Islam, because this is the one religion that erases from its society the race problem." As Hisham Aidi observes, "At least since Malcolm X, internationalist Islam has been a response to Western racism and imperialism."[35] Taken further, it might be argued that although they were living and operating in markedly different historical moments, both Malcolm X and Lupe Fiasco might be vying for a concept of a borderless Islamic nation that H. Samy Alim has labeled the transglobal hip-hop *umma* "where citizenship was based on faith rather than on contemporary nation-state distinction."[36] Nevertheless, there are two lessons to be learned from Malcolm X's post-hajj conversion that may illuminate Fiasco's stance as a prophetic black Muslim.

First, the combination of Sunni Islam and an emerging system of revolutionary international politics produced a meaningful paradigm for understanding jihad as a manifestation of prophetic religion in both principle and praxis. Although grossly maligned and misconstrued in the post–9/11 era as the result of a rising tide of Islamophobia in conjunction with the global war on terror, jihad actually refers to a constant struggle for social justice endorsed by Quranic teachings. This is also very much in keeping with the greater Islamic tradition that specifies that, as a devout Muslim himself, Fiasco asserts his interpretation of Quranic teachings that are keeping within the greater Islamic tradition of there being a dual essence to jihad—the first (*jihad bil nafs*) addresses "striving within the self"; the second (*jihad fi sabil Allah*) emphasizes "striving in the path of Allah"—but neither iteration of jihad mandates wanton bloodshed or any so-called clash of civilizations in order to be deemed truly faithful and observant Muslims.

Lastly, Fiasco is not only reacting to the circumstances of the world around us but also offers a level of introspection to those personal limits that work to prevent himself and others to speak out:

> A rebel in your thoughts, ain't going to make it halt
> If you don't become an actor, you'll never be a factor . . .
> I think that all the silence is worse than all the violence
> Fear is such a weak emotion that's why I despise it
> We scared of almost everything, afraid to even tell the truth
> So scared of what you think of me, I'm scared of even telling you
> Sometimes I'm like the only person I feel safe to tell it to . . .

As Lupe Fiasco illustrates in his verses, there is an entire generation of citizens coming of age within the body politic who feel betrayed by the collective inability of all Americans to articulate a more assertively progressive voice in matters of both US domestic and foreign policy. Furthermore, the shameful silence of too many people of true faith and good conscience regarding unjust, unrelenting, and unnecessary warfare becomes a steel trap that imprisons us all. In this sense, the sage warning of feminist writer and activist Audre Lorde is invaluable when she argues, "your silence will not protect you."[37] In the coming months and years, black religious leaders and scholars will need to come to the realization that silence has never been a shield and ignorance has never been an excuse when addressing issues of this magnitude.

Conclusion

In closing, whereas Obama never said he was a pacifist, Dr. Wright never said he was a political partisan, and Fiasco never said he was a policy maker, each in his own way demonstrates a path forward in the hopes of bringing these potential interlocutors into deeper, more meaningful interaction for the possible betterment of us all. It is this degree of moral clarity and accountability that prophetic voices like Lupe Fiasco and Jeremiah Wright are demanding from the US government writ large. Contrary to the conventional wisdom usually associated with realpolitik, the challenges to US foreign policy posed by Obama's political rise were rooted in a prophetic hope for America's more beneficent role in a shifting global order. Writing in the immediate aftermath of World War I—once believed by countless observers and survivors to be "the war to end all wars"—W. E. B. Du Bois opined: "the cause of war is preparation for war" in terms of the "preparation for wholesale murder" by wealthy, developed nations like the United States against their weaker, developing counterparts.[38]

Although proportionality, discrimination, and minimum force are still hallmarks of conventional just war theory, the variations of black prophetic discourse illustrated by Obama, Wright, and Fiasco articulate another, more urgent set of principles that must be considered. Whether prompted by the moral outrage of Fiasco and Wright or the optimistic pragmatism of Obama, their respective iterations of black prophetic discourse regarding the feasibility of waging just war in the modern world hinge on three key factors: truth, trust, and transparency. Despite their obvious differences, it is clear that all three men are bearing witness to the full burden of American imperialism from the underside of history. Therefore, they are operating in full awareness that the innermost workings of the American empire have rarely ever functioned in ways that have been truthful, trustworthy, and transparent with regard to people of color either at home or globally. Nonetheless, the serious consideration of black prophetic discourse as a means of creating a world order that could fathom and ultimately fulfill the vision of just war in our time is a challenge well worth the undertaking.

What is more, contemporary political leadership has not been properly attuned to these matters of black prophetic discourse in ways that resonate beyond the realms of religious studies and theological education. For the movers and shakers in America's national security apparatus—especially the military-industrial complex—their inclination has been to avoid, admonish, or abolish any radical critique of the existing status quo that seeks to influence national debates on international relations in terms of political activism and policy intervention. In other words, religious scholars and theological educators have not been able to help cultivate meaningful approaches to "just war" theory that move contemporary scholarship, ministry, activism, and broader civic engagement beyond moral principles and philosophical ideals toward practical applications. With only a few notable exceptions, contemporary religious scholarship has addressed the uses and abuses of US foreign policy insufficiently and intermittently. There are many factors that contribute to such a dilemma but, in the final analysis, the lack of cogent and critical insight on matters of faith and international relations by religious scholars has contributed in part to the considerable deficiencies of today's religious practitioners and believers alike from having greater voice and visibility regarding global war and peace.

Part Three

On Race/ing Belief

When White Is the "New Black": Religious Populism in the Age of Obama

Keri Day

Throughout the history of America, nonwhite populations such as African Americans have been "racialized," seen as possessing a "race," while white populations have simply been interpreted as the default, a non-racialized group that articulates the norm and standard against which all other nonwhite US citizens are judged. However, whiteness is increasingly "racialized," articulated as a racial or ethnic "other" under assault. Whiteness is understood as incurring political liability, rendering the history of white hegemony mute. Under the Obama presidency, white populism has intensified, coming to full expression with the 2016 election of Donald Trump. This chapter broadly explores how Christian religious fundamentalisms have fueled white populism in the United States, reshaping questions on race, racial injustice, and economic inequity under the Obama presidency. White religious logics and practices contribute to how white identity is now fretted over and pointed out so that the "new civil rights movement" is about focusing on how to combat practices of "white disenfranchisement." In American politics today, white suffering is re-casted as the "new black," the new oppressed subject within sociopolitical and economic spaces. This chapter offers a brief historical overview of whiteness, redefines what white populism is, investigates the social and political costs incurred by a white populist imagination, and concludes by asking how black religious leaders and thinkers might challenge a white populist agenda.

A brief historical view: The problem of whiteness

W. E. B. Du Bois notes that "the discovery of a personal whiteness among the world's people is a very modern thing—a nineteenth and twentieth century matter, indeed."[1] Du Bois offers a very important observation about the idea of race in the United States: that it is a modern creation. Within Western society, the racial categories of white and black are often treated as *biological* facts. Throughout American history, whiteness and blackness have been seen as two separate "races," which have been articulated as having an ontological status. In fact, it was assumed that the genetic differences between white and black populations were physiological facts beyond disputation. In 1920, Du Bois challenged this American assumption about race by speaking of whiteness in the language of "discovery," connecting it to the modern epoch that was characterized by the colonization and conquest of non-European lands along with the enforced enslavement of Africans in the Americas.

What Du Bois attempts to reclaim is race as a *contested* concept—that racial categories are socially constructed and culturally produced, grounded in historical narratives of Western colonization and conquest. There have been a number of black scholars in the humanities and social sciences that have attempted to challenge the interpretation of racial categories as rooted in biology through mapping the emergence of whiteness, white supremacy, and white privilege. To speak of race is often to speak about how it has adversely affected and impacted those who are marginalized and oppressed, such as black people in the United States. But merely talking about black pain and injury misses what has created blackness in the first place: whiteness. It is only when turning to white imperialism, hegemony, and colonialism that one can more deeply understand the insidious nature of racist logics and practices perpetrated upon brown and black people in the United States and even around the world.

Over the last several decades, a burgeoning field of literature in critical race theory and whiteness studies has shed light on how one might understand the construction of white supremacy and white privilege in this country. Whiteness studies have emerged as a way to explore the anatomy of a socially constructed whiteness that created blackness as a category through which to interpret non-European people as inferior and primitive. In speaking about the philosophical and theological foundations of racism in the West, scholars of whiteness studies acknowledge that one must move beyond discourses that solely focus on the problem of blackness.[2] It is important to name and expose white racist ideologies and narratives that denigrate and dehumanize brown and black people.

For a number of black and white scholars, part of understanding Western history and its effects on black people has been to investigate how the emergence of whiteness served as a discursive field out of which the idea of blackness appeared and was developed, marking non-European bodies as defiant, primitive, and "other."[3] Whiteness might be understood as a rhetorical and social-structural strategy that rationalized, justified, and ritualized the cultural and economic superiority of European communities over non-European peoples. White cultural superiority structured both the social systems and logics of economic exchange throughout the West, engendering ideologies and practices of racialized violence. The historical process by which white identity was created is important in grasping racial logics and racist systems that have disenfranchised people of color around the world.

For example, in the United States, whiteness was critically important to systems of slavery and Jim Crow/Jane Crow laws. The "white race" was invented to create a racially elite ruling social class that could oversee plantation economies (associated with slavery) in the eighteenth and nineteenth centuries. Central to the idea of whiteness is that it would be conferred upon all European working people in the United States. This conferral was important in order to mark all European citizens as biologically (naturally) superior to black and brown people in America such as black and Native

American groups. Interestingly, these racial categories were seen as natural and God-given to working-class whites although such logic went against their own interests, as they did not economically benefit from claims to cultural superiority that grounded plantation economies.

During Jim Crow, one can discern that whiteness in the United States possessed structural and spatial formations. Legal segregation created geographies of racism, in which racial categories spatially marked land and neighborhoods. Whiteness was used as a spatial and structural framework to control and contain black bodies within socially marked spaces.[4] Black bodies could not drink from the same water fountain as white bodies. Black people could not ride on the same train as white people. Black children could not attend the same schools as white children. Whiteness specified where black bodies could move and reside, demonstrating that whiteness was not simply ideological but *somatically* manifested itself in relation to black lives.

Christian religion has played a central role in the creation of whiteness. Historically, whiteness gains ideological and theological force through Christianity in the West. African American theologian Willie Jennings provides a generative account of *how Western Christian practices against black bodies first* presages the deep doctrinal and theological architecture that created and shaped early modern, missional hierarchal visions of different people, places, and societies. For instance, Jennings describes how the Portuguese pre-Enlightenment historian Zurara invokes a "scale of existence" with white bodies ranking at the highest end of the scale and black bodies ranking at the lowest end of the scale, leaving all other kinds of bodies placed between the white/black binary.[5] Zurara describes the aesthetic attributes of the African slaves being auctioned and sold during the North Atlantic slave trade. He writes that there are those "who are almost white—fair to look upon and well proportioned"; there are those who are "in between, like mulattos," and then there are those who are "black as Ethiopians, whose existence is deformed."[6] Eventually, these early descriptors began to mark darker, non-Christian bodies over and against white European Christian bodies. In fact, Jennings notes that in Zurara's historical accounts, Christian and black are contrasted with the former needing to overcome the latter.[7] Most importantly, this racial scale of existence grew in power and in service to Western expansion, domination, and exploitation into new non-Western lands and spaces.

However, this existence of scale is not the scientific taxonomies of racial hierarchy associated with modernity that relies on the notion of race as an essence. In contrast, this scale *is* theological because it refers to "seeing and touching multiple peoples and their lands at once and thinking them together" with an ecclesial and soteriological aim and end goal.[8] To put another way, this theological scale of value in relation to bodies *emerges from first touching, seeing, and encountering "othered bodies" and the land they resided on and then thinking these bodies together in relation to European bodies, with a soteriological end goal.* In other words, the trajectory of seeing, encountering, and touching black bodies inextricably gave rise to racialized ideas of Christian salvation as well as the form, content, and tone of Christian theology. As Western nations set out to colonize lands for economic reasons, missionary societies of Catholic and Protestant churches saw this as an opportunity to bring salvation to all "heathens" around the world.

Jennings forcefully argues that this "pre-Enlightenment" scale of existence established a new organizing reality for identities in which racial agency was a *theologically* articulated way of understanding European bodies "in relation to new spaces and new people in order to exert power over such people and spaces."[9] Before this scale of existence would contribute to a more modern scientific concept of race, this theological idea of race would offer a "distorted vision of creation that reduced theological anthropology to commodified bodies," ensuring that "people would forever carry their identities on their bodies."[10]

For Jennings, the problem with the historical trajectory of Western Christian theology then has been its insularity, which is marked by a theological imagination that has been in service to both European cultural superiority and the exchange logic of early capitalism. To use Jennings's words, Christian theology was forced and trapped "inside the intimacy of white existence,"[11] in which white existence was defined by the colonialist work of describing and subjugating non-European nations theologically, culturally, and politically. One cannot get underneath or grasp what has gone wrong with Western Christian tradition unless one turns to *this particular history of bodily practices*, investigating and deconstructing these historical moments and how these moments frame and legitimate Western Christian theology and its basic categories.

Historically, whiteness has had a kind of permanence, being interwoven into the DNA of Western societies such as the United States. Religions such as Christianity have been a central force in the creation and maintenance of whiteness as a system of structural power. Moreover, the colossal denials and silences surrounding white hegemony and white identity in relation to American racism are unsettling. Whiteness has structural power and has been the central regulating logic of racist, capitalist domination in the United States. One could argue that whiteness is a regulating ideology that drives globalization, as non-European communities are disproportionately affected by cultural and economic inequities and inequalities.

This brief historical narrative of whiteness enables one to see that to challenge and resist white racist structures, institutions, and practices means deconstructing and dismantling the ideological and institutional power of whiteness itself. Whiteness must be confronted and disassembled. When turning to our contemporary moment, one cannot fully interpret the intensification of racism or the preponderance of "reverse racism" that white populist movements claim to experience. Only through disclosing this history of whiteness can one see why white populist movements are merely a re-entrenchment of hegemonic logics used to put and keep blacks (and racially others) in their "place."

White populism redefined

In reviewing whiteness as a social and religio-structural force in America, white populism can be defined. Populism is often generally understood as the mobilization of a group of persons that feel their interests have been negated and violated by the ruling establishment.[12] It is argued that populist groups imagine themselves as "ordinary people" fighting established institutions that exclude them. I want to challenge this common understanding of populism. Populism is not merely about feelings of exclusion. Populists make the claim they represent "the people" alone—that their interests properly reflect the interests of the nation. As a result, populists *are always anti-pluralists*. It is an exclusionary form of identity politics that "the people" is single and homogeneous. Hence, political opponents are "enemies of the people" that must be converted or excluded altogether.[13]

White populism treats white interests and hegemony as the proper reflection of "the people," which leads to interpreting black interests not only as illegitimate but also as a threat to American national security and flourishing. In the United States, white populism emerged as early as the Reconstruction era in the United States in which southern whites felt that they were losing their ruling place within society due to the emancipation of African enslaved. White populist groups emerged in the South and North in order to protest against the American government, which was characterized as turning away from American national values (understood as white slave values). The federal government, in emancipating enslaved Africans, had also destroyed Southern plantation economies, which led white communities to feel as if their rights to economic self-determination had been taken from them.

Similar to this period, the dismantling of Jim Crow laws in the 1960s led to radical white populism. Many white southerners believed that the federal government abandoned American and biblical values when mandating integration of the "races." Radical white populism reemerged, appealing to biblical Christian values and national tradition as the guiding norms for maintaining segregation and black subordination. White communities genuinely felt like they had been socially and politically mistreated. It is important to remember that both Reconstruction and the dismantling of Jim Crow restructured the economy, allowing more African Americans to enter the Industrial Revolution which angered white communities who now felt they had to compete for jobs. Contemporary radical white populism can be more aptly interpreted as a re-entrenchment of past white nationalist ideology and hegemony, as such populist groups understand themselves as morally righteous and religiously justified through their appeal to biblical values and white nationalism (articulated as American patriotism).

As one can see, white populism has existed throughout American history. The current reemergence of radical white populism has been linked to the 2008 Recession and official election of President Barack Obama. In particular, the election of President Obama signaled to white populist groups that racism is a thing of the past. They articulate the election of a black man as proof that racial trauma and structural racism no longer exist. How can antiblack racism exist if an entire country elected a black man to the highest office of the land, as president? In fact, these groups argue that Obama's policies surrounding immigration, affirmative action, and health care prove that "reverse discrimination" against whites is now the new structural oppression. Working white communities also turn to the African American middle class as evidence that blacks are not economically marginalized and discriminated against. Are these legitimate claims? Are working-class white interests being rendered invisible? Or is radical white populism merely another instantiation of white hegemony that is linked to America's racist past?

The wages of whiteness in the era of Obama?

With the Obama presidency and the election of Trump, white rage has intensified, taking up residence in America's political spaces. White backlash to the Obama presidency has led to an articulation of whiteness as a category of oppression and marginalization. As a religious scholar, I am interested in investigating how white Christian religion has contributed to this radical white populist phenomenon. Has radical white populism led to the muting of white hegemony itself? Once Obama was elected to the office of President, white supremacy and institutional racism were seen as a "thing of the past." In fact, many white communities, particularly working-class communities, saw themselves as disenfranchised underneath the Obama administration. This feeling of disenfranchisement at the hands of people of color such as Mexican immigrants has fueled a white populist movement that sees its task as the renewing and reestablishment of American Christian values (read white Protestant values).

In the era of Obama, white populism has been costly in relation to the American democratic project of inclusion and equality. I think two areas in particular disclose how costly the wages of whiteness have been: (1) in how white populism has *racialized* economic problems and (2) in how Islam has been demonized as antithetical to American patriotism.

White populism *racializes* patterns of globalization and its material inequalities. For certain, working class and poor communities across racial affiliations have suffered from decades of economic restructuring. Sociologists speak about his restructuring as early as the 1960s. Black sociologists such as William Julius Wilson and Patricia Hill Collins capture the shifts in American political economy due to a movement from an industrial to postindustrial market. Because a postindustrial economy is a knowledge-based and technologically driven economy, the most qualified must have access to higher levels of education. Due to the modern industrial economy's transition from a producer to service economy in the 1970s, joblessness became a significant feature of poor racial communities and poor white communities. Not possessing the educational qualifications for a service-oriented economy, high school dropouts and high school graduates experienced a dwindling number of jobs with real earning potential. The postindustrial economy is characterized by greater demand for skilled labor and educated workers, which has led to a decline in the employment prospects for modestly educated and unskilled workers, who might be disproportionately black and Latino/a but affect unskilled workers across racial communities. Moreover, manufacturing jobs in the 1970s relocated, in which companies moved from urban areas in America to overseas locations. This shift in American political economy was part of a larger globalizing pattern that corporate elites and multinational corporations controlled.[14]

This shift in economy was adversely felt by white working-class communities (among other ethnic communities) and these communities held that their economic problems *were due to people of color* in the United States rather than corporate decision-making. White conservative voices encouraged working-class communities to interpret their perpetual material deprivation bound up with immigration of "third world" people to the United States as well as due to African Americans leeching off of the government. For instance, Mexican immigrants have been characterized as criminals and "illegal workers," taking jobs from white American citizens. One can discern that this argument imagines the American citizen through the logic of whiteness itself, characterizing all Mexican immigrants as illegal, dangerous, and unwanted. The problem with this conservative logic is that it ignores and/or dismisses how corporations relocated manufacturing jobs overseas in order to enlarge economic efficiency and profit.

Moreover, underneath Obama's administration, many white working-class communities interpreted Obama's modest economic recovery strategies as "socialist," a persistent conservative political belief that any social programs to help the poor is really about redistributing income and wealth from "hard working citizens" (read whites) to the underserving poor (being indolent people of color such as African Americans). As discussed, African Americans have been seen as noncitizens throughout the history of America. The impact of structural disparities on black people has not been seen by white conservative voices as due to legacies of racism. Instead, poor African Americans have been interpreted as moral failures because of their economic location. Consequently, as immigrants, African Americans are seen as responsible for the economic sufferings of white communities. Brought to fullest expression with the election of Donald Trump as president in November of 2016, these white communities interpret themselves as victims of reverse discrimination.

However, multinational companies and corporate elites have been responsible for widespread economic depression in this nation and around the world. The shift from an industrial economy to a postindustrial economy has been grounded in globalizing economic processes that have severely impoverished *all* American citizens and people of color around the world. For instance, the World Bank has established policy approaches based on free-market models that have economically devastated two-third worlds, which debunks the idea that "third world" workers are flourishing from American jobs. The World Bank and the International Monetary Fund's (IMF) policies have encouraged government deregulation, relaxed taxation, a reduction in public expenditure on welfare programs for the vulnerable (particularly women and children), and free trade, leading to the intensification of deprivation for many global communities. These policies have especially been implemented in crisis-ridden countries in the Global South such as Chile, Argentina, and post-Apartheid South Africa. Also known as "structural adjustment programs," these policies were mandated for countries who desired to secure loans through the World Bank and IMF. But these policies have been disastrous for these countries.[15]

These countries of the Global South have experienced intense poverty in the wake of globalizing process. For example, the gap between the rich and poor in these "developing" countries widened with the dismantling of welfare provisions. Poor women have also been disproportionately affected by globalizing processes as they constitute a large number of workers who remain chronically poor due to unethical corporate structures such as sweatshops. The American exploitation associated with North American Free Trade Agreement (NAFTA) is another example of why an influx of Mexican immigrants is due to American imperialist economics. Most Mexican farmers provided their local communities with corn crops. With the creation of NAFTA in 1994, multinational corporations moved into Mexico and crushed local farmers and businesses, contributing to chronic unemployment among farmers who had once provided communities with basic staple crops. In response to this economic recession, Mexican farmers and families began immigrating in record numbers seeking employment. Conservative white voices do not capture how American corporations have been responsible for economic problems American citizens experience. This history is concealed, which has fostered a white populist movement that continues to hold people of color as responsible for their material deprivation. As a result, white working-class communities' support of Trump is not shocking in the 2016 presidential campaign because Trump was simply tapping into the xenophobic, racist worldview associated with white populism.

Another cost associated with white populism has been its outright demonization of American Muslims. White populism argues that they experience cultural and religious oppression through Islamic violence. White voices often express themselves as under religious danger and even persecution by religious and ethnic minorities such as Muslims. It is important to note that the 9/11 attacks were interpreted as due to Islam rather than religious extremism. The Islamic religion after this national tragedy created an "us versus them" logic in which the patriotic responsibility was to punish and/or rid American society of "them," that is, Muslims. Islamic religion was characterized as desiring to religiously, culturally, and economically defeat Western countries such as the United States. The Patriot Act is one example of how unjust policy was used to racially and religiously target Arabs who were Muslims. On October 26, 2001, George Bush signed into law the Patriot Act, which was a law thought to be "appropriate" and "justified" in intercepting and obstructing terrorism. However, this act often led to warrantless, suspicious surveillances of religious and ethnic minorities such as American Arabs and other Middle Eastern Islamic communities. As a result, the 9/11 attacks in the United States intensified and even justified widespread beliefs that the Muslim world was an anathema to an American way of life, leading to rationalization and ritualization of structural racism and religious discrimination toward American Muslims.[16]

Interestingly, the religious and ethnic discrimination that white populism supports is wedded to whiteness itself, which articulates itself as simply wanting to return to the primacy of "Christian values." For radical white populism, America is a Christian nation, which precludes other religious traditions such as Islam from having any real influence in the public square. Such conservative voices link American identity to the narrative of a past Christian purity. This past Christian purity is seen as what has made America innocent and "great." America is innocent in the sense that it has "trusted God" to establish democracy and market freedoms in order to promote flourishing for all people, being a global beacon of hope. America is great in the sense that its economic empire is due to God granting favor to the United States due to its allegiance to biblical ideas at its founding. To leave this past Christian purity would produce moral and economic devastation for the country. In order to avoid this apocalyptic possibility, radical white populism invokes a return to Christian values so that America might maintain its moral and economic standing in the world.

But the Christian purity of America has always been a fiction. America's philosophy of "manifest destiny" established this nation as an economic superpower. America did not accrue economic wealth through living into democratic ideals of equality and justice. Rather, America established national wealth and power through the disenfranchisement and conquest of lands and peoples. The conquest of Native American lands and genocide of this land's people created the groundwork for the geographical assets of early colonial America. The forced enslavement of millions of Africans provided the free labor upon which America profited. The exploitation of Asian and Latino immigrant labor enabled America to economically rise. In other words, America's unlikely story of its emergence as a super power is tethered to colonization, conquest, genocide, and the dispossession and exploitation of people of color around the world. Radical white populism ignores and dismisses these alternative histories of America.

Combating a white populist imagination

How might black religious resources challenge a white populist imagination that articulates white as the "new black?" As discussed earlier in this chapter, white populists are essentially anti-pluralists. They do not believe that issues of racial or economic justice among ethnic communities are proper American interests. Instead, these interests are dangerous and threatening to the stability of America. They do not interpret these interests as part of "we the people." However, black leaders and thinkers have always advocated for the plural interests of the nation, particularly the interests of those marginalized and oppressed by white hegemony. Centering these plural interests were at the heart of American democracy for black thinkers and leaders. I want to briefly focus the rest of this chapter on two major leaders and thinkers: Maria Stewart and Frederick Douglass. These two leaders are illustrative examples of how American communities might combat this white populist imagination.

Maria Stewart should be interpreted as challenging the white populism of her day. An African American domestic servant who became an orator, teacher, and writer, Maria Stewart publicly offered a critique of white populist ideology. Being the first woman to speak to a "promiscuous" audience (audience of men and women), Stewart offered speeches supporting the abolition of slavery *and* women's rights. Having written two pamphlets on abolition and black autonomy, Stewart railed against how the abolition of slavery was seen as the rhetoric of troublemakers who were insistent on the breakdown of "law and order." Stewart used biblical themes such as the Exodus motif in order to highlight and challenge the contradictions of America understanding itself as the land of freedom and equality. Similar to the Exodus narrative, God is a God of the Oppressed who will deliver an oppressed people from under the demonic heel of white supremacy. This theme was often articulated in the meditations she wrote for publication.[17]

Stewart's public speaking career did not last long. It lasted for about three years due to her challenging white supremacy/white populism in America. Moreover, she makes a connection between white supremacy/white populism and black patriarchy. She decries how black women and girls are kept domesticated in kitchens, unable to fulfill their potential as black persons and women. Stewart's career ended when she publicly stated that black men "lacked the ambition and requisite courage" to address the oppressive realities of black women.[18] She demanded equal rights for African American women, and this highly contentious perspective led to her early retirement from public life. I think it is important to note however that Stewart understood how the white imagination worked: in ways that sponsored racial and gendered forms of oppression, even affecting black communities. She wanted to note these intersections, contending that the freedom and liberties of black women were bound up in racial *and* gender justice and parity.

What also marks Stewart's work is her vehement critique of northern racism in America. White populism in the nineteenth century was seen as an uneducated Southern thing. Racial apartheid and slavery were seen as pathologies of the South. However, during the nineteenth century, Stewart directly attached how white Northerners articulated their "interests" as objective and unlike the South. Stewart responded that the Northerners' practice of capitalism in the North, which relegated blacks to a form of economic neo-slavery and exploitation, was as insidious as the South's plantation economies and structures. While Northerners were planning meetings against the South, Stewart blew open the white racial ideology at work in the North, a white northern racial ideology which attempted to cover up forms of racist practice through speaking of capitalist interests and "progress." She reminded her readers or listeners that white racial ideology and the populism that resulted involved analyzing how racism, sexism, and capitalism intersected in structuring the economic life chances of blacks.

Similarly, during and after the Civil War, Frederick Douglass combats an insidious white populism that sees the African enslaved as responsible for an unjust war and the destruction of a moral way of life. For white plantation owners, free slave labor was the bedrock of their economic flourishing and cultural way of life. For America's slave society, this cultural way of life was both moral and theologically permissible. Churches supported the fight by white plantation owners and northern whites to uphold the dignity and sanctity of their cultural way of life, which held whites as ontologically superior to blacks. Douglass constantly critiques this white racial ideology as categorically false, demonstrating how this ideology was connected to the preservation of modes of economic production that secured wealth for whites.

Douglass exposes how white populist ideology was *false* ideology, being disconnected from and dishonest about the human sufferings of blacks. Douglass berates white Christian churches for professing love for God while intentionally ignoring love's requirements: the practice of empathy, care, compassion, and justice for one's neighbor, particularly the African enslaved neighbor, which meant ending slavery. How could Christian love and slavery coexist? Douglass recounts how one of his masters, Master Thomas, would justify his "bloody deeds" through quoting scripture.[19] In fact, white Christian churches that used religious sanction for their racist cruelty underwrote the inhumane practices of slaveholders. Christian religion was used to support cycles of violence within slavery. Douglass knew that white populist ideology *was a re-entrenchment of white supremacy rather than an objective articulation of white interests.*

In fact, Douglass was clear that there was a difference between "slaveholding religion" and the "Christianity of Christ." He argues that one must choose a side. He states "that to receive one [Christianity of Christ] as good, pure, and holy, is of necessity to reject the other as bad, corrupt, and wicked. To be the friend of the one, is of necessity to be the enemy of the other."[20] Slaveholding religion claiming to be Christianity was "the boldest of all frauds, and the grossest of all libels."[21] Douglass concludes his *Narrative* by describing slaveholding religion's horrible inconsistencies and contradictions when calling itself "Christian." He notes that white men who beat slaves within an inch of their life claim to be meek and lowly like Jesus. The white man who would rob Douglass of his earnings at the end of the week would be his Bible study class leader on Sunday morning. The white slaveholder who sells black women into prostitution piously stands up and promotes purity for women. White ministers who preach about injunctions to read the Bible do not allow slaves to read or write. White slaveholders and clergy who maintain the religious and moral importance of marriage deny this sacred right to millions of blacks who are enslaved. White men who sold and built churches also sold black slave babies to missionize abroad to heathen nations.[22] Yet, these same white men would argue that the dismantling of slavery was a violation of state's rights and an abrogation of their individual right to economic self-determination.

Douglass discloses that white populism is dangerous because it cloaks white supremacy and domination in the language of "white interests" and "reverse discrimination."

These are illustrative examples of how black religious leaders have challenged white populist ideology. Although I can only gesture in this direction, there are contemporary examples of how black religious leaders and social movements are responding to the organizing category and practice of whiteness and white populism in America. For instance, Black Lives Matter (BLM) is a movement that exposes and combats how whiteness as a structural program of violence against black bodies shows up in American institutions such as law enforcement (police brutality of black bodies). Although BLM did not emerge from black churches, a number of black churches continue to collaborate, march with, and support the methods and message of BLM. While BLM emerged in relation to numerous police killings such as Trayvon Martin, Mike Brown, Renisha McBride, Sandra Bland, Eric Garner, and countless others, this movement also articulates broader demands for America's racist institutions such as education and employment, which treat black lives as disposable. BLM is a movement that desires to defy, disrupt, and dismantle whiteness and white populism in America. As a result, BLM's goal is to show the persistence of structural racism in this country and how it shapes the maltreatment of black lives. BLM remains a critical movement to disrupting and ending whiteness and its multiple manifestations.

Conclusion

This chapter has investigated the reemergence of white populism in America. This chapter offered a brief historical overview of whiteness, redefined what white populism is, investigated the social and political costs incurred by a white populist imagination, and concluded by asking how black religious leaders and thinkers might challenge a white populist agenda. White populism certainly began to intensify with the election of Obama but it remains to be seen the ways in which it will take further hold in the new age of Trump.

In the Wake of Obama's Hope: Thoughts on Black Lives Matter, Moralism, and Re-imaging Race Struggle

Anthony B. Pinn

During the "age of Obama"[1] emerged a mode of praxis we have come to call the Black Lives Matter (BLM) movement. While it has received both popular and academic attention, in terms of its origin and consequences, in these pages, I want to explore briefly the nature of its challenge to public strategies and to the ideology framing of some earlier modalities of protest. That is to say, it, BLM, jettisons public endorsement of traditional religious sensibilities, mid-twentieth-century protest paradigms, and a naive narrative of American progress. And, instead, it reflects a more humanistic ethic framed in terms of a race-conscious moralism.[2]

In making this argument, I am not suggesting all participants or even all those who have a prominent profile within BLM activities identify as humanists or atheists. Rather, what I have in mind is the general ethos, the manner in which BLM tends toward a bracketing of religious faith and its accompanying theological commitments so as to avoid any narrowing of public activities or the underlying epistemological sensibilities for such activism.[3] And, in this manner, it privileges a non-religion-determined public arena, guided in large measure by the workings of logic and reason, without assumptions of a theological framed sense of morality. In fact, much of the constitution and ideological platform of BLM runs contrary to the general theological thinking of the Christian tradition some of the participants claim and that is typically associated with the form and content of civil rights praxis. With respect to moralism, I am not suggesting BLM reflects a debilitating sense of the tragic, nor a nihilistic posture toward social conditions. No, to the contrary, by BLM's moralism I mean to isolate its sharp and biting critique of national hypocrisy and inconsistency grounded in a sense of the tenacious nature of disregard. Finally, to historically and intellectually frame and situate this new mode of engagement—BLM—I turn to Du Bois's dualistic epistemology of race outlined in *Souls of Black Folk*.[4] Simply put, Obama, channeling social gospel–influenced civil rights approaches, concerned himself with the "Negro problem" about which Du Bois says the following: "Herein lie buried many things which if read with patience may show the strange meaning of being black here in the dawning of the Twentieth Century. This meaning is not without interest to you, Gentle Reader; for the problem of the Twentieth Century is the problem of the color-line."[5] Through this conceptualization, this theory of racial *othering*, Du Bois opens a conversation concerning the challenge of "incorporating" into the life of the nation the recently freed and their descents—a population distinct by its tangled relationship to the United States as both embedded in its history and despised for their disruptive presence. Enriching signs of belonging have been approached through faltering economic, educational, political, and social transfigurations: efforts to address material well-being bumped against a deeply embedded racial metaphysics; yet, as the civil rights movement and Obama's rhetoric suggest, failure to transform circumstances doesn't justify assumptions that such mechanisms ultimately can't work if undertaken in sincerity and with great effort.

This dilemma, the Negro problem, constitutes only one half of the larger epistemological platform rehearsed in *Souls*. The other half involves the African American on a metaphysical level: "They," Du Bois reflects, "approach me in a half-hesitant sort of way, eye me curiously or compassionately, and then, instead of saying directly, how does it feel to be a problem, they say, I know an excellent colored man in my town; or, I fought at Mechanicsville; or, Do not these Southern outrages make your blood boil? . . . To the real question, how does it feel to be a problem? I answer seldom a word."[6] *How does it feel to be a problem?* This question is the challenge of ontological disregard, of epistemological irrelevance, which makes possible the unrepented material and political brutalizing of African Americans. This is the manner in which black life is over determined and reified—reduced to an inconvenience. Du Bois seldom responded to this question, in part because it is seldom asked explicitly, although its impact is felt perpetually. BLM, however, has forced a surfacing of and confrontation with this query to the discomfort of conservatives and liberals alike.[7]

Obama and the failed attack on racial disregard

A well-educated and socially "acceptable" black man occupying the White House twice provides the contemporary setting for the new and technologically advanced[8] hyper visibility of black embodied humanity destroyed in compliance with the rule of white supremacy.[9] Or, as journalist Wesley Lowery reflected, "any façade of a postracial reality was soon melted away amid the all-consuming eight-year flame of racial reckoning that Barack Obama's election sparked. . . . As President Obama's second term toiled on, it became increasingly clear that talk of a postracial America was no more than cheap political punditry." Furthermore, he continues, "A new generation of black Americans were, if anything, as emboldened by our black president as they were unsurprised by the failure of his election to usher in a fantasy period of racial healing."[10] Such statements reflect the context of his presidency, which is Obama's campaigning on a rather simple, but compelling promise. He would serve as a catalyst for change by helping citizens realize and act on shared concerns and values. And, he understood his election as a successful litmus test of American possibility and democratic vision. "If there is anyone out there who still doubts that America is a place where all things are possible," he proclaimed during his acceptance speech on November 4, 2008: "who still wonders if the dream of our founders is alive in our time; who still questions the power of our democracy, tonight is your answer."[11]

Perhaps his most explicit framing of race and racism as part of the American legacy is to be found in his "A More Perfect Union" speech given in 2008 as a way to clarify his relationship to his former black theology influenced pastor, Rev. Jeremiah Wright. In it then senator Obama recognized the manner in which founding documents establishing the United States are "stained by this nation's original sin of slavery." Therefore, advancing the nation toward its better possibilities has required traditions of public protest, by means of which "Americans in successive generations . . . were willing to do their part—through protests and struggle, on the streets and in the courts, through a civil war and civil disobedience and always at great risk—to narrow that gap between the promise of our ideals and the reality of their time." He understood his campaign and eventual election(s) as the productive continuation of that tradition of effort.[12] Obama did not "disown" him, but rather distanced himself from Wright's vision-critique of the United States. He acknowledged racial inequality, but instead tamed the angry over injustice by de-racializing social pain and making it a more general American response that speaks to all suffering. In the face of such anger, he says, "I have asserted a firm conviction—a conviction rooted in my faith in God and my faith in the American people—that working together we can move beyond some of our old racial wounds, and that in fact we have no choice if we are to continue on the path of a more perfect union."[13] His second inaugural address maintained his commitment to "the promise of our democracy."[14] One might say Obama offered a new way of mapping life, one that privileged shared territory as opposed to the much more rugged and outlaying areas of exclusion and radical marginalization.[15]

Obama's claim to be concerned with change, with the advancement of the country, had to be played out in more than the political arena.[16] It also had to be true in terms of cultural vision, one giving rise in some quarters to a growing illusion of colorblindness and a sense of social debt paid in full—funneled through a narrative of American grit and hard work winning the day despite a national legacy of racial inequality: *a black president, who would serve two terms in office—and without a major scandal!* A prime example of this approach is neatly presented in Obama's 2013 speech at Morehouse College, in which is found the following: "Success may not come quickly or easily. But if you strive to do what's right, if you work harder and dream bigger, if you set an example in our own lives and do your part to help meet the challenges of our time, then I'm confident that, together, we will continue the never-ending task of perfecting our union."[17] He rests this confidence in a sense of respectability, a measure of "ownership" over the problems faced by African Americans, in accordance with the American narrative of self-help and brave determination: "It means taking full responsibility for our own lives—by demanding more from our fathers, and spending more time without children, and reading to them, and teaching them that while they may face challenges and discrimination in their own lives, they must never succumb to despair or cynicism; they must always believe that they can write their own destiny."[18] Again, the Negro problem so conceived is rectified through educational advancement, economic opportunity and community investment, and civil rights legislation opening access.[19]

Obama's adherence to a naive assumption concerning the mechanics of democracy and his allegiance to a racial "uplift," respectability politics ultimately failed to produce outcomes expected by many of his supporters. Regarding respectability politics, "young activist on the front lines today," writes Wesley Lowery, "refuse to poll-test their martyrs, a practice they see as yet another bastion of respectability politics. Insisting that the burden of proof rests with the body of the slain black man or woman is to argue that black life, on its own, does not matter."[20] It is not that the "age of Obama" didn't entail attention to failure, or to racial injustice. It did, as an early quotation in this chapter makes clear. However, the finger was pointed more often at victims of racial disregard, while the fundamental health of the democratic experiment was assumed. More to the point, according to Keeanga-Yamahtta Taylor, "while it may be surprising that a Black protest movement has emerged during the Obama presidency, the reluctance of his administration to address any of the substantive issues facing Black communities has meant that suffering has worsened in those communities over the course of Obama's term of office."[21] His is a political strategy that assumes a particular moral sensibility without recognizing just how *deeply* (and permanently) American moral values are stained by a long history of irrational racial hatred and white privilege. Furthermore, this privilege is a framing of life much of the nation wants to maintain at any cost. For Obama, the capacity of the United States for transformation is significant and this isn't fundamentally altered by its misdeeds because all developments are filtered through the American narrative expanded to include blacks into that specialness.[22] Yet, for others, the "age of Obama" may have "opened with profound hope," but "it ends with utter fear."[23]

We are living a legacy of racial violence operated by means of both crud and sophisticated technologies of disregard. Difference, in this case racial difference, is understood as a problem—a virus of sorts that must be controlled if not wiped out. The terror involved in this process of control isn't simply the threat of death, but the inability to anticipate what will trigger violent response to embodied, gendered blackness. Even compliance can be deadly, and docile bodies aren't safe from further abuse. Any sign of struggle—even for one's breath—can be understood as a threat to the safety of law enforcement and, as was the case for Eric Garner, can result in death. The jail cell as a place of confinement can also be a death chamber, as Sandra Bland's demise makes clear.[24]

Black Lives Matter

What started as a hashtag (#BlackLivesMatter), forged by black women in response to the systemic destruction of black life through state-sanctioned violence, grew into a web of organizations committed to the advance of the marginalized. Sparked to some degree by the killing of Trayvon Martin (2012), BLM—within popular imagination—is associated more deeply with the murder of Michael Brown (2013), in Ferguson, Missouri. Alicia Garza wrote an open letter sparked by these killings, and ended with the now famous (or infamous?) phrase: "black lives matter." Patrisse Cullors's response to the post resulted in a moral pronouncement linguistically and ideologically framing a movement.[25] There is irreverence lodged in BLM's battle cry—"this ain't your grand-mamma's civil rights movement." Shadowing it is a Sisyphusian hermeneutic: Collective vision for so long blurred by a haze of rights nostalgia is confronted now in graphic ways by a disturbing fact. There are no decipherable ground rules for survival if one happens to live in black flesh. "This land is your land; this land is my land," is a statement of hope, a wish, not a fact. As one activist has been reported to say, "why vote? Having a black president didn't keep the police from killing Mike Brown."[26]

Yet, as some have cautioned, BLM isn't simply about the killing of African Americans, nor is it a total rejection of civil rights movement strategies and sensibilities. No, it's a praxis-framed refinement in light of the current cultural "mood" and political setting; it pushes for a deeper interrogation of the strategies of exclusion and dehumanization that authorize violence and that desensitizes citizens to the murder of African Americans as anything other than justified. That is to say, as Garza phrases it, "what we are lifting up here is that we need a bigger vision than just Band-Aid reforms—we need to move toward a transformative vision that touches on what's at the root of the problems we are facing." Hence, rather than simply convicting police officers, attention must be given to state violence, and the systems of thought authorizing and supporting said violence.[27] I would suggest, BLM, on a fundamental level, challenges, through the public presentation of bodies, the metaphysical assumptions articulated through white supremacy that sanction aggressive racial disregard. As political scientist Frederick Harris has pointed out, the mid-twentieth-century movement for rights—the ideological and programmatic basis for much of Obama's thinking—addressed the physical and institutional markers of inequality. Yet, it failed to wrestle with and call popular attention to the undergirding ontological considerations and warping of thought that informed the very reason why black bodies were devalued and dehumanized.[28] BLM, however, operates on the assumption that attention to structural change is irrelevant without addressing the underlying justifications for the dehumanization of blacks.[29] Garza makes the points this way, "when [Opal Tometi, Patrisse Cullors and I] created Black Lives Matter, it absolutely was about: how do we live in a world that dehumanizes us and still be human? The fight is not just being able to keep breathing. The fight is actually to be able to walk down the street with your head held high—and feel like I belong here, or I deserve to be here, or I just have right to have a level of dignity."[30] This is not *Imago Dei* thinking in any way, although so many BLM participants are committed Christians. Rather, in a general sense, this turn to ontology is premised on historical and material markers of meaning. This is not to suggest the civil rights movement didn't pose an ontological challenge, it did. However, the difference is this: BLM is aware of the centrality of this ontological work—and I would argue has been more intentional regarding it—whereas the civil rights movement posed this sort of opposition as a secondary force. In a word, BLM's challenge(s) to the safeguards of whiteness take place responsive to a layered and dynamic arrangement of the status quo.[31]

BLM uses discourse and embodied engagement to cause disruption of ontological-epistemological assumptions. As the founders—Alicia Garza, Patrisse Cullors, and Opal Tometi—agree, "Black Lives Matter is an ideological and political intervention in a world where Black lives are systematically and intentionally targeted for demise. It is an affirmation of Black folks' contributions to this society, our humanity, and our resilience in the face of deadly oppression."[32] The sense of those at risk who must be safeguarded expands beyond the sense of humanity couched in the civil rights movement in that, according to Alicia Garza, "Black Lives Mater affirms the lives of Black Queer and trans folks, disabled folks, Black undocumented folks, folks with records, women and all Black lives along the gender spectrum. It centers those that have been marginalized within Black liberation movements."[33]

The civil rights movement and the work of Obama attempted greater access to resource and space. And, BLM not only seeks this access but also pushes deeper and urges an interrogation of the structuring of thought regarding subjectivity under girding, informing, and authorizing public behavior and access. While BLM has recently promoted a policy platform and some of the key figures have thought about "infrastructure for the long haul,"[34] its greatest impact involves this second challenge to modes of thought. Perhaps it is for this reason, Opal Tometi referred to BLM as "an affirmation for our people. It's a love note for our people, but it's also a demand."[35] In other words, BLM on a conceptual level disrupts normative discourse of whiteness by exposing the manner in which this discourse constitutes death. The goal involves more liberative framings of subjectivity, and from this new ontology might come sustained effort to foster space for robust and complex humanity. I argue this point is what Glenn Mackin highlights when arguing, "Black Lives Matter activists do not interrupt the racial inequalities that structure US society. They dramatize and contest them in ways that involve a coherent counterworld . . . Black Lives Matter activists do not just raise validity claims that can be subject to debate. They also expose and challenge dominant patterns of perception and interpretation."[36]

The very naming of BLM creates a social dissonance that surfaces the typically hidden structuring of racial disregard as "natural." And, rather than doing this through an appeal to theological knowledge and religious claims, it does this through the performance and rhetoric of expansive humanity "naturally" occupying time and space, and in so doing the dynamics of whiteness are exposed to view. Put differently, the codes determining the cultural climate are exposed, and in the exposing they are opened to reconfiguration based on an alternate sense of the look and presence of the subject.

The civil rights movement of the mid-century fostered dissonance for white Americans, but along these lines: Must I share my "stuff" with black-others? Are they entitled to the trappings of life I take for granted as belonging solely to those like me? BLM fosters dissonance on a more fundamental level, rendered along these lines: are these black-others human as I am human? Have I in my whiteness been wrong about them in their blackness? Does their blackness matter in a positive way? In both cases—civil rights and BLM—white supremacy is contested. But, with regard to the former, the material and political trappings of public life is the target of struggle. To reiterate an important point, for BLM, protest involves first an interrogation of the circumstances, logics, and technologies that construct the human and that under gird and make possible the material and political trappings of life. Second, it is about policy and programming.

BLM, over against the tendency of even more progressive religious organizations, has no desire to view transformation through an assumption history is teleological in nature and moving toward justice. Instead, BLM assumes a more humanistic alternative whereby inconvenient (for the status quo) presentation of black bodies in time and space provides a better means of asserting worth and value.[37] Furthermore, the more egalitarian approach of BLM, what has been referenced as "a horizontal ethic of organizing, which favors democratic inclusion at the grassroots level,"[38] opens and urges a greater sense of accountability and responsibility. There are no special skills, no divine calling serving as a litmus test for taking a stand and absorbing the risk of involvement. There is something more organic and synergistic about this de-centralizing of leadership. Of course, this is not to say there aren't key spokespersons highlighted by media, but this is not the same as saying the directives for engagement are centralized. More liberty with respect to approach is afforded as BLM moves away from civil rights top-down approach.[39] In other words, "I don't think," states Cathy Cohen, "we have often seen movements say that the common thread of blackness is not just the male body, or the presumed cis male body, but in fact that cis and trans black women can represent the intersectional positionality and oppression that black communities face."[40] This is both a hermeneutical and ethical transformation, which, based on diversity of the movement and its agendas points to the tangled nature of struggle and also allows for a more realistic depiction of outcomes. Reflecting a critique of the tendency to masculinize black protest highlighted by Hazel Carby, BLM urges awareness of the attack on black humanity without gender and sexuality boundaries in that blackness coded to all modes of gender and sexuality is despised and threatened with physical and/or social death.[41]

While, as many have noted, the involvement of women from various social locations isn't new to social struggle, the public leadership and centrality of these women in the re-imaging of black life is a noteworthy shift. That is to say, the civil rights movement, for instance, fought for racial justice while holding to, in significant ways, the social assumptions regarding gender and sexuality. With BLM, however, these social assumptions are interrogated and denied through the centrality of queer black women and men. In addition, BLM inclusion of black women and LBGTQ members of African American communities doesn't meet internally as strongly with theological objections in that church teachings, for instance, aren't allowed to trump an appreciation for the diversity of African American communities and the integrity of difference.[42] Even for those who maintain theistic conceptual maps, antiquated notions of sin and righteousness don't enter into conversation. Put another way, the idea that black lives matter to God as a theodical consideration is worked out, to some degree, in the civil rights movement's Christian dimension and platform. Yet, BLM is asking a different and more humanistic question: can black lives matter to and in US society?[43]

BLM's rejection of religious leadership isn't simply a matter of organizational preference. It is also an indictment of assumption and framing that offers an ungrounded depiction of meaning premised on an assumption of human value forged beyond the reach of history. For BLM there is no adequate response to the theodicy question; the theological wishes expressed by many fail to highlight the depth of disregard marking the historical moment and instead seek resolution either as future restitution or divine intervention in the social dynamics of belief beyond the abilities of humans. In the words of Obama and every other modern president, "God bless America!"

If one thinks in terms of the 'mood' of social struggle in the mid-twentieth century, civil rights activism was popularly framed by dream or nightmare—both articulated using a theological vocabulary and grammar.[44] BLM frames lucidity, or awareness, that is at least agnostic toward theological utterance. Over against either dreams or nightmares, BLM rhetorically and programmatically encourages the US citizenry to "stay woke."

While the civil rights movement and Obama, as its contemporary advocate, have an affective response to suffering-struggle akin to melancholy, BLM might be said to involve a performance of mourning. But this is mourning understood along the lines of what David McIvor posits when saying, mourning is constituted by "recognition and repair" rather than the effort to get over circumstance.[45] There is something perpetual about mourning, which takes away from it negative connotations and associations, and which highlights the strength and persistence of strategies of disregard that stem from white supremacy and that inform and effect public and private life. Under girding this mourning, I would suggest, is recognition that current circumstances aren't an aberration, a misstep, but the very framing of "American exceptionalism."

Situating Black Lives Matter

The attempt to understand BLM through a traditional platform of theologized racial transformation fails to capture its viewpoint, values, and organizational strategies. One might think about this along the lines suggested by Harvey Young, when writing, "if Barack Obama rode a wave of hope ('Yes We Can') to the White House in 2008, then the closing of the 'Age of Obama' might mark a return to skepticism. Antiblack racial violence and racism still exist."[46] I would agree with Young's push against the radical optimism of the Obama sensibility (borrowed from the civil rights movement and the social gospel), but rather than skepticism, I would suggest that the "closing of the 'Age of Obama'" is marked by the moralist stance I have suggested at numerous points in this chapter. Moralism here understood in the (W. E. B.) Du Boisian articulation of a strong critique of inconsistency and hypocrisy in social life, coupled with an ethical framing.[47]

As Du Bois used the written word to outline the nature of the absurdity we encounter as we approach the world, BLM uses tweets, posts, and blogs. In both cases, the work points out the link between racial anthropology and epidemiology—of difference as *disease*. The result for humanity, in this case African Americans, is not a sense of original sin along the lines of what Saint Augustine lamented and what every good Christian is to struggle against, but rather a warping of their being, a twisting of their meaning, and a manipulation of their inner ideal—what Du Bois hauntingly calls "tragic soul-life."[48] There are in this situation all the markings of a pervasive evil. The distinction between mid-twentieth-century racial activism (and Obama's extension of it) and BLM is premised on awareness of the tenacity and tendencies of white supremacy as a pervasive evil.[49]

The Negro problem could be addressed to the extent it entailed socioeconomic and political arrangements in line with modern white supremacy. Doing so was only a matter of discovering and applying the most appropriate tools that rejected the assumption blacks must be content in their inferior role or that blacks eventually face total elimination; either way, whites will remain the dominant force in the world.[50] Against the view defined by the Negro problem, the Negro *as a* problem sees the world in a way not resolved through inclusion nor is it resolved through the promises of faith within an ethos of degeneration. The "Negro as problem" probes into the world, and a fuller range of experience in the world, and comes to recognize that "the self is a battleground"—one, as BLM notes, surrounded by sanctioned death.[51]

In this sense, as Susan Mizruchi notes, death and blacks "have become synonymous in white minds."[52] Projection of blacks as death produced a type of sociocultural necrophobia, played out in various forms of disregards—as it must extreme the effort to control death through death—Martin, Brown, and others.[53] Kristin Hunter Lattany argues this isn't a superficial flaw, but rather killing and death are intrinsic to the logic of the nation. "We see," writes Lattany, "that America is not a glamour queen but a grisly skeleton, her only produce death . . . her only lessons how to kill and how to die."[54] What Neil Small says concerning the discussion of death within scholarship and as differentiated over time in the West is applicable here: "Death is the apotheosis of this grand dream of control and of the belief in the power of the ordered."[55] It is an odd arrangement: African Americans are projected as death within a context fighting to keep death at bay; and, participation in American life in any substantive way requires African Americans to participate in this troubling of the death they are projected as constituting.

BLM differs from Obama's stance in that for BLM experience of the world trumps surrender of certain categories of encounter in order to safeguard the possibility of happiness. It exposes the limitation of liberal, theological-political agendas.[56] There is no sure resolution, but effort must be made regardless. Obama hopes, but BLM raises a question that opens to moralist analysis: "Is such a hope justified"?

Whereas the national narrative seeks to deny tragedy, BLM points out the persistent of suffering—in fact making suffering synonymous with the cultural climate of the historical moment. BLM observes and notes the disregard, the danger, the violence, and the silence of the world in response to the demands for change. A theodical formulation of collective life that advantages whiteness as divine is replaced thereby with an anthropodicy of fragility.

BLM recognizes the absurdity of the African American's encounter with the world, a world defined by racial disregard and mechanisms for the creation of the African American as inferior. It is a world without comfort, but a world in which African Americans—through their dogged strength holding together warring ideals—revolt. That is to say, BLM, pulling the best of Du Bois into the twenty-first century, entails a lucid depiction of the world and the inability to develop strategies that ultimately change the dynamics of the world. BLM, then, recognizes the silence of the world, and Du Bois frames this in terms of the question—the question of questions—that the white world doesn't ask and, to which Du Bois has no answer. And so, the Negro *as* problem highlights the misery, or the tragic quality of life. Or, as Du Bois reflects early in *Souls*, "while sociologists gleefully count his bastards and his prostitutes, the very soul of the toiling, sweating black man is darkened by the shadow of a vast despair . . . a sickening despair that would disarm and discourage any nation save that black host to whom 'discouragement' is an unwritten world."[57] Again, the response of BLM to this situation outlined so long ago by Du Bois entails, I suggest, a stance containing sensibilities one might associate probing, pointing out hypocrisy, and critiquing the presence of disregard.

Like the moralists, BLM's diagnosis urges confrontation with beliefs—in this case the ability of the United States to address adequately its history of disregard. It pushes against comforting assumptions by highlighting and forcing viewers and participants to view human suffering without the affective and intellectual safeguard of linguistically or programmatically "flinching" and "blinking," so to speak.[58] This confrontation with suffering as intrinsic to the cultural climate encasing our approach to the world is embodied. There is no retreat from this predicament—no guaranteed solace that will ultimately take away this silence and offer in its stead comfort. The civil rights movement and advocates such as Obama long for a source of appeal, for some meaning safeguard by a cosmic force. For BLM life is drowned in suffering.[59]

In a sense, the goal is to confront the world and not be permanently bent by the weight of its silence regarding the destruction of black life. Those rendered epistemologically, when not physically, dead—and who are treated as if they are *the* ontology of death—fight. What keeps BLM going, to some extent I would suggest, is perhaps what moralism intends with an appeal to "lucidity"[60]—recognition, awareness, of circumstances as they are, and from that vantage point, think, "move," and "do."

Deporter-in-Chief: Why Reject Christian Hospitality?

Miguel A. De La Torre

When Donald Trump announced his candidacy for the presidency, he unapologetically used nativist fear to garner votes: "When Mexico sends its people, they're not sending their best. They're not sending you. They're not sending you. They're sending people that have lots of problems, and they're bringing those problems with us. They're bringing drugs. They're bringing crime. They're rapists. And some, I assume, are good people."[1]

In the presence of outright bigotry and ethnic discrimination, it is easy to forget the consequences of eight years of Obama's immigration policies and how the Latinx community has viewed his administration. In comparison to the Trump administration, the Obama administration may appear more hospitable, more benign; nonetheless, the immigration policies of his eight years in office were as damning to Latinxs as what four or eight years of a Trump presidency promises to be. And while many accomplishments exist for celebrating during the Obama years, specifically in the midst of a Trump whitelash, Obama's immigration policies have been devastating to migrants south of the border, so devastating that in 2014, Janet Murguía, president of the National Council of La Raza (a prominent Latinx advocacy group), labeled the president the "deporter-in-chief."[2]

During Obama's first term, immigration advocates consistently pressured the president to use executive authority to stop deportations; but instead he played it politically safe, claiming he lacked authority and was forced to wait for a congressional solution—an unlikely prospect considering six years of a Republican Congress hostile to Obama personally and immigration issues. To please his opponents in Congress in the hope they would in turn negotiate some grand bargain on immigration, Obama further militarized (euphemistically referred to as securing) the borders. "We respectfully disagree with the president on his ability to stop unnecessary deportations," Murguía said, "he can stop tearing families apart. He can stop throwing communities and businesses into chaos. He can stop turning a blind eye to the harm being done. He does have the power to stop this. Failure to act will be a shameful legacy for this his presidency."[3]

A shameful legacy?

While our immigration policies are broken, for the Latinx community, they are literally deadly. Gloria E. Anzaldúa captured the reality of the border for Latinxs when she wrote,

> The U.S-Mexican border *es una herida abierta* [an open wound] where the Third World grates against the first and bleeds. And before a scab forms it hemorrhages again, the lifeblood of two worlds merging to form a third country—a border culture. Borders are set up to define the places that are safe and unsafe, to distinguish us from them. A border is a dividing line, a narrow strip along a steep edge. A borderland is a vague and undetermined place created by the emotional residue of an unnatural boundary. It is in a constant state of transition. The prohibited and forbidden are its inhabitants.[4]

This *herida abierta* bleeds due to the deterrent policies of the US Border Patrol. Five preventable deaths occur among those crossing every four days;[5] deaths of mainly brown bodies invisible to the public consciousness. Even those who do not perish while crossing still bleed. One out of every ten migrants have reported some sort of physical abuse while in custody, and one in four reported verbal abuse.[6] Patrol agents have been known to kidnap and rape the undocumented, including brown girls as young as fourteen years old.[7] Agents have beaten individuals, like Jose Gutierrez Guzman, into a comatose state.[8] Since 2014, the Border Patrol has been involved in more fatal shootings than perhaps any other US law enforcement agency, developing a reputation for abuse and corruption. On average, between 2005 and 2012, one border agent was arrested each and every single day for some sort of misconduct.[9] Rather than dealing with these types of abuses and corruptions, the Obama administration—in its first year in office—directed the Border Patrol leadership to simply change its definition of "corruption" so as to underrepresent the number of incidents.[10]

And while Obama did inherit a broken immigration system, nonetheless, he bears responsibility for what has become the greatest human rights violations currently occurring within our country, a modern-day *Jaime y Juana Cuervo*.[11] Our current immigration policies—since 1994—are based on "prevention through deterrence." In an August 1, 2001, letter to the US Senate Committee on the Judiciary, Richard M. Stana from the US General Accounting Office wrote that the ultimate goal of the Border Patrol was "to make it so difficult and costly for aliens to attempt illegal entry that fewer individuals would try."[12] "Costly" does not solely mean a financial expense; deterrence becomes a euphemism for a policy based on the loss of life. Shifting migration traffic away from urban areas, militarizing the border, and building impregnable walls simply meant migrants undertook greater risk of injury or death when attempting to cross mountains, deserts, and rivers far from where walls and fences end. Migrants are calculatedly pushed toward 120,000 square miles of the Sonora Desert or over the mountain ranges north of Tecate.

Shifting migration to the most hostile and unforgiving lands purposely made migration deadly, a governmental policy engineered so some crossing the border would die; but that precisely was the ultimate goal, for their deaths are supposed to deter others from attempting similar hazardous crossings. The death of brown migrant bodies was not some unforeseen consequence, but an acceptable component of "collateral damage." The reality is no one was deterred; the reality is more deaths on the border. And while migrants always faced dangers while crossing borders, prior to the implementation of "prevention through deterrence" in 1994 (known as Operation Gatekeeper), migrant deaths were rare. Even after decades where no empirical evidence existing showed any actual deterrence occurring, we continued with a policy where desperate huddled masses of color were placed into life-threatening situations.

Obama had an opportunity to, at the very least, make our border policies more humane, saner, not dependent on a death-causing deterrence. When elected in 2008, Democrats controlled both Houses of Congress, making the prospects of passing comprehensive immigration reform doable. Unfortunately, the administration failed to act. Instead, during his entire term, the Obama administration deported more immigrants than the sum of all previous presidents of the twentieth century—a total of 2.5 million people between 2009 and 2015[13]—and these numbers do not even reflect his last year in office, 2016, for which data was unavailable at the time of this writing. The administration argued that the first priority for deportations was those who posed "threats to national security, border security, and public safety,"[14] boosting 91 percent of those deported in fiscal year 2015 were previously convicted of crimes.[15] It was argued in a 2014 speech that deportations involved "felons, not families. Criminals, not children. Gang members, not a mom who's working hard to provide for her kids. We'll prioritize, just like law enforcement does every day."[16] A neat dichotomy was created between the "good" and the "bad" immigrant with those being deported defined a bad, as criminals, while those who get to stay viewed as the good immigrant. Unfortunately, the reality where the undocumented find themselves is a bit more complex than simple dichotomies. How Obama's priority has been carried out has been destructive to brown lives, especially when millions of "bad" immigrants deported are characterized as criminals—what Trump would eventually call "bad *hombres*."[17]

Because 2.5 million individuals deported is a number too abstract to conceive, a multitude easily stereotyped, a face is required for at least one of these bad *hombres*. Sandra Lopez is such a face. She is but one of the millions of lives crushed under the immigration grinding wheel. Brought to this country when she was less than a month old, she attended public schools, where she flourished, excelling in her studies and graduating with honors. Barely speaking Spanish, Sandra was a typical American teenager with an unlimited future before her, until she wanted to attend Pima Community College. Lacking a Social Security card meant she would be unable to register for classes and achieve her dream of studying medical science. Instead, at nineteen years old, she took a menial job at a local butcher shop.

On September 1, 2010, a friend asked her to mail a package. Being late for work he needed a Good Samaritan to do him a minor favor. Sandra went to the local FedEx store, paying the cost with the $100 bill her friend gave her, and keeping the $14.59 in change for her troubles. Upon leaving the shop she was stopped and arrested because the package, unbeknownst to her, contained 3.4 pounds of marijuana. Charged with a Class 3 felony (possession of marijuana for sale) she plea bargained to secure the proceeds of an offense ($14.59) and was sentenced to time already served in jail. Once released from jail, immigration officials picked her up and began deportation procedures because she was, after all, a criminal. During her trial, the judge asked her if either of her parents was an American citizen, to which she responded "no" (even though her stepfather was). The judge said she had no relief and told her to sign a form (which she didn't understand) authorizing her deportation. Later that very night, she—like so many vulnerable women and children—was deported to a dangerous border town after all the social service aid offices were closed.

Sandra found herself in Mexico with about $30 in her pocket. If she had known to say her stepfather is a US citizen, she would not have been deported and her nightmare could have been avoided. On March 9, 2011, Sandra arrived in Nogales, Sonora, with limited Spanish skills and knowing no one. Sandra was deported to a country she never visited. Immediately, some women offered her food and shelter in exchange for prostituting herself. "*Mija*, we will help you survive and get back across the border," they promised. She approached a police officer to ask directions to the local humanitarian aid station, but instead the officer attempted to take advantage of her in exchange for his protection. She wandered the streets staying close to the border, as if that infernal wall, which snakes across the landscape, could provide some sense of security. At nights she slept in empty cargo cars by the train tracks close to the wall, as close to home as possible. One night, she decided to use her precious cash to pay for a room at a fleabag motel. She noticed through her motel window some *mafioso* pulling up with girls younger than herself; some seemed to be preadolescent. All appeared to be drugged by the way they staggered. Through the thin walls she could hear these girls scream for help as they were being abused. She barely slept, fearing the men would break down her door to come for her. The next day she left penniless to again wander the streets.

A week had gone by and this frightened teenager was growing desperate. It was then a tall strange man accosted her with a knife, grabbing her from behind. She broke loose and ran for her life. She ran toward home, as fast as she could, up the vehicle lanes of the DeConcini Port of Entry screaming for help, seeking asylum. Instead, she was charged with a felony for illegal reentry after a deportation. Rather than processing her as an asylum seeker, as she requested, the Border Patrol violated proper protocols and procedures. Since her arrest in 2011, Sandra has spent almost three years at Eloy Detention Center fighting her immigration case and, in a very real sense, fighting for a life. The flower of her youth spent behind bars due to a broken immigration system, she endured constant humiliations, strip and cavity searches, and being constantly taunted by guards who cursed and demeaned her.

The irony is since the implementation of Deferred Action for Childhood Arrivals (DACA), none of this needed to occur, if not for the felony of illegal reentry. But she didn't illegally reenter the United States; she was seeking asylum, fearing for her life. She was released on a $6,000 bail in November 2013, about a month before we sat down and I heard her story. Since then she obtained DREAMer status and has enrolled at Maricopa Community College. Her felony conviction that prevented DACA eligibility was eventually reduced to a misdemeanor conviction. Still, no young person who grew up in this country, whose parents paid taxes, should undergo what Sandra suffered. Unfortunately, Sandra is but one among millions of lives being broken by our immigration policies regardless of the rhetorical pledge of "felons, not families. Criminals, not children."

Considering Sandra's story, one might be inclined to celebrate Obama's 2008 executive order implementing DACA, allowing DREAMers who entered the United States prior to their sixteenth birthday, or received an honorable military discharge and were under thirty-one years of age to receive a work permit and two-year renewable deferred action from deportation. But before we rush to praise the Obama administration for probably its only redeeming immigration act, the timing of DACA's announcement raises eyebrows because it appears highly politically suspicious in nature. Facing an indifferent Latinx community just months before his 2008 reelection win; Obama signed the DACA executive order. His action motivated Latinxs to turn up on election day helping Obama secure a second term. Unfortunately, for the more than a-quarter-of-a-million immigrants (including Sandra) who benefited from DACA, they are at risk of losing this benefit under a Trump administration who while campaigning, promised to roll back Obama's executive order.

Sandra's story shows how Obama's immigration policies might prove to be more damaging than Trump's. While Trump used nativist fear of the Other to scare whites to voting for him, promising to protect them from the brown menace by deporting "all of the illegals," Obama presented a kinder, gentler policy which nonetheless has proven to be just as deadly. During Trump's transition period to the White House, he began to flip-flop on immigration, reducing expectations of deporting "all of the illegals" by providing numbers (2 to 3 million) for deportation, numbers similar to what Obama already accomplished during his term in office.[18] Trump will be able to accomplish this goal because Obama already built the necessary machinery to make it happen. Obama said all the right things concerning immigration while his policies devastated the Latinx community. He separated families; incarcerated over 85,000 unaccompanied minors (seventeen years old and younger) in detention centers[19]; called for the indefinite detention of thousands until they can prove citizenship[20]; militarized the border by signing a $600 million bill[21]; criminalized a segment of the population which benefited private prisons as Latinx, who comprise only 18 percent of the population, which now represents the largest presence in federal prisons due to immigration violations[22]; deported 7,000 children without a court hearing[23]; and as already mentioned, deported more brown bodies than all his predecessors combined. At least Trump is honest concerning his intentions. And yet we are quick to call Trump a racist for the same things he promises to do to brown bodies that Obama has actually been doing all along.

Probably the most shameful act the Obama administration took against immigrants was how Obama resolved the June 2014 immigration crises, when women and children started showing up at our southern borders. According to the Border Patrol, about 55,420 family members were apprehended on the US-Mexican border between October 2013 and June 2014—a nearly 500 percent increase over the same period during the previous year. Additionally, 57,525 unaccompanied minors were detained by the end of that June creating a humanitarian crisis on the border.[24] These families, who were mainly comprised of women and children, were primarily from Central America. They were escaping the rampant gang violence of their homelands—a violence whose roots can be traced to our own military involvements in their countries protecting US business interests (under the guise of fighting communism). Unlike most undocumented immigrants who tried to avoid detection by the Border Patrol, these women and children, once within the United States, sought border agents. They undertook their hallowing trek after rumors spread within their countries, specifically Guatemala, Honduras, and El Salvador, if they made it to the United States, they would be allowed to stay.

Obviously, they did not walk the entire journey, first through their own country, then through the whole of Mexico. Instead, they rode on top of a train called *la bestia*—the beast—a treacherous ride where the migrant might accidently fall off and either die under the wheels of the train or at best, lose a limb or two. Gangs patrol these trains, preying and robbing migrants of their meager possessions. Women and young girls are the most vulnerable, facing rape and abuse. Some of them, as a precaution, began taking birth control medicine months before they undertook their trek. Before Central American migrants get to face the abusive practices of the US Border Patrol, they must first survive the abusive practices of *los federales* of Mexico. The crises of so many women and children showing up on our border was not only a humanitarian problem, but for the Obama administration, a political nightmare, and the administration's response to the crises can only be described as inhumane and shameful.

By December 2014, a for-profit detention facility was opened in Dilley, Texas, with the capacity of housing 2,400 of these mothers along with their children. The Obama years has made us a nation where infants and children live behind bars! When seven House members undertook a fact-finding tour of the Dilley facilities, they were met with chants in Spanish: "We want freedom!"[25] At first, the situation appeared to be changing. On June 24, 2015, Homeland Security announced plans to end long-term detention of mothers and children caught crossing the border once they pass the first hurdle of the asylum process, an interview to voice their fears for returning home. However, by August 2015, the Obama administration, while agreeing with reforms implemented in June, nonetheless argued for ramping up detention facilities housing mothers and children as an effective tool in deterring border crossings.[26]

Also, by July 2014, the United States "outsourced" its women and children immigration problem. Mexico, at the request and with the assistance of the United States, began an unprecedented and merciless crackdown of refugees fleeing Central America. The United States provided Mexico with tens of millions of dollars for the fiscal year ending September 2015 to stop these migrants from ever reaching the US border. Mexico redirected 300–600 immigration agents to its southernmost border, conducting over 20,000 raids on the freight trains upon which immigrants ride, and at the bus stations, hotels, and highways they traverse while on their northward journey. During the first seven months of fiscal 2015, Mexican authorities apprehended 92,889 Central Americans trying to reach the United States (more than the 70,448 apprehended by the United States during the same period).[27]

When it comes to immigration, both Trump and Obama while embracing different rhetoric, nonetheless, have much in common. For the Latinx community, the consequences of an Obama or a Trump immigration policy hold little difference. What Trump proposes to do is not so different than what Obama has already done. Both men's similar actions toward the undocumented are made possible because both ignore why we have an immigration problem in the first place. The United States has a Latin American immigration crisis, yet a failure exists in recognizing its causes. The question too often ignored is why they come in the first place.

Why they come?

For conservatives, immigrants come to use up our social services, have their anchor babies, and commit crimes. For liberals, immigrants are searching for the American Dream, freedom, and opportunity. Both are wrong. We have an immigration problem due to US economic, political, and foreign policies which have pushed immigrants from their homelands in Latin America while simultaneously have pulled them in due to our unquenchable thirst for cheap labor. The United States has a Latin American immigration problem because for the past 200 years, thanks to Manifest Destiny, gunboat diplomacy, and neoliberalism, the wealth of the United States was based on stealing the cheap labor and natural resources of its neighboring countries to the south.

The pseudo-religious nineteenth-century ideology known as Manifest Destiny believed God gave Euro-Americans (like the biblical Hebrews) a new promised land encompassing the entire western hemisphere. James K. Polk, the eleventh president, was perhaps the ideology's staunchest supporter and advocate. While on the campaign trail, he promised to annex Texas and engage in a Mexican land grab if elected. Upon taking office, he deployed troops into Mexican territory, soliciting the desired response—having the Mexican army fire first upon the invading US army. The Mexican-American War ended with Mexico's capitulation, ceding half her territory. And as important as the new lands acquired were the resources tied to those lands—the gold of California, the oil of Texas, the silver of Nevada, the copper of New Mexico and Arizona, and all the rich minerals of Colorado—resources which served as seed money launching the eventual Industrial Revolution. This expansionist war, minimized by the false creation of the United States' historical mega-narrative, masked the fact that it was the empire that crossed the borders—not the other way around.

Besides the nineteenth-century practice of invading sovereign nations (a recurring theme when we consider Indigenous people), there was the twentieth-century policy of "gunboat diplomacy"[28] which unleashed a colonial venture depriving Latin American countries of their natural resources while providing the United States with an unlimited supply of cheap labor. President Theodore Roosevelt's foreign policy placed the full force of the US military, specifically the Marines, at the disposal of US corporations, specifically the United Fruit Company, to protect their business interest. Nicknamed "El Pulpo"—the Octopus—because its tentacles extended into every power structure within Central America, the United Fruit Company was able to set prices, taxes, and employee treatment free from local government intervention. Any nation in "our" hemisphere which attempted to claim its sovereignty to the detriment of US business interests could expect the United States to invade and set up a new government (hence the term "banana republic," coined in 1935 to describe servile dictatorships). It is no coincidence the rise of US banana consumption coincided with the rise of US imperialist actions throughout the Caribbean Basin. During the twentieth century, the

United States invaded at least twenty-one Caribbean Basin countries and participated in at least twenty-six CIA-led covert operations to institute regime change, even when some of those countries, like Guatemala, had democratically elected governments. This gunboat diplomacy laid the foundation for the enrichment of today's multinational corporations, a policy still in full operation, but under a different name: regime change. George W. Bush's "regime change" (gunboat diplomacy?) in Iraq benefited firms like that of then vice president's former company Halliburton, to a tune of $680-million no-bid reconstruction contracts.[29]

More important than territorial expansion during the nineteenth century was the United States' hegemonic attempt to control economies of other nations during the twentieth century. While empires of old, like Rome, relied on brute force, the US empire instead relies on economic force—not to disregard the fact that it also has the largest military apparatus ever known to humanity. Through its economic might, the United States dictates terms of trade with other nations, guaranteeing that benefits continue to flow northward toward the center and toward the elites from the countries that signed the trade agreements. Consider the consequences of implementing the 1994 North American Free Trade Agreement (NAFTA), which destroyed the Mexican agricultural sector.

Dumping US surplus corn on Mexico (about $4 billion a year during the first decade of NAFTA)[30] translated into a 70 percent drop in Mexican maize prices, while housing, food, and other living essentials increased by 247 percent.[31] In the first ten years of NAFTA, at least 1.3 million Mexican maize farmers lost their small plots of land unable to compete with cheaper US subsidized corn.[32] While Mexican farmers were squeezed out due to their inability to compete with US subsidized corn, US-owned transnational traders, like Cargill and Maseca, were able to step in and monopolize the corn sector through speculating on trading trends. They used their power within the market, for example, to manipulate movements on biofuel demand and thus artificially inflate the price of corn many times over.[33] Worsening the plight of the maize campesino were the structural adjustments imposed on Mexico by the World Bank in 1991, eliminating all government price supports and subsidies for corn.[34]

The United States has an immigration crisis, yet a failure exists in recognizing the reason why they come. The irony, a paradox conveniently ignored by conservative and liberal politicians, by Trump and Obama, and unknown to most citizens, is how US foreign policies are directly responsible for the growing US Latinx population. They come to escape the violence and terror the United States historically unleashed upon them in an effort to protect *Pax Americana*, a needed status quo if American foreign business interests are to flourish. An immigration problem exists because for almost two centuries, the United States has exploited—and continues to economically exploit—their neighbors to the south. The undocumented attempt the hazardous crossing because our foreign and trade policies from the nineteenth through the twenty-first century have created an economic situation in their countries where they are unable to feed their families. When one country builds roads into another country to extract, by brute force if necessary, their natural resources and their cheap labor, why should we be surprised when the inhabitants of those same countries take those same roads following all that has been stolen.

We should not be surprised when conservative-leaning politicians, like Trump, are hostile to Latinx immigration, ignoring the complex causes of the problem for easy nativist and xenophobic solutions. But liberal-leaning politicians also ignore their history, calling for a virtue of hospitality to undergird how they approach and treat the undocumented. When Obama gave his November 2014 immigration speech, he began by exulting the nation's virtue of hospitality: "For more than 200 years, our tradition of welcoming immigrants from around the world has given us a tremendous advantage over other nations."[35] Who could argue against hospitality? Who could argue against the president's words of welcome? This virtue becomes a religious and civic duty to assist (bring salvation to) these poor unfortunate souls. It is what Jesus would do.

Rejecting hospitality

Hospitality is a biblical concept, meaning more than just opening one's home to the stranger and inviting him or her in for a meal. The Hebrew biblical text reminds us all the patriarchs were aliens, as were the Jews during their time in Egypt as slaves, their forty years wandering in the desert, and their time in the Babylonian exile. Thus the concept of hospitality and offering justice to the sojourner is foundational and we are consistently reminded to care for the alien. The New Testament reminds us how Jesus was also an alien in Egypt and how others, while showing hospitality to strangers, entertained angels without realizing (Heb. 13:2). The biblical terms "stranger" or "sojourner" capture the predicament of today's undocumented immigration from Mexico or Central America to the United States. The terms connote the in-between space of being neither native-born nor a foreigner. As such, the alien lacks the benefits and protection ordinarily provided to those tied to the land due to their birthplace. Vulnerable to those who profit from their labor, aliens derive security from the biblical mandate of hospitality. So hospitality, while a good virtue to practice, is damning if misused, as is the case with how Obama approached immigration. Obama, as with most liberals, based his response to the immigration crises on the Christian concept of hospitality; a paternalistic approach ignoring the causes of immigration.

Part of the problem is a national narrative, embraced by the Obama administration, which ignores the roads built by the United States into the original homelands of Latinx (conquest, banana republics, NAFTA), causing these migrants to take those same roads following their stolen goods. Christian hospitality is the wrong approach. Hospitality assumes "I" own the house and due to my Christian generosity, I will share my possessions with you who has none. Missing is a historical understanding revealing how Latin American's cheap labor and stolen natural resources were responsible for building the house in the first place. Due to US conquest of lands, sponsored banana republics, and neoliberal agreements like NAFTA, Latin Americans hold a lien on this US house's title. Rather than speaking about the virtue of hospitality, it would historically be more accurate to speak about the responsibility of restitution.[36] Maybe the ethical question we should therefore be asking is not "why" are they coming, but, how does United States begin to make reparations for all it has stolen to create the present economic empire?

Final judgment

Based on actions taken by the Obama administration, Latinxs are very aware that immigration has not been a priority. This point was driven home during the final month of his term as president when the opportunity existed for him to take bold action. Over a hundred immigrant advocate organizations petitioned in December 2016 for Obama to shield from deportation up to 200,000 legal immigrants (holding proper green cards) with minor criminal records. If Obama would have used his pardon power before leaving office (which has never been used for civil violations— only criminal), he could have redeemed his legacy as deporter-in-chief. Such a pardon could have solely focused on the civil immigration violation, leaving the immigrants to still face any criminal violation without fear of deportation[37] And while 200,000 is but a small representation of the 11 million undocumented immigrants within the United States, at least it could have served as symbolic proof that Obama is unlike the man who replaced him; at least it could have depicted Obama as caring for the undocumented. Unfortunately, Obama didn't even make this small symbolic gesture, ending his term with a dismal record on immigration—a fail record as far as Latinxs are concerned.

"Now. Next." Confronting the Past and Shaping the Future[1]

Sharon Welch

Election disparities

On an unseasonably warm fall evening in November 2008, I joined thousands of people in Grant Park, Chicago, cheering the win in each state, and relishing the grand collective jubilation of shouts, dancing, cries, laughter, and hugs when the polls closed at 11:00 p.m. and we knew that we had done it. On the evening of November 8, 2016, the mood could not have been more different. My small watch party of close friends disbanded around midnight, certain that Clinton would eke out a victory, yet profoundly dispirited by the close margin. Discouragement was replaced with shock, disbelief, and dread when I awoke at 3:00 a.m. and discovered the results. The ride to downtown Chicago on the bus the next morning felt like a funeral procession.

How did we manage to achieve so much, and then lose it so rapidly, and so thoroughly? The words of Michael Dyson are telling: "we have, in the span of a few years, elected the nation's first black president and placed in the Oval Office the scariest racial demagogue in a generation. . . . The remarkable progress we seemed to make with the former has brought out the peril of the latter."[2]

The magnitude of what is at stake here is unquestionably immense—not just the outcome of this particular exercise in democracy, but the way in which white racism is poisoning the very future of democracy. Like many activists, I have always taken the fundamentals of democracy for granted, and worked to expand them. Now, the challenge is far different—not just the expansion of mechanisms to insure equal rights and justice for all, but the restoration of a social compact that has been grievously damaged, the restoration of a commitment to who we can be as Americans.

In his article in the *Atlantic Monthly* in January 2017, Ta-Nehisi Coates names this same dynamic, the depth of racism during the Obama presidential campaign and then the Obama presidency, and how many of us misread what it meant:

What Obama was able to offer white America is something very few African Americans could—trust. The vast majority of us are, necessarily, too crippled by our defenses to ever consider such a proposition. But Obama, through a mixture of ancestral connections and distance from the poisons of Jim Crow, can credibly and sincerely trust the majority population of this country. That trust is reinforced not contracted, by his blackness. . . . He stands firm in his own cultural traditions and says to the country virtual no black person can, but every president must: "I believe you."[3]

To the extent that such trust was warranted, and confirmed by being elected twice to the highest office in the land, many of us, myself included, did not think that Trump could win. Coates describes this conviction in his recounting of his conversation with President Obama "just after Columbus Day": "At this moment, the idea that a campaign so saturated in open bigotry, misogyny, chaos, and possible corruption could win a national election was ludicrous. This was America."[4]

This conviction was based on two realities: pride in what Obama had accomplished, even in the face of unprecedented levels of political obstruction, and a certainty that blatant racism, misogyny, and multiple forms of hatred were discrediting, not empowering, the Republican Party.

Coates provides a clear summary of some of the achievements of the Obama presidency:

Obama's accomplishments were real: a $1 billion settlement on behalf of black farmers, a Justice Department that exposed Ferguson's municipal plunder, the increased availability of Pell Grants (and their availability to some prisoners), and the slashing of the crack/cocaine disparity in sentencing guidelines, to name just a few. . . . There was a feeling that he'd erected a foundation upon which further progressive policy could be built. It's tempting to say that foundation is now endangered. The truth is, it was never safe.[5]

That foundation was endangered by blatant racism, expressed early and often. Coates describes some of the disturbing signs of what was being unleashed:

Racism greeted Obama in both his primary and general-election campaigns in 2008. Photos were circulated of him in Somali garb. Rush Limbaugh dubbed him "Barack the Magic Negro." Roger Stone, who would go on to advise the Trump campaign, claimed that Michelle Obama could be heard on tape yelling "Whitey." Detractors circulated emails claiming that the future first lady had written a racist senior thesis while at Princeton. A fifth of all West Virginia Democratic-primary voters in 2008 openly admitted that race had influenced their vote. Hillary Clinton trounced him by 67 to 26 percent.[6]

Too many of us dismissed the racism, some by arguing that the primary cause of support for Trump was economic; others by thinking that the blatant appeal to racism and bigotry in so many forms marked the death throes of white supremacy and of the Republican Party, not the birth pangs of their resurgence.

Coates describes how many saw the rise of the Tea Party and Trump as being "largely the discontented rumblings of a white working class threatened by the menace of globalization and crony capitalism. . . . Deindustrialization, globalization, and broad income inequality are real. And they have landed with at least as great a force upon black and Latino people in our country as upon white people. And yet these groups were strangely unrepresented in this new populism."[7]

What has been unfolding is far more than economic anxiety and discontent. As Coates state, our democracy is at risk and "one needn't stretch too far to conclude that an eight-year campaign of consistent and open racism aimed at the leader of the free world helped clear the way. . . . 'They rode the tiger. And now the tiger is eating them,' David Axelrod, speaking of the Republican party, told me. That was in October. His words proved too optimistic. The tiger would devour us all."[8]

"The tiger is devouring us all," and the challenge is clear. Michael Eric Dyson states that we as a nation are in grave need of moral repair, a repair only possible if white people join people of all races and learn from them the current costs and painful history of racial injustice:

> I know that when we get out of our own way and let the spirit of love and hope shine through we are a better people.
>
> But such love and hope can only come about if we first confront the poisonous history that has almost unmade our nation and undone our social compact. We must face up to what we as a country have made of the black people who have been the linch pin of democracy, the folk who saved American from itself, who redeemed it from the hypocrisy of proclaiming liberty and justice for all while denying all that liberty and justice should be to us.[9]

Since the election of Trump in 2016, I have been heartened by the upsurge in resistance and activism by people of all races, and I am equally aware of the need to do more, to understand more, and not merely repeat the activist strategies of the past.

What enabled the first victory of Barack Obama, and what propelled the backlash? To take up both questions poses profound challenges for political strategies and for the contours of the religious imagination. We are now challenged to confront the complexity of change, the vulnerability of positive change, and the multifaceted responsibilities of agents of change.

For all of these tasks, it is important to recognize a paradox—the galvanizing power and the intrinsic limitations of the prophetic imagination. It is also important to reckon honestly and forthrightly with the depth of white racism and the resilient power of human evil. While exploring both issues, I do not have definitive answers, but rather I am inviting you to join me in this struggle of finding ways to act more creatively, think more deeply, and name our work more precisely and evocatively.

Later in this chapter, I will explore the contours of constructive social engagement and the ethical and religious challenges of such work, but first, let us take up Dyson's challenge to confront the "poisonous history that has almost unmade our nation and undone our social compact."[10]

History and ongoing costs of racism

In this chapter, I explore what it means for whites to take seriously the critiques of Ta-Nehisi Coates, Michael Eric Dyson, Anthony Pinn, Carol Anderson, and Ibram Kendi, what they tell us about the brutal costs of racism, what they tell us about the historical drivers of racial injustice.

Dyson's description of the ongoing costs of racism is stark:

> The terror that black people experience is of two varieties. *Slow terror* is masked but malignant: it stalks black people in denied opportunities that others take for granted . . . black boys and girls being expelled from school at higher rates than their white peers; black men and women being harassed by unjust fines from local municipalities; having billions of dollars of their wealth drained off by shady financial instruments sold to blacks during the mortgage crisis; and e being imprisoned out of proportion to their percentage of the population. President Obama has referred to this kind of terror as a "slow rolling crisis." *Fast terror* is more dynamic, more explicitly lethal, more grossly evident. It is the spectacle of black death in public displays of vengeance and violence directed against defenseless black bodies.[11]

Anthony Pinn describes another key dimension of this terror, seen so blatantly in the police killings of black citizens, and in the acquittal of police officers for those crimes:

> We are living a legacy of racial violence. . . . The terror involved in this process of control isn't simply the threat of death, but the inability to anticipate what will trigger violent responses to blackness. As with Philando Castile in Minnesota— the land of "nice-ness"—compliance can be deadly. Any sign of struggle—even for one's breath—can be understood as a threat to the safety of law enforcement and, as was the case for Eric Garner, can result in death. The jail cell as a place of confinement can also be a death chamber, as Sandra Bland's demise makes clear. There are no decipherable ground rules for survival if one happens to lie in black flesh.[12]

Pinn makes another point, crucial for all of us committed to expanding racial justice and containing white supremacy to address: white supremacy mutates, ending one form does not mean that it will not reemerge in other forms. "That is the genius of white supremacy: it mutates and transforms, and it gives up a little in order to present the illusion of fundamental change. It finds ways to blame victims for the violence perpetuated against them."[13]

For whites to confront the mutation and spread of white supremacy means that we must forthrightly see it for what it is, and not attempt to deny it, or minimize it. As an example of such denial, some white commentators attributed the support of Trump more to economic anxiety than to a resurgence of racism. Michael Eric Dyson clearly points out the fallacy of that line of reasoning:

> When the defender of whiteness proclaim that it is not whiteness that was at stake in electing Trump, but, instead, the ache of poverty and class, what they mostly always fail to mention is that millions of black and brown folk are poor, or working class, too. It is only the white lower and middle classes whose silent suffering is portrayed as having got a president elected. As important as their economic vulnerability is, it is not the major engine of their disgust; rather it is the fury of whiteness unlashed, of whiteness unbonded, of whiteness made, not less white, but even white by its class rage, a rage that oddly leaves aside solidarity with millions of other hurting souls whose only reason for exclusion is their color.[14]

The problem with the claim that Trump voters were primarily working class and motivated by economic security is twofold: a convincing array of data shows that Trump supporters were not primarily working class, and some of that same data also shows that his supporters were primarily motivated by racial animus and racial resentment.

First, I will discuss the fallacy of limiting the support for Trump to the white working class. In an article for the June 5, 2017, *Washington Post*, Nicolas Carnes, a professor of public policy, and political scientist Noam Lupu make a strong claim:

> Media coverage of the 2016 election often emphasized Donald Trump's appeal to the working class. *The Atlantic* said that "the billionaire developer is building a blue-collar foundation." The Associated Press wondered what "Trump's success in attracting white, working-class voters" would mean for his general election strategy. On Nov. 9, *The New York Times* front-page article about Trump's victory characterized it as "a decisive demonstration of power by a largely overlooked coalition of mostly blue collar white and working-class voters."
>
> There's just one problem: this account is wrong. Trump voters were not mostly working-class people.[15]

Carnes and Lupu are not alone in challenging this narrative. As early as May 2016, Nate Silver took on "the mythology of Trump's working class support." Looking at the data from exit polls in the primary, Silver found that Trump voters were actually more affluent than most Americans:

> As compared with most Americans, Trump's voters are better off. The median household income of a Trump voter so far in the primaries is about $72,000, based on estimates derived from exit polls and Census Bureau data. That's lower than the $91,000 median for Kasich voters. But it's well above the national median household income of about $56,000. It's also higher than the median income for Hillary Clinton and Bernie Sanders supporters, which is around $61,000 for both.[16]

These numbers hold even when race is factored in:

> Since almost all of Trump's voters so far in the primaries have been non-Hispanic whites, we can ask whether they make lower incomes than other white Americans. . . . The answer is "no." The median household income for non-Hispanic whites is about $62,000, still a fair bit lower than the $72,000 median for Trump voters.[17]

Silvers points out that 27 percent of Americans have incomes of less than $30,000, and more of those voted for Clinton and Sanders than for Trump: "Only 12% of Trump voters have incomes below $30,000. . . . For Clinton and Sanders the numbers were 17% and 18%."[18] Silvers also challenged the characterization of Trump supporters as being relatively uneducated:

> Likewise, although about 44 percent of Trump supporters have college degrees, according to exit polls—lower than the 50 percent for Cruz supporters or 65 percent for Kasich supporters—that's still higher than the 33 percent of non-Hispanic white adults, or the 29 percent of American adults overall, who have at least a bachelor's degree.[19]

While much of the media focused on economic anxiety as the primary driver of support for Trump, political scientists were finding a vastly different story. Jason McDaniel and Sean McElwe writing for "The New West: official blog of the Western Political Association" March and August 24, 2016, also addressed this issue:

> What explains the rise of Donald Trump?
>
> There are many potential answers, but over the course of the campaign two competing theories have emerged. The first holds that Trump's message appeals to working-class white voters who've seen their incomes remain stagnant, manufacturing jobs, vanish, and inequality skyrocket in recent decades. The root cause of Trumpism, in this view, is economic insecurity. The other, blunter theory is that Trump's fans flock to him for the same reason elites view him as an existential threat to American democracy: his open appeals to racist, white nationalist sentiment.
>
> Both of these theories have some truth to them. But polling data suggests that racial attitudes, including racial resentment and explicit racial stereotypes, are the more important factor. What's more, the evidence presented below shows that racial attitudes uniquely predict support for Trump, compared to the other Republican candidates.[20]

McDaniel and McElwe base their conclusions on the American National Election 2016 Pilot Study. The political scientist Thomas Wood describes the value of the American National Election Survey: "The ANES has been conducted since 1948. . . . This incredibly rich, publicly funded data source allows us to put elections into historical perspective, examining how much each factor affected the vote in 2016 compared with other recent elections."[21] Among the many questions are specific ones about implicit racial resentment and explicit racial animus.

The poll measures racial animus by asking the following questions: First, it asked respondents how important their race is to their identity. Second, it asked respondents whether they think the words "lazy" and "violent" describe black people, Muslims, and Hispanics "extremely well," "very well," "moderately well," "slightly well," or "not well at all."[22]

The poll also measures implicit racial resentment, "racist attitudes [that] are expressed in a way that is seemingly neutral, but still animates racial anger." The survey asked respondents their level of agreement on four statements related to racial resentment, which we then combined to a single metric:

> Irish, Italian, Jewish, and many other minorities overcome prejudice and worked their way up. Black people should do the same without any special favors.
>
>   It's really a matter of some people not trying hard enough; if black people would only try harder they could be just as well-off as whites.
>
>   Over the past few years, black people have gotten less than they deserve.
>
>   Generations of slavery and discrimination have created conditions that make it difficult for black people to work their way out of the lower class.[23]

The results were clear:

> Support for Trump increased along with measured racial animus . . . increased levels of overt racial stereotyping among white respondents—as measured by belief that black people, Muslims, and Hispanics are "lazy" or "violent"—strongly increases support for Trump, even after controlling for other factors. The opposite is true, however, when it comes to support for Marco Rubio.
>
>   The same story is true for racial resentment. The more troubling respondents' answers on the four resentment questions were, the likelier they were to support Trump. There is no such relationship between racial resentment and support for Marco Rubio or the other major Republican contenders.[24]

The data first seen in primary exit polls were confirmed in exit polls from the November election. Jon Henley writing for the *Guardian* stated that

> in the end according to exit polls, the election result seems to have been more about the clear backing of America's white and wealthy voters for Donald Trump—including white graduates, and white female voters. . . . Of the one in three Americans who earn less than $50,000 a year, a majority voted for Clinton. A majority of those who earn more backed Trump.[25]

The data is telling: "Broken down by income bracket, 52% of voters earning less than $50,000 a year—who make up 36% of the electorate—voted for Clinton, and 41% for Trump. But among the 64% of American voters who earn more than $50,000 a year, 49% chose Trump, and 47% Clinton."[26]

In looking at the American National Election Studies data from the November election, Thomas Wood makes an important point. Trump had less appeal to wealthy Republicans than Republican candidates in the past, and more from poor Americans than Republicans had received in the past: "While the wealthy are usually most likely to vote for the Republican, they didn't this time; and while the poor are usually less likely to vote for the Republican, they were unusually supportive of Trump. And the degree to which the wealthy disdained the 2016 Republican candidate was without recent historical precedent."[27]

Despite these changes in relative support, the evidence so far still shows that the majority of Trump's supporters were not working class. While wealthy voters were less likely to vote Republican in the past, and the poor more likely to vote for Trump, looking at the same data, Carnes and Lupu find that Trump supporters overall "were mostly affluent Republicans." While possibly less wealthy in the past, of those who did vote for Trump, incomes were high: "Among people who said they voted for Trump in the general election, 35 percent had household incomes under $50,000 per year. . . . In the general election, like the primary, about two thirds of Trump supporters came from the better-off half of the economy."[28]

The same is true of education. Carnes and Lupu discredit the claim that it was primarily uneducated working-class whites who supported Trump. While it is true that a large number of Trump supporters did not have college degrees (69 percent), that number does not mean lack of affluence, nor is it unrepresentative of the number of the voting population without college degrees:

> The truth is more complicated: many of the voters without college educations who supported Trump were relatively affluent . . . among white people without college degrees who voted for Trump, nearly 60 percent were in the top half of the income distribution. In fact, one in five white Trump voters without a college degree had a household income over $100,000.
>
> In short, the narrative that attributes Trump's victor to a "coalition of mostly blue-collar white and working-class voters" just doesn't square with the 2016 election data . . . white non-Hispanic voters without college degrees making below the median household income made up only 25 percent of Trump voters. That's a far cry from the working-class-fueled victory many journalists have imagined.[29]

The primary determinant in support for Trump was not class, but it was race, and it was also racial animus and resentment. First, Henley provides the data that shows the clear support of whites of all genders and ages for Trump:

> What appears to have made the biggest difference on the night was the turnout for Trump of white voters across the board—of both sexes, almost all ages and education levels, and from mid and higher income levels.
>
> White voters, who make up 69% of the total, voted 58% for Trump and 37% for Clinton. Non-white voters, who make up 31% of the electorate, voted 74% for Clinton and 21% for Trump. White men opted 63% for Trump and 31% for Clinton; white women voted 53% for Trump and 43% for Clinton.[30]

To many of us, this was surprisingly, and ominously, even true of white young voters: "More 18–29 year old whites voted for Trump (48%) than for Clinton (43%). Trump collected just 9% of black votes from the same age group, and 24% of Latinos."[31]

It was, however, not just race but racial resentment and animus that predicted support for Trump, and lack of such animus and resentment that predicted support for Clinton. Wood states that "[since] 1988, we've never seen such a clear correspondence between vote choice and racial perceptions. The biggest movement was among those who voted for the Democrat, who were far less likely to agree with attitudes coded as more racially biased."[32] The opposite was true for those who voted for Trump. For these voters, "moving from 50th to the 75th percentile" in the racial attitudes scale "made someone 20 percent more likely to vote for Trump."[33]

While more results will certainly emerge, the data so far is clear. The drivers in this election were not primarily income and wealth levels, but were racial animus and racial resentment, and what is being unleashed by this campaign is explicit white nationalist racist violence. What the voting numbers miss is the depth of the vitriol and the extent of the violence that has been unleashed. This was seen in the murder of nine people in Charleston, South Carolina, by Dylann Roof. It is also present in the spread of "Alt-Fight Clubs." Alan Feuer and Jeremy W. Peters describe the rise of this form of explicit white identity–based violence in the June 3, 2017, issue of *The New York Times*:

> Part fight club, part Western-pride fraternity, the Alt-Knights and similar groups recruit battalions of mainly young white men for one-off confrontations with their ideological enemies—the black-clad left-wing militants who disrupted President Trump's inauguration and have protested against the appearance of conservative speakers on college campuses.[34]

Other similar groups are the Proud Boys and the Oath Keepers. The Oath Keepers is primarily made up of "current and former law enforcement officers and military veterans." These groups bond on the joint dynamic of the claim to be "white, proud, Western chauvinists" and on violent hazing. "Some groups like the Proud Boys have initiation rituals that include violent hazing and require an oath of fealty to Western civilization."[35]

These groups are not alone in explicit calls to white nationalism. Beginning in December 2016, Richard Spencer of the National Policy Institute began a campaign to cultivate white identity at over sixty college campuses through the spring of 2017, and such campaigns are ongoing.

Now—what is the lesson of this for our ongoing challenges against racism and for racial justice? How can whites nurture their best and contain, maybe even prevent, their worst? Again, the insights of African American scholars are essential.

This is not the first time in US history when we have seen these kinds of violent attacks on the dignity, equality, and the very lives of African American people. Two very different accounts of the history of white racism are equally instructive: Ibram Kendi's *Stamped from the Beginning: The Definitive History of Racist Ideas in America* and Carol Anderson's *White Rage: The Unspoken Truth of Our Racial Divide*.

The lessons here are stark. In his thorough study of the history of racist ideas in the United States, Ibram Kendi discovers a dimension of white supremacy that is essential for us to recognize as we work against racism and for racial justice. Hatred and ignorance are real, yet Kendi claims that the drivers of such poisons, and such terror, are policies with racially deleterious effects, chosen out of white self-interest, not out of explicitly racist intentions, and only later defended and maintained by racist ideas:

> Hate and ignorance have not driven the history of racist ideas in America. Racist policies have driven the history of racist ideas in America. . . . Time and again, racist ideas have not been cooked up from the boiling pot of ignorance and hate. Time and again, powerful and brilliant men and women have produced racist ideas in order to justify the racist policies of their era, in order to redirect the blame for their era's racial disparities away from those policies and onto Black people.
>
> Racial discrimination—racist ideas—ignorance/hate: this is the causal relationship driving America's history of race relations.[36]

Kendi's argument is essential to understand as we take up the work of dismantling racist structures. While the effects of many policies have undoubtedly damaged the lives and limited the opportunities of black Americans, Kendi argues that these policies were most often based on self-interest, not on explicit racist intentions:

> Their own racist ideas usually did not dictate the decisions of the most powerful Americans when they instituted, defended, and tolerated discriminatory policies that affected millions of Black lives over the course of American history. Racially discriminatory policies have usually sprung from economic, political, and cultural self-interests. . . . Politicians seeking higher office have primarily created and defended discriminatory policies out of political self-interest—not racist ideas. Capitalists seeking to increase profit margins have primarily created and defended discriminatory policies out of economic self-interest—not racist ideas.[37]

When it becomes clear that black lives are harmed by policies, the blame is laid to the supposed inferiority of black people, and not to the effects of the policies:

> When we look back on our history, we often wonder why so many Americans did not resist slave trading, enslaving, segregating, or now, mass incarcerating. The reason is, again, racist ideas. The principle function of racist ideas in American history has been the suppression of resistance to racial discrimination and its resulting racial disparities. The beneficiaries of slavery, segregation, and mass incarceration have produced racist ideas of Black people being best suited for or deserving of the confines of slavery, segregation, or the jail cell. Consumers of these racist ideas have been led to believe there is something wrong with Black people and not the policies that have enslaved, oppressed, and confined so many Black people.[38]

A related dynamic is found in the manipulation of whites who are often damaged by the same economic and social policies, not changing policies to provide educational and economic opportunities, but providing the putative satisfactions of the "wages of whiteness." One example given by Kendi of this phenomenon is found after Reconstruction. Here he summarizes W. E. B. Du Bois's analysis of this phenomenon, one that is still at work today:

> After the Civil War, Black and White commoners came together to build democratic state governments providing public resources for the masses of southerners. White elites overthrew these governments by securing the loyalty of White commoners, a feat accomplished not by offering them higher wages, but by holding up the rewards of the lucrative "public and psychological wage." From Du Bois, historians now term these rewards the "wages of whiteness": they were the privileges that would accrue to Whites through application of racist ideas and segregation. And to receive them, White laborers needed only stand shoulder to shoulder with White elites on lynched and raped and exploited Black bodies.[39]

In the work of Carol Anderson, we also find another essential account of the many forms that white supremacy has taken, and what triggers the attacks by white Americans on black freedom, dignity, and equality. Her interpretation differs from that of Kendi, and adds another layer that is essential to see, understand, contain, and redress:

> The trigger for white rage, inevitably, is black advancement. It is not the mere presence of black people that is the problem; rather, it is blackness with ambition, with drive, with purpose, with aspirations, and with demands for full and equal citizenship. It is blackness that refuses to accept subjugation, to give up.[40]

Anderson goes on to state that the election of Obama was the "ultimate advancement, and thus the ultimate affront":[41]

> The truth is, white rage has undermined democracy, warped the Constitution, weakened the nation's ability to compete economically, squandered billions of dollars on baseless incarceration, rendered an entire region sick, poor, and woefully undereducation, and left cities nothing less than decimated. All this havoc has been wreaked simply because African Americans wanted to work, get an education, live in decent communities, raise their families, and vote.[42]

In his book *1919, The Year of Racial Violence: How African Americans Fought Back*, David F. Krugler also explores the manifestations of white rage examined by Anderson. Here is his description of the extreme white violence that followed Reconstruction:

> After the Civil War, white opposition to abolition and to citizenship for African Americans ushered in a new era of racialized mob violence. Reconstruction, directed by congressional Republicans and policed by federal troops, enabled black men's participation in the democratic process as voters and officeholders.... Despite

the presence of federal troops, white southerners deployed violence in a sustained campaign to topple the new Republican majorities, oust black officeholders, and disenfranchise black voters. At times, the violence resembled warfare: between 1865 and 1875, whites in Louisiana killed 2,141 blacks and wounded another 2,115. B7 1877, the formal end of Reconstruction, the "redemption" of the South was complete: mob terrorism had suppressed black voting rights.[43]

Krugler rightly states that the use of the language of "race riot" for attacks like these are fundamentally misleading, both implying spontaneity and hiding the fact that the violence was planned and initiated by white Americans. He argues that a more accurate term is antiblack collective violence: "Race riot implies that rioters of all races were equally responsible for the violence, but almost all of the year's conflict resulted from white-on-black violence. . . . African Americans were not so much rioting as fighting back, counter-attacking, repelling violence; above all, resisting."[44]

The lessons from history are stark: when policies fail, there is a resurgence of racism. When policies succeed, there is also a resurgence of racism. What can stop this pernicious scapegoating and fear of black Americans by white Americans?

We cannot live out our vision of an inclusive and multiracial democracy until we see the patterns, and until whites join people of other races and take up our roles in containing and preventing such violence. We live in a time in which there is still a call to an expansive and vibrant democracy. The trust that Coates saw in the Obama presidency for white Americans has been destroyed, but the challenge for us to be more together, and the invitation for us to be more together remains. The words of Anderson, Dyson, and Kendi are compelling.

The words of Michael Eric Dyson are clear. Whites must begin by acknowledging the deadly scope and impact of white privilege:

> Beloved, to be white is to know that you have at your own hand, or by extension, through institutionalized means, the power to take black life with impunity. It's the power of life and death that gives whiteness its force, its imperative. White life is worth more than black life.[45]

Given this reality, Dyson states that

> the most radical action a white person can take is to acknowledge this denied privilege, to say, "Yes, you're right. In our institutional structures, and in deep psychological structures, our underlying assumption is that our lives are worth more than yours."[46]

Once we who are right have seen this stark reality, what must we do? Again Dyson is clear. We can work for a genuinely inclusive democracy when we confront both the scope of white violence and the depth of our dependence upon black Americans for the very ideals and vibrancy of an inclusive democracy:

> You must swim in the vast ocean of blackness and then realize you have been buoyed all along on its sustaining view of democracy. What would this nation be

without the efforts of Frederick Douglass and Martin Luther King, Jr., to make it behave according to its ideals? What would it be had not Diane Nash and Fannie Lou Hamer given their all to quench the fires of hate?

When we confront racial catastrophe, black folk insist on fighting back. We have given this country the spiritual will and the moral maturity it lost in the bitter divorce of principle and practice. Our nation can only reach its best destiny when that recognition grounds our shared culture and existence. We want what you want. We want to pursue our dreams without the hindrance of racism. We want to raise our children in safety and send them to good schools. We want our communities to overflow with opportunity and support. We want good jobs and health care. We want gorgeous parks and lovely homes. We want affordable markets and department stores nearby. And we don't want to die at the hands of either the cops or other black folk.[47]

Anderson challenges us to refuse to follow Trump and his attempt to "take our country back":

It's time instead that we take our country forward into the future, a better future.

It is time to defuse the power of white rage. It is time to move into that future. It is a future where the right to vote is unfettered by discriminatory restrictions that prevent millions of American citizens from having any say in their own government.

The future is one that invests in our children by making access to good schools the norm, not the exception, and certainly not dependent upon zip code. . . . Why use property taxes as the basis for funding schools when that method rewards discriminatory public policy and perpetuates the inequalities that undermine our society?

The future is one that takes seriously a justice system whose enormous powers are actually used to serve and protect.[48]

I agree with Kendi that we can do far more in our work against racism and for racial justice than protest. We can use institutional power wisely and well, and in so doing, end the discrimination that limits fundamental opportunities for black Americans and fuels racist ideas for white Americans:

Any effective solution to eradicating American racism must involve Americans committed to antiracist policies seizing and maintaining power over institutions, neighborhoods, counties, states, nations—the word. . . . An antiracist America can only be guaranteed if principled antiracists are in power, and then antiracist policies become the law of the land, and then antiracist ideas become the common sense of the people, and then the antiracist common sense of the people holds those antiracist leaders and policies accountable.[49]

What does it take to join this work? I think that here, too, Kendi is right. The motivation for white participation in antiracism has been, and continues to be, enlightened self-interest: "Antiracists do not have to be self-less. Antiracists merely have to have intelligent self-interest, and to stop consuming those ideas racist ideas that have engendered so much unintelligent self-interest over the years."[50] Kendi gives an early example of such intelligent and expansive self-interest:

> The 1688 Germantown Petition Against Slavery was the inaugural antiracist tract among European settlers in colonial America. Beginning with this piece, the Golden Rule would forever inspire the cause of White antiracists. Antiracists of all races—whether out of altruism or intelligent self-interest—would always recognize that preserving racial hierarchy simultaneously preserves ethnic, gender, class, sexual, age, and religious hierarchies. Human hierarchies of any kind, they understood, would do little more than oppress all of humanity.[51]

While it is possible for whites to nurture and cultivate intelligent self-interest, the lessons of Anthony Pinn are also clear. There is a need for ongoing vigilance because of the multiple and mutating forms of white supremacy. When we take up these challenges, those of ongoing vigilance and the implementation of just political, economic, and educational policies, the types of activism proposed are multiple, all important, all worth ongoing experimentation and innovation. Dyson describes ten actions that are equally vital, ranging from reparations to developing racial literacy and cultivating an inclusive civic imagination.[52]

Pinn adds another dimension to our work. His challenge for humanist institutions applies to all institutions. It is vital that we "make acknowledgement of white privilege central to the mission and aims" of the organization, acknowledge the way white supremacy is operating and has operated in this particular organization, include racial minorities in this acknowledgment "by centralizing the concerns and insights of those who suffer from white privilege," act in response to these particular areas, for example, housing, "literally diversify the boards of our organizations, the chairs of various committees," and "repeat steps 1–5 again . . . and again."[53]

Kendi also calls for systematic oversight of such policy work, and calls for the creation of an agency "that aggressively investigates the disparities and punishes conscious and unconscious discriminators. This agency would also work toward equalizing the wealth and power of Black and White neighborhoods and their institutions, with a clear mission of repairing the inequities caused by discrimination."[54] In regard to the latter, such agencies do not have to be invented. I am fortunate to work with one, the Cook County Commission on Social Innovation. This organization was created by the president of the Cook County Board of Commissioners, Toni Preckwinkle, in April 2016. It is chaired by a Latino public official with a long history of commitment to social and economic justice, Jesus Chuy Garcia, and the vice chair is a white activist, Marc Lane. Lane is an attorney who is one of the major movers in the field of impact investing, creating the legal framework for people to use their wealth for the larger common good. The chairs of the various committees are racially diverse: 59 percent are black, Latinx, and Asian. The purpose of the committee is clear: to provide economic development for the black and Latinx communities of Chicago in a way that is not gentrification, but genuine empowerment for these communities and their current residents. In addition, it is hoped that this creative cooperation between businesses, nonprofits, and county government can serve as a model for other cities who share the same goals. Writing about the Commission for Forbes, Anne Fields reports that "the hope is that a creative all-hands-on-deck partnership between government, nonprofits and businesses with a social purpose might boost economic development and opportunities for the area's many impoverished residents."[55]

I will now take up a core challenge posed by Kendi. For those of us who are antiracist and have institutional power, or gain such power, how do we use it accountably and well? What does it take to create policies that are genuinely equitable? The challenges here are threefold:

1. there are tested and plausible strategies for addressing both implicit bias and structural racism that can be implemented;
2. intrinsic to these strategies is deliberate and ongoing attention to the frequent disparity between intent and impact;
3. the work of policy development and implementation is not clear cut and is often at odds with the prophetic imagination.

First, as an example of the second point, Bill Clinton did not intend to inaugurate the new Jim Crow with his war on drugs policies, yet as Michelle Alexander has demonstrated in her work, that impact is real, is a fundamental affront to human rights, and can be and must be rectified.[56]For an example of how this can be done, see the May 2015 report of President Obama's task force on twenty-first-century policing.[57]

There is strong evidence on how to contain and prevent implicit bias and structural racism in the work of behavioral public policy, the work of the Engagement Scholarship Consortium, and global efforts to create forms of economic life that are environmentally sound and socially just.[58] What has not yet been fully engaged is containing and preventing explicit white nationalism, white identity politics, and the resurgence of white collective antiblack violence.

Let us take up the basic challenge of constructive political change and the paradoxical ways in which the prophetic imagination is both a catalyst for such work and can yet shortchange the catalytic power of this work. In Gary Dorrien's study of the Obama presidency, he writes of progressives of all races who were disappointed in Obama's health care reform and his not fighting for the public option. "For many of them, winning was important, but trying was even more important: Obama settled too easily for a half loaf that he could win."[59]

In Dyson's interviews with President Obama, Dyson documents Obama's description of this same process, yet does not appear to himself fully grasp its significance. Also, while in this passage President Obama is addressing African American critics, the same critique can rightly be made of white progressives and liberals. In this passage, Obama is speaking of the particularity of "targeted strategies versus broad-based ones," a focus on "universal programs" that will provide better opportunities for whites as well as minorities. The fundamental issue, though, is larger. He is addressing

> a very practical political reality that some of my African American critics don't have to worry about because they're pundits or they're preachers, so they've just

got a different role to play. I've got to put together coalitions that allow me to get legislation through a House and a Senate that results in a bill on my desk that I can sign into law. Looking me straight in the eye, Obama rebuked the idealism of two of his most vocal black critics: "I have to appropriate dollars for any program which has to go through ways and means committees, or appropriations committees, that are not dominated by folks who read Cornel West or listen to Michael Eric Dyson." . . . "I don't always have the luxury of speaking prophetically . . . or in theory . . . I've got the job of governing and delivering to the people who desperately need help."[60]

Barack Obama was not the first progressive leader to honestly engage this challenge. We can see the same dynamic in the political leadership of Nelson Mandela and Ronald Dellums, and learn from their reflections on this essential component of social change. In his autobiography, Nelson Mandela stated that "it is a relatively simple proposition to keep a movement together when you are fighting against a common enemy. But creating a policy when that enemy is across the negotiating table is another matter altogether."[61] Congressman Ronald Dellums also explored the challenge of moving from protest to the creation of effective policy solutions. In *Lying Down with the Lions*, Dellums recounts the history of his work in politics and the commitments and strategies that have shaped his work, a career grounded in two factors: an ongoing openness to listening to the stories of injustice and hope of those who were marginalized and exploited, and an astute understanding of the nature of the democratic process.

Although affirming the "moral certitude" and "righteous rage" of those who are oppressed, Dellums's own political engagement led him away from denunciations of other people and social structures. Dellums recounts that he had early on to make a choice: was he going to be a "rhetorical activist" or "an effective legislator committed to securing social change through the process of governance?"[62]

I had not come to Congress to attack and alienate my colleagues; I had come to challenge their ideas. I needed to step back from the personal . . . . I had to return to the educative role that Dr. King had laid out in his challenge to leadership. I needed to become better informed, to understand my opponents and be able to best them in open debate. I had to bring them along with me, not demand that they reject themselves . . . . I could not be content with a role as the radical outsider if I wanted people to pay heed to our radical ideas. I needed to develop arguments that my fellow legislators could take home to *their* constituents and imagine articulating at *their* constituents' day meetings.[63]

This is as a lesson that many progressives have yet to learn. We know how to create forms of public witness that denounce what is wrong—demonstrations, boycotts, sit-ins. What is harder, however, is finding the means of providing energizing and compelling public support for what *may* be right. How do we show support for, and engage critically and creatively in, the messy and ambiguous process of change? While it is true that our victories are most often partial, their impact may be real and may even be a catalyst for further change.

As an example of this process, let us return to the matter of health care. We did not get the public option on health care, but Dorrien describes the significance of what was gained under Obama, and what is now under direct attack:

> But covering 34 million people was a colossal achievement. No one should go bankrupt because of an illness. Obama risked his presidency in order to help the poorest and most vulnerable people in American society. He knew very well that doing so would pay few political dividends and would carry a huge political downside. He took for granted that opponents would legally challenge the mandate that makes reform affordable. . . . There may be a majority in the electoral system and the courts that are willing to ensure that poor and vulnerable people are not excluded from having the medical system work for them. And perhaps there is not. Obama has put into play the very fundamental question: What kind of country should we want to be?[64]

What kind of country are we becoming, and what kind of country do we still want to be? The challenge of the crafting of policies that nurture and respect equal opportunity for all remains, and now, we are seeing the need for other types of policies. What specific policies can contain now and possibly prevent in the future collective antiblack violence by white nationalists? I do not have an answer; a new exploration is underway. My wager in shaping both types of policies includes a specific recasting of the religious imagination, that is, in one way, an affirmation of Dyson, in another, not. Dyson writes, "We will not surrender because we know that faith is greater than fear, good triumphant over evil, love more noble than hate."[65]

My wager—given the recent debacle and tragic history—for whites is that *our evil is as strong as our good*. It can be contained, but may never be eradicated. Our hopes, and our efforts, require resolute attention to the former and constant vigilance in regard to the latter.

As we resolutely craft policies to contain our evil now and prevent its resurgence in the future, we must grapple with the ethical challenges of using power wisely. Here we encounter the limits of prophetic imagination—the ethical challenges of using power wisely cannot be grasped by either the logic of prophetic critique or prophetic vision. Our challenge is, then, what to call the work of responding genuinely to prophetic critique and doing all that is in our power to bring a prophetic vision to life? The language of reform, of pragmatism, is too mild, missing both the urgency of the work and the extent of the change being sought. The language of revolution is too purist, missing the complexity of the work and the intrinsic ambiguity of the process. Our work may fail in some regards, and yet be catalytic in others. Reforms may be ingredients for further change, or may remain insufficient. In other settings I have written more about this third stage of constructive social engagement, and am still searching for the language that holds the complexity, danger, and promise of the structural work of implementation that may follow the constitutive work of critique and inclusion.[66]

What sustains and empowers here is a simple conviction, as applicable to the contours of daily life as to the challenges of making history. My friend HK Hall, lifelong antiracist activist in his personal, professional, and political life, told me about the understandings of life expressed by people in their nineties and hundreds who are as fully engaged now as ever. In a documentary about aging, Carl Reiner described his philosophy of life in two words: "now" and "next."[67]

Now—we must see the horrific costs of racism and the dangers of its expansion. Far from the death knell of white rage and extremism in the United States, we may be seeing the birth pangs of another resurgence of white antiblack anti-immigrant violence, the birth pangs of a white identity grounded in fear, exclusion, and domination.

Next—this is the time for resolute, thorough, innovative action.

In this dialectic, it is ironic that the prophetic imagination is both a compelling gift, and at times, a damaging limitation. The power of the prophetic imagination is to name what is wrong, and name what can be, with courage and power.

The prophetic imagination does not, however, know how to work with the inevitable messiness and complexity of the move from prophetic critique and vision to just implementations. The prophetic imagination can see it and denounce this complexity, but not work with it in catalytic ways. As we try to do that, the language of pragmatism is also limited, lacking both the intense impetus for the work of social justice and the irony and costs of the failures and foibles of even the progressive vanguard.

Perhaps what is required is not simple pragmatism, but alchemy.

I have long found the words of the legal scholar Patricia Williams to be evocative and inspiring, and offer them to you, to us, as we continue our struggle to restore, maintain, and expand the very soul of democracy:

> To say that blacks never fully believed in rights is true. Yet it is also true that blacks believed in them so much and so hard that we gave them life where there was none before. . . . This was the resurrection of life from ashes four hundred years old. The making of something out of nothing took immense alchemical fire—the fusion of a whole nation and the kindling of several generations. . . . But if it took this long to breathe life into a form whose shape had already been forged by society, and which is therefore idealistically if not ideologically accessible, imagine how long the struggle would be without even that sense of definition, without the power of that familiar vision.
>
> In discarding rights altogether, one discards a symbol too deeply enmeshed in the psyche of the oppressed to lose without trauma and much resistance. Instead, society must *give* them away. Unlock them from reification by giving them to slaves. Give them to trees. Give them to cows. Give them to history. Give them to rivers and rocks. Give to all of society's objects and untouchables the rights of privacy, integrity, and self-assertion; give them distance and respect. Flood them with the animating spirit that rights mythology fires in this country's most oppressed psyches, and wash away the shrouds of inanimate-object status, so that we may say not that we own gold but that a luminous golden spirit owns us.[68]

Notes

Introduction

1 See "Inside Obama's Sweeping Victory" at: http://www.pewresearch.org/2008/11/05/inside-obamas-sweeping-victory/.

2 https://www.usnews.com/news/campaign-2008/articles/2008/11/06/young-voters-powered-obamas-victory-while-shrugging-off-slacker-image.

3 http://www.huffingtonpost.com/garrett-graff/why-yes-we-can-inspires_b_84838.html.

4 http://www.latimes.com/world/la-fg-worldreax6-2008nov06-story.html.

5 Tim Shipman, "Conservative backlash begins against Barak Obama," *The Telegraph.* Reviewed at: http://www.telegraph.co.uk/news/worldnews/barackobama/3464679/Conservative-backlash-begins-against-Barack-Obama.html.

6 "After Obama's win, white blacklash festers in US," found at: https://www.csmonitor.com/USA/Politics/2008/1117/p03s01-uspo.html.

7 In addition to President Obama's own monographs, *Dreams from My Father: A Story of Race and Inheritance* (1995) and *The Audacity of Hope: Thoughts on Reclaiming the American Dream* (New York: Crown, 2006), also see T. Denean Sharpley-Whiting, ed., *The Speech: Race and Barack Obama's "A More Perfect Union"* (London: Bloomsbury, 2009); Thomas J. Sugrue, *Not Even Past: Barack Obama and the Burden of Race* (Princeton: Princeton University Press, 2009); David Remnick, *The Bridge: The Life and Rise of Barack Obama* (New York: Knopf, 2010); Jonathan Alter, *The Promise: President Obama, Year One* (New York: Simon and Schuster, 2010); William Jelani Cobb, *The Substance of Hope: Barack Obama and the Paradox of Progress* (New York: Walker Books, 2010); Michael Tesler and David O. Sears, *Obama's Race: The 2008 Election and the Dream of a Post-Racial America* (Chicago: University of Chicago Press, 2010); Peniel E. Joseph, *Dark Days, Bright Nights: From Black Power to Barack Obama* (New York: Basic Civitas Books, 2010); James T. Kloppenberg, *Reading Obama: Dreams, Hope, and the American Political Tradition* (Princeton: Princeton University Press, 2011); Randall Kennedy, *The Persistence of the Color Line: Racial Politics and the Obama Presidency* (New York: Vintage, 2011); Fredrick Harris, *The Price of the Ticket: Barack Obama and Rise and Decline of Black Politics* (New York: Oxford University Press, 2012); Jodi Kantor, *The Obamas* (New York: Little Brown and Company, 2012); Jenny Scott, *A Singular Woman: The Untold Story of Barack Obama's Mother* (New York: Penguin, 2011); Sally H. Jacobs, *The Other Barack: The Bold and Reckless Life of President Obama's Father* (New York: Public Affairs, 2011); David Maraniss, *Barack Obama: The Story* (New York: Simon & Schuster, 2012); Jonathan Alter, *The Center Holds: Obama and His Enemies* (New York: Simon & Schuster, 2013); Michael Eric Dyson, *The Black Presidency: Barack Obama and the Politics of Race in America* (Boston: Houghton Mifflin Harcourt, 2016); E. J. Dionne Jr. and Joy-Ann Reid eds., *We Are the Change We Seek: The Speeches of Barack Obama* (London: Bloomsbury, 2017); and David J. Garrow, *Rising Star: The Making of Barack Obama* (New York: William Morrow, 2017).

8 Kloppenberg, *Reading Obama*, xxxvii.

9 Ta-Nehisi Coates, "My President Was Black: A History of the First African American White House – and What Came Next," *The Atlantic* (January/February 2017). https://www.theatlantic.com/magazine/archive/2017/01/my-president-was-black/508793/.

10 Kloppenberg, *Reading Obama*, 83.

11 Jerry Harris and Carl Davidson, "Obama: The New Contours of Power," *Race & Class* 50, no. 1 (2009): 2.

12 Full acceptance speech transcript: http://abcnews.go.com/Politics/Vote2008/story?id=6181477.

13 This paragraph is from: Anthony Pinn, "Getting Wright Wrong: Preaching Is Not Policy", *Religion Dispatches* (July 3, 2009). At: http://religiondispatches.org/getting-wright-wrong-preaching-is-not-policy/.

14 Harris and Davidson, "Obama," 4.

15 See, for example, the *Washington Post* article: https://www.washingtonpost.com/opinions/obamas-risky-embrace-of-occupy-wall-street/2011/10/19/gIQA2pQf1L_story.html?utm_term=.ca3ed7397457.

16 See, for example, Jürgen Habermas, *The Structural Transformation of the Public Sphere* (Cambridge: MIT Press, 1991); Jürgen Habermas, *Theory of Communicative Actions*, vols. 1–2 (Boston: Beacon Press, 1985) and Nancy Frazer, "Rethinking the Public Sphere: A Contribution to the Critique of Actually Existing Democracy," *Social Text*, 25/26 (1990): 56–80; Nancy Fraser, *Justice Interruptus: Critical Reflections on the "Postsocialist" Condition* (New York: Routledge, 1997).

17 David Frum, "Republicans Must Change to Win," *Financial Times* (July 5, 2008): 11; George F. Will, "Republicans: Save Your Party, Don't Give to Trump", *Washington Post* (June 22, 2016); and Jeff Flake, *Conscience of a Conservative: A Rejection of Destructive Politics and a Return to Principle* (New York: Random House, 2017).

18 Obama, *The Audacity of Hope*, 205.

19 Stephen Prothero, *Religious Literacy: What Every American Needs to Know—and Doesn't* (New York: HarperCollins Publisher, 2008).

20 Obama, *The Audacity of Hope,* 207.

21 Anthony B. Pinn, *Understanding & Transforming the Black Church* (Eugene, OR: Cascade Books, 2010), 124.

22 Andrew Billingsley, *Mighty Like a River: The Black Church and Social Reform* (New York: Oxford University Press, 2003), 170–81; Sharpley-Whiting, ed., *The Speech*; Jeremiah A. Wright Jr., *A Sankofa Moment: The History of Trinity United Church of Christ* (Dallas, TX: St. Paul Press, 2010); Susan Williams Smith, *The Book of Jeremiah: The Life and Ministry of Jeremiah A. Wright Jr.* (Cleveland, OH: Pilgrim Press, 2013); and Carl A. Grant and Shelby J. Grant, *The Moment: Barack Obama, Jeremiah Wright, and the Firestorm at Trinity United Church of Christ* (Lanham, MD: Rowman and Littlefield, 2013).

23 Researchers for years to come will have to contemplate and consider very deeply the significance of the first black US president being brought into the fold of the black church tradition by a pastor who was a proud and prophetic exemplar of black liberation theology both in theory and praxis. A book such as this is at least an initial attempt at such an endeavor.

24 Stephen Marche, "The Obama Years," *Los Angeles Review of Books* (November 30, 2016). https://lareviewofbooks.org/article/the-obama-years/#!.

25 E. J. Dionne Jr. and Joy-Ann Reid, "Introduction," in E. J. Dionne Jr. and Joy-Ann Reid, eds., *We Are the Change We Seek: The Speeches of Barack Obama* (London: Bloomsbury Press, 2017), xvii.

26 The numerous books written about President Barack Obama essentially tend to fall into three general categories: personal and family biographies, contemporary political analyses of his presidency (both critical and celebratory), and explorations of race and racism in American society based on his identity. In addition to Obama's own monographs, *Dreams from My Father* and *The Audacity of Hope*, one can also see Kantor, *The Obamas*, Scott, *A Singular Woman*, Jacobs, *The Other Barack*, and Maraniss, *Barack Obama* as representative texts focused on Obama's personal and family history. With regard to books focused on the political impact of the Obama years, there are works such as Paul Street, *Barack Obama and the Future of American Politics* (New York: Routledge, 2009), Eric Alterman, *Kabuki Democracy: The System vs. Barack Obama* (New York: Nation Books, 2011), Kloppenberg, *Reading Obama*, Remnick, *The Bridge*, Alter, *The Promise*, Richard Wolffe, *Renegade: The Making of a President* (New York: Broadway Books, 2010), Gary Dorrien, *The Obama Question: A Progressive Perspective* (New York: Rowman & Littlefield Publishers, 2012), and Alter, *The Center Holds* among others. For obvious reasons, the books concentrating on his complicated "mixed race" identity and its perceived impact on culture and society have been legion. Among the most notable works of this ilk is Johnny B. Hill, *The First Black President: Barack Obama, Race, Politics, and the American Dream* (New York: Palgrave Macmillan, 2009), Sharpley-Whiting, ed., *The Speech*, Sugrue, *Not Even Past*, Joseph, *Dark Days, Bright Nights*, Cobb, *The Substance of Hope*, Tesler and Sears, *Obama's Race*, Kennedy, *The Persistence of the Color Line*, Harris, *The Price of the Ticket*, Eddie S. Glaude Jr., *Democracy in Black: How Race Still Enslaves the American Soul* (New York: Broadway Books, 2016), and Dyson, *The Black Presidency*.

27 Andrew Sullivan, "Goodbye to All that: Why Obama Matters," *The Atlantic* (December 2007). Found at: https://www.theatlantic.com/magazine/archive/2007/12/goodbye-to-all-that-why-obama-matters/306445/.

Chapter 1

1 Michelle A. Vu, "Why Some Evangelicals Won't Vote for Romney," *Christian Post* (October 16, 2007). http://www.christianpost.com/news/why-some-evangelicals-won-t-vote-for-romney-29718/ (accessed January 15, 2017).

2 Vu, "Why Some Evangelicals Won't Vote for Romney."

3 Romney's own great-grandfather fled to Mexico in the 1880s to avoid imprisonment under anti-bigamy laws.

4 Craig Foster, *A Different God? Mitt Romney, the Religious Right, and the Mormon Question* (Salt Lake City, UT: Greg Kofford Books, 2008), 189–91. For an accessible and thorough introduction to Romney's "religion problem" during the 2007–08 campaign, see Ibid.

5 Edward S. Herman and David Peterson, "Jeremiah Wright in the Propaganda System," *Monthly Review* 60, no. 4 (September 2008): 6–7. For an accessible and thorough introduction to the Obama-Wright relationship, see Clarence E. Walker and Gregory D. Smithers, *The Preacher and the Politician* (Charlottesville, The University of Virginia, 2012 (reprint)).

6 Such scholarship exists, the findings of which suggest that the more familiar voters are with a marginalized religious and/or racial minority culture, the less affected they will be by controversies that sensationalize these cultures. Brian McKenzie, "Barack

Obama, Jeremiah Wright, and Public Opinion in the 2008 Presidential Primaries," *Political Psychology* 32, no. 6 (2011): 943–61. David E. Campbell, John C. Green, and J. Quinn Monson, "The Stained Glass Ceiling: Social Contact and Mitt Romney's 'Religion Problem,'" *Political Behavior* 34, no. 2 (June 2012): 277–99.

7 On the "white American republic" of the late nineteenth century during which the "Mormon" and "black" problems were most fully articulated, see Edward Blum, *Reforging the White Republic: Race, Religion, and American Nationalism, 1865-1898* (Baton Rouge: Louisiana State University Press, 2005). On the white American republic's contemporary descendent, "white Christian America," see Robert P. Jones, *The End of White Christian America* (New York: Simon & Schuster: 2016). On the "Mormon" and "black" problems as both racial and religious histories, see W. Paul Reeve, *Religion of a Different Color: Race and the Mormon Struggle for Whiteness* (New York: Oxford University Press, 2015); Curtis Evans, *The Burden of Black Religion* (New York: Oxford University Press, 2008).

8 On Obama's religion as a proxy for his race, see Kevin Healey, "The Pastor in the Basement: Discourses of Authenticity in the Networked Public Sphere," *Symbolic Interaction* 33, no. 4 (October 2010): 526–51.

9 Walker and Smithers, *The Preacher and the Politician*, 16.

10 Ibid. See also, Bernard W. Bell, "President Obama, the Rev. Dr. Jeremiah Wright, and the African American Jeremiadic Tradition," *The Massachusetts Review* 50, no. 3 (Autumn 2009): 332–43.

11 Herman and Peterson, "Jeremiah Wright in the Propaganda System," 6–7.

12 Mark Steyn, "Uncle Jeremiah: Barack Obama and His Cookie-cutter Race Huckster," *The National Review* (March 15, 2008). http://www.nationalreview.com/node/223934/ print (accessed January 16, 2017).

13 Most of media produced contemporaneous with the controversy and the scholarship produced since have focused on Wright as a black liberation theologian and as a proponent of Afrocentrist politics. Yet, there are elements of Wright's career that signify a politics of respectability. Wright transformed Trinity from a church with less than 100 regular attendees to, by the time he retired in early 2008, a church with some 8,000 parishioners, among which were some of black Chicago's most prominent figures, including Oprah Winfrey and Common. Trinity was the largest black church in the predominantly white UCC, which brought fame to Trinity and to the denomination, and state-wide and national recognition (including several honorary doctorates and presidential commendations) to Wright himself. Just two days before the controversy broke, the Illinois General Assembly passed an official resolution congratulating Wright on his retirement. House Resolution: HR1073, "Congrats-Rev. Jeremiah Wright" (March 11, 2008). http://www.ilga.gov/legislation/BillStatus.asp?Do cNum=1073&GAID=9&DocTypeID=HR&LegID=38304&SessionID=51&SpecSess= &Session=&GA=95 (accessed January 20, 2017).

14 Brian Ross, Rehab el-Buri, "Obama's Pastor: God Damn America, U.S. to Blame for 9/11," *ABC News* (March 13, 2008). http://abcnews.go.com/Blotter/story?id=4443788 (accessed January 20, 2017).

15 On "the Preferential Option for the Poor and Oppressed" and its connection to racial minorities, see Dwight Hopkins, *Heart and Head: Black Theology Past, Present, and Future* (New York: Palgrave, 2002), 53–76.

16 On Wright's Christian Afrocentrism, see the edited volume of his sermons in Dr. Jeremiah Wright, *Africans Who Shaped Our Faith* (Durham, NC: Urban Ministries, 1995). As black preachers had done for centuries, Wright connected the present plight of

African Americans in America with Israelite captivity in Egypt and Babylon. But Wright did not simply assert that the African American experiences of bondage and racial oppression were akin to the experiences of the ancient Israelites. He implied that African Americans were *actual kin* of the ancient Israelites. Therefore "Africans" by blood were heirs to the most ancient and sacred covenants. Ibid., 20. On African-Israelite connections and the contemporary communities they form, see Tudor Parfitt, *Black Jews in Africa and the Americas* (Cambridge, MA: Harvard University Press, 2013).

17 Dr. James H. Cone, "Toward a Black Theology," *Ebony* (August 1970): 114; Alex Haley, Malcolm X, *The Autobiography of Malcolm X* (New York: Ballantine Books, 1992), 31–32; W. E. B. Du Bois, *The Souls of Black Folk: Essays and Sketches* (Chicago: A. C. McClurg & Co, 1903), 3.

18 In at least one sermon, Wright's deployed the term "Negro" to signify the African Americans—"Colin Powell, Chappie James, Roy Wilkins, and Ralph Bunche"—who spoke against Martin Luther King's (Jeremiah-like) decision to oppose the American colonial effort in Vietnam in 1967. In doing so, Wright differentiated between these "Negro" black Americans, whose souls and minds remain divided, and those "Africans" who have woken up to their true selves. In the same sermon, Wright emphasized the importance of African Americans to embrace "African" names. He even attempted a unique exegetical—perhaps midrashic—move to claim that "MLK" is an (almost) African name. "MLK-Zadok means 'King of righteousness'". Wright, *Africans Who Shaped Our Faith*, 121–24.

19 Barack Obama, *Dreams from My Father: A Story of Race and Inheritance* (Broadway Books, 2004), 294.

20 Obama, *Dreams from My Father*.

21 Reeve, *Religion of a Different Color*.

22 Ibid., 6.

23 On race as a signifier, see Sut Jhally (Producer; Director), *Staurt Hall: Race, the Floating Signifier* (Northampton, MA: Media Education Foundation, 1998). See also, Brian Fung, "The Uncanny Valley: What Robot Theory Tells Us about Mitt Romney," *The Atlantic* (January 31, 2012). http://www.theatlantic.com/politics/archive/2012/01/the-uncanny-valley-what-robot-theory-tells-us-about-mitt-romney/252235/ (accessed January 16, 2017).

24 "Robotic-Looking, Special Underwear-Wearing Mormon Mitt Romney Gives Commencement Speech at Coe College in Iowa," May 7, 2006, state29.blogspot.com. (The post seems to have been removed, but another blogger captured the text, and offered his own commentary, here: http://goodpoliticaldebatepromotingalgorithm.blogspot.com/2006/05/re-bigoted-rant.html (accessed January 16, 2017)). Romney as a robot became a widespread (and upon reflection perhaps a racially troubling) meme during the 2012 election. Asawin Suebsaeng, "Romney or Robot: The Quiz" (March 21, 2012). http://www.motherjones.com/politics/2012/03/mitt-romney-robot-quiz (accessed January 16, 2017); Hal Boyd, "Friends Say Mitt Romney Not as Stiff or Robotic as Media Portrays," *Deseret News* (August 19, 2011), http://www.deseretnews.com/article/700172041/Friends-say-Mitt-Romney-not-as-stiff-or-robotic-as-media-portrays.html (accessed January 16, 2017).

25 Barton Gellman, "Dreams from His Mother," *Time* (June 4, 2012). http://content.time.com/time/subscriber/article/0,33009,2115636,00.html (accessed December 12, 2017).

26 Mark Leibovich, "Polished and Upbeat, Romney Tries to Connect," *The New York Times* (June 16, 2007). http://www.nytimes.com/2007/06/16/us/politics/16romney.html (accessed January 16, 2017).

27 Andrew Sullivan, "Mormon Sacred Underwear," *The Atlantic* (November 24, 2006). http://www.theatlantic.com/daily-dish/archive/2006/11/mormon-sacred-underwear/232160/ (accessed January 16, 2017).

28 Maureen Dowd, "Mitt's No J.F.K.," *The New York Times* (December 9, 2007). http://www.nytimes.com/2007/12/09/opinion/09dowd.html?n=Top/Opinion/Editorials%20and%20Op-Ed/Op-Ed/Columnists/Maureen%20Dowd (accessed January 16, 2017).

29 Scott Keeter, "Public Opinion about Mormons," *Pew* (December 4, 2007). http://www.pewresearch.org/2007/12/04/public-opinion-about-mormons/ (accessed January 28, 2017).

30 Foster, *A Different God?* 189–91.

31 Ibid.

32 Mitt Romney, "Faith in America," *NPR* (December 6, 2007). http://www.npr.org/templates/story/story.php?storyId=16969460 (accessed January 28, 2017).

33 Thomas J. Carty, *A Catholic in The White House: Religion, Politics, and John F. Kennedy's Presidential Campaign* (New York: Palgrave, 2004), 59–62.

34 Romney, "Faith in America." Ironically, Kennedy's martyrdom reinforced the relationship between the presidency and what Robert Bellah first described as "civil religion in America." Robert N. Bellah, "Civil Religion in America," *Daedalus* 96, no. 1 (Winter 1967): 1–21.

35 To be sure, many white evangelicals were deeply disappointed that the "born-again" Carter failed to engage in the culture wars, which led directly to the rise of the "Moral Majority" in the late 1970s. This brought about a paradigm shift in white evangelicals' relationship with politics, with the two dominant political parties, and with particular politicians. By the time George W. Bush ran for the presidency as evangelical in 2000, the definition of an "evangelical" politician had changed to such a degree that Carter, the first candidate to inaugurate the identity in modern presidential politics, would not have been seen as one. D. Michael Lindsay, *Faith in the Halls of Power: How Evangelicals Joined the American Elite* (New York: Oxford University Press, 2008), 16–26, 54–56.

36 Romney, "Faith in America."

37 Ibid. Though this litany of religions is limited to the "Abrahamic Faiths" and though it reflects some problematic religious illiteracy (e.g., the Jews' traditions are not ahistorical, as Romney declares), it also sounds a lot like the Christian pluralism championed by Diana Eck. Diana L. Eck, "Prospects for Pluralism: Voice and Vision in the Study of Religion," *Journal of the American Academy of Religion* 75, no. 4 (2007): 743–76.

38 Romney, "Faith in America."

39 Patrick Henry, "'And I Don't Care What It Is': The Tradition-History of a Civil Religion Proof-Text," *Journal of the American Academy of Religion* 49, no. 1 (1981): 35–47.

40 Romney, "Faith in America."

41 Ibid.

42 "Romney's Announcement in Dearborn, Michigan," *The New York Times* (February 13, 2007). http://www.nytimes.com/2007/02/13/us/politics/13romney-text.html?pagewanted=print (accessed January 23, 2017).

43 Romney, "Faith in America."

44 Ibid.

45 Ibid.

46 Jan Shipps, "Making Saints: In the Early Days and the Latter Days," in Marie Cornwall et al. eds., *Contemporary Mormonism: Social Science Perspectives* (Urbana: University of Illinois Press, 2001), 64–86.

47 Bruce Kinney, *Mormonism: The Islam of America* (New York: H. Revell Co., 1912), 35, 136, 172, 152. See also, Josiah Strong, *Our Country: Its Possible Future and Its Present Crisis* (New York: Baker and Taylor Co., 1885), 61–64.

48 Barack Obama, "On My Faith and My Church," *Huffington Post* (March 14, 2008). http://www.huffingtonpost.com/barack-obama/on-my-faith-and-my-church_b_91623.html (accessed January 28, 2017).

49 Ben Smith, "Wright Leaves Obama Campaign," *Politico* (March 14, 2008). http://www.politico.com/blogs/ben-smith/2008/03/wright-leaves-obama-campaign-007039 (accessed January 28, 2017).

50 On Obama's speechwriters' role in shaping the speech, see Nedra Pickler, "From Greek Mythology, Obama Learned a Lesson," *USA TODAY* (June 4, 2008). http://usatoday30. usatoday.com/news/politics/2008-06-04-2310712963_x.htm (accessed January 25, 2017). It's also important to note that Obama had been reflecting on these themes his whole public career. Kloppenberg, *Reading Obama*, 208–15.

51 Barack Obama, "A More Perfect Union," *NPR* (March 18, 2008). http://www.npr.org/ templates/story/story.php?storyId=88478467 (accessed January 28, 2017). Gary Wills rightfully sees parallels between Obama's "A More Perfect Union" speech and Lincoln's "Cooper Union Address." "Both used a campaign occasion to rise a higher vision of America's future. Both argued intelligently for a closer union in the cause of progress." And in some measure, both speeches are credited with electing the two men president. But I also find connections to Lincoln's "House Divided" speech in that Obama and Lincoln spoke to the moral and practical unsustainability of a divided nation; for Lincoln between North and South; for Obama between black and white. Gary Wills, "Two Speeches on Race," *The New York Review of Books* (May 1, 2008). http://www. nybooks.com/articles/2008/05/01/two-speeches-on-race/ (accessed January 25, 2017).

52 Obama, "A More Perfect Union."

53 Ibid. Yet, as Ta-Nehisi Coates has written, Obama's notion of what we might call a theology of "black America" was qualitatively different from Wright's. "Obama offered black America a convenient narrative that could be meshed with the larger American story," Coates has written. "It was a narrative premised on Crispus Attucks, not the black slaves who escaped plantations and fought for the British; on the 54th Massachusetts, not Nat Turner; on stoic and saintly Rosa Parks, not young and pregnant Claudette Colvin; on a Christlike Martin Luther King Jr., not an avenging Malcolm X. Jeremiah Wright's presence threatened to rupture that comfortable narrative by symbolizing that which makes integration impossible—black rage." Ta-Nehisi Coates, "Fear of a Black President," *The Atlantic* (September 2012). https:// www.theatlantic.com/magazine/archive/2012/09/fear-of-a-black-president/309064/ (accessed December 11, 2017).

54 Obama, "A More Perfect Union."

55 Ibid.

56 Ibid. W. E. B. Du Bois, "The Talented Tenth," in Booker T. Washington et al. eds., *The Negro Problem* (New York: James Pott & Company, 1903) 31–76.

57 Obama, "A More Perfect Union."

58 Thomas Frank, *What's the Matter with Kansas* (New York: Holt, 2005). See also, David Roediger, *The Wages of Whiteness* (New York: Verso, 2007).

59 Obama, "A More Perfect Union."

60 Ibid. Obama was clearly speaking to black American fathers in particular. Dyson, *The Black Presidency* 132–34.

61 Gellman, "Dreams from His Mother."

62 Obama, "A More Perfect Union."

63 Romney, "Faith in America."

64 Foster, *A Different God?* 190–91.

65 Thomas Burr, "Hang-ups over Mormonism Proved Romney's Undoing," *Salt Lake Tribune* (February 10, 2008). http://archive.sltrib.com/story.php?ref=/ci_8221611 (accessed January 30, 2017).

66 Max Perry Mueller, "Twice-told Tale: Telling Two Histories of Mormon-Black Relations during the 2012 Presidential Election," in Randall Balmer and Jana Reiss, eds., *Mormonism and American Politics* (Columbia University Press, 2015), 155–74.

67 "Transcript of Mitt Romney's Speech on Donald Trump," *The New York Times* (March 3, 2016). https://www.nytimes.com/2016/03/04/us/politics/mitt-romney-speech.html (accessed January 30, 2017).

68 On the history of anti-Mormonism, see J. Spencer Fluhman, "'A Peculiar People': Anti-Mormonism and the Making of Religion in Nineteenth-Century America* (Chapel Hill: The University of North Carolina Press, 2012).

69 Max Perry Mueller, "Why Mormons Don't Like Trump," *Slate* (August 4, 2016). http://www.slate.com/articles/news_and_politics/politics/2016/08/why_mormons_don_t_like_donald_trump.html (accessed January 30, 2017).

70 Trump underperformed Romney who took the state with 72.6 percent in 2012. Trump got 45 percent to Hillary Clinton's 27 percent and McMullin's 21 percent. Max Perry Mueller, "Not My Choir," *Slate* (January 19, 2017), http://www.slate.com/articles/news_and_politics/politics/2017/01/make_america_s_choir_great_again.html (accessed January 30, 2017).

71 Hendrik Hertzberg, "Obama Wins," *The New Yorker* (November 17, 2008): 40; Kloppenberg, *Reading Obama*, 208–15.

72 Stanley Kurtz, "'Context,' You Say? A Guide to the Radical Theology of the Rev. Jeremiah Wright," *The National Review* (May 19, 2008): 28–29.

73 "Growing Number of Americans Say Obama is a Muslim," Pew Research Center (August 18, 2010). http://www.pewforum.org/2010/08/18/growing-number-of-americans-say-obama-is-a-muslim/ (accessed January 15, 2017).

74 The same poll found that 20 percent of American adults believed he was born outside the United States. Peter Schroeder, "Poll: 43 Percent of Republicans Believe Obama is a Muslim," *The Hill* (September 13, 2015). http://thehill.com/blogs/blog-briefing-room/news/253515-poll-43-percent-of-republicans-believe-obama-is-a-muslim (accessed January 15, 2017).

75 "Remarks by the President in Eulogy for the Honorable Reverend Clementa Pinckney," *The White House* (June 26, 2015). https://www.whitehouse.gov/the-press-office/2015/06/26/remarks-president-eulogy-honorable-reverend-clementa-pinckney (accessed January 30, 2017).

76 This work began even before the start of Obama's second term. Kloppenberg, *Reading Obama*.

Chapter 2

1 An earlier version of "Political Spirituality" first appeared as "Epilogue: Political Spirituality, or The Oprahfication of Obama," in *Oprah: The Gospel of an Icon*, by Kathryn Lofton (Berkeley: University of California Press, 2011), 213–22.

2 In a 2004 interview, Obama and Oprah discussed the similarity between their names, "Oprah Talks to Barack Obama," *O, The Oprah Magazine* 5, no. 11 (November 2004): 288. For more on the branding of the Obama campaign, see Steven Heller, "The 'O' in Obama," *New York Times* (November 20, 2008); Hendrik Hertzberg, "Comment: Obama Wins," *New Yorker* (November 17, 2008): 39; Philip Kennicott, "The Power of Brand-Old Message Art," *Washington Post* (January 13, 2009); "Selling the President: Get Your Obama Hot Sauce," *The Week* (January 30, 2009): 17.

3 On the life stories Oprah and Obama tell about themselves, see Jennifer Buckendorff, "The Oprah Way," *Salon.com* (January 24, 2005); Jodi Kantor, "A First Family that Reflects a Nation's Diversity," *New York Times* (January 21, 2009); David Remnick, "The Joshua Generation," *New Yorker* (November 17, 2008): 72; Brian Stelter, "Following the Script: Obama, McCain, and the *West Wing*," *New York Times* (October 30, 2008).

4 For the religious and cultural communities of Oprah and Obama, see "Bill Cosby mulls his show's possible impact on Obama's election," *Associated Press* (November 12, 2008); John Blake, "Black first family 'changes everything'," *CNN.com* (January 15, 2009); Caitlin Flanagan and Benjamin Schwarz, "Showdown in the Big Tent," *New York Times* (December 6, 2008); Michelle Goldberg, "Obama's Divisive Choice of Rick Warren," *ReligionDispatches.org* (December 18, 2008); James Hannaham, "Obama: Don't Pander to Homophobes," *Salon.com* (October 26, 2007); "How They See Us: An African President for America," *The Week* (February 6, 2009): 16; Allison Samuels, "Something Wasn't Wright, So Oprah Left His Church," *Newsweek* (May 12, 2008): 8; Majorie Valbrun, "The Trouble With Transcending Race," *TheRoot.com* (April 30, 2008); Jeff Zeleny, "A New Wind Is Blowing in Chicago," *New York Times* (November 20, 2008).

5 On the styles of Oprah and Obama, see John Dickerson, "Professor Obama's First Seminar," *Slate.com* (February 10, 2009); Maureen Dowd, "The First Shrink," *New York Times* (April 5,2009); Jodi Kantor, "The Long Run: Teaching Law, Testing Ideas, Obama Stood Slightly Apart," *New York Times* (July 30, 2008); Lisa Miller, "Is Obama the Antichrist?" *Newsweek* (November 24, 2008): 18; Amy Sullivan, "An Antichrist Obama in McCain Ad?" *Time* (August 8, 2008); Fareed Zakaria, "The Global Elite: Barack Obama," *Newsweek* (December 29, 2008/January 5, 2009): 37.

6 In a 2004 interview, Obama demonstrated his religious amalgamation in response to the question, "What do you believe?"

> I am a Christian. So, I have a deep faith. So I draw from the Christian faith. On the other hand, I was born in Hawaii where obviously there are a lot of Eastern influences. I lived in Indonesia, the largest Muslim country in the world, between the ages of six and ten. My father was from Kenya, and although he was probably most accurately labeled an agnostic, his father was Muslim. And I'd say, probably, intellectually I've drawn as much from Judaism as any other faith. So, I'm rooted in the Christian tradition. I believe that there are many paths to the same place, and that is a belief that there is a higher power, a belief that we are connected as a people. That there are values that transcend race or culture, that move us forward, and there's an obligation for all of us individually as well as collectively to take responsibility to make those values lived. And so, part of my project in life was probably to spend the first forty years of my life figuring out what I did believe—I'm forty-two now—and it's not that I had it all completely worked out, but I'm spending a lot of time now trying to apply what I believe and trying to live up to those values.

From "Obama's Fascinating Interview with Cathleen Falsani," *BeliefNet.com* (November 11, 2008).

7 Jon Meacham, "Who We Are Now," *Newsweek* (January 26, 2009): 40; Judith Warner, "Tears to Remember," *New York Times* (November 6, 2008).

8 Quoted in "Race: Has American Entered a New Era?" *The Week* (November 21, 2008): 8.

9 Kinney Littlefield, "Oprah Winfrey Is Tired and Tearful But Still Enjoying Her TV Power," *Pittsburgh Post-Gazette* (May 19, 1997): D2.

10 Quoted in "Gossip," *The Week* (February 6, 2009): 10.

11 "Is War The Only Answer?" *The Oprah Winfrey Show* (October 1, 2001).

12 "Vice President Al Gore," *The Oprah Winfrey Show* (September 11, 2000). For a discussion of Oprah's interviews with Bush, Clinton, Gore, and Kerry, see Lee Siegel, "Thank You for Sharing: The Strange Genius of Oprah," *The New Republic* 234, no. 21/22 (June 15 and 12, 2006): 20.

13 "Oprah Talks To Barack Obama", 250. Fareed Zakaria invoked Max Weber to explain Barack Obama's charisma, writing that he is "set apart from ordinary men and treated as endowed with supernatural, superhuman, or at least specifically exceptional powers or qualities." With Weber on his side, Zakaria writes that for some supporters Obama is "the One" whose "birth, background and eloquence . . . give him almost magical qualities." Zakaria, "The Global Elite," 37.

14 "Oprah Talks to Barack Obama," 290.

15 Jeff Zeleny, "Oprah Winfrey Hits Campaign Trail for Obama," *New York Times* (December 9, 2007).

16 In "The Role of Celebrity Endorsements in Politics: Oprah, Obama, and the 2008 Democratic Primary," University of Maryland economists Craig Garthwaite and Timothy J. Moore argued that "our results suggest that Oprah Winfrey's endorsement of Barack Obama prior to the 2008 Democratic Presidential Primary generated a statistically and qualitatively significant increase in the number of votes received as well as in the total number of votes cast." p. 3 Currently posted at http://econ-server. umd.edu/~garthwaite/celebrityendorsements_garthwaitemoore.pdf.

17 Remnick, "The Joshua Generation," 80.

18 "Oprah Talks To Barack Obama," 251.

19 Zadie Smith, "Speaking in Tongues," *New York Review of Books* 56, no. 3 (February 26, 2009).

20 Jann S. Wenner, "A Conversation with Barack Obama," *Rolling Stone* (July 10–24, 2008): 72–73.

21 Leonard Downie Jr. and Sara Rafsky, "The Obama Administration and the Press," *Committee to Protect Journalists* (October 10, 2013).

22 Aside from the obvious comparisons to charismatic individuals from religious contexts, Ronald Reagan, especially in his careful self-invention, supplies a strong parallel to Barack Obama. On the conscientious construction of the Reagan iconography, see Will Bunch, *Tear Down This Myth: How the Reagan Legacy Has Distorted Our Politics and Haunts Our Future* (New York: Free Press, 2009); William Kleinknecht, *The Man Who Sold the World: Ronald Reagan and the Betrayal of Main Street America* (New York: Nation Books, 2009).

Chapter 3

1 Eduardo Bonilla-Silva, *Racism Without Racists: Color-Blind Racism and the Persistence of Racial Inequality in the United States* (Lanham: Rowman & Littlefield, 2010);

Dyson, *The Black Presidency*; Mark S. Ferrara, *Barack Obama and the Rhetoric of Hope* (Jefferson: McFarland, 2013).

2 Barbara Dianne Savage, *Your Spirits Walk Beside Us: The Politics of Black Religion* (Cambridge, MA: Harvard University Press, 2008); Sugrue, *Not Even Past.*

3 "Do 59 percent of Americans believe Barack Obama is Muslim?" http://www. politifact.com/punditfact/statements/2015/nov/23/arsalan-iftikhar/do-59-percent-americans-believe-barack-obama-musli/ (accessed November 29, 2016).

4 For instance, the English "hello" is derived from "hallow" and is rooted in the concept of wholeness as healthfulness, in the sense by which the sick wish to become whole again.

5 "Remarks by the President on a New Beginning." http://www.whitehouse.gov/ the_press_office/Remarks-by-the-President-at-Cairo-University-6-04-09 (accessed December 5, 2016).

6 "Remarks by the President at Cairo University, 6-04-09." https://obamawhitehouse. archives.gov/the-press-office/remarks-president-cairo-university-6-04-09 (accessed November 4, 2016).

7 "Obama's Most Dangerous Drone Tactic is Here to Stay." http://foreignpolicy. com/2016/04/05/obamas-most-dangerous-drone-tactic-is-here-to-stay/ (accessed December 5, 2016). Jameel Jaffer and American Civil Liberties Union, eds., *The Drone Memos: Targeted Killing, Secrecy, and the Law* (New York: The New Press, 2016).

8 "Secret 'Kill List' Proves a Test of Obama's Principles and Will." http://www.nytimes. com/2012/05/29/world/obamas-leadership-in-war-on-al-qaeda.html (accessed February 12, 2017). Inderjeet Parmar, Linda B. Miller, and Mark Ledwidge, eds., *Obama and the World: New Directions in US Foreign Policy*, Second edition, Routledge Studies in US Foreign Policy (London and New York: Routledge, Taylor & Francis Group, 2014). Linda Miller, "The United States and the Arab Spring: Now and Then in the Middle East," in Portman et al., eds., *Obama and the World.*

9 "Get the Data: Obama's Terror Drones." https://www.thebureauinvestigates. com/2012/02/04/get-the-data-obamas-terror-drones/ (accessed December 6, 2016). "Obama's Most Dangerous Drone Tactic is Here to Stay." http://foreignpolicy. com/2016/04/05/obamas-most-dangerous-drone-tactic-is-here-to-stay/ (accessed December 5, 2016). Jaffer and American Civil Liberties Union, *The Drone Memos.*

10 David E. Sanger, *Confront and Conceal: Obama's Secret Wars and Surprising Use of American Power* (New York: Crown Publishers, 2012), 21. Ibid.; David Cortright, Rachel Fairhurst, and Kristen Wall, eds., *Drones and the Future of Armed Conflict: Ethical, Legal, and Strategic Implications* (Chicago: The University of Chicago Press, 2015); William M. Arkin, *Unmanned: Drones, Data, and the Illusion of Perfect Warfare*, First edition (New York: Little, Brown and Company, 2015).

11 Arkin, *Unmanned*; Jaffer and American Civil Liberties Union, *The Drone Memos.*

12 https://www.stimson.org/content/grading-progress-us-drone-policy-0 (accessed February 15, 2017).

13 Ashley Moore, "American Muslim Minorities: The New Human Rights Struggle," *Human Rights and Human Welfare: An Online Journal of Academic Literature Review.* http://www.du.edu/korbel/hrhw/researchdigest/minority/Muslim.pdf (accessed December 7, 2016). "Trump's Proposed Muslim Registry Echoes Bush-Era Program." http://www.npr.org/2016/11/24/503279102/trumps-proposed-muslim-registry-echoes-bush-era-program (accessed April 18, 2017).

14 Sylvester A. Johnson and Steven Weitzman, *The FBI and Religion: Faith and National Security During and After 9/11* (Berkeley: University of California Press, 2017).

15 "Remarks by the President on Trayvon Martin." https://www.whitehouse.gov/the-press-office/2013/07/19/remarks-president-trayvon-martin (accessed December 7, 2016). Dyson, *The Black Presidency*; Jaffer and American Civil Liberties Union, *The Drone Memos*; Arkin, *Unmanned*.

16 "Cornel West: Obama's Response to Trayvon Martin Case Belies Failure to Challenge 'New Jim Crow.'" https://www.democracynow.org/2013/7/22/cornel_west_obamas_response_to_trayvon (accessed December 7, 2016).

17 Parmar, Miller, and Ledwidge, *Obama and the World*.

18 Besheer Mohamed, "A New Estimate of the US Muslim Population." http://www.pewresearch.org/fact-tank/2016/01/06/a-new-estimate-of-the-u-s-muslim-population/ (accessed December 14, 2016).

19 Savage, *Your Spirits Walk Beside Us*; Dawn-Marie Gibson, *A History of the Nation of Islam: Race, Islam, and the Quest for Freedom* (Santa Barbara, CA: Praeger, 2012).

20 Jeffrey Haas, *The Assassination of Fred Hampton : How the FBI and the Chicago Police Murdered a Black Panther* (Chicago, IL: Lawrence Hill Books and Chicago Review Press, 2010).

21 Gibson, *A History of the Nation of Islam*, 170–71. Throughout Obama's presidency, abysmal lapses occurred in his security detail. Among these was the white male intruder who was allowed to breach the White House lawn and run inside the premises before being tackled. Also of note was Secret Service's decision to allow a random security officer to accompany Obama's detail on an elevator ride. "Armed Outside Guard Was Allowed on Elevator With President, Officials Say." https://www.nytimes.com/2014/10/01/us/armed-man-boarded-elevator-with-obama-official-reports.html?_r=0 (accessed May 31, 2017).

22 Christopher S. Chivvis, *Toppling Qaddafi: Libya and the Limits of Liberal Intervention* (Cambridge: Cambridge University Press, 2014).

23 Chivvis, *Toppling Qaddafi*.

24 "African Migrants Targeted in Libya." http://www.aljazeera.com/news/africa/2011/02/201122865814378541.html (accessed April 20, 2017).

25 "Farrakhan Press Conference on Libya, President Obama and Col. Gadhafi," (March 31, 2011). https://www.youtube.com/watch?v=6EwiGk9TXCE (accessed January 17, 2017).

26 Antoine J. Banks, "The Public's Anger: White Racial Attitudes and Opinions Toward Health Care Reform" *Political Behavior* 36, no. 3 (September 2014): 493–514.

27 Ashley Alman, "Larry Klayman Tells Obama 'To Put The Quran Down' At Veterans Rally." http://www.huffingtonpost.com/2013/10/13/larry-klayman-obama-quran_n_4094589.html (accessed January 18, 2017).

28 "Operation American Spring is Still Waiting for Its Millions of Patriots." http://www.theatlantic.com/politics/archive/2014/05/operation-american-spring-is-still-waiting-for-its-millions-of-patriots/371092/ (accessed January 18, 2017).

29 Richard W. Stevenson, "Officials to Block Qaddafi Gift to Farrakhan," *The New York Times* (August 28, 1996). http://www.nytimes.com/1996/08/28/us/officials-to-block-qaddafi-gift-to-farrakhan.html.

30 Theodore Roosevelt, Woodrow Wilson, and "Jimmy" Carter were also recipients of the Nobel Peace Prize. Former vice-president Al Gore also became a recipient in 2007.

31 "The Nobel Peace Prize for 2009 to President Barack Obama—Press Release." http://www.nobelprize.org/nobel_prizes/peace/laureates/2009/press.html (accessed January 20, 2017).

32 John Sifton, "A Brief History of Drones." https://www.thenation.com/article/brief-history-drones/ (accessed January 20, 2017).

33 Ian G. R. Shaw, "The Rise of the Predator Empire: Tracing the History of U.S. Drones", Understanding Empire, (2014). https://understandingempire.wordpress.com/2-0-a-brief-history-of-u-s-drones/ (accessed January 20, 2017).

34 "Nobel Secretary Regrets Obama Peace Prize." http://www.bbc.com/news/world-europe-34277960 accessed 1/20/2017.

35 Human Rights Watch, "Guantanamo by the Numbers." http://www.humanrightsfirst.org/resource/guantanamo-numbers (accessed January 17, 2017).

36 Human Rights Watch, "Guantanamo by the Numbers." http://www.humanrightsfirst.org/resource/guantanamo-numbers (accessed January 17, 2017).

37 Talal Asad, *Formations of the Secular : Christianity, Islam, Modernity*, Cultural Memory in the Present (Stanford, CA: Stanford University Press, 2003).

38 Edward E. Curtis IV, *The Call of Bilal: Islam in the African Diaspora* (Chapel Hill: The University of North Carolina Press, 2014).

Chapter 4

1 "How Many Lives?" in *Off Our Backs: A Women's News Journal* 2, no. 1. Special Issue: September, 1971.

2 See, for instance, Michelle Ye Hee Lee, "Does the United States Really Have 5 percent of the world's population and one quarter of the world's prisoners?" *The Washington Post*, April 30, 2015. https://www.washingtonpost.com/news/fact-checker/wp/2015/04/30/does-the-united-states-really-have-five-percent-of-worlds-population-and-one-quarter-of-the-worlds-prisoners/

3 Lynette N. Tannis writes, "In the United States, we have more federal, state, and local jails and prisons than we have two- and four-year-granting colleges and universities. For example, in 2013, there were 4,726 degree-granting institutions, compared to the 5,104 federal and state prisons and local jails. These numbers do not account for the more than 2,500 juvenile facilities nationwide, 49 percent of which are owned by non- and for-profit organizations." Lynette N. Tannis, "Foreword: A Crime for a Crime? The Landscape of Correctional Education in the United States," *Harvard Educational Review* 87, no. 1 (Spring 2017): 75.

4 Marie Gottshalk, *Caught: The Prison State and the Lockdown of American Politics* (Princeton, NJ: Princeton University Press, 2015), 258.

5 President Obama relies on the distinction between violent and nonviolent offenders for his vision of criminal justice reform. See, for instance, President Barack Obama, "Remarks by the President at the NAACP Conference," given at Pennsylvania Convention Center, Philadelphia, PA, released by the Office of the Press Secretary, The White House (July 14, 2015), https://obamawhitehouse.archives.gov/the-press-office/2015/07/14/remarks-president-naacp-conference; President Barack Obama, "Remarks by the President after Visit at the El Reno Federal Correctional Institution," El Reno, OK, released by the Office of the Press Secretary, The White House (July 16, 2015), https://obamawhitehouse.archives.gov/the-press-office/2015/07/16/remarks-president-after-visit-el-reno-federal-correctional-institution.

On the insufficient and misleading concepts of "violent" and "non-violent" crime, see Allegra McLeod, "Prison Abolition and Grounded Justice," *UCLA Law Review* (2015): 1167–71. On the misinterpretation of statistics regarding violent and nonviolent offenders, see Michelle Alexander, *The New Jim Crow: Mass Incarceration in the Age of Colorblindness* (New York: The New Press, 2010), 101–02.

6   As Allegra McLeod has put it, "reducing social risk by physically isolating and caging entire populations is not morally defensible, even if abandoning such practices may increase some forms of social disorder." McLeod, "Prison Abolition," 1171.

7   Pope Francis, "Visit to the Detainees at Curran-Frumhold Correctional Facility: Address of the Holy Father," *Philadelphia* (Sunday, September 27, 2015), https://w2.vatican.va/content/francesco/en/speeches/2015/september/documents/papa-francesco_20150927_usa-detenuti.html.

8   *City of God* 1.15; translation my own. "neque enim aliunde beata ciuitas, aliunde homo, cum aliud ciuitas non sit quam concors hominum multitudo."

9   Pope Francis, "Apostolic Letter *Misericordia et misera*" (November 20, 2016), §20. https://w2.vatican.va/content/francesco/en/apost_letters/documents/papa-francesco-lettera-ap_20161120_misericordia-et-misera.html.

10 Ibid., preface.

11 Ibid., §2.

12 Augustine, "Commentary on the Gospel of John, 33," in *Political Writings*, eds. E. M. Atkins and R. J. Dodaro, trans. E. M. Atkins (New York: Cambridge University Press, 2007), 33.1; 101.

13 Ibid.

14 Ibid., 33.2; 102; translation adapted. Italics are in the original and indicate when Augustine is quoting scripture.

15 Ibid.

16 Ibid., 33.3; 102.

17 Ibid., 33.4; 103.

18 Ibid.

19 Ibid.

20 Ibid.

21 Ibid.

22 Ibid.

23 Ibid., 33.5; 104.

24 Ibid.

25 Ibid., 33.2; 102.

26 Ibid., 33.5; 104.

27 Ibid.

28 Ibid., 33.6; 105.

29 Ibid., 33.5; 105.

30 Augustine's scriptural sources are lost to us except in his quotations of them. There was no single, recognized version of a Latin text to which Augustine and his readers could refer. In addition, prior to the Vulagate, the Latin translations of the older testament were derived from the Greek Septuagint rather than the Hebrew scriptures. Dennis Brown, "Jerome and the Vulgate," in *A History of Biblical Interpretation, volume 1*, eds. Alan J. Hauser and Duane F. Watson (Grand Rapids, MI: Eerdmans, 2003), 355–79; Philip Burton, *The Old Latin Gospels: A Study of Their Texts and Language* (Oxford: Oxford University Press, 2000), 3–4; Görge K. Hasselhoff, "Revising the Vulgate: Jerome and his Jewish Interlocutors," *Zeitschrift für Religions und Geistesgeschichte* 64, no. 3 (2012): 209–21.

31 Mt. 7:3, *Biblia Sacra Vulgata. Editio quinta*, eds. Roger Gryson and Robert Weber (German Bible Society: 2006).

32 Augustine, *Homilies on the Gospel of John 1-40*, ed. Boniface Ramsey, trans. Edmund Hill, vol. I/12, *The Works of Saint Augustine: A Translation for the 21st Century* (Hyde Park, NY: New City Press, 2009), 528n12.

33 Augustine, "Commentary on the Gospel of John, 33," trans. E. M. Atkins, 33.5; 105.

34 Ibid.

35 Ibid., 33.5; 104. The recommendation resonates with another avid reader of the fourth gospel, Richard Meux Benson, an Anglican reformer who founded the Society of St. John the Evangelist in the mid-nineteenth century: that he should have "a heart of stone towards myself, a heart of flesh towards my neighbor, and a heart of flame towards God" (quote found in Rowan Williams, *Where God Happens: Discovering Christ in One Another* (Boston: New Seeds, 2005), 30–31).

36 Augustine, "Commentary on the Gospel of John, 33," trans. E. M. Atkins, 33.5; 104.

37 Augustine, *The City of God Against the Pagans*, trans. R. W. Dyson, Cambridge Texts in the History of Political Thought (New York: Cambridge University Press, 1998), 1.26; 39. Translation adapted by author. "nos per aurem conscientiam conuenimus, occultorum nobis iudicium non usurpamus."

38 In the ancient world, sight is privileged as the sense that yields knowledge. In fact, in Greek, the word for "I know" translates literally as "I have seen" (*oida*). Augustine, however, teaches his readers that conscience is discerned in a much less direct and less immediate way: through the ear.

39 Augustine, "Commentary on the Gospel of John, 33," trans. E. M. Atkins, 33.5; 104.

40 Ibid., 33.5; 105.

41 Ibid., 33.6; 105.

42 Ibid.

43 In remarks during the conclave in which he was elected pope in 2013, then Cardinal Jorge Mario Bergoglio exhorted his fellow cardinals: "The Church is called to come out of herself and to go to the peripheries, not only geographically, but also the existential peripheries: the mystery of sin, of pain, of injustice, of ignorance and indifference to religion, of intellectual currents, and of all misery." Quoted in John Gehring, *The Francis Effect: A Radical Pope's Challenge to the American Catholic Church* (Lanham, MD: Rowman & Littlefield, 2015), 150.

44 Bryan Stevenson, *Just Mercy: A Story of Justice and Redemption* (New York: Random House, 2014), 308–09.

45 Pope Francis, "Apostolic Letter *Misericordia et misera*," §20.

46 Jed S. Rakoff, "Why Innocent People Plead Guilty," *New York Review of Books*, November 20, 2014 Issue, http://www.nybooks.com/articles/2014/11/20/why-innocent-people-plead-guilty/

47 The rate of incarceration of those innocent is impossible to determine. Yet, Daniel Medwed writes, "Even assuming that the error rate in the criminal justice system hovers around 1 percent of felony cases, a figure smaller than many scholars estimate, that means thousands of innocent people live behind bars." That is, of the 2.2 million people incarcerated at any given time, we are caging at least 22,000 people who are innocent of the charges for which they are convicted. Daniel S. Medwed, *Prosecution Complex: America's Race to Convict and Its Impact on the Innocent* (New York: New York University Press, 2012), 3.

48 Brady Heiner, "The Procedural Entrapment of Mass Incarceration: Prosecution, Race, and the Unfinished Project of American Abolition," *Philosophy and Social Criticism* 42, no. 6 (2016): 606.

49 The disparities become apparent when we consider the overrepresentation of black and brown people in the prison population: the American prison population is 39 percent black and 40 percent white, though only 13 percent of the American population is black while 64 percent is white. Or to put it another way: 1 in every 106 white men is incarcerated; for Hispanic men that rate increases to 1 in 36, and

for black men to 1 in 15. In addition, 75 percent of women who are incarcerated are survivors of intimate violence in adulthood, while 82 percent survived severe physical or sexual abuse as children. Prison Policy Initiative, "Racial and ethnic disparities in prisons and jails," Compiled from 2010 Census, Summary File 1, https://www.prisonpolicy.org/reports/pie2017.html; American Civil Liberties Union, "Combatting Mass Incarceration—The Facts," https://www.aclu.org/infographic-combating-mass-incarceration-facts?redirect=combating-mass-incarceration-facts-0.

50 Gottschalk, *Caught*, 278–79. The effect is cyclical as well; higher rates of incarceration exacerbate preexisting social inequality. See Adriaan Lanni, "The Future of Community Justice," *Harvard Civil Rights-Civil Liberties Law Review* 40 (2005): 388–39.

51 Laura Magnali and Harmon L. Wray, *Beyond Prisons: A New Interfaith Paradigm for Our Failed Prison System* (Minneapolis, MN: Fortress Press, 2006), 148–49. For an in-depth exploration of how teen girls, in particular, are impacted by and resist the encroachment of the carceral state within their communities, see the special issue of *Violence against Women* co-edited by Mariame Kaba and Michelle VanNatta. Mariame Kaba and Michelle VanNatta, "Guest Editors' Introduction," *Violence against Women* 13, no. 12 (December 2007): 1223–28.

52 "Those who have experienced violence know that crime is much more complex than the legal procedure reflects. They know that their perception of 'the truth' shifts as their understanding of the crime deepens. They also know that they need to be able to tell this truth over and over again as their understanding changes, in order to weave what was lost in the act of violence into their lives and into the history of their communities." Ibid., 149.

53 "How Many Lives?"

54 Ibid.

55 While the language surrounding the purposes of "corrections" varies from state to state, Gilmore notes that California removed the language of "rehabilitation" from its correctional documents. Ruth Wilson Gilmore, *Golden Gulag: Prisons, Surplus, Crisis, and Opposition in Globalizing California* (Berkeley, CA: University of California Press, 2007), 88–89.

56 Gilmore, *Golden Gulag*, 14.

57 McLeod, "Prison Abolition," 1171.

58 Pope Francis, "Visit to Detainees."
    And it is not just those convicted of crimes that suffer in our current system. One prison officer reported: "I was a happy-go-lucky guy when I married my wife, but she tells me over the years I became more serious. . . . Lots of officers have gotten divorced, become drinkers or too rough and bossy with their family. The job changes you. You have to be on edge all of the time." New York Civil Liberties Union Report, "Boxed In: The True Cost of Extreme Isolation in New York's Prisons" (2012): 36. https://www.nyclu.org/sites/default/files/publications/nyclu_boxedin_FINAL.pdf.

59 Ibid.

60 Ibid.

61 Pope Francis, "Apostolic Letter *Misericordia et misera*," §1.

62 Ibid.

Chapter 5

1 "Transcript, Barack Obama's Inaugural Address," *New York Times*, January 20, 2009. On Bush spending priorities from both a conservative and a liberal perspective, see

Veronique de Rugy, "Spending Under President George W. Bush," Working paper 09-04 (March 2009), Mercatus Center, George Mason University; John Cassidy, "Reagan, Bush, and Obama: We Are All Still Keynesians," *The New Yorker*, June 4, 2012, online at http://www.newyorker.com/news/john-cassidy/reagan-bush-and-obama-we-are-all-still-keynesians (accessed December 5, 2014).

2 George Packer, "Let Us Now Set Aside Childish Things," *The New Yorker*, January 20, 2009.

3 "Obama Wants to Expand Role of Religious Groups," *New York Times*, July 2, 2008; "White House Faith Office to Expand," *New York Times*, February 9, 2009; "Despite a Decade of Controversy, the 'Faith-Based Initiative' Endures," *New York Times*, July 31, 2009; "White House Picks Church-State Lawyer Melissa Rogers to Head Faith Office," *Washington Post*, March 13, 2013.

4 "Text of New President's Address at Inauguration," *Washington Post*, March 5, 1933.

5 Gary Scott Smith, *Faith and the Presidency from George Washington to George W. Bush* (New York: Oxford University Press, 2006), 191–220; Alison Collis Greene, "The End of 'The Protestant Era'?" *Church History* 80, no. 3 (September 2011): 600–10.

6 "Text of New President's Address at Inauguration."

7 Josephine Chapin Brown, *Public Relief, 1929-1939* (New York: Octagon Books, 1971), 175–; Michael B. Katz, *In the Shadow of the Poorhouse: A Social History of Welfare in America*, 2nd ed. (New York: Basic Books, 1996 [1986]), 224–31; Dorothy M. Brown and Elizabeth McKeown, *The Poor Belong To Us: Catholic Charities and American Welfare* (Cambridge, MA: Harvard University Press, 1997), 163–73.

8 Nocolaus Mills, Roosevelt, and the Affordable Care Act, July 16, 2013, *Huffington Post* [http://www.huffingtonpost.com/nicolaus-mills/roosevelt-and-the-afforda_b_3600103.html]; Al Carroll, "Franklin Roosevelt and the New Deal Compared to Obamacare," Daily Kos, May 27, 2014 [http://www.dailykos.com/story/2014/05/27/1298267/-Franklin-Roosevelt-and-the-New-Deal-Compared-to-Obamacare].

9 Alison Collis Greene, "'A Divine Revelation?': Southern Churches Respond to the New Deal," in *Religion and American Politics*, ed. Andrew Preston et al. (Philadelphia: University of Pennsylvania Press, forthcoming, 2015); John P. Bartkowski and Helen A. Regis, *Charitable Choices: Religion, Race, and Poverty in the Post-Welfare Era* (New York: New York University Press, 2003), 1–6; Axel R. Schäfer, *Piety and Public Funding: Evangelicals and the State in Modern America* (Philadelphia: University of Pennsylvania Press, 2012), 1–20, 194–214. I rely most heavily on Schäfer's examples and argument, focused primarily on conservatives, as I describe transitions in public funding of religious agencies from the 1940s to the present.

10 Axel R. Schäfer, "The Cold War State and the Resurgence of Evangelicalism: A Study of the Public Funding of Religion Since 1945," *Radical History Review* 99 (Fall 2007): 33, 42.

11 See, for instance, recent comments by Joni Ernst: O. Kay Henderson, "Ernst carries concealed weapon '90 percent of the time'" (with audio), Radio Iowa, August 20, 2013, http://www.radioiowa.com/2013/08/20/ernst-carries-concealed-weapon-90-percent-of-the-time-audio/ (accessed December 5, 2014).

12 Marvin Olasky, *The Tragedy of American Compassion* (Washington, DC: Regnery, 1992); Franklin Graham, "'This Week' Transcript: God and Government," ABC News website, http://abcnews.go.com/ThisWeek/week-transcript-god-government/story?id=13446238#.TySHQ-NSSs0 (accessed January 28, 2012). I have written briefly about Graham's comments before. See Greene, "Let's Remember History, When Religious Institutions Welcomed Government Support," The Table, *Religion*

and Politics, June 4, 2012, http://religionandpolitics.org/2012/06/04/lets-remember-history-when-religious-institutions-welcomed-government-support/.

13   Katz, *In the Shadow of the Poorhouse*, xiv; Theda Skocpol, *Protecting Soldiers and Mothers: The Political Origins of Social Policy in the United States* (Cambridge: Belknap Press, 1992). This body of scholarship is enormous and varied. See also, Michele Landis Dauber, *The Sympathetic State: Disaster Relief and the Origins of the American Welfare State* (Chicago: University of Chicago Press, 2012); Ange-Marie Hancock, *The Politics of Disgust: The Public Identity of the Welfare Queen* (New York: New York University Press, 2004); Linda Gordon, *Pitied But Not Entitled: Single Mothers and the History of Welfare, 1890-1935* (New York: Free Press, 1994).

14   Lizabeth Cohen, *Making a New Deal: Industrial Workers in Chicago, 1919-1939* (New York: Cambridge University Press, 1990), 1–9, 213–89; David M. Kennedy, *Freedom from Fear: The American People in Depression and War* (New York: Oxford University Press, 1999), 88. For a southern comparison, see Elna Green, *This Business of Relief: Confronting Poverty in a Southern City, 1740-1940* (Athens: University of Georgia Press, 2003).

15   Bureau of the Census, *Census of the United States, 1930;* Bureau of the Census, *Census of Religious Bodies: 1926, Part I* (Washington, DC: Government Printing Office, 1930): 466–67, 580–82, 632–34.

16   Elna Green (ed.), *Before the New Deal: Social Welfare in the South, 1830-1930* (Athens, GA: University of Georgia Press, 1999), ix–xviii; Jennifer Ann Trost, *Gateway to Justice: The Juvenile Court and Progressive Child Welfare in Memphis* (Athens: University of Georgia Press, 2006), 65; Skocpol, *Protecting Soldiers and Mothers*, 102–51, *Directory: Social Welfare Agencies* (Memphis, TN: Council of Social Agencies of Memphis and Shelby County, 1941), 9–11, 14–15; US Department of Labor, Children's Bureau, *Mothers' Aid, 1931*, Bureau Publication 220 (Washington, DC: Government Printing Office, 1933), 1, 7–9, 14, 17, 26; Charles O. Lee, *1931 Annual Report, Memphis Community Fund*, Memphis-Charities-Community Fund Clippings File, Memphis-Community Chest Clippings File, Memphis Public Library, Memphis, Tennessee (MPL), p.10; Skocpol, *Protecting Soldiers and Mothers*, 424–79.

17   Enid Baird, *Public and Private Aid in Urban Areas, 1929-1938* (Washington, DC: Social Security Board, 1942), 115; Trost, *Gateway to Justice*, 64–67, 136–38; "All Creeds Meet at Welfare School," *Memphis Commercial-Appeal*, July 9, 1932; *Open Your Heart: Memphis Cares for Her Own*, Memphis Community Fund, 1928, back page, MPL.

18   *Twelfth Annual Appeal of the Memphis Community Fund*, 1933, 12; *1931 Annual Report, Memphis Community Fund*, 2. On nutrition, see "A Nutrition Investigation of Negro Tenants in the Yazoo Mississippi Delta," *Bulletin*, Mississippi Agricultural Experiment Station, A & M College, no. 254, Starkville, Mississippi: Mississippi State University, 1928.

19   *1940 Annual Report, Memphis Community Fund, with Historical Supplement, Memphis, Tennessee*, Mayor Watkins Overton Papers, MPL; *Open Your Heart: Memphis Cares for Her Own*, Memphis Community Fund, 1928, back page, Memphis-Community Chest Clippings File, MPL.

20   "Hunger-1931," *The Nation*, February 11, 1931, 151–52; *Statistical Abstract of the United States, 1941*, (Washington, DC: Government Printing Office, 1942), 741; Nan Elizabeth Woodruff, *As Rare As Rain: Federal Relief in the Great Southern Drought of 1930-31* (Urbana: University of Illinois Press, 1985), 30–36, 50–52; "$962,000 Is Obtained for Drought Relief," *New York Times*, January 22, 1931, 3.

21   *Twelfth Annual Appeal of the Memphis Community Fund*, 1933, 12; *1931 Annual Report, Memphis Community Fund*, 2; "Boys, Old Men—All Poor and Hungry, Swarm to Salvation Army for Shelter," *Memphis Press-Scimitar*, February 9, 1933.

22   *1931 Annual Report*, Memphis Community Fund, 4, 9.

23   Marsha Wedell, *Elite Women and the Reform Impulse in Memphis, 1875-1915* (Knoxville: University of Tennessee Press, 1991), 106–07; David Beito, *From Mutual Aid to the Welfare State: Fraternal Societies and Social Services, 1890-1967* (Chapel Hill: University of North Carolina Press, 2000), 1–16, 181–221; Benson Y. Landis and George Edmund Haynes, *Cotton-Growing Communities Study no. 2: Case Studies of 10 Rural Communities and 10 Plantations in Arkansas* (New York: Federal Council of Churches, 1935), 9, 21.

24   Rosemary D. Marcuss and Richard E. Kane, "U.S. National Income and Product Statistics: Born of the Great Depression and World War II," *Survey of Current Business* (February 2007): 32–46; "Bowing Out 1931," *New Orleans Christian Advocate*, January 7, 1932, 4; Samuel C. Kincheloe, *Research Memorandum on Religion in the Depression* (New York, NY: Social Science Research Council, 1937), 17, 23, 28.

25   "Our Present Denominational Situation," *(Arkansas) Baptist Advance*, August 7, 1930, 1, 9.

26   Corrington Gill, "Unemployment Relief," *American Economic Review* 25, no. 1 (March 1935): 176–85; Kennedy, *Freedom from Fear*, 84–85; "Fund Shakeup Nears; R.F.C. Drops Support," *Memphis Commercial Appeal*, June 26, 1933.

27   Baker, *Public Relief*, 184–90; Kennedy, *Freedom from Fear*, 131–59.

28   Brown, *Public Relief*, 172–90 (quotation on 90).

29   Brown and McKeown, *The Poor Belong to Us*, 164–66.

30   Baird, *Public and Private Aid*, 86–151.

31   *Final Statistical Report of the FERA*, 102–04; Brown, *Public Relief*, 205.

32   J. F. Dodd, School Director, Supt. of Sunday School, Alpena Pass, Arkansas, to Welfare Society, Washington, D.C., October 9, 1934, Box 264, Correspondence with Government Departments, Eleanor Roosevelt Papers, Franklin D. Roosevelt Presidential Library and Archives, Hyde Park, NY [FDR Library]; Secretary to Mrs. Roosevelt to J. F. Dodd, October 12, 1934, Box 264, Eleanor Roosevelt Papers, FDR Library.

33   I. C. Franklin, Port Gibson, Mississippi, to Franklin D. Roosevelt, October 16, 1935, Folder: Mississippi, Box 30, President's Personal File 21A-Church Matters, [Clergy Letters], FDR Library.

34   John B. Kirby, *Black Americans in the Roosevelt Era: Liberalism and Race* (Knoxville: University of Tennessee Press, 1980), 24. See also Ira Katznelson, *Fear Itself: The New Deal and the Origins of Our Time* (New York: Liveright, 2013); Harvard Sitkoff, *A New Deal for Blacks: The Emergence of Civil Rights as a National Issue: The Depression Decade* (New York: Oxford University Press, 2009 [1978]).

35   For more detail about these results, see Greene, "A Divine Revelation?" For more detail on the Roosevelt administration's motivation in sending out the letter, and the controversy it provoked, see Matthew Avery Sutton, "Was FDR the Antichrist? The Birth of Fundamentalist Antiliberalism in a Global Age," *Journal of American History* 98, no. 4 (January 2012): 1052–74.

36   John S. Chadwick (ed.), *Christian Advocate*, Nashville, Tennessee, October 3, 1935, Authors and educators folder, Box 35, Clergy Letters, FDR Library.

37   John S. Chadwick of the *Christian Advocate*, Nashville, Tennessee and Dadeville, Alabama, October 3, 1935, Authors and Educators folder, box 35, CL.

38   Rev. R. L. Phelps, Synod of Mississippi, PCUSA, September 30, 1935, Church Officials folder, box 35, CL.

39   On the South and the New Deal, see Katznelson, *Fear Itself*; Glenda Elizabeth Gilmore, *Defying Dixie: The Radical Roots of Civil Rights, 1919-1950* (New York: W. W. Norton, 2008); Roger Biles, *The South and the New Deal*. Lexington: University Press of Kentucky, 1994.

40   Schäfer, *Piety and Public Funding*, 1–59, 123–62; Peter Dobkin Hall, "Historical Perspectives on Religion, Government, and Social Welfare in America," in *Can Charitable Choice Work? Covering Religion's Impact on Urban Affairs and Social Services*, ed. Andrew Walsh (Philadelphia: Pew Charitable Trusts), http://www. trincoll.edu/depts/csrpl/Charitable%20Choice%20book/hall.pdf (accessed October 15, 2014).

41   Schäfer, "The Cold War State and the Resurgence of Evangelicalism," 28–34.

42   Bartkowski and Regis, *Charitable Choices*, 1–59.

43   Ibid., Schäfer, *Piety and Public Funding*, 210–14.

Chapter 6

1   While 53% of white female voters voted for Trump, this support varied along class lines. A majority of white women with college degrees (51%) voted for Clinton and 62% of women without a college degree voted for Trump. Katie Rogers, "White Women Helped Elect Donald Trump," *The New York Times*, November 9, 2016, sec. Politics.

2   For a more detailed ethical analysis of neoliberalism and economic globalization see Rebecca Todd Peters, *In Search of the Good Life: The Ethics of Globalization* (New York: Continuum, 2004), esp. ch. 3.

3   All data is this paragraph taken from the World Wealth and Income Database, http:// wid.world/country/usa/ (accessed February 27, 2017).

4   Karl Marx and Ernest Mandel, *Capital: Volume 1: A Critique of Political Economy*, Translated by Ben Fowkes, Reprint edition, London; New York, N.Y: Penguin Classics, 1990, Part 8.

5   David R. Loy, "The Religion of the Market," *Journal of the American Academy of Religion* 65, no. 2 (Summer 1997): 275–90.

6   Heath W. Carter, *Union Made: Working People and the Rise of Social Christianity in Chicago*, New York: Oxford University Press, 2015.

7   Gary Dorrien, *Soul in Society*, Minneapolis: Fortress Press, 1995; Gary Dorrien, *Social Ethics in the Making: Interpreting an American Tradition*, Malden, Mass: Wiley-Blackwell, 2010.

8   Francis Fukuyama, "The End of History?" *The National Interest* (Summer 1989): 3–18.

9   Daniel Yergin and Joseph Stanislaw, *The Commanding Heights: The Battle between Government and the Marketplace That is Remaking The Modern World* (New York: Simon and Schuster, 1998), 149.

10 Jim Cullen, The American Dream: A Short History of an Idea That Shaped a Nation (New York: Oxford, 2003).

11 Walmart Company Facts, available on Walmart website: http://corporate.walmart. com/newsroom/company-facts (accessed May 26, 2017).

12 Jackie Wattles, "Wal-Mart Increasing Wages; Union Says It's All Show," CNN Money (January 20, 2016). http://money.cnn.com/2016/01/20/news/companies/walmart-pay-raise-wages/ (accessed May 26, 2017).

13 Roger Bybee, "Auto Task Force Outsources Jobs," *In These Times* (June 12, 2009).

14 Ha-Joon Chang, *23 Things They Don't Tell You About Capitalism* (New York: Bloomsbury, 2010), 194–95.

15 Evidence of this racial resentment was abundant in the remarkable attitudes and opinions that many white people held about President Obama throughout his presidency. While Obama clearly identifies himself as Christian and has attended and been active in Christian churches throughout his life, by the end of his Presidency, one poll showed that 43 percent of Republicans and 54 percent of Trump supporters identified Obama as Muslim. After a concerted campaign by Obama's detractors to compromise his legitimacy by questioning his citizenship, by the end of Obama's presidency 20 percent of the electorate believed that Obama was not born in the United States, with some polls showing that as many as 72 percent of registered Republicans questioning his citizenship status. For the record, Obama was born in Hawaii in 1961, two years after Hawaii became a state.

16 See Arlie Russell Hochschild, *Strangers in Their Own Land: Anger and Mourning on the American Right*, New York: The New Press, 2016 for a riveting analysis of the increasing anger of rural white US Americans and the political right.

17 CNN exit polls, http://www.cnn.com/election/results/exit-polls.

18 For evangelical and right-wing Christians, "traditional family values" is itself code for the disapproval of not only same-sex relationships but also the increasing sexual independence of women made possible, in part, by contraception and abortion as well as the increased rates of divorce, single-parent households, and children born to non-married women. Charles Murray provides an excellent example of this kind of right-wing analysis about the "loss" of traditional (Christian) values in *Coming Apart: The State of White American 1960-2010* (New York: Crown Forum, 2012).

19 CNN exit polls, http://www.cnn.com/election/results/exit-polls.

20 Data taken from United Food and Commercial Workers International Union website, "Wal-Mart Quick Facts." http://www.ufcw.org/take_action/walmart_workers_campaign_info/facts_and_figures/walmartgeneralinfo.cfm (accessed July 9, 2009); and Jeff M. Sellers, "Corporation's Plan in Only Slightly Worse Than Its Chain Competitors," *Christianity Today* (May 2005).

21 Ken Jacobs, Ian Perry, and Jenifer MacGillvary, "The High Public Cost of Low Wages: Poverty-Level Wages Cost U.S. Taxpayers $152.8 Billion Each Year in Public Support for Working Families," Berkeley: UC Berkeley Center for Labor Research and Education, April 2015.

22 John Schmitt, "How Good is the Economy at Creating Good Jobs?" *Center for Economic and Policy Research* (October 2005): 1.

23 Sean F. Reardon and Kendra Bischoff, "Growth in the Residential Segregation of Families by Income, 1970-2009," Stanford University, November 2011, http://graphics8.nytimes.com/packages/pdf/national/RussellSageIncomeSegregationreport.pdf (accessed December 22, 2011).

24 US Census Bureau, Table 2. Poverty Status of People by Family Relationship, Race, and Hispanic Origin: 1959–2015, https://www.census.gov/data/tables/time-series/demo/income-poverty/historical-poverty-people.html (accessed May 29, 2017).

25 US Census Bureau, Table 18. Workers as a Proportion of All Poor People, https://www.census.gov/data/tables/time-series/demo/income-poverty/historical-poverty-people.html (accessed May 29, 2017).

26 Information on the most recent United Auto Worker contract settlement from 2007 indicates that assembly-line workers for GM, Chrysler, and Ford all make approximately $28 an hour. See http://www.uaw.org/contracts/index.php (accessed July 9, 2009).

27 Pamela Sparr, *Mortgaging Women's Lives: Feminist Critiques of Structural Adjustment* (London: Zed Books, 1994).

28 W. E. B. Du Bois and David Levering Lewis, *Black Reconstruction in America (The Oxford W. E. B. Du Bois): An Essay Toward a History of the Part Which Black Folk Played in the Attempt to Reconstruct Democracy in America, 1860–1880,* edited by Henry Louis Gates, Oxford University Press, 2014.

29 Larry M. Bartels, *Unequal Democracy: The Political Economy of the New Gilded Age,* Second edition, New York: Princeton University Press, 2016.

Chapter 7

1 In this article, I focus on cisgender women as the primary users of birth control pills, IUDs, and EC. Obviously, "women" does not exhaust the category of people who use these contraceptive methods: transmen, gender nonconforming, and nonbinary people also use—and, under the Affordable Care Act, are entitled to cost-free access to—all FDA–approved methods of birth control.

2 Susan A. Cohen, "Abortion and Women of Color: The Bigger Picture," Guttmacher Policy Review, August 6, 2008. https://www.guttmacher.org/gpr/2008/08/abortion-and-women-color-bigger-picture; Nancy Northup, Center for Reproductive Rights, "Supplemental Information about the United States Scheduled for Review during the Committee for the Elimination of Racial Discrimination Committee's 72nd Session," December 19, 2007, 5; "Women of Color Need Improved Information and Access to Effective Contraception," Bixby Center for Global Reproductive Health, University of California, San Francisco, https://bixbycenter.ucsf.edu/news/women-color-need-improved-information-and-access-effective-contraception (accessed July 1, 2017).

3 *Burwell v. Hobby Lobby,* 573 U.S. 1 (2014) (Ginsburg dissenting).

4 Christine Dehlendorf et al., "Disparities in Family Planning," *American Journal of Obstetrics and Gynecology* 202, no. 3 (2010): 214–20.

5 With all due respect to Kendrick Lamar.

6 *Reynolds v. U.S.* (1878) and *Burwell v. Hobby Lobby* (2014) respectively, notwithstanding the recent decision in *Trinity Lutheran Church of Columbia, Inc. v. Comer* (2017).

7 Adjudication of Supreme Court cases addressing the free exercise of mainstream, primarily conservative Christianities was at its height during the Reagan administration.

8 *Reynolds v. U.S.,* 98 US 145 (1878).

9 Ibid.

10 Ibid. This decision compared polygyny with human sacrifice and widow self-immolation, denigrating LDS practice through comparison with "eastern" religions. On this point, see Timothy Marr, *The Cultural Roots of American Islamicism* (Cambridge: Cambridge University Press, 2006).

11 *Reynolds v. U.S.*, 98 US 145 (1878), emphasis added.

12 Sarah Barringer Gordon, *The Mormon Question: Polygamy and Constitutional Conflict in Nineteenth-Century America* (Chapel Hill: The University of North Carolina Press, 2002), 5.

13 As quoted in *Reynolds v. U.S.*, 98 US 145 (1878).

14 The Republican Party Platform of 1856 referred to Mormon polygamy, with slavery, as the "twin relics of barbarism." As quoted in Arland Thorton, "The International Fight Against Barbarism: Historical and Comparative Perspectives on Marriage Timing, Consent, and Polygamy," in *Modern Polygamy in the United States: Historical, Cultural, and Legal Issues,* eds. Cardell Jacobsen and Lara Burton (New York: Oxford University Press, 2011), 277.

15 *Reynold's* position on free exercise was further clarified in three subsequent cases: *Murphy v. Ramsey* (1885); *Davis v. Beason* (1889); and *the Late Corporation of LDS v. U.S.* (1890). This last case disenfranchised Utahan women. Utah's territorial legislature had voted for women's suffrage in February 1869. Church president Brigham Young's grandniece, Sarah Young, was reportedly the first American woman to vote in a municipal election. Gordon, *The Mormon Question,* 180.

16 See also *Cleveland v. U.S.* (1946), which confirmed the unconstitutionality of the Mann Act, forbidding the transportation of women across state lines for the purposes of plural marriage.

17 The major exceptions in this precedent involve the constitutionality of blue laws, social security, and tax codes as pertaining to religious practice.

18 *Sherbert v. Verner*, 374 US 398 (1963).

19 *Employment Division, Department of Human Resources of Oregon v. Smith,* 494 US 872 (1990).

20 Ibid.

21 Ibid.

22 Winnifred Fallers Sullivan, "The World That Smith Made," in *The Politics of Religious Freedom,* eds. Winnifred Fallers Sullivan, Elizabeth Shakman Hurd, Saba Mahmood, and Peter G. Danchin (Chicago: The University of Chicago Press, 2015), 234.

23 *Religious Freedom Restoration Act of 1993*, HR 1308, 103rd Congress, 1st session, *Congressional Record.*

24 Sullivan, "The World that Smith Made," 235.

25 Free exercise cases involving mainstream Christian parties include *U.S. v. MacIntosh* (1931), *Hamilton v. the Regents of the University of California* (1934), *in re: Summers* (1945), *U.S. v. Hull Church* (1968), *McDaniel v. Paty* (1977), *Bob Jones University v. U.S.* (1982), *Alamo Foundation v. Secretary of Labor* (1985), *Ohio Rights Commission v. Dayton Christian Schools* (1986), *Frazee v. Illinois Department of Employment Security* (1989), *Jimmy Swaggart Ministries v. Board of Equalization of California* (1990), *Locke v. Davey* (2004), *Christian Legal Society v. Martinez* (2009), *Hosanna Tabor v. EEOC* (2011), *Burwell v. Hobby Lobby* (2014), and *Trinity Lutheran v. Comer* (granted January 2016).

    The Obama presidency is second only to the Reagan presidency in cases brought by or against mainstream Christian actors. There were five such cases brought before the Court from 1981 to 1989. Reflects broader cultural trend toward self-perception of conservative Christians as embattled, following political consolidation of New Christian Right in 1970s. Get text from Satan chapter.

    This list excludes *Pierce v. Society of Sisters* (1925), as Roman Catholics were politically vulnerable, lacking meaningful legislative representation, and publicly suspect, arguably until the mid-twentieth century. That John F. Kennedy had to reassure the body politic his allegiance to country over Rome is worth consideration on this point. See his speech to the Greater Houston Ministerial Association on September 12, 1960. "Transcript: JFK's Speech on His Religion," National Public Radio, December 5, 2007, http://www.npr.org/templates/story/story.php?storyId=16920600.

26 "Margaret Sanger, The Mike Wallace Interview, Sept. 21, 1957" Harry Ransom Center at the University of Texas at Austin, http://www.hrc.utexas.edu/multimedia/video/2008/wallace/sanger_margaret_t.html (accessed July 1, 2017). Sanger opened the first US "birth control clinic" in 1916 and the American Birth Control League in 1921. The latter has become the Planned Parenthood Federation of America.

27 The Roman Catholic Magisterium's opposition to birth control failed to discourage the majority of American Roman Catholics from using contraception. By the mid-1960s, 45 percent of Roman Catholics were using some form of birth control; by the mid-1970s, 60 percent of Catholic women were using contraceptives. Patricia Miller, *Good Catholics: The Battle Over Abortion in the Catholic Church* (Oakland: University of California Press, 2014), 14, 33.

28 Ibid., 36, as well as James C. Mohr, *Abortion in America* (New York: Oxford University Press, 1978), 207–08. Public anxieties regarding Catholics "outbreeding the competition" informed early-twentieth-century discourse regarding birth control and abortion as well—see the Sanger interview above.

29 Miller, *Good Catholics*, 16, citing the Bishops' Resolution at 1930 Lambeth Conference: "Where there is a clearly felt moral obligation to limit or avoid parenthood, the method must be decided on Christian principles. The primary and obvious method is complete abstinence from intercourse (as far as may be necessary) in a life of discipleship and self-control lived in the power of the Holy Spirit. Nevertheless, *in those cases where there is such a clearly felt moral obligation to limit or avoid parenthood, and where there is a morally sound reason for avoiding complete abstinence, the Conference agrees that other methods may be used, provided that this is done in the light of the same Christian principles.* The Conference records its strong condemnation of the use of any methods of conception-control for motives of selfishness, luxury, or mere convenience" (emphasis added).

30 Miller, *Good Catholics*, 16.

31 Married Baptist couples were theologically permitted to use contraception. Ibid., 181.

32 In referring to a catholicization of public morality, I draw on the dual operation of "c/Catholic": both specifically referring to the Roman Catholic Church, and the denotation of Catholic as "universal." It is important to note that the meaningful inclusion of Roman Catholic theology as an articulation of national values pertains exclusively to matters of sexuality, often to the exclusion of other theological priorities (capital punishment, ecology, etc.).

33 Michael Warner, "Ruse of 'Secular Humanism,'" *The Immanent Frame*, http://blogs.ssrc.org/tif/2008/09/22/the-ruse-of-secular-humanism/ (accessed July 1, 2017); Daniel Williams, *God's Own Party: The Making of the Christian Right* (New York: Oxford University Press, 2010), 5. Popular attitudes toward increased "sexual liberation" contributed to conservative Christians' increasing self-perception as embattled. This self-perception corresponds with a significant increase in late-twentieth-century Supreme Court free exercise cases regarding mainstream Christian actors.

34 Tracy Fessenden, "Sex and the Subject of Religion," *The Immanent Frame*, http://blogs.ssrc.org/tif/2008/01/10/sex-and-the-subject-of-religion/ (accessed July 1, 2017); Miller, *Good Catholics*, 72.

35 Some early push-back re: bishops' support for antiabortion legislation from other denominations, who felt Catholics overstepped their bounds. General board of American Baptist Churches accused bishops of "violat[ing] the theological and moral sensitivities, and hence the freedom, of other church bodies." Quoted Miller 72.

36 As Daniel Williams suggests: "By the end of the 1960s, [evangelicals and fundamentalists'] fear of cooperating with Catholics had dissipated in the midst of their concerns over secularism and moral decline. The sexual revolution, sex education, race riots, the counterculture, increases in drug use, and the beginning of the feminist movement convinced them that the nation had lost its Christian identity and that the family was under attack. At such a time, evangelicals—and eventually many fundamentalists, as well—decided that it was imperative to unite with socially conservative allies, even if they happened to be Catholic." *God's Own Party*, 5.

37 Miller, *Good Catholics*, 88.

38 Ibid., 89, 91.

39 Ibid., 92; Francis X. Clines, "Pope Ends U.S. Visit with Capital Mass Affirming Doctrine," *New York Times*, October 8, 1979. Regarding the papal conflation of contraception with abortion, see also Miller, *Good Catholics*, 133.

40 "Under the Reagan administration, US family planning policy had become a tool of John Paul II's vision." Ibid., 148, 150. Early 1980s evangelical concerns regarding contraception mostly dealt with young women's access to birth control without parental consent. See Ronald Reagan's "evil empire" speech on March 8, 1983, *Los Angeles Times*, http://www.latimes.com/la-reagan-empire-story.html (accessed July 1, 2017).

41 Miller, *Good Catholics*, 175.

42 Ibid., 202. Miller calls GW Bush's outreach to Catholics "unprecedented." Princeton natural law scholar Robert George noted that "in 1960, John Kennedy went from Washington down to Texas to assure Protestant preachers that he would not obey the pope. In 2001, George Bush came from Texas up to Washington to assure a group of Catholic bishops that he would." Ibid.

43 Ibid., 207.

44 Ibid., 179–80.

45 Ibid., 182.

46 Ibid., 183.

47 Ibid., 98 percent of women report having used contraception at some points in their lives; two-thirds of women childbearing age use contraception.

48 Ibid., 184.

49 Ibid.

50 Ibid.

51 Ibid., 185–86.

52 Ibid., 255, quoting Albert Mohler's "Can Christians Use Birth Control?," May 8, 2006, http://www.albertmohler.com/2006/05/08/can-christians-use-birth-control/.

53 Miller, *Good Catholics*, 255.

54 Ibid.

55 Ibid., 249.

56 Ibid., 250.

57 Ibid.

58 Ibid.

59 Ibid.

60 Ibid., 302, quoting W. D. Mosher and J. Jones, "Use of contraception in the United States: 1982-2000," *Vital Health Statistics* 23 (2010): 1–44.

61 Laurie Sobel, Adara Beamsederfer, and Alina Salganicoff, "Private Insurance Coverage of Contraception," The Henry J. Kaiser Family Foundation, December 7, 2016. http://www.kff.org/womens-health-policy/issue-brief/private-insurance-coverage-of-contraception/. See also Nora V. Becker and Daniel Polsky: "The average percentages of out-of-pocket spending for oral contraceptive pill prescriptions and IUDs insertions by women using those methods both dropped by 20 percentage points after implementation of the ACA mandate." "Women Saw Large Decrease In Out-Of-Pocket Spending For Contraceptives After ACA Mandate Removed Cost Sharing," *Health Affairs* 34, no. 7 (July 2015): 1204–11.

62 Ibid., Usha Ranji et al., "Ten Ways That the House American Health Care Act Could Affect Women," The Henry J. Kaiser Family Foundation, May 8, 2017, http://www.kff.org/womens-health-policy/issue-brief/ten-ways-that-the-house-american-health-care-act-could-affect-women/#Contraceptive.

63 Richard Adams, "Joe Biden: This Is a Big Fucking Deal," *The Guardian,* March 23, 2010, https://www.theguardian.com/world/richard-adams-blog/2010/mar/23/joe-biden-obama-big-fucking-deal-overheard.

64 Kinsey Hasstedt, "Abortion Coverage Under the Affordable Care Act: Advancing Transparency, Ensuring Choice, and Facilitating Access," *Guttmacher Policy Review*, April 9, 2015, https://www.guttmacher.org/gpr/2015/04/abortion-coverage-under-affordable-care-act-advancing-transparency-ensuring-choice-and

65 Nina Agrawal, "Abortion Rate Declines to Historic Low, with Obamacare a Likely Contributor," *Los Angeles Times,* January 18, 2017, http://www.latimes.com/nation/la-na-us-abortion-rates-20170117-story.html.

66 *Burwell v. Hobby Lobby*, 573 U.S. 37 (2014). Alito cites *Thomas v. Review Board of the Indiana Employment Security Division* (1981) to support this position. *Thomas'* plaintiff was a Jehovah's Witness who objected to his company's transfer of operations to weapons manufacturing.

67 *Burwell v. Hobby Lobby*, 573 U.S. 38 (2014).

68 Ibid., 16–17, 21.

69 Ibid., 3.

70 Ibid., 45.

71 Ibid., 46.

72 Ibid., 18 (emphasis added).

73 Ibid., 4. Justice Anthony Kennedy concurred, observing that while "the health of female employees" is a "legitimate and compelling" government interest and free exercise may not "unduly restrict other persons, such as employees," the contraceptive mandate is not the least restrictive means of pursuing that interest. Ibid., (Kennedy concurring).

74 Ibid., (Ginsburg dissenting), 24.

75 Without insurance, the cost for IUDs is equivalent to a month's wages at minimum wage. Almost one-third of women would change their method of contraception if cost were not a factor, and only a quarter of women got IUDs after finding out their cost before the ACA. Studies suggest that when the cost of IUDs is below $50, women are eleven times more likely to have one implanted. Ibid.

76 Ibid., (Ginsburg dissenting), 6.

77 Ibid., 2. Nineteen senators who voted for RFRA in 1993 entered an amicus brief on the Hobby Lobby case, stating that "Congress could not have anticipated, and did not intend, such a broad and unprecedented expansion of RFRA. Nor did Congress intend for courts to permit for-profit corporations and their shareholders to use

RFRA to deny female employees access to health care benefits to which they are otherwise entitled." "Statement of Interest," *Brief for Senators Murray* et al., 2–3.

78 573 U.S. 9 (2014), (Ginsburg dissenting).

79 Ibid., 27.

80 Ibid., 28.

81 Ibid., 31–32.

82 Ibid., 32.

83 Ibid., 13. Justices Kagan and Breyer concur with the entirety of Ginsburg's dissent, excepting this portion of her argument. They find no reason to establish whether for-profit corporations can sue under RFRA. 573 U.S. 1 (2014) (Breyer and Kagan dissenting).

84 Ibid., 13. On this point, see also the documentary film *The Corporation* (2004, dir. Mark Achbar and Jennifer Abbot), which proposes that if a corporation were analyzed on the basis of its behavior, it would be diagnosed as psychopathic, http://thecorporation.com.

85 Ibid., 8.

86 Ibid., 20.

87 Ibid., 21.

88 Ibid., 22.

89 Ibid., 23.

90 Ibid.

91 "Today's decision elides entirely the distinction between the sincerity of a challenger's religious belief and the substantiality of the burden placed on the challenger." Ibid., 22.

92 Ibid., 27.

93 Ibid., 2.

94 "Public Funded Family Planning Yields Numerous Positive Health Outcomes While Saving Taxpayer Dollars," Guttmacher Institute, January 9, 2015, https://www.guttmacher.org/news-release/2015/publicly funded-family-planning-yields-numerous-positive-health-outcomes-while.

95 Winnifred Fallers Sullivan, "The Impossibility of Religious Freedom," *The Immanent Frame*, http://blogs.ssrc.org/tif/2014/07/08/impossibility-of-religious-freedom/ (accessed July 1, 2017); Sarah Imhoff, "The Supreme Court's Faith in Belief," *The Immanent Frame*, http://blogs.ssrc.org/tif/2014/12/16/the-supreme-courts-faith-in-belief/ (accessed July 1, 2017).

96 Jason Bivins, "Embattled Majority: Religion and Its Despisers in America (Or: The Long-Lurching Wreck of American Public Life)," *Religion in American History*, http://usreligion.blogspot.com/2012/11/embattled-majority-religion-and-its.html (accessed July 1, 2017). This sense of racial embattlement has intensified in the past year. See Samuel Sommers and Michael Norton, "White People Think Racism Is Getting Worse. Against White People," *Washington Post*, July 21, 2016, https://www.washingtonpost.com/posteverything/wp/2016/07/21/white-people-think-racism-is-getting-worse-against-white-people/?utm_term=.a4d6ff7b6e79 CNN commentator Van Jones dubbed this phenomenon "white lash" in the context of the 2016 election. John Blake, "This Is What 'Whitelash' Looks Like," CNN, November 19, 2016, http://www.cnn.com/2016/11/11/us/obama-trump-white-backlash/index.html.

97 Martha J. Bailey, Brad Hershbein, and Amalia R. Miller, "The Opt-In Revolution? Contraception and the Gender Gap in Wages," *American Economic Journal. Applied Economics* 4, no. 3 (2012): 225–54; and Martha Bailey, Olga Malkova, and Johannes

Norling, "Do Family Planning Programs Decrease Poverty? Evidence from Public Census Data," *CESifo Economic Studies* 60, no. 2 (June 2014): 312–37.

98 "Unintended Pregnancy in the United States," Guttmacher Institute, September 2016, https://www.guttmacher.org/fact-sheet/unintended-pregnancy-united-states

99 LB Finer and SK Henshaw, "Disparities in Rates of Unintended Pregnancy in the United States, 1994 and 2001," *Perspectives in Sex and Reproductive Health* 38, no. 2 (2006): 90–96.

100 Dehlendorf, "Disparities in Family Planning," 216.

101 Susan A. Cohen, "Abortion and Women of Color: The Bigger Picture," *Guttmacher Policy Review*, August 6, 2008, https://www.guttmacher.org/gpr/2008/08/abortion-and-women-color-bigger-picture.

102 Nancy Northup, Center for Reproductive Rights, "Supplemental Information about the United States Scheduled for Review during the Committee for the Elimination of Racial Discrimination Committee's 72nd Session," December 19, 2007, 5.

103 Marcela Howell and Ann M. Starrs, "For Women of Color, Access to Vital Health Services Is Threatened," *The Hill*, July 26, 2017, http://thehill.com/blogs/pundits-blog/healthcare/343996-for-women-of-color-access-to-vital-health-services-is

104 Arkansas, Colorado, Georgia, Hawaii, Indiana, Maine, Michigan, Montana, Nevada, North Carolina, Oklahoma, South Carolina, South Dakota, Texas, Utah, West Virginia, Wyoming. Arkansas and—famously—Indiana passed. "2015 State Religious Freedom Restoration Legislation," National Conference of State Legislatures, September 3, 2015, http://www.ncsl.org/research/civil-and-criminal-justice/2015-state-rfra-legislation.aspx.

105 Dana Llebelson, "Arkansas Governor Says He Won't Sign 'Religious Freedom' Bill Until Changes Are Made," *Huffington Post*, April 1, 2015, http://www.huffingtonpost.com/2015/04/01/religious-freedom_n_6985090.html.

106 House Bill 1228, 90th General Assembly, Regular Session (Arkansas 2015), http://guides.library.cornell.edu/c.php?g=134360&p=881263. Arizona Governor Jan Brewer vetoed a similar bill in 2014.

107 Tony Cook and Brian Eason, "Gov. Mike Pence Signs RFRA Fix," *The Indianapolis Star*, April 1, 2015, http://www.indystar.com/story/news/politics/2015/04/01/indiana-rfra-deal-sets-limited-protections-for-lgbt/70766920/. More recently, a US District Judge just made Kentucky taxpayers responsible for the $220,000 in court costs incurred by couples who sued Rowan County clerk Kim Davis for refusing to issue marriage licenses to same-sex couples after the landmark decision *Obergefell v. Hodges* (2015) legalized same-sex marriages. Amy Held, "Kentucky Must Pay Attorney Fees For Couples Who Sued Kim Davis, Judge Says," *National Public Radio*, July 21, 2017, http://www.npr.org/sections/thetwo-way/2017/07/21/538592022/kentucky-must-pay-attorney-fees-for-couples-who-sued-kim-davis-says-judge.

108 The Supreme Court agreed to hear *Masterpiece Cake Shop v. Colorado Civil Rights Commission* in June 2017. The case closely resembles *Ingersoll v. Arlene's Flowers*, in which the Washington State Supreme Court found for the plaintiffs, Curt Freed and Robert Ingersoll. In both cases, the owners of the businesses refused services to same-sex couples on the grounds of conservative Christian conscience. See Adam Liptak, "Justices to Hear Case on Religious Objections to Same-Sex Marriage," *New York Times*, June 26, 2017, https://www.nytimes.com/2017/06/26/us/politics/supreme-court-wedding-cake-gay-couple-masterpiece-cakeshop.html; and "Washington State Supreme Court Rules Florist Discriminated Against Same-Sex Couple by Refusing Wedding-Related Service," *American Civil Liberties Union*,

February 16, 2017, https://www.aclu.org/news/washington-state-supreme-court-rules-florist-discriminated-against-same-sex-couple-refusing.

109 Miller, *Good Catholics*, 258.

110 Zubik v. Burwell was brought by petitioners on behalf of religious organizations claiming that filing religious exemption paperwork to the ACA's contraceptive mandate constituted a substantial burden on those organizations' free exercise. Regarding Gorsuch's position on abortion and contraception, see Corey Brettschneider, "Gorsuch, Abortion, and the Concept of Personhood," *New York Times,* March 21, 2017, https://www.nytimes.com/2017/03/21/opinion/gorsuch-abortion-and-the-concept-of-personhood.html.

111 Donald J. Trump, "My Vision for a Culture of Life," *Washington Examiner,* January 23, 2016, http://www.washingtonexaminer.com/donald-trump-op-ed-my-vision-for-a-culture-of-life/article/2581271; Elizabeth Landers, "Vice President Mike Pence Speech Right at Home at March for Life," *CNN,* January 27, 2017, http://www.cnn.com/2017/01/27/politics/mike-pence-march-for-life-speech/index.html.

112 Executive Order of May 4, 2017, Promoting Free Speech and Religious Liberty, https://www.whitehouse.gov/the-press-office/2017/05/04/presidential-executive-order-promoting-free-speech-and-religious-liberty (accessed July 1, 2017).

113 Olga Khazan, "Tom Price: 'Not One' Woman Struggled to Afford Birth Control," *The Atlantic,* November 29, 2016, https://www.theatlantic.com/health/archive/2016/11/tom-price-not-one-woman-cant-afford-birth-control/509003/.

114 "Survey: Nearly Three in Four Voters in America Support Fully Covering Prescription Birth Control," Planned Parenthood Federation of America, January 30, 2014, https://www.plannedparenthood.org/about-us/newsroom/press-releases/survey-nearly-three-four-voters-america-support-fully-covering-prescription-birth-control.

115 Megan Goodwin, "Planned Parenthood? Forsaking American Women for the Mother of All Bombs," *Religion Bulletin,* May 16, 2017, http://bulletin.equinoxpub.com/2017/05/theorizing-religion-in-the-age-of-trump-megan-goodwin/

116 Antonia Blumberg, "These Congressmen Are Trying to Curb Religious Freedom Abuses," *Huffington Post,* July 13, 2017, http://www.huffingtonpost.com/entry/do-no-harm-act_us_5967c542e4b03389bb160cb5?section=us_religion.

Chapter 8

1 "Bill O'Reilly Confronts Rapper Lupe Fiasco Over Calling Obama a 'Terrorist'" O'Reilly Factor television program (June 20, 2011) *YouTube* (June 20, 2011), https://youtu.be/eqtkdSM1CJk.

2 See Jürgen Habermas's *The Structural Transformation of the Public Sphere: An Inquiry into a Category of Bourgeois Society* (Cambridge, MA: MIT Press, 1989), I have incorporated several important critiques into my overall understanding of the public sphere as a historic and conceptual framework. Among these are Evelyn Brooks Higginbotham, *Righteous Discontent: The Women's Movement in the Black Baptist Church, 1880–1920* (Cambridge, MA: Harvard University Press, 1993), 7–13; Nancy Fraser, "Rethinking the Public Sphere: A Contribution to the Critique of Actually Existing Democracy," in *Habermas and the Public Sphere*, ed. Craig Calhoun (Cambridge, MA: MIT Press, 1992), 109–42; Craig Calhoun, "Civil Society and the Public Sphere," *Public Culture* 5 (1993): 267–80; Jeffrey Alexander and Philip Smith,

"The Discourse of American Civil Society: A New Proposal for Cultural Studies," *Theory and Society* 22 (1993): 151–207; Adam B. Seligman, *The Idea of Civil Society* (Princeton: Princeton University Press, 1992); Marshall Battani et al., "Cultures' Structures: Making Meaning in the Public Sphere," *Theory and Society* 26 (December 1997): 781–812; Earl Lewis, *In Their Own Interests: Race, Class, and Power in Twentieth-Century Norfolk, Virginia* (Berkeley: University of California Press, 1991), 5–6, 81–84, 188–94; and Carl Boggs, "The Great Retreat: Decline of the Public Sphere in Late Twentieth-Century America," *Theory and Society* 26 (December 1997): 741–80.

3 Some of these ideas were initially explored in "More Than Conquerors: Just War Theory and the Need for a Black Christian Antiwar Movement," *Black Theology: An International Journal* 9, no. 2 (2011): 136–60.

4 Text of "Obama's Nobel Remarks," *New York Times*, December 11, 2009, http://www.nytimes.com/2009/12/11/world/europe/11prexy.text.html.

5 Ibid.

6 Ibid.

7 Peter Beinart, *The Good Fight: Why Liberals—And Only Liberals—Can Win the War on Terror and Make America Great Again* (New York: Harper, 2008).

8 Barack H. Obama, *The Audacity of Hope: Thoughts on Reclaiming the American Dream* (New York: Crown, 2006), 271–323.

9 "Remarks of the President on a New Beginning," *New York Times* (2009).

10 Walid Phares, *The Coming Revolution: The Struggle for Freedom in the Middle East* (New York: Simon and Schuster, 2010).

11 Anthony N. Celso, "Obama and the Arab Spring: The Strategic Confusion of a Realist-Idealist," *Journal of Political Sciences & Public Affairs* 2, no. 2 (2014): 2.

12 Fareed Zakaria, *The Post-American World* (New York: W. W. Norton & Company, 2008).

13 Zbigniew Brzezinski, *Strategic Vision: America and the Crisis of Global Power* (New York: Basic Books, 2012), 122.

14 Kenneth R. Himes OFM, *Drones and the Ethics of Targeted Killing* (Lanham, MD: Rowman & Littlefield, 2015); Scott Shane, "Targeted Killing Comes to Define War on Terror," *New York Times* (April 7, 2013), http://www.nytimes.com/2013/04/08/world/targeted-killing-comes-to-define-war-on-terror.html?rref=collection%2Fbyline%2Fscott-shane&action=click&contentCollection=undefined&region=stream&module=stream_unit&version=search&contentPlacement=1&pgtype=collection.

15 Alex Emmons, "After 8 Years of Expanding Presidential War Powers, Obama Insists They Are Limited," *The Intercept* (December 6, 2016), https://theintercept.com/2016/12/06/after-8-years-of-expanding-them-obama-insists-that-presidential-war-powers-are-limited/.

16 Jeremy Scahill, "Trump May Not Finish His Term but the Assassination Complex Will Live On," *TheIntercept.com* (August 21, 2017), https://static.theintercept.com/amp/trump-may-not-survive-his-term-but-the-assassination-complex-will.html.

17 Uri Friedman, "Targeted Killings: A Short History," *Foreign Policy* (August 13, 2012), http://foreignpolicy.com/2012/08/13/targeted-killings-a-short-history/.

18 Barack H. Obama, "What I Am Opposed to Is a Dumb War: Speech against the Iraq War (Chicago, IL October 2, 2002)," in *We Are the Change We Seek: The Speeches of Barack Obama*, eds. E. J. Dionne and Joy-Ann Reid (London: Bloomsbury, 2017), 1–4.

19 Reinhold Niebuhr, *The Irony of American History* (1952; Chicago: University of Chicago Press, 2008), 174.

20 Ibid., 4–5.

21 Ibid., 5.

22 Ibid., 40–41.

23 Full text of Rev. Jeremiah A. Wright Jr., "Confusing God and Government" sermon (April 18, 2003), http://www.blackpast.org/?q=2008-rev-jeremiah-wright-confusing-god-and-government.

24 Ibid.

25 Ibid.

26 Juan M. Floyd-Thomas, "More Than Conquerors: Just War Theory and the Need for a Black Christian Antiwar Movement," *Black Theology: An International Journal* 9, no. 2 (2011): 136–60.

27 See T. Denean Sharpley-Whiting (ed.), *The Speech: Race and Barack Obama's "A More Perfect Union"* (London: Bloomsbury, 2009).

28 Jeffrey O. G. Ogbar, "Message from the Grassroots: Hip Hop Activism, Millennials, and the Race for the White House," in *The Hip Hop & Obama Reader*, eds. Travis L. Gosa and Erik Nielson (New York: Oxford University Press, 2015), 47.

29 Hisham Aidi, "Jihadis in the Hood: Race, Urban Islam, and the War on Terror," *Middle East Report*, no. 224 (Autumn 2002): 37.

30 Juan M. Floyd-Thomas, "A Jihad of Words: The Evolution of African American Islam and Contemporary Hip Hop," in *Noise and Spirit: The Religious and Spiritual Sensibilities of Rap Music*, ed. Anthony B. Pinn (New York: University Press, 2003), 75–109; H. Samy Alim, "Re-inventing Islam with Unique Modern Tones: Muslim Hip Hop Artists as Verbal Mujahidin," *Souls: A Critical Journal of Black Politics, Culture, and Society* 8, no. 4 (2006): 45–58; and Torie Rose DeGhett, "'Record! I Am Arab:' Paranoid Arab Boys, Global Ciphers, and Hip Hop Nationalism," in *The Hip Hop & Obama Reader*, eds. Travis L. Gosa and Erik Nielson (New York: Oxford University Press, 2015), 94–106.

31 Scott Heins, "Method Man Speaks Out On 'P.L.O. Style' & Black-Palestinian Solidarity in a New Interview," *OkayPlayer.com*.

32 See Chalmers Johnson, *Blowback: The Costs and Consequences of American Empire* (New York: Henry Holt and Company, 2001).

33 Juan M. Floyd-Thomas, "More than Conquerors: Just War Theory and the Need for a Black Christian Antiwar Movement," *Black Theology: An International Journal* 9, no. 2 (2011): 136–60.

34 Saladin Ambar, *Malcolm X at Oxford Union: Racial Politics in a Global Era* (New York: Oxford University Press, 2014); Graeme Abernathy, *The Iconography of Malcolm X* (Lawrence: University Press of Kansas, 2013), 214; a sample recording of these last lines of the Malcolm X's Oxford Union speech can be heard on Mos Def, "Supermagic," *The Ecstatic*, Downtown, DWT70055, 2009. Video footage and complete transcript of the Oxford Union debate is available via the *Liberator Magazine*, http://weblog.liberatormagazine.com/2010/12/malcolm-x-ascended-extremism-in-defense.html.

35 Hishaam D. Aidi, "Let Us Be Moors: Race, Islam, and 'Connected Histories,'" in *Black Routes to Islam*, 123.

36 H. Samy Alim, "A New Research Agenda: Exploring the Transglobal Hip Hop *Umma*," in *The Hip Hop and Religion Reader*, eds. Monica R. Miller and Anthony B. Pinn (London: Routledge, 2015), 54.

37 Audre Lorde, "The Transformation of Silence into Language and Action," *Sister Outsider: Essays and Speeches* (Freedom, CA: The Crossing Press, 1984), 41.

38 W. E. B. Du Bois, *Darkwater: Voices From Within the Veil* (1920: Mineola, NY: Dover Publications, 1999), 26.

Chapter 9

1 W. E. B. Du Bois, *Darkwater* (1920), Republished in Roediger (Black on White), 1998, 184.

2 Refer scholars who write about whiteness studies: Richard Delgado and Jean Stefancic (eds.), *Critical White Studies: Looking Behind the Mirror* (Philadelphia: Temple University Press, 1997); Robert Jensen, *The Heart of Whiteness: Confronting Race, Racism, and White Privilege* (San Francisco: City Light Publishers, 2005); Steve Martinot, *The Machinery of Whiteness: Studies in the Structure of Racialization* (Philadelphia: Temple University Press, 2010); and Jennifer Harvey, *Whiteness and Morality: Pursuing Racial Justice through Reparations and Sovereignty* (New York: Palgrave Macmillan, 2012).

3 See seminal works by these African American scholars who focus on race and racisms in the West and the United States: Charles Long, *Significations: Signs, Symbols, and Images in the Interpretation of Religion* (Aurora, CO: The Davies Group Publishers, 1999); David Theo Goldberg, *Racist Culture: Philosophy and the Politics of Meaning* (Hoboken, NJ: Blackwell Publishers, 1993); Hortense Spillers, *Black, White, and In Color: Essays on American Literature and Culture* (Chicago: University of Chicago Press, 2003); and Alexander Weheliye, *Habeas Viscus: Racializing Assemblages, Biopolitics, and Black Feminist Theories of the Human* (Durham: Duke University Press, 2014).

4 See this text on how whiteness and racism are inscribed into geographies: Caroline Bressey and Claire Dwyer (eds.), *New Geographies of Race and Racism* (New York: Routledge, 2016).

5 Willie Jennings, *The Christian Imagination: Theology and the Origins of Race* (New Haven: Yale University Press, 2010), 23.

6 Jennings, *The Christian Imagination*.

7 Ibid.

8 William Jennings, *The Christian Imagination*, 26.

9 Ibid., 59.

10 Ibid.

11 William Jennings, *The Christian Imagination*, 241.

12 Jan-Werner Muller, *What is Populism?* (Philadelphia: University of Pennsylvania Press, 2016), 3.

13 Jan-Werner Muller, *What is Populism?* 3–5.

14 To read more about this economic restructuring, refer to: William Julius Wilson, *The Truly Disadvantaged: The Inner City, the Underclass, and Public Policy* (Chicago: University of Chicago Press, 1987) and *When Work Disappears: The World of the New Urban Poor* (New York: Vintage, 1997); Marcellus Andrews, *The Political Economy of Hope and Fear* (New York: New York University Press, 2001); Patricia Hill Collins, *Black Feminist Thought: Knowledge, Consciousness and the Politics of Empowerment* (New York: Routledge, 2000); and bell hooks, *Where We Stand: Class Matters* (New York: Routledge, 2000).

15 See these texts on the adverse impact the World Bank and IMF have had on the Global South: Amartya Sen, *Development as Freedom* (New York: Anchor, 2000); Joseph Stiglitz, *Globalization and Its Discontents* (New York: W. W. Norton & Company, 2003) and *The Price of Inequality: How Today's Divided Society Endangers Our Future* (New York: W. W. Norton & Company, 2013); and Martha Nussbaum, *Women and Human Development: The Capabilities Approach* (Cambridge: Cambridge University Press, 2001).

16 See Alia Malek (ed.), *Patriot Acts: Narratives of Post-9/11 Injustices* (San Francisco: McSweeney's Publishing, 2011).

17 See Marilyn Richardson, *Maria Stewart, America's First Black Woman Political Writer: Essays and Speeches*, 4th Printing edition (Bloomington: Indiana University Press, 1987).

18 Maria W. Stewart, *Meditations from the Pen of Mrs. Maria W. Stewart* (London: Forgotten Books, 2016). This little volume was first delivered as a speech by Stewart in 1832 to the First African Baptist Church and Society of Boston, Massachusetts.

19 Frederick Douglass, *Narrative of the Life of Frederick Douglass*, Unabridged Edition (New York: Dover, 1995), 68. Originally published by the Anti-Slavery Office in Boston, MA in 1845.

20 Frederick Douglass, *Narrative of the Life of Frederick Douglass* 153.

21 Ibid.

22 Frederick Douglass, *Narrative of the Life of Frederick Douglass* 154.

Chapter 10

1 By this phrase, I mean his initial campaign through the end of his second term in office—complete with its vision of collective life fueled by a synergistic commitment to liberal religiosity in the mode of the social gospel and the democratic hopefulness of the civil rights movement.

2 By humanism I mean a human center mode of thought and practice without debt to theistic sensibilities and transhistorical concerns. For a sense of what I mean by humanism as presented here see Pinn, *African American Humanist Principles* (New York: Palgrave Macmillan, 2004); Pinn, *The End of God-Talk: An African American Humanist Theology* (New York: Oxford University Press, 2012); Pinn, *When Colorblindness Isn't the Answer: Humanism and the Challenge of Race* (Durham: Pitchstone Publishing, 2017). By moralism I mean to highlight a hermeneutic concerned with pointing out the hypocrisies and inconsistencies within social structures and mechanisms of collective life.

3 In fact, this is the similar to the mode of public activism I tried to turn attention toward in *What Has the Black Church to Do With Public Life?* (New York: Palgrave Macmillan, 2013). In discussing religion here, I have in mind traditional definitions of religion as opposed to my particular theory—religion as a quest for complex subjectivity.

4 I make use of Du Bois here because of the manner in which theories of race from the early twentieth century moving forward respond to his work. They either embrace his conceptual framework (e.g., double-consciousness, the "color-line"), or critique his thinking. In either case, Du Bois is foundational to contemporary thinking on race.

5 W. E. B. Du Bois, *The Souls of Black Folk*, edited by Henry Louis Gate, Jr., and Terri Hume Oliver, Norton Critical Edition (New York: W. W. Norton & Company, 1999), 5.

6 W. E. B. Du Bois, *The Souls of Black Folk*, edited by Henry Louis Gate, Jr., and Terri Hume Oliver, Norton Critical Edition (New York: W. W. Norton & Company, 1999), 9.

7 My work on Du Bois's "The Negro as a Problem" was presented first as the 2017 William James Lecture at Harvard Divinity School, March 9, 2017. A more expansive wrestling with the "problem soul" and African American moralism will take place in my volume *Religion and the Meaning of Things* to be published by Oxford University Press.

8 William J. Maxwell, "Born-Again, Seen-Again James Baldwin: Post-Postracial Criticism and the Literary History of Black Lives Matter", *American Literary History* 28, no. 4 (2016): 813.

9 Rickey Hill and Tazinski P. Lee, "The Killing of Black People by the US State is as American as Apple Pie: Groundwork Toward a Critique," *Journal of Race & Policy* 16 (2015): 5–22.

10 Wesley Lowery, *They Can't Kill Us All: Ferguson, Baltimore, and a New Era in America's Racial Justice Movement* (New York: Little, Brown and Company, 2016), 14, 15.

11 Obama, "Election Night Victory Speech," Grant Park, Illinois, November 4, 2008. See: http://obamaspeeches.com/E11-Barack-Obama-Election-Night-Victory-Speech-Grant-Park-Illinois-November-4-2008.htm (accessed May 31, 2017).

12 See http://www.nytimes.com/2008/03/18/us/politics/18text-obama.html (accessed May 31, 2017).

13 See http://www.nytimes.com/2008/03/18/us/politics/18text-obama.html (accessed May 31, 2017).

14 https://obamawhitehouse.archives.gov/the-press-office/2013/01/21/inaugural-address-president-barack-obama (accessed May 31, 2017).

15 Read this statement in light of Eric Foner's "Teaching the History of Radicalism in the Age of Obama", *The Nation* (January 2/9, 2017): 76–80.

16 Some of these ideas are drawn from a piece I wrote for *Religion Dispatches*, published on June 16, 2009.

17 "Remarks by the President at Morehouse College Commencement Ceremony," May 19, 2013. See https://obamawhitehouse.archives.gov/the-press-office/2013/05/19/remarks-president-morehouse-college-commencement-ceremony (accessed May 30, 2017).

18 See http://www.nytimes.com/2008/03/18/us/politics/18text-obama.html (accessed May 31, 2017).

19 "In the white community, the path to a more perfect union means acknowledging that what ails the African-American community does not just exist in the minds of black people; that the legacy of discrimination—and current incidents of discrimination, while less overt than in the past—are real and must be addressed. Not just with words, but with deeds—by investing in our schools and our communities; by enforcing our civil rights laws and ensuring fairness in our criminal justice system; by providing this generation with ladders of opportunity that were unavailable for previous generations. It requires all Americans to realize that your dreams do not have to come at the expense of my dreams; that investing in the health, welfare, and education of black and brown and white children will ultimately help all of America prosper." See http://www.nytimes.com/2008/03/18/us/politics/18text-obama.html (accessed May 31, 2017).

20 Wesley Lowery, *They Can't Kill Us All: Ferguson, Baltimore, and a New Era in America's Racial Justice Movement* (New York: Little, Brown and Company, 2016), 195–96.

21 Keeanga-Yamahtta Taylor, *From #BlackLivesMatter to Black Liberation* (Chicago: Haymarket Books, 2016), 10.

22 When reflecting on Black Lives Matter, he had this to say: "Once you've highlighted an issue and brought it to people's attention and shined a spotlight, and elected officials or people who are in a position to start bringing about change are ready to sit down with you, then you can't just keep on yelling at them." Quoted in Brian P. Jones, "Black Lives Matter and the Struggle for Freedom", *Review of the Month* (April 2016): 1.

23 Kai Wright, "Black Life and Death in the Age of Obama," *The Nation* (January 2–9, 2017). See https://www.thenation.com/article/black-life-and-death-in-the-age-of-obama/ (accessed May 30, 2017).

24 Some of this material is drawn from: Anthony B. Pinn, "On Struggle In Our Historical Moment," *Huffington Post,* July 12, 2016, http://www.huffingtonpost.com/anthony-b-pinn/on-struggle-in-our-histor_b_10930544.html.

25 Hailey Wallace, "The Making of a Movement" *Black Enterprise.Com* (July/August 2016): 65.

26 Wesley Lowery, *They Can't Kill Us All: Ferguson, Baltimore, and a New Era in America's Racial Justice Movement* (New York: Little, Brown and Company, 2016), 101.

27 Mychal Denzel Smith, "A Q&A with Alicia Garza, Co-Founder of #BlackLivesMatter," *The Nation* (March 24, 2015). See: https://www.thenation.com/article/qa-alicia-garza-co-founder-blacklivesmatter/ (accessed May 31, 2017).

28 Frederick C. Harris, "The Next Civil Rights Movement?" *Dissent* (Summer 2015): 34.

29 Mychal Denzel Smith, "A Q&A With Opal Tometi, Co-Founder of #BlackLivesMatter," *The Nation* (June 2, 2015). See https://www.thenation.com/article/qa-opal-tometi-co-founder-blacklivesmatter/ (accessed May 31, 2017).

30 Mychal Denzel Smith, "A Q&A with Alicia Garza, Co-Founder of #BlackLivesMatter," *The Nation* (March 24, 2015). See https://www.thenation.com/article/qa-alicia-garza-co-founder-blacklivesmatter/ (accessed May 31, 2017).

31 Kate Driscoll Derickson, "The Racial State and Resistance in Ferguson and Beyond", *Urban Studies* 53, no. 11 (2016): 2223.

32 Alicia Garza, "A Herstory of the #BlackLivesMatter Movement", *Feministwire*, http://thefeministwire.com/2014/10/blacklivesmatter-2/.

33 Alicia Garza, "A Herstory of the #BlackLivesMatter Movement", *Feministwire*, http://thefeministwire.com/2014/10/blacklivesmatter-2/.

34 Karin Kamp, "Black Lives Matter Co-Founder Alicia Garza on the Global Movement for Black Lives," *BillMoyers.com* (October 3, 2016). See http://billmoyers.com/story/black-lives-matter/ (accessed May 31, 2017).

35 Mychal Denzel Smith, "A Q&A With Opal Tometi, Co-Founder of #BlackLivesMatter," *The Nation* (June 2, 2015). See https://www.thenation.com/article/qa-opal-tometi-co-founder-blacklivesmatter/ (accessed May 31, 2017).

36 Glenn Mackin, "Black Lives Matter and the Concept of the Counterworld," *Philosophy and Rhetoric* 49, no. 4 (2016): 462.

37 In this way, BLM is a challenge to both a limited sense of personhood and justice within the civil rights movement and the theological rationale for such exclusion offered in so many religious discourses.

38 Jelani Cobb, "The Matter of Black Lives," *The New Yorker* (March 14, 2016). See http://www.newyorker.com/magazine/2016/03/14/where-is-black-lives-matter-headed (accessed May 31, 2017).

39 If there are figures rightly called leaders within the Black Lives Matter movement, they work not based on a model entailing a central figure providing agenda and instructions. But rather, it is a model of leadership nurturing of skills, capacity, and persistence within the group—not "do it my way!" Rather, "how should we do our work so as to maximize our diversity of talents and abilities?"

40 Cathy J. Cohen and Sarah J. Jackson, "As a Feminist: A Conversation with Cathy J. Cohen on Black Lives Matter, Feminism and Contemporary Activism," *Signs* 41, no. 4 (2016): 783.

41 Hazel Carby, *Race Men* (Cambridge, MA: Harvard University Press, 2000).

42 Jermaine M. McDonald, "Ferguson and Baltimore According to Dr. King: How Competing Interpretations of King's Legacy Frame the Public Discourse on Black Lives Matter," *Journal of the Society of Christian Ethics* 36, no. 2 (2016): 141–58.

43 Christian theologian, Shawn Copeland recognizes this turn when writing, "the principles of Black Lives Matter movement constitute a kind of platform for renewed black humanism (or natural theology) that struggles for the survival, liberation, and

flourishing of the black human being as self and as subject." See M. Shawn Copeland, "Memory, #BlackLivesMatter, and Theologians," *Political Theology* 17, no. 1 (January 2016): 2.

44   See for example: James H. Cone, *Martin, Malcolm & America: A Dream or a Nightmare* (Maryknoll, NY: Orbis Books, 1991).

45   David W. McIvor, *Mourning in America: Race and the Politics of Loss* (Ithaca: Cornell University Press, 2016), xii.

46   Harvey Young, "Pessimism and the Age of Obama", *American Literary History* 28, no. 4 (Winter 2016): 855.

47   In terms of Du Bois, I frame this in terms of Souls of Black Folk. Elsewhere I also connect this tradition to a later source—Albert Camus. A prime example of this philosophy in the work of Camus is: *The Myth of Sisyphus and Other Essays* (New York: Vintage International, 1991).

48   Du Bois, *Souls*, 138.

49   The election and re-election of Obama pointed to the tenacious and thick presence of disregard, a fog of disregard intense enough to withstand the winds of change. BLM points out the confrontation with the "how does it feel to be a problem" (i.e., the Negro as Problem) equation represented by Du Bois and notes that it can't be captured through language and rationale argument, but rather the very answer is embodied, it is about the occupation of time and space in ways that confront, twist and force new consideration.

50   W. E. B. Du Bois, "The Negro Problem" (From The Negro, 1915) found in David Levering Lewis (ed.), *W. E. B. Du Bois: A Reader* (New York: Henry Holt and Company, 1995), 48, 49, 50, 51.

51   Pericles Lewis, "James's Sick Souls," *The Henry James Review* 22, no. 3 (Fall 2001): 251.

52   Susan Mizruchi, "Neighbors, Strangers, Corpses: Death and Sympathy in the Early Writings of W. E. B. Du Bois," in *The Souls of Black Folk: W. E. B. Du Bois*, eds. Henry L. Gates, Jr., and Terri Hume Oliver (New York: W. W. Norton & Company, 1999), 274.

53   What the lynching of Sam Hose meant to Du Bois, the killing of a black man accused of being with a white prostitute meant to Wright. In both cases the every present threat of death confronted all dimensions of life, and there was no relief available.

54   Kristin Hunter Lattany, "Off-Timing: Stepping to the Different Drummer," in *Lure and Loathing: Essays on Race, Identity, and the Ambivalence of Assimilation*, ed. Gerald Early (New York: The Penguin Press, 1993), 164.

55   Neil Small, "Death and difference," in *Death, Gender and Ethnicity*, eds. David Field, Jenny Hockey, and Neil Small (London: Routledge, 1997), 208–09.

56   Zamir, *Dark Voices: W. E. B. Du Bois and American Thought, 1888-1903* (Chicago: The University of Chicago Press, 1995), 133.

57   Du Bois, *Souls*, 12–13; Stephanie J. Shaw, *W. E. B. Du Bois and the Souls of Black Folk* (Chapel Hill: The University of North Carolina Press, 2013), 38–40. Shaw also offers a more positive assessment of double-consciousness than most, finding in it not a strict political or economic statement regarding leadership of the race and Du Bois place within the hierarchy, nor as a hopeless situation, but rather as a statement concerning the inner workings of African Americans as they approach life within a society marked by racial disregard (41–42).

58   Robert Zaretsky, *A Life Worth Living: Albert Camus and the Quest for Meaning* (Cambridge, MA: Harvard University Press, 2013), 7.

59   Robert Zaretsky, *A Life Worth Living: Albert Camus and the Quest for Meaning* (Cambridge, MA: Harvard University Press, 2013), 8.

60   Jean Kellogg, *Dark Prophets of Hope* (Chicago: Loyola University Press, 1975), 89–100.

Chapter 11

1 Michelle Ye Hee Lee, "Donald Trump's False Comments Connecting Mexican Immigration and Crime," *The Washington Post*, July 8, 2015.

2 Suzanne Gamboa, "Deporter-in-Chief Label Ups the Pressure for Action from Obama," *NBC News*, March 6, 2014.

3 Rebecca Kaplan, "Obama is 'Deporter-in-Chief,' Says Prominent Latino Group," *CBS News*, March 4, 2014.

4 Gloria E. Anzaldúa, *Borderlands/La Frontera: The New Mestiza* (San Francisco: Spinsters/Aunt Lute, 1987), 3.

5 Santos and Zemansky, "Arizons Desert Swallows Migrants on Riskier Trails," May 20, 2013.

6 The Center for Latin American Studies, *In the Shadow of the Wall: Family Separation, Immigration Enforcement and Security* (Tucson: Arizona University, 2013), 24.

7 Ildefonso Ortiz, "Agent Sexually Assaults Family, Kidnaps Girl, Commits Suicide," *The Brownsville Herald*, March 13, 2014.

8 https://www.youtube.com/watch?v=xomI5NK01gc.

9 Garrett M. Graff, "The Green Monster: How the Border Patrol became America's Most Out-of-Control Law Enforcement Agency," *Politico Magazine* (November/December 2014).

10 Ibid.

11 Jim and Jane Crow.

12 Richard M. Stana, *INS Southwest Border Strategy: Resource and Impact Issues Remain After Seven Years* (Washington, DC: US General Accounting Office, 2001), 1.

13 United States Department of Homeland Security, *Yearbook of Immigration Statistics: 2015* (Washington, DC: United State Department of Homeland Security, Office of Immigration Statistics, 2016), 103–07.

14 John Charles Johnson, Secretary of the United States Department of Homeland Security, "Memorandum: Policies for the Apprehension, Detention and Removal of Undocumented Immigrants," November 20, 2014, 3.

15 Serena Marshall, "Obama Has Deported More People than Any Other President," *ABC News*, August 26, 2016.

16 President Barack Obama, "Transcript: Obama's Immigration Speech," *The Washington Post*, November 20, 2014.

17 Adam Kealoha Causey, "To Some, Trump's 'Bad Hombres' is Much More than a Botched Spanish Word," *PBS News Hour*, October 20, 2016.

18 Amy B. Wang, "Donald Trump Plans to Immediately Deport 2 Million to 3 Million Undocumented Immigrants," *The Washington Post*, November 14, 2016.

19 Jens Manuel Krogstad, Ana Gonzalez-Barrera, and Mark Hugo Lopez, "Children 12 and Under are Fastest Growing Group of Unaccompanied Minors at United State Border," *Pew Research Center*, July 22, 2014.

20 Eyder Peralta, "You Say You're an American, But What If You Had to Prove It or Be Deported?" *NPR*, December 22, 2016.

21 Julia Preston, "Obama Signs Border Bill to Increase Surveillance," *The New York Times*, August 13, 2010.

22 Solomon Moore, "Study Shows Sharp Rise in Latino Federal Convicts," *The New York Times*, February 18, 2009; and Jennifer Steinhaur, "Bipartisan Push Builds to Relax Sentencing Laws," *New York Times*, July 28, 2015.

23 Cedar Attanasio, "Deporter in Chief: Obama Ordered 7,000 Immigrant Children to Be Deported without a Court Hearing," *Latin Times*, March 16, 2016.

24 "Arizona Protestors Mistake Busload of YMCA campers for Immigrant Children," *CBS News*, July 16, 2014.

25 "Rep. Roybal-Allard, House Democrats Recap Trip to Family Detention Facilities," *Congressional Hispanic Caucus*, June 24, 2015.

26 Chico Harlan, "Inside the Administration's $1 Billion Deal to Detain Central American Asylum Seekers," *The Washington Post*, August 14, 2016.

27 Sonia Nazario, "The Refugees at Our Door: We Are Paying Mexico to Keep People from Reaching Our Borders, People Who Are Fleeing Central American Violence," *The New York Times*, October 10, 2015.

28 Gunboat diplomacy, like big stick diplomacy, refers to the US pursuit of foreign policy objectives through the display of military might, specifically through the use of naval power in the Caribbean Basin. This normative twentieth-century US international policy constituted a direct threat of violence and warfare toward any nation who would choose to pursue its own sovereign destiny by refusing to agree to the terms imposed by the superior hegemonic imperial force.

29 For a complete detailed description of these transactions, see Miguel A. De La Torre, *Doing Christian Ethics from the Margins*, 2nd ed. (Maryknol: Orbis Books, 2014), 97–101.

30 Alexei Barrionuevo, "Mountains of Corn and a Sea of Farm Subsidies," *The New York Times*, November 9, 2005.

31 Ann Aurelia López, *The Farmworkers' Journal* (Berkeley: University of California Press, 2007), 7–9, 41.

32 Labor Council for Latin American Advancement (LCLAA), *Another America Is Possible: The Impact of NAFTA on the United State Latino Community and Lessons for Future Trade Agreements*, Product ID 9013 (Washington, DC: Public Citizen's Global Trade Watch, 2004), 4–8.

33 Walden Bello, "The World Bank, the IMF, and the Multinationals: Manufacturing the World Food Crises," *The Nation*, June 8, 2008.

34 Miguel A. De La Torre, *Trails of Hope and Terror: Testimonies on Immigration* (Maryknoll, NY: Orbis Books, 2009), 39.

35 President Barack Obama, "Transcript: Obama's Immigration Speech," *The Washington Post*, November 20, 2014.

36 Miguel A. De La Torre, *Trails of Hope and Terror: Testimonies on Immigration* (Maryknoll, NY: Orbis Books, 2009), 9–14.

37 Caitlin Dickerson, "A Creative Plea from Immigrants, and a Ticking Clock for Obama," *The New York Times*, December 21, 2016.

Chapter 12

1 Carl Reiner, "If You're Not in the Obit, Eat Breakfast," June 5, 2017, documentary on HBO. Directed by Danny Gold.

2 Michael Eric Dyson, *Tears We Cannot Stop: A Sermon to White America* (New York: St. Martin's Press, 2017), 3.

3 Coates, "My President Was Black," 20–313.

4 Ibid., 21.

5 Ibid., 28.

6 Ibid., 30.

7 Ibid., 33–34.

8 Ibid., 34.

  9 Dyson, *Tears We Cannot Stop*, 4–5.

10 Ibid., 5.

11 Dyson, *The Black Presidency*, 209.

12 Pinn, "On Struggle in Our Historical Moment."

13 Ibid., 2.

14 Dyson, *Tears We Cannot Stop*, 220.

15 Nicholas Carnes and Noam Lupu, "It's Time to Bust the Myth: Most Trump Voters were not Working Class," *The Washington Post* (June 5, 2017): 1.

16 Nate Silver, "The Mythology of Trump's 'Working Class' Support: His voters are better off economically compared with most Americans." http//fivethirtyeight.com/features/the-mythology-of-trumps-working-class-support/, 2. Filed May 3, 2016.

17 Silver "The Mythology of Trump's 'Working Class' Support," 5.

18 Ibid.

19 Ibid.

20 Jason McDaniel and Sean McElwe, *The New West: Official Blog of the Western Political Association*. March 27, 2016; August 24, 2016, 1.

21 Thomas Wood, "Racism Motivated Trump Voters More than Authoritarianism," *The Washington Post*, April 17, 2017.

22 McDaniel and McElwe, *The New West*, 1.

23 Ibid.

24 Ibid., 2.

25 Jon Henley, "White and Wealthy Voters Gave Victory to Donald Trump, Exit Polls Show," *The Guardian* November 9, 2016 https://www.theguardian.com/us-news/2016/nov/09/white-voters-victory-donald-trump-exit-polls.

26 Henley, "White and Wealthy Voters Gave," 2.

27 Wood, "Racism Motivated Trump Voters More than Authoritarianism," 2.

28 Carnes and Lupu, "It's Time to Bust the Myth," 2.

29 Ibid., 2–3.

30 Henley, *The Guardian*, 1–2.

31 Ibid., 2.

32 Wood, "Racism Motivated Trump Voters More than Authoritarianism," 2.

33 Ibid., 3.

34 Alan Feuer and Jeremy W. Peters, *The New York Times*, (June 3, 2017), A1, A13.

35 Ibid., A13.

36 Ibram X. Kendi, *Stamped From the Beginning: The Definitive History of Racist Ideas in America* (New York: Nation Books, 2016), 9.

37 Kendi, *Stamped From the Beginning*, 9, 10.

38 Ibid., 10.

39 Ibid., 331.

40 Carol Anderson, *White Rage: The Unspoken Truth of Our Racial Divide* (New York: Bloomsbury, 2016), 4.

41 Anderson, *White Rage*, 5.

42 Ibid., 6.

43 David F. Krugler, *1919, The Year of Racial Violence: How African Americans Fought Back* (New York: Cambridge University Press, 2015), 9.

44 Krugler, *1919, The Year of Racial Violence*, 11.

45 Dyson, *Tears We Cannot Stop*, 104.

46 Ibid.

47 Ibid., 134, 142.

48 Anderson, *White Rage*, 161–62.

49 Kendi, *Stamped From the Beginning*, 510.

50 Ibid., 504

51 Ibid., 52.

52 Dyson, *Tears We Cannot Stop*, 197–212.

53 Anthony B. Pinn, *When Colorblindness Isn't the Answer: Humanism and the Challenge of Race* (Durham, North Carolina: Pitchstone Publishing and Washington, DC: Institute for Humanist Studies, Forthcoming), 75–78.

54 Kendi, *Stamped From the Beginning*, 507.

55 Anne Field, https://www.forbes.com/sites/annefield/2016/06/20/chicagos-commission-on-social-innovation-enlisting-impact-entrepreneurs-to-boost-the-economy/#2a86832a69a8, 1.

56 Alexander, *The New Jim Crow*, 56–57.

57 President's Task Force on Twenty-First Century Policing. Final Report of the President's Task Force on Twenty-First Century Policing. (Washington, DC: Office of Community Oriented Policing Services, 2015). While the Trump administration is not implementing these policies, they are being implemented at the city level by many jurisdictions. I am fortunate to work with one such educational effort that is being led by the attorneys Al and Adam Gerhardstein on providing tools for communities that are committed to containing police violence and enhancing community safety. The training is called "Achieving Safe Communities Through Strategies that Eliminate Racial Bias and Reduce Arrests." Al and Adam Gerhardstein describe the work of the training as follows:

> Hands-on, practical training on how to keep your community safe while also reducing the arrests of people of color. Learn how to study and address racially biased policing in your community. Hear from leading civil rights attorneys, police officers, community advocates, criminal justice academics, and politicians. Instructors are mostly from Cincinnati, Ohio, which has been implementing a collaborative agreement between the DOJ, City, FOP, and the black community to stop racially biased policing since 2002. You will be given concrete assignments to help you identify bias in your community's policing strategy, address that bias, and build stronger police-community relations.

58 For in-depth studies of how to identify and contain implicit bias, see the following work: Daniel Kahneman, *Thinking, Fast and Slow* (New York: Farrar, Straus and Giroux, 2011); Elda Shafir, ed., *The Behavioral Foundations of Public Policy* (Princeton: Princeton University Press, 2013); and the work of the Engagement Scholarship Consortium, *Journal of Community Engagement and Scholarship*. For in-depth studies of how to identify and challenge structural forms of injustice, see Iris Marion Young, *Justice and the Politics of Difference*, Second edition (Princeton: Princeton University Press, 2011); Kwame Anthony Appiah, *The Honor Code: How Moral Revolutions Happen* (New York: W. W. Norton & Company, 2010); Steven Pinker, *The Better Angels of Our Nature: Why Violence Has Declined* (New York: Viking Penguin, 2011); Van Jones with Ariane Conrad, *The Green Collar Economy: How One Solution Can Fix Our Two Biggest Problems* (New York: HarperOne, 2008); Abhijit V. Banerjee and Esther Duflo, *Poor Economics: A Radical Rethinking of the Way to Fight Global Poverty* (Philadelphia: Public Affairs, 2011): Marc J. Lane, *Social Enterprise: Empowering Mission-Driven Entrepreneurs* (Chicago: ABA Publishing, American Bar Association, 2011); Marc Lane, *The Mission-Driven Venture: Business Solutions to the World's Most Vexing Social Problems* (Hoboken, NJ: Jossey-Bass, 2015).

59 Dorrien, *The Obama Question*, 119.
60 Dyson, *The Black Presidency*, 161, 162.
61 Nelson Mandela, *Long Walk to Freedom: The Autobiography of Nelson Mandela* (Boston: Little, Brown and Company, 1994, 1995), 593.
62 Ronald V. Dellums and H. Lee Alterman, *Lying Down with the Lions* (Boston: Beacon Press, 2000).
63 Dellums and Alterman, *Lying Down with the* Lions.
64 Dorrien, *The Obama Question*, 121.
65 Dyson, *Tears We Cannot Stop*, 227.
66 Sharon D. Welch, "The Machiavellian Dilemma: Paradoxes and Perils of Democratic Governance," *Tikkun* (May/June 2010) and Sharon D. Welch, "In Praise of Imperfect Commitment: An Ethic of Power, Professionalism and Risk," in George E. DeMartino and Deirdre N. McCloskey, eds., *The Oxford Handbook of Professional Economic Ethics* (Oxford: Oxford University Press, 2016), 55–70.
67 Carl Reiner, "If You're Not in the Obit, Eat Breakfast," June 5, 2017, documentary on HBO. Directed by Danny Gold.
68 Patricia J. Williams, *The Alchemy of Race and Rights: Diary of a Law Professor* (Cambridge: Harvard University Press, 1991), 163, 165.

Bibliography

"Bill Cosby Mulls His Show's Possible Impact on Obama's Election," *Associated Press*, November 12, 2008.

"Bowing Out 1931." *New Orleans Christian Advocate*, January 7, 1932.

"Fund Shakeup Nears; R.F.C. Drops Support." *Memphis Commercial Appeal*, June 26, 1933.

"How many lives?" *Off OurBacks: A Women's News Journal* 2, no. 1. (September 1971), www.jstor.org/stable/25771344.

"How they see us: An African president for America." *The Week*, February 6, 2009.

"Nobel Secretary Regrets Obama Peace Prize." *BBC*, September 17, 2015. http://www.bbc.com/news/world-europe-34277960

"Our Present Denominational Situation." *(Arkansas) Baptist Advance*, August 7, 1930.

"Race: Has America entered a New Era?" *The Week*, November 21, 2008.

"Selling the president: Get your Obama Hot Sauce." *The Week*, January 30, 2009.

"Text of New President's Address at Inauguration." *Washington Post*, March 5, 1933.

Abernethy, Graeme. *The Iconography of Malcolm X*. Lawrence, KS: University Press of Kansas, 2013.

Adams, Richard. "Joe Biden: This Is a Big Fucking Deal." *The Guardian*, March 23, 2010. https://www.theguardian.com/world/richard-adams-blog/2010/mar/23/joe-biden-obama-big-fucking-deal-overheard.

Agrawal, Nina. "Abortion Rate Declines to Historic Low, with Obamacare a Likely Contributor." *Los Angeles Times*, January 18, 2017. http://www.latimes.com/nation/la-na-us-abortion-rates-20170117-story.html.

Aidi, Hishaam D. "Jihadi's in the Hood: Race, Urban Islam, and the War on Terror." *Middle East Report* 224 (Autumn 2002): 36–43. http://www.jstor.org/stable/1559422.

Aidi, Hishaam D. "Let Us Be Moors: Race, Islam, and 'Connected Histories.'" In *Black Routes to Islam*, edited by Manning Marable and Hishaam D. Aidi. New York: Palgrave Macmillan, 2009.

Alexander, Jeffrey, and Philip Smith. "The Discourse of American Civil Society: A New Proposal for Cultural Studies." *Theory and Society* 22 (1993): 151–207.

Alexander, Michelle, and Cornel West. *The New Jim Crow: Mass Incarceration in the Age of Colorblindness*. New York: The New Press, 2012.

Alim, H. Samy. "Re-inventing Islam with Unique Modern Tones: Muslim Hip Hop Artists as Verbal Mujahidin." *Souls: A Critical Journal of Black Politics, Culture, and Society* 8, no. 4 (2006): 45–58.

Alim, H. Samy. "A New Research Agenda: Exploring the Transglobal Hip Hop *Umma*." In *The Hip Hop and Religion Reader*, edited by Monica R. Miller and Anthony B. Pinn. London: Routledge, 2015.

Alman, Ashley. "Larry Klayman Tells Obama 'To Put The Quran Down' At Veterans Rally." *Huffington Post*, October 14, 2013. http://www.huffingtonpost.com/2013/10/13/larry-klayman-obama-quran_n_4094589.html.

Alter, Jonathan. *The Promise: President Obama, Year One*. New York: Simon & Schuster, 2010.

Alter, Jonathan. *The Center Holds: Obama and His Enemies.* New York: Simon & Schuster, 2013.

Alterman, Eric. *Kabuki Democracy: The System vs. Barack Obama.* New York: Nation Books, 2011.

Ambar, Saladin. *Malcolm X at Oxford Union: Racial Politics in a Global Era.* Oxford and New York, NY: Oxford University Press, 2014.

American Civil Liberties Union. "Combatting Mass Incarceration – The Facts." https://www.aclu.org/infographic-combating-mass-incarceration-facts?redirect=combating-mass-incarceration-facts-0.

American Civil Liberties Union. "Washington State Supreme Court Rules Florist Discriminated Against Same-Sex Couple by Refusing Wedding-Related Service." February 16, 2017. https://www.aclu.org/news/washington-state-supreme-court-rules-florist-discriminated-against-same-sex-couple-refusing.

Anderson, Carol. *White Rage: The Unspoken Truth of Our Racial Divide.* Reprint ed. New York: Bloomsbury USA, 2017.

Andrews, Marcellus W. *The Political Economy of Hope and Fear.* New York: New York University Press, 2001.

Anzaldua, Gloria. *Borderlands/La Frontera: The New Mestiza.* 4th ed. San Francisco: Aunt Lute Books, 2012.

Appiah, Kwame Anthony. *The Honor Code: How Moral Revolutions Happen.* Reprint ed. New York: W. W. Norton & Company, 2011.

Arkin, William M. *Unmanned: Drones, Data, and the Illusion of Perfect Warfare.* New York: Little, Brown and Company, 2015.

Asad, Talal. *Formations of the Secular: Christianity, Islam, Modernity.* Stanford, California: Stanford University Press, 2003.

Attanasio, Cedar. "Deporter in Chief: Obama Ordered 7,000 Immigrant Children to be Deported Without a Court Hearing." *Latin Times*, March 16, 2016.

Augustine. *Sermons 1-19*, translated by O. P. Edmund Hill. Brooklyn, NY: New City Press, 1990.

Augustine. *Augustine: The City of God against the Pagans*, edited by R. W. Dyson. Cambridge and New York: Cambridge University Press, 1998.

Augustine. *Augustine: Political Writings*, edited by E. M. Atkins, and R. J. Dodaro. Cambridge, UK and New York: Cambridge University Press, 2001.

Augustine. "Commentary on the Gospel of John, 33." In *Political Writings*, edited by E. M. Atkins and R. J. Dodaro. New York: Cambridge University Press, 2007.

Augustine. *Homilies on the Gospel of John 1-40*, translated by O. P. Edmund Hill. Hyde Park, NY: New City Press, 2009.

Bailey, Martha J., Brad Hershbein, and Amalia R. Miller. "The Opt-In Revolution? Contraception and the Gender Gap in Wages." *American Economic Journal of Applied Economics* 4, no. 3 (2012): 225–54.

Bailey, Martha J., Brad Hershbein, Amalia R. Miller, Olga Malkova, and Johannes Norling. "Do Family Planning Programs Decrease Poverty? Evidence from Public Census Data." *CESifo Economic Studies* 60, no. 2 (June 2014): 31237.

Baird, Enid. *Public and Private Aid in 116 Urban Areas, 1929-38: With Supplement for 1939 and 1940.* Washington DC: Federal security agency, Social Security Board, 1942.

Baker, Thomas H. *Memphis Commercial Appeal: The History of a Southern Newspaper.* Baton Rouge: Louisiana State University Press, 1971.

Balmer, Randall, and Jana Riess, eds. *Mormonism and American Politics.* New York: Columbia University Press, 2015.

Banerjee, Abhijit, and Esther Duflo. *Poor Economics: A Radical Rethinking of the Way to Fight Global Poverty.* Reprint ed. New York: Public Affairs, 2012.

Barrionuevo, Alexei. "Mountains of Corn and a Sea of Farm Subsidies." *The New York Times,* November 9, 2005.

Bartkowski, John P., and Helen A. Regis. *Charitable Choices: Religion, Race, and Poverty in the Post-Welfare Era.* New York: New York University Press, 2003.

Battani, Marshall, David R. Hall, and Rosemary Powers "Cultures' Structures: Making Meaning in the Public Sphere." *Theory and Society* 26 (December 1997): 781–812.

Becker, Nora V., and Daniel Polsky. "Women Saw Large Decrease In Out-Of-Pocket Spending For Contraceptives After ACA Mandate Removed Cost Sharing." *Health Affairs* 34, no.7 (July 2015):1204–11.

Beito, David T. *From Mutual Aid to the Welfare State: Fraternal Societies and Social Services, 1890-1967.* Chapel Hill: The University of North Carolina Press, 2000.

Bell, Bernard W. "President Obama, the Rev. Dr. Jeremiah Wright, and the African American Jeremiadic Tradition." *The Massachusetts Review* 50, no. 3 (Autumn 2009): 332–43.

Bellah, Robert N. "Civil Religion in America." *Daedalus* 96, no. 1 (Winter 1967): 1–21.

Bello, Walden. "The World Bank, the IMF, and the Multinationals: Manufacturing the World Food Crises." *The Nation,* June 8, 2008.

Biles, Roger. *The South and the New Deal.* Lexington: University Press of Kentucky, 2006.

Billingsley, Andrew. *Mighty Like a River: The Black Church and Social Reform.* New York and Oxford: Oxford University Press, 2003.

Bivins, Jason. "Embattled Majority: Religion and Its Despisers in America or The Long-Lurching Wreck of American Public Life." *Religion in American History,* November 2012. http://usreligion.blogspot.com/2012/11/embattled-majority-religion-and-its.html.

Bixby Center for Global Reproductive Health. "Women of Color Need Improved Information and Access to Effective Contraception." *University of California, San Francisco.* https://bixbycenter.ucsf.edu/news/women-color-need-improved-information-and-access-effective-contraception.

Blake, John. "Black first family 'changes everything.'" *CNN.com,* January 15, 2009.

Blake, John. "This Is What 'Whitelash' Looks Like." *CNN,* November 19, 2016. http://www.cnn.com/2016/11/11/us/obama-trump-white-backlash/index.html.

Blum, Edward J., and John Stauffer. *Reforging the White Republic: Race, Religion, and American Nationalism, 1865-1898.* Baton Rouge: LSU Press, 2015.

Blumberg, Antonia. "These Congressmen Are Trying to Curb Religious Freedom Abuses." *Huffington Post,* July 13, 2017. http://www.huffingtonpost.com/entry/do-no-harm-act_us_5967c542e4b03389bb160cb5?section=us_religion.

Boggs, Carl. "The Great Retreat: Decline of the Public Sphere in Late Twentieth-Century America." *Theory and Society* 26 (December 1997): 741–80.

Boorstein, Michelle. "White House Picks Church-State Lawyer Melissa Rogers to Head Faith Office." *Washington Post,* March 13, 2013.

Boyd, Hal. "Friends Say Mitt Romney Not as Stiff or Robotic as Media Portrays." *Deseret News,* August 19, 2011. http://www.deseretnews.com/article/700172041/Friends-say-Mitt-Romney-not-as-stiff-or-robotic-as-media-portrays.html.

Bressey, Caroline. *New Geographies of Race and Racism,* edited by Claire Dwyer. New York: Routledge, 2016.

Brettschneider, Corey. "Gorsuch, Abortion, and the Concept of Personhood." *New York Times*, March 21, 2017. https://www.nytimes.com/2017/03/21/opinion/gorsuch-abortion-and-the-concept-of-personhood.html.

Brown, Dennis. "Jerome and the Vulgate." In *A History of Biblical Interpretation, Volume 1: The Ancient Period*, edited by Alan J. Hauser and Duane F. Watson, 355–79. Grand Rapids, MI: Eerdmans, 2003.

Brown, Dorothy M., and Elizabeth McKeown. *The Poor Belong to Us: Catholic Charities and American Welfare*. Cambridge, MA: Harvard University Press, 2000.

Brown, Josephine Chapin. *Public Relief, 1929-1939*. New York: Octagon Books, 1971.

Brzezinski, Zbigniew. *Strategic Vision: America and the Crisis of Global Power*. Reprint ed. New York: Basic Books, 2013.

Buckendorff, Jennifer. "The Oprah Way." *Salon.com*, January 24, 2005.

Bunch, Will. *Tear Down This Myth: The Right-Wing Distortion of the Reagan Legacy*. Reprint ed. New York: Free Press, 2009.

Bureau of the Census. *Census of Religious Bodies: 1926, Part I*. Washington DC: Government Printing Office, 1930.

Bureau of the Census. *Census of the United States, 1930*. Washington DC: Government Printing Office, 1930.

Bureau of the Census. *Statistical Abstract of the United States, 1941*. Washington DC: Government Printing Office, 1942.

Burr, Thomas. "Hang-ups over Mormonism Proved Romney's Undoing." *Salt Lake Tribune*, February 10, 2008. http://archive.sltrib.com/story.php?ref=/ci_8221611

Burton, Philip. *The Old Latin Gospels: A Study of Their Texts and Language*. New York: Clarendon Press, 2001.

Bybee, Roger. "Auto Task Force Outsources Jobs." *In These Times*, June 12, 2009.

Calhoun, Craig. "Civil Society and the Public Sphere." *Public Culture* 5 (1993): 267–80.

Calhoun, Craig, ed. *Habermas and the Public Sphere*. Reprint ed. Cambridge, MA: The MIT Press, 1993.

Campbell, David E., John C. Green, and J. Quinn Monson. "The Stained Glass Ceiling: Social Contact and Mitt Romney's 'Religion Problem.'" *Political Behavior* 34, no. 2 (June 2012): 277–99.

Camus, Albert. *The Myth of Sisyphus and Other Essays*, translated by Justin O'Brien. New York: Vintage, 1991.

Carby, Hazel V. *Race Men*. Cambridge, MA and London: Harvard University Press, 2000.

Carnes, Nicholas, and Noam Lupu. "It's Time to bust the Myth: Most Trump Voters Were Not Working Class." *The Washington Post*, June 5, 2017.

Carroll, Al. "Franklin Roosevelt and the New Deal Compared to Obamacare." *Daily Kos*, May 27, 2014. http://www.dailykos.com/story/2014/05/27/1298267/-Franklin-Roosevelt-and-the-New-Deal-Compared-to-Obamacare.

Carty, T. *A Catholic in the White House?: Religion, Politics, and John F. Kennedy's Presidential Campaign*. New York; Basingstoke: Palgrave Macmillan, 2004.

Cassidy, John. "Reagan, Bush, and Obama: We Are All Still Keynesians." *The New Yorker*, June 4, 2012. http://www.newyorker.com/news/john-cassidy/reagan-bush-and-obama-we-are-all-still-keynesians.

Causey, Adam Kealoha. "To Some, Trump's 'Bad Hombres' is Much More than a Botched Spanish Word." *PBS News Hour*, October 20, 2016.

Celso, Anthony N. "Obama and the Arab Spring: The Strategic Confusion of a Realist-Idealist." *Journal of Political Sciences & Public Affairs* 2, no. 2 (2014). doi:10.4172/2332-0761.1000115.

The Center for Latin American Studies. *In the Shadow of the Wall: Family Separation, Immigration Enforcement and Security.* Tucson: Arizona University, 2013.

Chang, Ha-Joon. *23 Things They Don't Tell You About Capitalism.* Reprint ed. New York: Bloomsbury Press, 2012.

Chivvis, Christopher S. *Toppling Qaddafi: Libya and the Limits of Liberal Intervention.* New York, NY, USA: Cambridge University Press, 2013.

Chu, Henry. "From the archives: World reaction to Obama victory: Elation." *LA Times,* November 8, 2008. http://www.latimes.com/world/la-fg-worldreax6-2008nov06-story.html.

Clines, Francis X. "Pope Ends U.S. Visit with Capital Mass Affirming Doctrine." *New York Times,* Oct 8 1979.

Coates, Ta-Nehisi. "My President Was Black: A History of the First African American White House – and What Came Next." *The Atlantic,* January/February 2017. https://www.theatlantic.com/magazine/archive/2017/01/my-president-was-black/508793/.

Cobb, William Jelani. *The Substance of Hope: Barack Obama and the Paradox of Progress.* Walker Books, 2010.

Cobb, William Jelani. "The Matter of Black Lives." *The New Yorker,* March 14, 2016. http://www.newyorker.com/magazine/2016/03/14/where-is-black-lives-matter-headed.

Cohen, Cathy J., and Sarah J. Jackson. "As a Feminist: A Conversation with Cathy J. Cohen on Black Lives Matter, Feminism and Contemporary Activism." *Signs* 41, no. 4 (2016): 775–92. https://doi.org/10.1086/685115.

Cohen, Lizabeth. *Making a New Deal: Industrial Workers in Chicago, 1919-1939.* 2nd ed. Cambridge: Cambridge University Press, 2008.

Cohen, Susan A. "Abortion and Women of Color: The Bigger Picture." *Guttmacher Policy Review,* August 6, 2008. https://www.guttmacher.org/gpr/2008/08/abortion-and-women-color-bigger-picture.

Collins, Patricia Hill. *Black Feminist Thought: Knowledge, Consciousness, and the Politics of Empowerment.* New York: Routledge, 2008.

Cone, James H. "Toward a Black Theology." *Ebony,* August 1970.

Cone, James H. *Martin & Malcolm & America: A Dream or a Nightmare.* 20th Anniversary ed. Orbis Books, 2012.

Cook, Tony, and Brian Eason. "Gov. Mike Pence Signs RFRA Fix." *The Indianapolis Star,* April 1, 2015. http://www.indystar.com/story/news/politics/2015/04/01/indiana-rfra-deal-sets-limited-protections-for-lgbt/70766920/.

Copeland, M. Shawn. "Memory, #BlackLivesMatter, and Theologians." *Political Theology* 17, no. 1 (January 2016): 1–3. https://doi.org/10.1080/1462317X.2016.1134137.

The Corporation. Directed by Mark Achbar and Jennifer Abbot. 2004. http://thecorporation.com

Cortright, David, Rachel Fairhurst, and Kristen Wall, eds. *Drones and the Future of Armed Conflict: Ethical, Legal, and Strategic Implications.* Chicago: University of Chicago Press, 2015.

Cullen, Jim. *The American Dream: A Short History of an Idea That Shaped a Nation.* 9th ed. Oxford: Oxford University Press, 2004.

Curtis IV, Edward E. *The Call of Bilal: Islam in the African Diaspora.* Chapel Hill: The University of North Carolina Press, 2014.

Dauber, Michele Landis. *The Sympathetic State: Disaster Relief and the Origins of the American Welfare State.* Chicago: University of Chicago Press, 2012.

DeGhett, Torie Rose. "'Record! I Am Arab:' Paranoid Arab Boys, Global Ciphers, and Hip Hop Nationalism." In *The Hip Hop & Obama Reader*, edited by Travis L. Gosa and Erik Nielson, 94–106. New York: Oxford University Press, 2015.

Dehlendorf, Christine, Maria Isabel Rodriguez, Kira Levy, Sonya Borrero, and Jody Steinauer. "Disparities in Family Planning." *American Journal of Obstetrics and Gynecology* 202, no. 3 (2010): 214–20.

Delgado, Richard, and Jean Stefancic, eds. *Critical White Studies: Looking Behind the Mirror*. Philadelphia: Temple University Press, 1997.

Dellums, Ronald V., and H. Lee Halterman. *Lying Down with the Lions*. Boston: Beacon Press, 2000.

DeMartino, George F., and Deirdre N. McCloskey, eds. *The Oxford Handbook of Professional Economic Ethics*. New York, NY: Oxford University Press, 2016.

Dickens, Dorothy. "A Nutrition Investigation of Negro Tenants in the Yazoo Mississippi Delta." *Bulletin*, Mississippi Agricultural Experiment Station, A & M College, no. 254, Starkville, Mississippi: Mississippi State University, 1928.

Derickson, Kate Driscoll. "The Racial State and Resistance in Ferguson and Beyond." *Urban Studies* 53, no. 11 (August 2016): 2223–37. https://doi.org/10.1177/0042098016647296.

Dickerson, Caitlin. "A Creative Plea from Immigrants, and a Ticking Clock for Obama." *The New York Times*, December 21, 2016.

Dickerson, John. "Professor Obama's First Seminar." *Slate.com*, February 10, 2009.

Dionne Jr., E. J. and Joy-Ann Reid. Introduction to *We Are the Change We Seek: The Speeches of Barack Obama*, edited by E. J. Dionne, Jr. and Joy-Ann Reid. London: Bloomsbury Press, 2017.

Dorrien, Gary. *The Obama Question: A Progressive Perspective*. Lanham: Rowman & Littlefield Publishers, 2012.

Douglass, Frederick. *Narrative of the Life of Frederick Douglass*. New York: Dover Publications, 1995.

Dowd, Maureen. "Mitt's No J.F.K." *The New York Times*, December 9, 2007. http://www.nytimes.com/2007/12/09/opinion/09dowd.html?n=Top/Opinion/Editorials%20and%20Op-Ed/Op-Ed/Columnists/Maureen%20Dowd.

Dowd, Maureen. "The First Shrink." *New York Times*, April 5, 2009.

Downie Jr., Leonard and Sara Rafsky. "The Obama Administration and the Press." *Committee to Protect Journalists*, October 10, 2013.

Du Bois, W. E. B. "The Talented Tenth." In *The Negro Problem*, edited by Booker T. Washington, 31–76. New York: James Pott & Company, 1903.

Du Bois, W. E. B. "The Negro Problem (From The Negro, 1915)." In *W. E. B. Du Bois: A Reader*, edited by David Levering Lewis,48–54. New York: Henry Holt and Company, 1995.

Du Bois, W. E. B. *Darkwater: Voices from Within the Veil*. New York: Dover Publications, 1999.

Du Bois, W. E. B. *The Souls of Black Folk, A Norton Critical Edition*, edited by Henry Louis Gates. Jr., and Terri Hume Oliver. New York: W. W. Norton & Company, 1999.

Dyson, Michael Eric. *The Black Presidency: Barack Obama and the Politics of Race in America*. Boston: Houghton Mifflin Harcourt, 2016.

Dyson, Michael Eric. *Tears We Cannot Stop: A Sermon to White America*. New York: St. Martin's Press, 2017.

Early, Gerald, ed. *Lure and Loathing: Essays on Race, Identity, and the Ambivalence of Assimilation*. New York, NY: Penguin Books, 1994.

Eck, Diana L. "Prospects for Pluralism: Voice and Vision in the Study of Religion." *Journal of the American Academy of Religion* 75, no. 4 (2007): 743–76.

Elizabeth, Nan. "$962,000 Is Obtained for Drought Relief." *New York Times*, January 22, 1931.

Emmons, Alex. "After 8 Years of Expanding Presidential War Powers, Obama Insists They Are Limited." *The Intercept*, December 6, 2016. https://theintercept.com/2016/12/06/after-8-years-of-expanding-them-obama-insists-that-presidential-war-powers-are-limited/.

Evans, Curtis J. *The Burden of Black Religion.* Oxford and New York: Oxford University Press, 2008.

Fessenden, Tracy. "Sex and the Subject of Religion." *The Immanent Frame*, January 10, 2008. http://blogs.ssrc.org/tif/2008/01/10/sex-and-the-subject-of-religion/.

Field, Anne. "Chicago's Commission On Social Innovation: Enlisting Impact Entrepreneurs To Boost The Economy." *Forbes*, June 20, 2016. https://www.forbes.com/sites/annefield/2016/06/20/chicagos-commission-on-social-innovation-enlisting-impact-entrepreneurs-to-boost-the-economy/#2a86832a69a8.

Field, David, Jenny Hockey, and Neil Small, eds. *Death, Gender and Ethnicity.* New York: Routledge, 1997.

Finer, Lawrence B. and Stanley K. Henshaw. "Disparities in Rates of Unintended Pregnancy in the United States, 1994 and 2001." *Perspectives in Sex and Reproductive Health* 38, no. 2 (2006): 90–96.

Flake, Jeff. *Conscience of a Conservative: A Rejection of Destructive Politics and a Return to Principle.* New York: Random House, 2017.

Flanagan, Caitlin, and Benjamin Schwarz. "Showdown in the Big Tent." *New York Times*, December 6, 2008.

Floyd-Thomas, Juan M. "A Jihad of Words: The Evolution of African American Islam and Contemporary Hip Hop." In *Noise and Spirit: The Religious and Spiritual Sensibilities of Rap Music*, edited by Anthony B. Pinn, 75–109. New York: University Press, 2003.

Floyd-Thomas, Juan M. "More Than Conquerors: Just War Theory and the Need for a Black Christian Antiwar Movement." *Black Theology: An International Journal* 9, no. 2 (2011): 136–60. https://doi.org/10.1558/blth.v9i2.136

Foner, Eric. "Teaching the History of Radicalism in the Age of Obama." *The Nation*, January 2, 2017.

Foster, Craig L. *A Different God?: Mitt Romney, the Religious Right, and the Mormon Question.* Draper, UT: Greg Kofford Books Inc, 2008.

Fraser, Nancy. "Rethinking the Public Sphere: A Contribution to the Critique of Actually Existing Democracy." *Social Text*, no. 25/26 (1990): 56–80. http://www.jstor.org/stable/466240.

Fraser, Nancy. "Rethinking the Public Sphere: A Contribution to the Critique of Actually Existing Democracy." In *Habermas and the Public Sphere*, edited by Craig Calhoun, 109–42. Cambridge, MA: MIT Press, 1992.

Fraser, Nancy. *Justice Interruptus: Critical Reflections on the "Postsocialist" Condition.* New York: Routledge, 1996.

Friedman, Uri. "Targeted Killings: A Short History." *Foreign Policy*, August 13, 2012. http://foreignpolicy.com/2012/08/13/targeted-killigs-a-short-history/.

Frum, David. "Republicans Must Change to Win." *Financial Times*, July 5, 2008.

Fukuyama, Francis. "The End of History?" *The National Interest*, Summer 1989.

Fung, Brian. "The Uncanny Valley: What Robot Theory Tells Us about Mitt Romney." *The Atlantic*, January 31, 2012. http://www.theatlantic.com/politics/archive/2012/01/the-uncanny-valley-what-robot-theory-tells-us-about-mitt-romney/252235/.

Gamboa, Suzanne. "Deporter-in-Chief Label Ups the Pressure for Action from Obama." *NBC News*, March 6, 2014.

Garrow, David. *Rising Star: The Making of Barack Obama*. William Morrow, 2017.

Garza, Alicia. "A Herstory of the #BlackLivesMatter Movement." *The Feminist Wire*, October 7, 2014. http://thefeministwire.com/2014/10/blacklivesmatter-2/.

Gehring, John. *The Francis Effect: A Radical Pope's Challenge to the American Catholic Church*. Lanham: Rowman & Littlefield Publishers, 2015.

Gerson, Michael. "Obama's Risky Embrace of Occupy Wall Street." *The Washington Post*, October 20, 2011. https://www.washingtonpost.com/opinions/obamas-risky-embrace-of-occupy-wall-street/2011/10/19/gIQA2pQf1L_story.html?utm_term=.a53d3b0a8bc6

Gibson, Dawn-Marie. *A History of the Nation of Islam: Race, Islam, and the Quest for Freedom*. Santa Barbara, California: Praeger, 2012.

Gill, Corrington. "Unemployment Relief." *American Economic Review* 25, no. 1 (March 1935): 176–85.

Gilmore, Glenda Elizabeth. *Defying Dixie: The Radical Roots of Civil Rights, 1919-1950*. Reprint ed. New York: W. W. Norton & Company, 2009.

Gilmore, Ruth Wilson. *Golden Gulag: Prisons, Surplus, Crisis, and Opposition in Globalizing California*. Berkeley: University of California Press, 2007.

Glaude Jr., Eddie S. *Democracy in Black: How Race Still Enslaves the American Soul*. Reprint ed. New York: Broadway Books, 2017.

Goldberg, David Theo. *Racist Culture: Philosophy and the Politics of Meaning*. Oxford, England and Cambridge, MA: Blackwell, 1993.

Goldberg, Michelle. "Obama's Divisive Choice of Rick Warren." *ReligionDispatches.org*, December 18, 2008.

Goodwin, Megan. "Planned Parenthood? Forsaking American Women for the Mother of All Bombs." *Religion Bulletin*, May 16, 2017. http://bulletin.equinoxpub.com/2017/05/theorizing-religion-in-the-age-of-trump-megan-goodwin/.

Gordon, Linda. *Pitied but Not Entitled: Single Mothers and the History of Welfare*. New York: Free Press, 1994.

Gosa, Travis L., and Erik Nielson, eds. *The Hip Hop & Obama Reader*. New York: Oxford University Press, 2015.

Gottschalk, Marie. *Caught: The Prison State and the Lockdown of American Politics*. Revised ed. Princeton, NJ: Princeton University Press, 2016.

Graff, Garrett M. "The Green Monster: How the Border Patrol became America's Most Out-of-Control Law Enforcement Agency." *Politico Magazine*, November/December 2014. https://www.politico.com/magazine/story/2014/10/border-patrol-the-green-monster-112220.

Graham, Franklin. "'This Week' Transcript: God and Government." *ABC News*. http://abcnews.go.com/ThisWeek/week-transcript-god-government/story?id=13446238#.TySHQ-NSSs0.

Green, Elna, ed. *Before the New Deal: Social Welfare in the South, 1830-1930*. Athens, GA: University of Georgia Press, 1999.

Green, Elna, ed. *This Business of Relief: Confronting Poverty in a Southern City, 1740–1940*. Athens: University of Georgia Press, 2003.

Greene, Alison Collis. "The End of 'The Protestant Era'?" *Church History* 80, no. 3 (September 2011): 600–10.

Greene, Alison Collis. "Let's Remember History, When Religious Institutions Welcomed Government Support." *Religion and Politics*, June 4, 2012. http://religionandpolitics. org/2012/06/04/lets-remember-history-when-religious-institutions-welcomed-government-support/.

Greene, Alison Collis. "'A Divine Revelation?': Southern Churches Respond to the New Deal." In *Faithful Republic: Religion and Politics in the 20th Century United States*, edited by Andrew Preston, Bruce J. Schulman, and Julian E. Zelzer University of Pennsylvania Press, forthcoming 2015.

Guttmacher Institute. "Unintended Pregnancy in the United States." September 2016. https://www.guttmacher.org/fact-sheet/unintended-pregnancy-united-states.

Haas, Jeffrey. *The Assassination of Fred Hampton: How the FBI and the Chicago Police Murdered a Black Panther*. Chicago, IL: Chicago Review Press, 2011.

Habermas, Jürgen. *The Structural Transformation of the Public Sphere: An Inquiry into a Category of Bourgeois Society*. 6th ed. Cambridge, MA: The MIT Press, 1991.

Hall, Peter Dobkin. "Historical Perspectives on Religion, Government, and Social Welfare in America." In *Can Charitable Choice Work? Covering Religion's Impact on Urban Affairs and Social Services*, edited by Andrew Walsh. Hartford, CT: Pew Program on Religion and the News Media and the Leonard E. Greenberg Center for the Study of Religion in Public Life, 2001.

Hall, Stuart. *Stuart Hall: Race, the Floating Signifier*. Northampton, MA: Media Education Foundation, 1998.

Hancock, Ange-Marie. *The Politics of Disgust: The Public Identity of the Welfare Queen*. New York: New York University Press, 2004.

Hannaham, James. "Obama: Don't Pander to Homophobes." *Salon.com*, October 26, 2007.

Harlan, Chico. "Inside the Administration's $1 Billion Deal to Detain Central American Asylum Seekers." *The Washington Post*, August 14, 2016.

Harris, Fredrick C. *The Price of the Ticket: Barack Obama and the Rise and Decline of Black Politics*. Reprint ed. New York: Oxford University Press, 2014.

Harris, Frederick C. "The Next Civil Rights Movement?" *Dissent* 62, no. 3 (Summer 2015): 34–40. doi:10.1353/dss.2015.0051.

Harris, Jerry, and Carl Davidson. "Obama: The New Contours of Power." *Race & Class* 50, no. 4 (2009): 1–19. https://doi.org/10.1177/0306396809102993.

Harvey, J. *Whiteness and Morality: Pursuing Racial Justice Through Reparations and Sovereignty*. New York: Palgrave Macmillan, 2012.

Hasselhoff, Görge K. "Revising the Vulgate: Jerome and his Jewish Interlocutors." *Zeitschrift für Religions und Geistesgeschichte* 64, no. 3 (2012): 209–21.

Hasstedt, Kinsey. "Abortion Coverage Under the Affordable Care Act: Advancing Transparency, Ensuring Choice, and Facilitating Access." *Guttmacher Policy Review*, April 9, 2015. https://www.guttmacher.org/gpr/2015/04/abortion-coverage-under-affordable-care-act-advancing-transparency-ensuring-choice-and.

Hauser, Alan J., and Duane F. Watson, eds. *A History of Biblical Interpretation, Volume 1: The Ancient Period*. Grand Rapids, MI: Eerdmans, 2003.

Healey, Kevin. "The Pastor in the Basement: Discourses of Authenticity in the Networked Public Sphere." *Symbolic Interaction* 33, no. 4 (October 2010): 526–51.

Heiner, Brady. "The Procedural Entrapment of Mass Incarceration: Prosecution, Race, and the Unfinished Project of American Abolition." *Philosophy and Social Criticism* 42, no. 6 (2016): 594–631.

Held, Amy. "Kentucky Must Pay Attorney Fees For Couples Who Sued Kim Davis, Judge Says." *National Public Radio*, July 21, 2017. http://www.npr.org/sections/thetwo-way/2017/07/21/538592022/kentucky-must-pay-attorney-fees-for-couples-who-sued-kim-davis-says-judge.

Heller, Steven. "The 'O' in Obama." *New York Times*, November 20, 2008.

Henderson, Kay and Joni Ernst. "Ernst Carries Concealed Weapon '90 Percent of the Time.'" *Radio Iowa*, August 20, 2013. http://www.radioiowa.com/2013/08/20/ernst-carries-concealed-weapon-90-percent-of-the-time-audio/.

Henry, Patrick. "'And I Don't Care What It Is': The Tradition-History of a Civil Religion Proof-Text." *Journal of the American Academy of Religion* 49, no. 1 (1981): 35–47.

Herman Edward S., and David Peterson. "Jeremiah Wright in the Propaganda System." *Monthly Review* 60, no. 4 (September 2008), https://monthlyreview.org/2008/09/01/jeremiah-wright-in-the-propaganda-system/.

Hertzberg, Hendrik. "Obama Wins." *The New Yorker*, November 17, 2008.

Higginbotham, Evelyn Brooks. *Righteous Discontent: The Women's Movement in the Black Baptist Church, 1880–1920*. Cambridge, MA: Harvard University Press, 1994.

Hill, J. B. *The First Black President: Barack Obama, Race, Politics, and the American Dream*. New York: Palgrave Macmillan, 2009.

Hill, Rickey, and Tazinski P. Lee. "The Killing of Black People by the US State is as American as Apple Pie: Groundwork Toward a Critique." *Journal of Race & Policy* 2, no. 2 (2015): 5–22.

Hippo, Augustine. *City of God*, translated by Henry Bettenson. New York: Penguin Classics, 2004.

Hooks, bell. *Where We Stand: Class Matters*. New York: Routledge, 2000.

Hopkins, D. *Heart and Head: Black Theology Past, Present, and Future*. New York: Palgrave Macmillan, 2002.

House Resolution: HR1073."Congrats-Rev. Jeremiah Wright." March 11, 2008. http://www.ilga.gov/legislation/BillStatus.asp?DocNum=1073&GAID=9&DocTypeID=HR&LegID=38304&SessionID=51&SpecSess=&Session=&GA=95.

Howell, Marcela, and Ann M. Starrs. "For Women of Color, Access to Vital Health Services Is Threatened." *The Hill*, July 26, 2017. http://thehill.com/blogs/pundits-blog/healthcare/343996-for-women-of-color-access-to-vital-health-services-is.

Human Rights Watch. "Guantanamo by the Numbers." *Human Rights First*, December 12, 2017. http://www.humanrightsfirst.org/resource/guantanamo-numbers.

Imhoff, Sarah. "The Supreme Court's Faith in Belief." *The Immanent Frame*, December 16, 2014. http://blogs.ssrc.org/tif/2014/12/16/the-supreme-courts-faith-in-belief/.

Jacobs, Ken, Ian Perry, and Jenifer MacGillvary. *The High Public Cost of Low Wages: Poverty-Level Wages Cost U.S. Taxpayers $152.8 Billion Each Year in Public Support for Working Families*. Berkeley: UC Berkeley Center for Labor Research and Education, April 2015.

Jacobs, Sally H. *The Other Barack: The Bold and Reckless Life of President Obama's Father*. New York: Public Affairs, 2011.

Jacobson, Cardell, and Lara Burton, eds. *Modern Polygamy in the United States: Historical, Cultural, and Legal Issues*. Oxford and New York: Oxford University Press, 2011.

Jaffer, Jameel, ed. *The Drone Memos: Targeted Killing, Secrecy, and the Law*. New York: The New Press, 2016.

Jennings, Willie James. *The Christian Imagination: Theology and the Origins of Race*. New Haven: Yale University Press, 2011.

Jensen, Robert. *The Heart of Whiteness: Confronting Race, Racism and White Privilege*. San Francisco, CA: City Lights Publishers, 2005.

Jhally, Sut. *Stuart Hall: Race, the Floating Signifier.* Northampton, MA: Media Education Foundation, 1998.

Johnson, Chalmers. *Blowback: The Costs and Consequences of American Empire.* New York: Holt Paperbacks, 2004.

Johnson, Patrik. "After Obama's win, white backlash festers in US." *The Christian Science Monitor*, November 17, 2008. https://www.csmonitor.com/USA/Politics/2008/1117/p03s01-uspo.html.

Johnson, Sylvester A., and Steven Weitzman, eds. *The FBI and Religion: Faith and National Security before and after 9/11.* Oakland, California: University of California Press, 2017.

Jones, Brian P. "Black Lives Matter and the Struggle for Freedom." *Review of the Month*, April 2016.

Jones, Robert P. *The End of White Christian America.* New York: Simon & Schuster, 2017.

Jones, Van, and Ariane Conrad. *The Green Collar Economy: How One Solution Can Fix Our Two Biggest Problems.* New York, NJ: HarperOne, 2009.

Joseph, Peniel E. *Dark Days, Bright Nights: From Black Power to Barack Obama.* New York, NY: Civitas Books, 2010.

Kaba, Mariame, and Michelle VanNatta. "Guest Editors' Introduction." *Violence against Women* 13, no. 12 (December 2007): 1223–28.

Kahneman, Daniel. *Thinking, Fast and Slow.* New York: Farrar, Straus and Giroux, 2013.

Kamp, Karin. "Black Lives Matter Co-Founder Alicia Garza on the Global Movement for Black Lives." *BillMoyers.com*, October 3, 2016. http://billmoyers.com/story/black-lives-matter/.

Kantor, Jodi. "The Long Run: Teaching Law, Testing Ideas, Obama Stood Slightly Apart." *New York Times*, July 30, 2008.

Kantor, Jodi. "A First Family That Reflects A Nation's Diversity." *New York Times*, January 21, 2009.

Kantor, Jodi. *The Obamas.* New York, NY: Back Bay Books, 2012.

Kaplan, Rebecca. "Obama is 'Deporter-in-Chief,' Says Prominent Latino Group." *CBS News*, March 4, 2014.

Katz, Michael B. *In the Shadow of the Poorhouse: A Social History of Welfare in America.* 4th ed. New York: Basic Books, 1986.

Katznelson, Ira. *Fear Itself: The New Deal and the Origins of Our Time.* New York, NY: Liveright, 2014.

Keeter, Scott. "Public Opinion about Mormons." *Pew Internet & American Life Project*, December 4, 2007. http://www.pewresearch.org/2007/12/04/public-opinion-about-mormons/.

Kellogg, Jean Defrees. *Dark Prophets of Hope.* Chicago: Loyola Press, 1975.

Kendi, Ibram X. *Stamped from the Beginning: The Definitive History of Racist Ideas in America.* Reprint ed. New York: Nation Books, 2017.

Kennedy, David M. *Freedom from Fear: The American People in Depression and War, 1929-1945.* Reprint ed. New York, NY: Oxford University Press, 2001.

Kennedy, John F. "Transcript: JFK's Speech on His Religion." *National Public Radio*, December 5, 2007. http://www.npr.org/templates/story/story.php?storyId=16920600.

Kennedy, Randall. *The Persistence of the Color Line: Racial Politics and the Obama Presidency.* Reprint ed. Vintage, 2012.

Kennicott, Philip. "The Power of Brand-Old Message Art." *Washington Post*, January 13, 2009.

Khazan, Olga. "Tom Price: 'Not One' Woman Struggled to Afford Birth Control." *The Atlantic*, November 29, 2016. https://www.theatlantic.com/health/archive/2016/11/tom-price-not-one-woman-cant-afford-birth-control/509003/.

Kincheloe, Samuel C. *Research Memorandum on Religion in the Depression*. New York, NY: Social Science Research Council, 1937.

Kinney, Bruce. *Mormonism: The Islam of America*. London: Forgotten Books, 2012.

Kirby, John B. *Black Americans in the Roosevelt Era: Liberalism and Race*. Knoxville: University of Tennessee Press, 1982.

Kleinknecht, William. *The Man Who Sold the World: Ronald Reagan and the Betrayal of Main Street America*. New York: Nation Books, 2010.

Kloppenberg, James T. *Reading Obama: Dreams, Hope, and the American Political Tradition*. Princeton, NJ: Princeton University Press, 2010.

Kountoupes, Dina L., Karen S. Oberhauser, Carolyn Hughes, Sara J. Dykstra, Moya L. Alfonso, Karen Bogues, Meredith Russo, and Cassandra E. Simon. *Journal of Community Engagement and Scholarship, Vol. 1 No. 1: Fall 2008*, edited by Cassandra E. Simon. Tuscaloosa: University Alabama Press, 2008.

Krogstad, Jens Manuel, Ana Gonzalez-Barrera, and Mark Hugo Lopez. "Children 12 and Under are Fastest Growing Group of Unaccompanied Minors at United State Border." *Pew Internet & American Life Project*, July 22, 2014. http://www.pewresearch.org/fact-tank/2014/07/22/children-12-and-under-are-fastest-growing-group-of-unaccompanied-minors-at-u-s-border/.

Krugler, David F. *1919, The Year of Racial Violence: How African Americans Fought Back*. New York, NY: Cambridge University Press, 2014.

Kurtz, Stanley. "'Context,' You Say? A Guide to the Radical Theology of the Rev. Jeremiah Wright." *The National Review*, May 19, 2008.

Labor Council for Latin American Advancement (LCLAA). *Another America Is Possible: The Impact of NAFTA on the United State Latino Community and Lessons for Future Trade Agreements, Product ID 9013*. Washington DC: Public Citizen's Global Trade Watch, 2004.

Landers, Elizabeth. "Vice President Mike Pence Speech Right at Home at March for Life." *CNN*, January 27, 2017. http://www.cnn.com/2017/01/27/politics/mike-pence-march-for-life-speech/index.html.

Landis, Benson Y., and George Edmund Haynes. *Cotton-Growing Communities Study no. 2: Case Studies of 10 Rural Communities and 10 Plantations in Arkansas*. New York: Federal Council of Churches, 1935.

Lane, Marc J. *Social Enterprise: Empowering Mission-Driven Entrepreneurs*. Chicago, IL: American Bar Association, 2012.

Lane, Marc J. *The Mission-Driven Venture: Business Solutions to the World's Most Vexing Social Problems*. Hoboken, New Jersey: Wiley, 2015.

Lanni, Adriaan. "The Future of Community Justice." *Harvard Civil Rights-Civil Liberties Law Review* 40 (2005): 388–89.

Lattany, Kristin Hunter. "Off-Timing: Stepping to the Different Drummer." In *Lure and Loathing: Essays on Race, Identity, and the Ambivalence of Assimilation*, edited by Gerald Early, 163–75. New York: The Penguin Press, 1993.

Lee, Charles O. *1931 Annual Report, Memphis Community Fund*. Memphis, TN: Memphis-Charities-Community Fund Clippings File, Memphis-Community Chest Clippings File, Memphis Public Library, Memphis, Tennessee (MPL).

Lee, Michelle Ye Hee. "Donald Trump's False Comments Connecting Mexican Immigration and Crime." *The Washington Post*, July 8, 2015.

Lee, Charles O.. *Open Your Heart: Memphis Cares for Her Own.* Memphis Community Fund, 1928.

Leibovich, Mark. "Polished and Upbeat, Romney Tries to Connect." *The New York Times,* June 16, 2007. http://www.nytimes.com/2007/06/16/us/politics/16romney.html.

Lewis, David Levering, ed. *W. E. B. Du Bois: A Reader.* New York: Holt Paperbacks, 1995.

Lewis, Earl. *In Their Own Interests: Race, Class and Power in Twentieth-Century Norfolk, Virginia.* Berkeley, CA: University of California Press, 1993.

Lewis, Pericles "James's Sick Souls." *The Henry James Review* 22, no. 3 (Fall 2001): 248–58. doi:10.1353/hjr.2001.0030.

Liptak, Adam. "Justices to Hear Case on Religious Objections to Same-Sex Marriage." *New York Times,* June 26, 2017. https://www.nytimes.com/2017/06/26/us/politics/supreme-court-wedding-cake-gay-couple-masterpiece-cakeshop.html.

Littlefield, Kinney. "Oprah Winfrey Is Tired and Tearful But Still Enjoying Her TV Power." *Pittsburgh Post-Gazette,* May 19, 1997.

Llebelson, Dana. "Arkansas Governor Says He Won't Sign 'Religious Freedom' Bill Until Changes Are Made." *Huffington Post,* April 1, 2015. http://www.huffingtonpost.com/2015/04/01/religious-freedom_n_6985090.html.

Long, Charles H. *Significations: Signs, Symbols, and Images in the Interpretation of Religion.* 2nd ed. Aurora, Colorado: The Davies Group Publishers, 1999.

Lopez, Ann Aurelia. *The Farmworkers' Journey.* Berkeley: University of California Press, 2007.

Lowery, Wesley. *They Can't Kill Us All: The Story of the Struggle for Black Lives.* Reprint ed. New York, NY: Back Bay Books, 2017.

Loy, David R. "The Religion of the Market." *Journal of the American Academy of Religion* 65, no. 2 (Summer 1997): 275–90.

Mackin, Glenn. "Black Lives Matter and the Concept of the Counterworld." *Philosophy and Rhetoric* 49, no. 4 (2016): 459–81. https://muse.jhu.edu/article/638145.

Magnali, Laura, and Harmon L. Wray. *Beyond Prisons: A New Interfaith Paradigm for Our Failed Prison System.* Minneapolis, MN: Fortress Press, 2009.

Malcolm X, Alex Haley, and Attallah Shabazz. *The Autobiography of Malcolm X: As Told to Alex Haley.* New York: Ballantine Books, 1992.

Malek, Alia, ed. *Patriot Acts: Narratives of Post-9/11 Injustice.* San Francisco: McSweeney's, 2011.

Mandela, Nelson. *Long Walk to Freedom: The Autobiography of Nelson Mandela.* Boston: Back Bay Books, 1995.

Marable, M., and Hishaam D. Aidi, eds. *Black Routes to Islam.* New York, NY: Palgrave Macmillan, 2009.

Maraniss, David. *Barack Obama: The Story.* New York: Simon & Schuster, 2013.

Marche, Stephen. "The Obama Years." *Los Angeles Review of Books,* November 30, 2016. https://lareviewofbooks.org/article/the-obama-years/.

Marcuss, Rosemary D. and Richard E. Kane. "U.S. National Income and Product Statistics: Born of the Great Depression and World War II." *Survey of Current Business* (February 2007): 32–46.

Marr, Timothy. *The Cultural Roots of American Islamicism.* Cambridge: Cambridge University Press, 2006.

Marshall, Serena. "Obama Has Deported More People Than Any Other President." *ABC News,* August 26, 2016.

Martinot, Steve. *The Machinery of Whiteness: Studies in the Structure of Racialization.* Philadelphia: Temple University Press, 2010.

Maxwell, William J. "Born-Again, Seen-Again James Baldwin: Post-Postracial Criticism and the Literary History of Black Lives Matter." *American Literary History* 28, no. 4 (Winter 2016): 812–27. https://muse.jhu.edu/article/641260.

McDonald, Jermaine M. "Ferguson and Baltimore According to Dr. King: How Competing Interpretations of King's Legacy Frame the Public Discourse on Black Lives Matter." *Journal of the Society of Christian Ethics* 36, no. 2 (2016): 141–58. doi:10.1353/sce.2016.0035.

McIvor, David W. *Mourning in America: Race and the Politics of Loss.* Ithaca and London: Cornell University Press, 2016.

McKenzie, Brian. "Barack Obama, Jeremiah Wright, and Public Opinion in the 2008 Presidential Primaries," *Political Psychology* 32, no. 6 (2011): 943–61.

McLeod, Allegra. "Prison Abolition and Grounded Justice." *UCLA Law Review* (2015): 1167–71.

Meacham, Jon. "Who We Are Now." *Newsweek*, January 26, 2009.

Media, Nobel. "The Nobel Peace Prize for 2009 to President Barack Obama – Press Release." *Nobel Media AB*, October 9, 2009. http://www.nobelprize.org/nobel_prizes/peace/laureates/2009/press.html

Medwed, Daniel S. *Prosecution Complex: America's Race to Convict and Its Impact on the Innocent.* Reprint ed. New York: New York University Press, 2013.

Miller, Linda. "The United States and the Arab Spring: Now and Then in the Middle East." In *Obama and the World: New Directions in US Foreign Policy*, edited by Inderjeet Parmar, Inderjeet Parmar, Linda Miller, and Mark Ledwidge. New York: Routledge, 2014.

Miller, Lisa. "Is Obama the Antichrist?" *Newsweek*, November 24, 2008.

Miller, Monica R., and Anthony B. Pinn, eds. *The Hip Hop and Religion Reader.* New York: Routledge, 2014.

Miller, Patricia. *Good Catholics: The Battle over Abortion in the Catholic Church.* Reprint ed. Berkeley: University of California Press, 2014.

Mills, Nicolaus. "Roosevelt and the Affordable Care Act." *Huffington Post*, July 16, 2013. http://www.huffingtonpost.com/nicolaus-mills/roosevelt-and-the-afforda_b_3600103.html.

Mizruchi, Susan. "Neighbors, Strangers, Corpses: Death and Sympathy in the Early Writings of W. E. B. Du Bois." In *The Souls of Black Folk: W. E. B. Du Bois*, edited by Henry L. Gates, Jr., and Terri Hume Oliver. New York: W. W. Norton & Company, 1999.

Mohamed, Besheer. "A New Estimate of the US Muslim Population." *Pew Internet & American Life Project.* http://www.pewresearch.org/fact-tank/2016/01/06/a-new-estimate-of-the-u-s-muslim-population/

Mohr, James C. *Abortion in America: The Origins and Evolution of National Policy.* Oxford: Oxford University Press, 1979.

Moore, Ashley. "American Muslim Minorities: The New Human Rights Struggle." *Human Rights and Human Welfare: An Online Journal of Academic Literature Review*, 2009. http://www.du.edu/korbel/hrhw/researchdigest/minority/Muslim.pdf.

Moore, Solomon. "Study Shows Sharp Rise in Latino Federal Convicts." *The New York Times*, February 18, 2009.

Mosher, W. D., and J. Jones. "Use of contraception in the United States: 1982-2000." *Vital Health Statistics* 23 (2010): 1–44.

Mueller, Max Perry. "Twice-told Tale: Telling Two Histories of Mormon-Black Relations during the 2012 Presidential Election." In *Mormonism and American Politics*, edited by Randall Balmer and Jana Reiss, 155–74. Columbia University Press, 2015.

Mueller, Max Perry. "Why Mormons Don't Like Trump." *Slate*, August 4, 2016. http://www.slate.com/articles/news_and_politics/politics/2016/08/why_mormons_don_t_like_donald_trump.html.

Mueller, Max Perry. "Not My Choir." *Slate*, January 19, 2017. http://www.slate.com/articles/news_and_politics/politics/2017/01/make_america_s_choir_great_again.html.

Muller, Jan-Werner. *What Is Populism?* Philadelphia: University of Pennsylvania Press, 2016.

Murray, Charles. *Coming Apart: The State of White America, 1960-2010*. Reprint ed. New York, NY: Crown Forum, 2013.

Nazario, Sonia. "The Refugees at Our Door: We are Paying Mexico to Keep People from Reaching Our Borders, People Who Are Fleeing Central American Violence." *The New York Times*, October 10, 2015.

New York Civil Liberties Union. "Boxed In: The True Cost of Extreme Isolation in New York's Prisons." 2012. https://www.nyclu.org/sites/default/files/publications/nyclu_boxedin_FINAL.pdf.

Niebuhr, Reinhold, and Andrew J. Bacevich. *The Irony of American History*. Reprint ed. Chicago: University of Chicago Press, 2008.

Noll, Mark A., and Luke E. Harlow, eds. *Religion and American Politics: From the Colonial Period to the Present*. 2nd ed. Oxford and New York: Oxford University Press, 2007.

Northup, Nancy. "Supplemental Information about the United States Scheduled for Review during the Committee for the Elimination of Racial Discrimination Committee's 72nd Session." *Center for Reproductive Rights*, December 19, 2007.

Obama, Barack. *Dreams from My Father: A Story of Race and Inheritance*. New York: Broadway Books, 2004.

Obama, Barack. *The Audacity of Hope: Thoughts on Reclaiming the American Dream*. New York: Broadway Books, 2007.

Obama, Barack. "A More Perfect Union." *National Public Radio*, March 18, 2008. http://www.npr.org/templates/story/story.php?storyId=88478467

Obama, Barack. "On My Faith and My Church." *Huffington Post*, March 14, 2008. http://www.huffingtonpost.com/barack-obama/on-my-faith-and-my-church_b_91623.html.

Obama, Barack. "Transcript, Barack Obama's Inaugural Address." *New York Times*, January 20, 2009.

Obama, Barack. "Transcript: Obama's Immigration Speech." *The Washington Post*, November 20, 2014.

Obama, Barack. "Remarks by the President in Eulogy for the Honorable Reverend Clementa Pinkney." *The White House*, June 26, 2015. https://www.whitehouse.gov/the-press-office/2015/06/26/remarks-president-eulogy-honorable-reverend-clementa-pinckney.

Obama, Barack. "Remarks by the President after Visit at the El Reno Federal Correctional Institution." El Reno, OK, released by the Office of the Press Secretary, *The White House*, July 16, 2015. https://obamawhitehouse.archives.gov/the-press-office/2015/07/16/remarks-president-after-visit-el-reno-federal-correctional-institution.

Obama, Barack. "What I Am Opposed to Is a Dumb War: Speech against the Iraq War (Chicago, IL October 2, 2002)." In *We Are the Change We Seek: The Speeches of Barack Obama*, edited by E. J. Dionne and Joy-Ann Reid. London: Bloomsbury, 2017.

OFM and Kenneth R. Himes. *Drones and the Ethics of Targeted Killing*. Lanham, MD: Rowman & Littlefield Publishers, 2015.

Ogbar, Jeffrey O. G. "Message from the Grassroots: Hip Hop Activism, Millennials, and the Race for the White House." In *The Hip Hop & Obama Reader*, edited by Travis L. Gosa and Erik Nielson. New York: Oxford University Press, 2015.

Ohlheiser, Abby. "'Operation American Spring' Is Still Waiting for Its Millions of Patriots." *The Atlantic*, May 16, 2014. https://www.theatlantic.com/politics/archive/2014/05/operation-american-spring-is-still-waiting-for-its-millions-of-patriots/371092/.

Ortiz, Ildefonso. "Agent Sexually Assaults Family, Kidnaps Girl, Commits Suicide." *The Brownsville Herald*, March 13, 2014.

Packer, George. "Let Us Now Set Aside Childish Things." *The New Yorker*, January 20, 2009.

Parfitt, Tudor. *Black Jews in Africa and the Americas*. Cambridge, MA: Harvard University Press, 2013.

Parmar, Inderjeet, Linda B. Miller, and Mark Ledwidge, eds. *Obama and the World: New Directions in US Foreign Policy*. 2nd ed. New York: Routledge, 2014.

Pennsylvania Convention Center, Philadelphia, PA, released by the Office of the Press Secretary, *The White House*, July 14, 2015. https://obamawhitehouse.archives.gov/the-press-office/2015/07/14/remarks-president-naacp-conference.

Peralta, Eyder. "You Say You're an American, But What If You had to Prove It or Be Deported?" *NPR*, December 22, 2016.

Peters, Rebecca Todd. *In Search of the Good Life: The Ethics of Globalization*. New York, NY: Bloomsbury Academic, 2006.

Pew Research Center. "Inside Obama's Sweeping Victory." *Pew Internet & American Life Project*, November 5, 2008. http://www.pewresearch.org/2008/11/05/inside-obamas-sweeping-victory/.

Pew Research Center. "Growing Number of Americans Say Obama is a Muslim." *Pew Internet & American Life Project*, August 18, 2010. http://www.pewforum.org/2010/08/18/growing-number-of-americans-say-obama-is-a-muslim/.

Phares, Walid. *The Coming Revolution: Struggle for Freedom in the Middle East*. New York: Threshold Editions, 2010.

Pickler, Nedra. "From Greek Mythology, Obama Learned a Lesson." *USA Today*, June 4, 2008. http://usatoday30.usatoday.com/news/politics/2008-06-04-2310712963_x.html.

Pinker, Steven. *The Better Angels of Our Nature: Why Violence Has Declined*. Reprint ed. New York, Toronto and London: Penguin Books, 2012.

Pinn, Anthony B., ed. *Noise and Spirit: The Religious and Spiritual Sensibilities of Rap Music*. First Printing. New York: New York University Press, 2003.

Pinn, Anthony B., ed. *African American Humanist Principles: Living and Thinking Like the Children of Nimrod*. New York: Palgrave Macmillan, 2004.

Pinn, Anthony B., ed. "Getting Wright Wrong: Preaching Is Not Policy." *Religion Dispatches*, July 3, 2009. http://religiondispatches.org/getting-wright-wrong-preaching-is-not-policy/.

Pinn, Anthony B., ed. *Understanding and Transforming the Black Church*: Eugene, OR: Wipf & Stock Publishers, 2010.

Pinn, Anthony B., ed. *The End of God-Talk: An African American Humanist Theology*. New York: Oxford University Press, 2012.

Pinn, Anthony B., ed. *What Has the Black Church to Do with Public Life?* New York: Palgrave Pivot, 2013.

Pinn, Anthony B., ed. "On Struggle In Our Historical Moment." *Huffington Post*, July 12, 2016. http://www.huffingtonpost.com/anthony-b-pinn/on-struggle-in-our-histor_b_10930544.html

Pinn, Anthony B., ed. *When Colorblindness Isn't the Answer: Humanism and the Challenge of Race*. Durham and Washington DC: Pitchstone Publishing, 2017.

Planned Parenthood Federation of America. "Survey: Nearly Three in Four Voters in America Support Fully Covering Prescription Birth Control." January 30, 2014. https://www.plannedparenthood.org/about-us/newsroom/press-releases/survey-nearly-three-four-voters-america-support-fully-covering-prescription-birth-control.

Pope Francis. "Visit to the Detainees at Curran-Frumhold Correctional Facility: Address of the Holy Father." September 27, 2015.

Pope Francis. "Apostolic Letter *Misericordia Et Misera*." §20. November 20, 2016. https://w2.vatican.va/content/francesco/en/apost_letters/documents/papa-francesco-lettera-ap_20161120_misericordia-et-misera.html

Preston, Julia. "Obama Signs Border Bill to Increase Surveillance." *The New York Times*, August 13, 2010.

Prison Policy Initiative. "Racial and Ethnic Disparities in Prisons and Jails." Compiled from 2010 Census, Summary File 1. https://www.prisonpolicy.org/reports/pie2017.html.

Prothero, Stephen. *Religious Literacy: What Every American Needs to Know—and Doesn't*. Reprint ed. New York, NY: HarperOne, 2008.

Rakoff, Jed S. "Why Innocent People Plead Guilty." *New York Review of Books*, November 20, 2014. http://www.nybooks.com/articles/2014/11/20/why-innocent-people-plead-guilty/.

Ranji, Usha, Usha Ranji, Alina Salganicoff, Laurie Sobel, and Caroline Rosenzweig. "Ten Ways That the House American Health Care Act Could Affect Women." *The Henry J. Kaiser Family Foundation*, May 8, 2017. http://www.kff.org/womens-health-policy/issue-brief/ten-ways-that-the-house-american-health-care-act-could-affect-women/#Contraceptive.

Reardon, Sean F. and Kendra Bischoff. "Growth in the Residential Segregation of Families by Income, 1970-2009." *Stanford University*, November 2011. http://graphics8.nytimes.com/packages/pdf/national/RussellSageIncomeSegregationreport.pdf.

Reeve, Paul W. *Religion of a Different Color: Race and the Mormon Struggle for Whiteness*. Reprint ed. New York: Oxford University Press, 2017.

Reiner, Carl. *If You're Not in the Obit, Eat Breakfast*, directed by Danny Gold. HBO Films, 2017.

Remnick, David. "The Joshua Generation." *New Yorker*, November 17, 2008.

Remnick, David. *The Bridge: The Life and Rise of Barack Obama*. Reprint ed. New York: Vintage, 2011.

Richardson, Marilyn. *Maria Stewart, America's First Black Woman Political Writer: Essays and Speeches*. Bloomington: Indiana University Press, 1987.

Robbins, A. "Hunger-1931." *The Nation*, February 11, 1931.

Romney, Mitt. "Faith in America." *National Public Radio*, December 6, 2007. http://www.npr.org/templates/story/story.php?storyId=16969460.

Romney, Mitt. "Romney's Announcement in Dearborn, Michigan." *The New York Times*, February 13, 2007. http://www.nytimes.com/2007/02/13/us/politics/13romney-text.html?pagewanted=print.

Romney, Mitt. "Transcript of Mitt Romney's Speech on Donald Trump." *The New York Times*, March 3, 2016. https://www.nytimes.com/2016/03/04/us/politics/mitt-romney-speech.html.

Ross, Brian and Rehab el-Buri. "Obama's Pastor: God Damn America, U.S. to Blame for 9/11." *ABC News*, March 13, 2008. http://abcnews.go.com/Blotter/story?id=4443788.

Rugy, Veronique de. "Spending Under President George W. Bush." *Mercatus Center, George Mason University*, March 2009.

Samuels, Allison. "Something Wasn't Wright, So Oprah Left His Church." *Newsweek*, May 12, 2008.

Sanger, David E. *Confront and Conceal: Obama's Secret Wars and Surprising Use of American Power*. New York: Broadway Books, 2013.

Savage, Barbara Dianne. *Your Spirits Walk Beside Us: The Politics of Black Religion*. Cambridge, MA: Belknap Press, 2008.

Scahill, Jeremy. "Trump May Not Finish His Term But The Assassination Complex Will Live On." *The Intercept*, August 21, 2017. https://static.theintercept.com/amp/trump-may-not-survive-his-term-but-the-assassination-complex-will.html.

Schäfer, Axel R. "The Cold War State and the Resurgence of Evangelicalism: A Study of the Public Funding of Religion Since 1945." *Radical History Review* 99 (Fall 2007): 19–50.

Schäfer, Axel R. *Piety and Public Funding: Evangelicals and the State in Modern America*. Philadelphia: University of Pennsylvania Press, 2012.

Schmidt, Michael S. and Michael D. Shear. "Armed Outside Guard Was Allowed on Elevator With President, Officials Say." https://www.nytimes.com/2014/10/01/us/armed-man-boarded-elevator-with-obama-official-reports.html?_r=0.

Schmitt, John. "How Good is the Economy at Creating Good Jobs?" *Center for Economic and Policy Research*, October 2005.

Schroeder, Peter. "Poll: 43 Percent of Republicans Believe Obama is a Muslim." *The Hill*, September 13, 2015. http://thehill.com/blogs/blog-briefing-room/news/253515-poll-43-percent-of-republicans-believe-obama-is-a-muslim.

Scott, Jenny. *A Singular Woman: The Untold Story of Barack Obama's Mother*. Reprint ed. New York: Riverhead Books, 2012.

Seligman, Adam B. *The Idea of Civil Society*. Reprint ed. Princeton, NJ: Princeton University Press, 1995.

Sellers, Jeff M. "Corporation's Plan in Only Slightly Worse Than Its Chain Competitors." *Christianity Today*, May 2005.

Sen, Amartya. *Development as Freedom*. Reprint ed. New York: Anchor, 2000.

Shafir, Eldar, ed. *The Behavioral Foundations of Public Policy*. Princeton: Princeton University Press, 2012.

Shane, Scott. "Targeted Killing Comes to Define War on Terror." *New York Times*, April 7, 2013. http://www.nytimes.com/2013/04/08/world/targeted-killing-comes-to-define-war-on-terror.html?rref=collection%2Fbyline%2Fscott-shane&action=click&contentCollection=undefined&region=stream&module=stream_unit&version=search&contentPlacement=1&pgtype=collection.

Shaw, Ian G. R. "The Rise of the Predator Empire: Tracing the History of U.S. Drones", Understanding Empire." *Understanding Empire*, 2014. https://understandingempire.wordpress.com/2-0-a-brief-history-of-u-s-drones/.

Shaw, Stephanie J. *W. E. B. Du Bois and The Souls of Black Folk*. Reprint ed. Chapel Hill: The University of North Carolina Press, 2015.

Shipman, Tim. "Conservative backlash Begins Against Barack Obama." *The Telegraph*, November 15, 2008. http://www.telegraph.co.uk/news/worldnews/barackobama/3464679/Conservative-backlash-begins-against-Barack-Obama.html.

Shipps, Jan. "Making Saints: In the Early Days and the Latter Days." In *Contemporary Mormonism: Social Science Perspectives*, edited by Marie Cornwall et al., 64–87. Urbana: University of Illinois Press, 2001.

Siegel, Lee. "Thank You for Sharing: The Strange Genius of Oprah." *The New Republic* 234, no. 21/22 (June 2006): 21–22.

Sifton, John. "A Brief History of Drones." *The Nation*, February 7, 2012. https://www.thenation.com/article/brief-history-drones/.

Silver, Nate. "The Mythology of Trump's 'Working Class' Support: His voters are better off economically compared with most Americans." *FiveThirtyEight*, May 3, 2016. http://fivethirtyeight.com/features/the-mythology-of-trumps-working-class-support/.

Sitkoff, Harvard. *A New Deal for Blacks: The Emergence of Civil Rights as a National Issue: The Depression Decade*. Anniversary ed. New York: Oxford University Press, 2008.

Skocpol, Theda. *Protecting Soldiers and Mothers: The Political Origins of Social Policy in United States*. Reprint ed. Harvard: Belknap Press, 1995.

Small, Neil. "Death and Difference." In *Death, Gender and Ethnicity*, edited by David Field, Jenny Hockey, and Neil Small. London: Routledge, 1997.

Smith, Ben. "Wright Leaves Obama Campaign." *Politico*, March 14, 2008. http://www.politico.com/blogs/ben-smith/2008/03/wright-leaves-obama-campaign-007039.

Smith, Mychal Denzel. "A Q&A with Alicia Garza, Co-Founder of #BlackLivesMatter." *The Nation*, March 24, 2015. https://www.thenation.com/article/qa-alicia-garza-co-founder-blacklivesmatter/.

Smith, Mychal Denzel. "A Q&A With Opal Tometi, Co-Founder of #BlackLivesMatter." *The Nation*, June 2, 2015. https://www.thenation.com/article/qa-opal-tometi-co-founder-blacklivesmatter/.

Smith, Gary Scott. *Faith and the Presidency From George Washington to George W. Bush*. New York: Oxford University Press, 2009.

Smith, Susan Williams. *The Book of Jeremiah: The Life and Ministry of Jeremiah A. Wright, Jr*. Boston: The Pilgrim Press, 2014.

Smith, Zadie. "Speaking in Tongues." *New York Review of Books*, February 26, 2009.

Sobel, Laurie, Adara Beamsederfer, and Alina Salganicoff. "Private Insurance Coverage of Contraception." *The Henry J. Kaiser Family Foundation*, December 7, 2016. http://www.kff.org/womens-health-policy/issue-brief/private-insurance-coverage-of-contraception/.

Sommers, Samuel and Michael Norton. "White People Think Racism Is Getting Worse. Against White People." *Washington Post*, July 21, 2016. https://www.washingtonpost.com/posteverything/wp/2016/07/21/white-people-think-racism-is-getting-worse-against-white-people/?utm_term=.a4d6ff7b6e79.

Sparr, Pamela, ed. *Mortgaging Women's Lives: Feminist Critiques of Structural Adjustment*. Atlantic Highlands, NJ: Zed Books, 1993.

Spillers, Hortense J. *Black, White, and in Color: Essays on American Literature and Culture*. Chicago: University of Chicago Press, 2003.

Stana, Richard M. *INS Southwest Border Strategy: Resource and Impact Issues Remain After Seven Years*. Washington DC: US General Accounting Office, 2001.

Steinfels, Peter. "Despite a Decade of Controversy, the 'Faith-Based Initiative' Endures." *New York Times*, July 31, 2009.

Steinhaur, Jennifer. "Bipartisan Push Builds to Relax Sentencing Laws." *New York Times, July* 15, 2008. https://www.nytimes.com/2015/07/29/us/push-to-scale-back-sentencing-laws-gains-momentum.html.

Stelter, Brian "Following the Script: Obama, McCain, and the *West Wing*." *New York Times,* October 30, 2008.

Stevenson, Bryan. *Just Mercy: A Story of Justice and Redemption.* Reprint ed. New York: Spiegel & Grau, 2015.

Stevenson, Richard W. "Officials to Block Qaddafi Gift to Farrakhan." *The New York Times,* August 28, 1996. http://www.nytimes.com/1996/08/28/us/officials-to-block-qaddafi-gift-to-farrakhan.html.

Stewart, Maria W. *Meditations from the Pen of Mrs. Maria W. Stewart: (Widow Of The Late James W. Stewart) Now Matron Of The Freedman's Hospital, And Presented In 1832 .. Of Boston, Mass.. - Primary Source Edition.* Charleston, SC: Nabu Press, 2014.

Steyn, Mark. "Uncle Jeremiah: Barack Obama and His Cookie-cutter Race Huckster." *The National Review,* March 15, 2008. http://www.nationalreview.com/node/223934/print.

Stiglitz, Joseph E. *Globalization And Its Discontents by Joseph E Stiglitz.* New York: W. W. Norton & Company, 2003.

Stiglitz, Joseph E. The Price of Inequality: How Today's Divided Society Endangers Our Future. New York: W. W. Norton & Company, 2012.

Street, Paul. *Barack Obama and the Future of American Politics.* New York: Routledge, 2008.

Strong, Josiah. *Our Country: Its Possible Future and Its Present Crisis.* London: Forgotten Books, 2017.

Suebsaeng, Asawin. "Romney or Robot: The Quiz." March 21, 2012, http://www.motherjones.com/politics/2012/03/mitt-romney-robot-quiz.

Sugrue, Thomas J. *Not Even Past: Barack Obama and the Burden of Race.* Princeton, NJ: Princeton University Press, 2010.

Sullivan, Amy "An Antichrist Obama in McCain Ad?" *Time,* August 8, 2008.

Sullivan, Andrew. "Mormon Sacred Underwear." *The Atlantic,* November 24, 2006. http://www.theatlantic.com/daily-dish/archive/2006/11/mormon-sacred-underwear/232160/

Sullivan, Andrew. "Goodbye to All that: Why Obama Matters." *The Atlantic,* December 2007. https://www.theatlantic.com/magazine/archive/2007/12/goodbye-to-all-that-why-obama-matters/306445/.

Sullivan, Winnifred Fallers. "The Impossibility of Religious Freedom." *The Immanent Frame,* July 08, 2014. http://blogs.ssrc.org/tif/2014/07/08/impossibility-of-religious-freedom/.

Sullivan, Winnifred Fallers. "The World That Smith Made." In *The Politics of Religious Freedom,* edited by Winnifred Fallers Sullivan, Elizabeth Shakman Hurd, Saba Mahmood, and Peter G. Danchin, 231–40. Chicago: The University of Chicago Press, 2015.

Sullivan, Winnifred Fallers, Elizabeth Shakman Hurd, Saba Mahmood, and Peter G. Danchin, eds. *Politics of Religious Freedom.* Chicago: University of Chicago Press, 2015.

Sutton, Matthew Avery. ""Was FDR the Antichrist? The Birth of Fundamentalist Anti-liberalism in a Global Age." *Journal of American History* 98, no. 4 (January 2012): 1052–74.

Tannis, Lynette N. "Foreword: A Crime for a Crime? The Landscape of Correctional Education in the United States." *Harvard Educational Review* 87, no. 1 (Spring 2017): 74–80.

Taylor, Keeanga-Yamahtta. *From #BlackLivesMatter to Black Liberation*. Chicago, IL: Haymarket Books, 2016.

Tesler, Michael, and David O. Sears. *Obama's Race: The 2008 Election and the Dream of a Post-Racial America*. Chicago Studies in American Politics ed. Chicago: University of Chicago Press, 2010.

Thornton, Arland. "The International Fight Against Barbarism: Historical and Comparative Perspectives on Marriage Timing, Consent, and Polygamy." In *Modern Polygamy in the United States: Historical, Cultural, and Legal Issues*, edited by Cardell Jacobsen and Lara Burton. New York: Oxford University Press, 2011.

Torre, Miguel A. De La. *Trails of Hope and Terror: Testimonies on Immigration*. Maryknoll, NY: Orbis Books, 2009.

Torre, Miguel A. De La. *Doing Christian Ethics from the Margins: 2nd Edition Revised and Expanded*. 2nd ed. Maryknoll: Orbis Books, 2014.

Trost, Jennifer, Kermit Hall, Paul Finkelman, and Timothy Huebner. *Gateway to Justice: The Juvenile Court and Progressive Child Welfare in a Southern City*. Athens, GA: University of Georgia Press, 2005.

Trump, Donald J. "My Vision for a Culture of Life." *Washington Examiner*, January 23, 2016. http://www.washingtonexaminer.com/donald-trump-op-ed-my-vision-for-a-culture-of-life/article/2581271.

US Census Bureau. "Table 18: Workers as a Proportion of All Poor People." https://www.census.gov/data/tables/time-series/demo/income-poverty/historical-poverty-people.html

US Census Bureau. "Table 2: Poverty Status of People by Family Relationship, Race, and Hispanic Origin: 1959-2015."

US Department of Labor, Children's Bureau. *Mothers' Aid, 1931*. Bureau Publication 220, Washington DC: Government Printing Office, 1933.

United States Department of Homeland Security. *Yearbook of Immigration Statistics: 2015*. Washington DC: United State Department of Homeland Security, Office of Immigration Statistics, 2016.

Valbrun, Marjorie. "The Trouble With Transcending Race." *TheRoot.com*, April 30, 2008.

Vu, Michelle A. "Why Some Evangelicals Won't Vote for Romney." *Christian Post*. October 16, 2007. http://www.christianpost.com/news/why-some-evangelicals-won-t-vote-for-romney-29718/.

Walker, Clarence E., and Gregory D. Smithers. *The Preacher and the Politician: Jeremiah Wright, Barack Obama, and Race in America*. Reprint ed. Charlottesville: University of Virginia Press, 2012.

Wallace, Hailey. "The Making of a Movement." *Black Enterprise.Com*, July/August 2016.

Wallace, Mike. "Margaret Sanger, The Mike Wallace Interview, Sept. 21, 1957." Harry Ransom Center at the University of Texas at Austin. http://www.hrc.utexas.edu/multimedia/video/2008/wallace/sanger_margaret_t.html.

Wang, Amy B. "Donald Trump Plans to Immediately Deport 2 Million to 3 Million Undocumented Immigrants." *The Washington Post*, November 14, 2016.

Warner, Judith. "Tears to Remember." *New York Times*, November 6, 2008. https://opinionator.blogs.nytimes.com/2008/11/06/title/.

Warner, Michael. "Ruse of 'Secular Humanism.'" *The Immanent Frame*, September 22, 2008. http://blogs.ssrc.org/tif/2008/09/22/the-ruse-of-secular-humanism/.

Washington, Booker T., W. E. B. Du Bois, Charles W. Chestnutt, Wilford H. Smith, H. T. Kealing, Paul Laurence Dunbar, and T. Thomas Fortune. *The Negro Problem*. CreateSpace Independent Publishing Platform, 2017.

Wattles, Jackie. "Wal-Mart Increasing Wages; Union Says it's All Show." *CNN Money*, January 20, 2016. http://money.cnn.com/2016/01/20/news/companies/walmart-pay-raise-wages/.

Weber, Robert, and Roger Gryson, eds. *Biblia Sacra Vulgata*. Stuttgart: Deutsche Bibelgesellschaft, 1983.

Welch, Sharon D. "The Machiavellian Dilemma: Paradoxes and Perils of Democratic Governance." *Tikkun* 25, no. 3 (May/June 2010): 19–22. https://muse.jhu.edu/article/594669.

Welch, Sharon D. "In Praise of Imperfect Commitment: An Ethic of Power, Professionalism and Risk." In *The Oxford Handbook of Professional Economic Ethics*, edited by George E. DeMartino and Deirdre N. McCloskey, 55–70. Oxford: Oxford University Press, 2016.

Wedell, Marsha. *Elite Women and the Reform Impulse in Memphis, 1875-1915*. Knoxville: University of Tennessee Press, 1991.

Weheliye, Alexander G. *Habeas Viscus: Racializing Assemblages, Biopolitics, and Black Feminist Theories of the Human*. Durham: Duke University Press Books, 2014.

Wenner, Jann S. "A Conversation With Barack Obama." *Rolling Stone*, July 10, 2008.

West, Cornel. "Cornel West: Obama's Response to Trayvon Martin Case Belies Failure to Challenge 'New Jim Crow.'" https://www.democracynow.org/2013/7/22/cornel_west_obamas_response_to_trayvon.

Whiting, Tracy, ed. *The Speech: Race and Barack Obama's "A More Perfect Union."* New York: Bloomsbury USA, 2009.

Will, George F. "Republicans: Save Your Party, Don't Give To Trump." *Washington Post*, June 22, 2016.

Williams, Daniel. *God's Own Party: The Making of the Christian Right*. New York: Oxford University Press, 2010.

Williams, Patricia J. *The Alchemy of Race and Rights: Diary of a Law Professor*. Cambridge: Harvard University Press, 1991.

Williams, Rowan, Laurence Freeman, and Desmond Tutu. *Where God Happens: Discovering Christ in One Another*. Boston, MA: New Seeds, 2007.

Wills, Gary. "Two Speeches on Race." *The New York Review of Books*, May 1, 2008, http://www.nybooks.com/articles/2008/05/01/two-speeches-on-race/.

Wilson, William Julius. *When Work Disappears: The World of the New Urban Poor*. New York, NY: Vintage, 1997.

Wilson, William Julius. *The Truly Disadvantaged: The Inner City, the Underclass, and Public Policy*. 2nd ed. Chicago and London: University of Chicago Press, 2012.

Wind, Rebecca. "Public Funded Family Planning Yields Numerous Positive Health Outcomes While Saving Taxpayer Dollars." *Guttmacher Institute*, January 9, 2015. https://www.guttmacher.org/news-release/2015/publicly-funded-family-planning-yields-numerous-positive-health-outcomes-while

Winfrey, Oprah. "Oprah Talks To Barack Obama." *O, The Oprah Magazine* 5, no. 11 (November 2004): 248; 288.

Wolffe, Richard. *Renegade: The Making of a President*. Reprint ed. New York: Broadway Books, 2010.

Wood, Thomas. "Racism Motivated Trump Voters More than Authoritarianism." *The Washington Post*, April 17, 2017.

Woodruff, Nan. *As Rare as Rain: Federal Relief in the Great Southern Drought of 1930-31*. Urbana: University of Illinois Press, 1985.

Wright, Jeremiah. *Africans Who Shaped Our Faith*. Chicago, IL: Urban Ministries, 1995.

Wright Jr., Jeremiah A. *A Sankofa Moment: The History of Trinity United Church of Christ.* Dallas, TX: St. Paul Press, 2010.

Wright, Kai. "Black Life and Death in the Age of Obama." *The Nation*, January 2, 2017. https://www.thenation.com/article/black-life-and-death-in-the-age-of-obama/.

Yergin, Daniel, and Joseph Stanislaw. *The Commanding Heights: The Battle between Government and the Marketplace That Is Remaking the Modern World.* New York, NY: Simon & Schuster, 1998.

Young, Harvey. "Pessimism and the Age of Obama." *American Literary History 28*, no. 4 (Winter 2016): 854–58. https://muse.jhu.edu/article/641264.

Young, Iris Marion, and Danielle S. Allen. *Justice and the Politics of Difference.* Princeton, NJ: Princeton University Press, 2011.

Zakaria, Fareed. "The Global Elite: Barack Obama." *Newsweek*, December 29, 2008.

Zakaria, Fareed. *The Post-American World.* New York: W. W. Norton & Company, 2009.

Zamir, Shamoon. *Dark Voices: W. E. B. Du Bois and American Thought, 1888-1903.* Chicago: University of Chicago Press, 1995.

Zaretsky, Robert. *A Life Worth Living: Albert Camus and the Quest for Meaning.* Reprint ed. Cambridge, MA: Belknap Press: An Imprint of Harvard University Press, 2016.

Zeleny, Jeff. "Oprah Winfrey Hits Campaign Trail for Obama." *New York Times*, (December 9, 2007).

Zeleny, Jeff. "A New Wind Is Blowing in Chicago." *New York Times*, November 20, 2008.

Zeleny, Jeff and Laurie Goodstean. "White House Faith Office to Expand." *New York Times*, February 9, 2009.

Zeleny, Dorothy Jeff and Brian Knowlton. "Obama Wants to Expand Role of Religious Groups." *New York Times*, July 2, 2008.

Zwier, Carl A. Grant *The Moment: Barack Obama, Jeremiah Wright, and the Firestorm at Trinity United Church of Christ.* Lanham, MD: Rowman & Littlefield Publishers, 2012.

Index